REAL
NASCAR

REAL NASCAR

WHITE LIGHTNING, RED CLAY,
— AND — BIG BILL FRANCE

Daniel S. Pierce

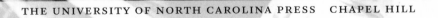

THE UNIVERSITY OF NORTH CAROLINA PRESS   CHAPEL HILL

Parts of this book have been reprinted with permission in revised form from
"The Most Southern Sport on Earth: NASCAR and the Unions," *Southern Cultures*
7, no. 2 (2001): 8–33, and "'Bib Overalls and Bad Teeth': Stock Car Racing and the
Piedmont Working Class," *Atlanta History* 46, no. 2 (2004): 26–41.

The paper in this book meets the guidelines for permanence and durability of
the Committee on Production Guidelines for Book Longevity of the Council on
Library Resources. The University of North Carolina Press has been a member of
the Green Press Initiative since 2003.

Library of Congress Cataloging-in-Publication Data
Pierce, Daniel S.
Real NASCAR : white lightning, red clay, and Big Bill France / Daniel S. Pierce.
p. cm.
Includes bibliographical references and index.
ISBN 978-0-8078-3384-1 (cloth : alk. paper)
1. Stock car racing—History. 2. NASCAR (Association) I. Title.
GV1029.9.S74P54 2010
796.72—dc22   2009039436

14 13 12 11 10   5 4 3 2 1

For Don Good

and in memory of Wayne Good

Contents

Illustrations

REAL
NASCAR

Introduction

In the Beginning . . . There Was Bristol

I grew up within earshot of the Asheville Speedway—or "New Asheville" as it was generally called in my childhood years—the local bastion of stock car racing. Like most Ashevillians who were not race fans, I considered the Friday night races noisy nuisances and the people who frequented the track rednecks. My opinion of racing and race fans did not change appreciably over the years, not even when my potluck roommate at Western Carolina University and soon-to-be best friend, Don Good, turned out to be a die-hard stock car racing fan whose fondest memories were of weekends spent camping with his truck driver father, Wayne, in the infield of the Charlotte Motor Speedway. Indeed, I doubt whether I ever saw more than a few minutes of a televised race, and I knew little about the sport other than having a passing knowledge of the on-track exploits of Richard Petty (I did grow up in North Carolina) and Darrell Waltrip (I happened to be teaching school in a town near Waltrip's Franklin, Tennessee, home when he was winning championships in Junior Johnson's car in the 1980s).

All of that changed on August 27, 1994, when Don, now a college professor and administrator, convinced me to go with him to the night Winston Cup race at Bristol Motor Speedway. As a southern historian—and also as an individual in his late thirties who had quit trying to run from his redneck roots—I felt I owed it to myself to see at least one race, so I agreed to go. Unbeknownst to me, the race Don had invited me to attend was, and still is, generally considered the most exciting race on the NASCAR circuit and the toughest ticket to acquire. It is hard to describe what I encountered on that August night. I was astounded by the sight of all the souvenir trailers around the track and the obvious loyalty of the fans, almost all attired in colorful T-shirts and hats announcing their allegiance to a favorite driver. The strange mixture of smells was equally overwhelming: an olio of carnival food, sweat, exhaust fumes, burning rubber, and high-octane gasoline.

At the time, the track held 70,000 or so fans, and it was jammed; even the grassy bank at the exit of the fourth turn was full of folks sitting on blankets. I lost count at more than one hundred as we climbed the seemingly innumerable steps of the new aluminum grandstand on the backstretch near the entrance to turn three. The rows of brightly colored team race car haulers—painted to match the paint job on the cars—parked in the infield added to the carnival scene. As the race neared, my anticipation grew when the crowd rose and a pastor delivered an invocation. After the invocation, Lee Greenwood sang "God Bless the U.S.A."—I cannot count the number of races I have been to where Greenwood sang this song—and the national anthem, and the fans roared their approval of an earsplitting flyover of air force jets in tight formation. The excitement of the fans intensified as the cars lined up on pit road and someone gave the command "Gentlemen, start your engines." I did not anticipate how loud the cars would be; in fact, I could barely communicate with Don over the unmuffled roar of the engines. The pace car pulled out onto the track followed by the brightly colored race cars, waxed to a high sheen to reflect the track lights. Seemingly all 70,000 fans inside the track rose to their feet in anticipation of the green flag.

When the green flag flew, the decibel level jumped tenfold. I had never heard anything like this assault on my eardrums in my life. Now I understood why people around me were wearing earplugs. Bristol Motor Speedway is a particularly loud facility, as the grandstands completely enclose the .533-mile track, which in turn sits in a bowl in the surrounding hills. You could literally feel the sound. After 5 laps—of a total 500—I knew I would never last the race without earplugs. Fortunately, the ends of the strap that I had on my sunglasses fit into my ears perfectly and muffled the sound. When I later asked Don why he did not warn me about the intense noise, he told me that he believed you had not really been to the races unless your ears rang for two or three days afterward. I will say I have chosen to forgo that particular racing pleasure.

Comfortable now with my improvised ear protection, I settled down to observe the sights in front of me. Television coverage provides no real sense of the speed of these cars. Although the average speed (mph) of the cars at Bristol is only in the high 120s, they were a blur as they made laps at a little more than fifteen seconds. The action on the track was intense;

in fact, one of the attractions of Bristol is that there is pretty much a guarantee that someone will wreck, or be wrecked, and the yellow caution flag will be brought out at least every fifty laps. Cautions are good because they give you a brief respite from the noise, and the excitement builds once again as the cars bunch up for another green flag start.

As fun and visceral as the racing was, it was almost as fun watching the fans around me. I had been a student at one time at the University of North Carolina–Chapel Hill and had witnessed extreme fan intensity in the Carmichael Auditorium student section as one of Dean Smith's teams battled the hated Lefty Driesel–led Maryland Terrapins on national television. I had been a graduate student at both the University of Alabama and the University of Tennessee and had seen fans foaming at the mouth at any number of football games. I thought I had seen the pinnacle of rabid fandom when I attended a University of Kentucky basketball game in Rupp Arena. I thought I had seen it all, until I went to my first NASCAR race. In particular, I will never forget the guy sitting about five rows in front of us — an unbelievable number of beer cans scattered at his feet before the race even began — who stood up every lap for 500 laps and saluted Dale Earnhardt's car with an extended middle finger.

Rusty Wallace won the race by little more than a car length. I was worn out but had learned a lot in that first session. I learned that when it came to Dale Earnhardt, there was no middle ground — you loved him or you hated him — although in all honesty I had yet to form a strong opinion. I learned that this new kid Jeff Gordon was pretty good and had a neat-looking car, what with the rainbow colors that my kids would come to love. I learned that while the stars of the day — Darrell Waltrip, Bill Elliott, Dale Earnhardt, Rusty Wallace, Harry Gant — had lots of fans, NASCAR fans were pretty democratic and even Mississippi driver Lake Speed, the unfortunately named Dick Trickle, and Dave Marcis, the journeyman driver from my hometown of Asheville, North Carolina, had their followings. Indeed, one of my most vivid race memories is of a guy in 1995 at a Bristol race wearing a blue hard hat with a can of Spam — Lake Speed's sponsor at the time — epoxied to the top. I learned that there was a lot more to stock car racing than rednecks driving in circles; not only was it exciting, but there was a lot going on out there for the thinking person, like pit strategy, tire stagger, and loose or tight cars. I guess the most important thing I learned was that stock car racing was a heck of a lot of fun.

Needless to say, my first taste of the exciting racing, overwhelming noise, and overall carnival atmosphere hooked me. Not a year has gone by since that 1994 race at Bristol that I have not attended at least one race in NASCAR's top division. When I am not at a race, I usually watch it on television or tune in to it on the radio. I well remember almost wrecking myself on I-26 returning to Asheville from Columbia, South Carolina, during the 1999 Bristol night race when I listened to the radio announcers describe the action as Dale Earnhardt put Terry Labonte into the wall on the last lap to win the race. I started going to local weekly races at the Asheville Speedway, which were almost as fun and exciting as—and a lot cheaper than—the Cup races. I mourned with thousands of other western North Carolina race fans when the owner sold that grand old track and the city turned it into a park in 1999 and with millions around the nation when Dale Earnhardt died in 2001. One of the first things I do every day is go to Jay Adamczyk's Website—www.jayski.com—to check out the latest NASCAR news and gossip. I have to admit it: yes, I am a NASCAR fan.

While I enjoy the racing on a personal level, I also became keenly interested in and fascinated by the history of the sport. The outlandish stories of the antics of early stock car racers immediately attracted me and compelled me to look deeper into the sport. Stories of Lloyd Seay and Roy Hall hauling liquor from Dawsonville, Georgia, to Atlanta one night and winning races at Lakewood Speedway the next day in the same car; of Fonty Flock winning the Southern 500 at Darlington Speedway wearing Bermuda shorts and argyle socks; of his brother Tim racing with a monkey—named Jocko Flocko—in his racecar; of discovering the colorful women racers in NASCAR's top division in the late 1940s and early '50s, Sara Christian, Louise Smith, and Ethel Mobley; of Curtis Turner doing any number of outlandish things including landing his airplane on an Easley, South Carolina, street on a Sunday morning so a buddy could go to his house to resupply their depleted stock of liquor; of Buck Baker discovering that the beer he had poured into a douche bag to sip on during a race had turned to pure suds after a few laps; of Richard Petty winning seventeen races in a row; of tire-iron fights, wild parties, and any number of like antics.

I also learned of the courage, toughness, utter fearlessness, and legendary cool of NASCAR's great champions. The first champion in NASCAR's top division, Red Byron, had a custom-built stirrup bolted to his clutch pedal to hold his mangled left leg—the result of a B-24 bomber crash during World War II—in place. The best drivers in the early days of the Darlington Raceway, knowing it was the fastest way around the track, regularly slapped the metal guardrail with the right rear quarter panel of their cars as they exited the turns, creating the legendary "Darlington stripe," a badge of honor for the gutsiest drivers. David Pearson, perhaps the coolest of the cool, demonstrated the ultimate in composure when he kept his car engine running to limp across the finish line at 20 mph to win the 1976 Daytona 500 after Richard Petty had clipped his front end and wrecked them both in the last turn of the race. Three years later, fans across the nation watched amazed as Donnie Allison and Cale Yarborough came into that same turn on the last lap of the 500 beating and banging and wrecked each other, allowing Petty to win the race. Cameras quickly panned from Petty's victory lap to a brawl in the infield, Yarborough versus Donnie and Bobby Allison, who had stopped to check on his brother. Fans, and the participants, still argue over who was at fault.

I also became fascinated by the culture that surrounds the sport and by the passionate loyalty of its fans. Stories abound about the lengths that fans will go to demonstrate their love for the sport and their loyalty to its heroes. Two incidents that occurred in my hometown of Asheville, North Carolina, will suffice to communicate the passion that many, especially in the Piedmont South, feel for this sport. In 1999, knowing that he would soon die, James Carver made an interesting request of his family. "I want to be brought around the track. Promise me when I die, you'll have them take me around." The track of which he spoke was the Asheville Motor Speedway, where Carver had spent many happy hours during his fifty-two-year life. As a child, he had walked two hours to the track despite the confinement of leg braces, the result of a bout with polio. One of eleven children in a working-class family, he could not afford a ticket but would sit on the bank outside the track and cheer for local favorites Boscoe Lowe, Bob Pressley, and Jack Ingram. When NASCAR's top division came to town, he eagerly watched his heroes Richard Petty, Junior Johnson, and David Pearson. As an adult, he never missed a race. He knew he could never emulate his heroes and race around the narrow track, beating and banging door to door with other young men, but he could vicariously experience the sense of freedom and excitement by watching and cheering. As reporter Susan Reinhardt observed: "He followed the races as if they were his calling."

When Carver died of a massive heart attack, family members convinced speedway and funeral home officials to honor his last request. Family and friends gathered in the grandstands and stood as a car bearing checkered flags on each side pulled onto the track. A black hearse carrying James Carver's remains followed, and a stock car with its throaty roar providing appropriate accompaniment to the scene brought up the rear of the procession. Carver's daughter Lisa yelled out, "Daddy, I love you." One sister commented, "At least he got to do it," while another observed, "He's happy now. I bet he's smiling too."[1]

Further evidence of the passion of NASCAR fans came after the death of Dale Earnhardt in a wreck on the last lap of the Daytona 500 on February 18, 2001. The outpouring of grief shocked the national news media as thousands dropped what they were doing all over the country and proceeded to make the pilgrimage to the Piedmont of North Carolina to pay their respects. The nation has rarely experienced such a widespread state of mourning for an individual who was not president of the United States or Elvis Presley. There are innumerable tales of the dedication of Earnhardt's fans, but an obituary that appeared in the *Asheville Citizen-Times* on December 8, 2005, for "Tommy" Lester Homer Boone Jr. of nearby Mars Hill particularly caught my attention. After listing his parents and three brothers, who had already passed, the second paragraph concluded with these words: "and he is also preceded in death by his hero, Dale Earnhardt."[2]

The primary goal of this book is to attempt to explain why James Carver and Tommy Boone—and hundreds of thousands, if not millions, of others who grew up in the Piedmont South and now throughout the nation—held, and hold, such strong feelings for stock car racing. The book is also intended be a comprehensive, chronological narrative history of the sport of stock car racing in the South from its earliest days up until the retirement of NASCAR founder Bill France Sr. and the entry of the R. J. Reynolds Tobacco Company and its Winston brand as the sponsor of NASCAR's top series in the early 1970s. I believe the sport is worthy of serious study, and my hope is that this book will help launch more such studies.[3]

I also hope this book will be read both by individuals who care nothing for NASCAR but want to understand the appeal of the sport and by stock car racing aficionados, who, I believe, will find much in this volume that is fresh and new. The story of the rise and growth of NASCAR in the South is one that is incredibly exciting, entertaining, and compelling, and I hope I have been successful in communicating that to the reader.

One of the necessary aspects of building such a narrative on the history of stock car racing and NASCAR in the South is to include only those stories that can be verified. Much of what has passed for NASCAR history is shrouded in myth, and even the better histories of the sport lack any sort of historical documentation. Many of the tales they relate have been repeated over and over, each author borrowing from the other and none actually verifying the stories' authenticity. A major goal, then, of this work is to attempt to separate the myths of stock car racing's early days from documented fact.

The challenges in attempting to do this in terms of documentation and source material are significant. NASCAR is a family-owned business that tightly controls access to its historical documents and is intensely protective of its image. The archives of NASCAR and its sister business, International Speedway Corporation, are not open to the public, and anyone who has a direct connection with these organizations generally toes the party line. Another difficulty, particularly in researching the first part of this book, is that people are often reluctant to talk about illegal activities with which their family members or friends may have been associated. Surprisingly, they will generally tell you if they have been involved themselves.

Despite these limitations, however, I have been able to find sources that have helped me tell this fascinating story. Newspapers—both local and racing—and magazines have been especially helpful in placing southern stock car racing in its proper context and in the history of American motorsports. The availability of interviews with many of the most important participants in the sport's history has been invaluable. There are several extensive collections of oral histories related to NASCAR history and southern stock car racing, including those found in published works and the NASCAR-related oral histories held at the Atlanta History Center. I have supplemented these collections with interviews I myself conducted, which are held in Special Collections of the Ramsey Library at the University of North Carolina at Asheville. Indeed, one of the great pleasures in researching and writing this book has been meeting and interviewing some of the sport's legendary figures, all of whom I have found to be gracious, generous, and forthcoming. There are also a number of good published works on important figures in southern stock car racing, including autobiographies and excellent biographies. Books on aspects of NASCAR history written by journalists have also been extremely useful. The challenge, of course, comes in weighing oral testimony, taking into account that memories are often selective, self-serving, less than totally candid, and faulty. I have attempted to verify statements by checking a variety of sources and have simply left out material that seemed outlandish or unlikely.

One of the most persistent stories in almost every account of the early days of NASCAR, and one that bears particular scrutiny, is the alleged role of moonshiners and bootleggers in the origins of the sport.[4] As it is usually told, the sport grew out of informal races between liquor-running drivers in their souped-up cars. According to H. A. "Humpy" Wheeler, at "the average race in 1950, particularly in western North Carolina or maybe the Peach Bowl down in Georgia, maybe 25 to 30 percent of the participants had run or was running moonshine at the time. And probably that many mechanics had either built or worked on moonshine cars."[5] Ned Jarrett estimates that "at least half the people I was racing against at Hickory and North Wilkesboro [in the early 1950s] were in bootlegging."[6]

Some observers, particularly academics, have wanted to question the validity of these stories. Geographer Richard Pillsbury asserts, "It seems questionable that moonshining has been a significant force in the development of stock car racing as we know it today."[7] Sociologist Jim Wright offers no qualifiers when he argues, "The idea that NASCAR was created by or was at least a tolerant, much less congenial, home for a gang of wild-eyed whiskey-runners is nonsense."[8] NASCAR founder Bill France Sr. regularly downplayed the alleged connection between moonshining and NASCAR's founding, and NASCAR itself has consistently ignored accounts that attempt to show a link to the illegal alcohol business.[9]

Early on in this project, I would have argued that such tales vastly exaggerated the role of moonshining and bootlegging in the sport's origins and early years. On closer inspection, however, I have discovered that, if anything, NASCAR's connection to the manufacturing, transportation, and sale of illegal alcohol has been both underestimated and misunderstood. Indeed, the deeper I looked into southern stock car racing's early history, the more liquor I found. To be sure, there is no disputing the fact that significant numbers of the early drivers in stock car racing—especially the most successful ones—had their initial high-speed driving experiences evading the law at the wheel of a souped-up 1939 or '40 Ford V-8 loaded with 120 gallons of illegal whiskey. What most chroniclers of stock car racing and NASCAR have failed to note, however, is that a large percentage of the early mechanics, car owners, promoters, and track owners had deep ties to the illegal alcohol business. It would not be an exaggeration to say that the sport was built on the proceeds of the manufacture, transport, and sale of hundreds of thousands, if not millions, of cases of white liquor—and legally produced but illegally sold bootleg "red" liquor—in the Piedmont region of the South and its adjacent foothills.

As important as the liquor haulers were in the origins of NASCAR, no individual played a greater role in the sport's beginnings, development, and growth than William Henry Getty "Big Bill" France. Although there is plenty of mythology out there about the 6'6" France's dominating role in the sport, his importance cannot be overestimated. He raced in the first major stock car race in the South, became one of the leading early drivers, moved on to dominate promotion of the sport in the Piedmont after World War II, became the founder and owner of NASCAR as well as one of its most important track owners, and formed the key relationships to corporate America that laid the foundation for the sport to grow to national prominence. France's—and now the France family's—dominance of NASCAR is unprecedented in the history of American sport. While most families earn millions in other businesses and then move into an ownership role in professional sports, France arrived in Daytona Beach in 1935 virtually penniless and turned his interests in stock car racing into an enterprise worth billions of dollars. The France story is tightly woven into this account of NASCAR's history.

The final goal of this book, one that most histories of NASCAR and southern stock car racing fail to accomplish, is to place the sport in its proper historical and cultural context. Southern stock car racing cannot be properly understood without understanding its strong connections to a particular region, to a particular time, and to a particular group of people. In addition, NASCAR history is American sports history and, most important, is central to understanding American motorsports history.

In examining NASCAR in its formative years—and the earlier stock car racing from which it emerged—I have come to some conclusions that I believe are crucial to properly understanding this sport, especially at a time when NASCAR itself has sought to clean up its history and present an approved version of its heritage to the American public. First, NASCAR, in its origins and early growth, was not a sport popular in all of the South. For much of its early history it was nurtured and grew out of the Piedmont region of the South, stretching roughly from Richmond, Virginia, in an arc to Birmingham, Alabama. Indeed, the "NASCAR South" is the South of red clay, not black loam; yeoman farmers, not plantation slavery; and cotton mills, rather than cotton fields. Second, I have come to agree with historian Pete Daniel—who explored the early days of NASCAR in a chapter in his book *Unfinished Revolution: The South in the 1950s*—that in its origins stock car racing was an "enthusiasm of the vulgus": a sport primarily developed by and for white, working-class men of the Piedmont and adjacent foothills.[10]

Third, NASCAR has a unique place in the history of American sports and the history of motorsports. Southern stock car racing emerged in the Piedmont in the late 1930s and early 1940s, an era that already had a significant amount of professional motor racing of several varieties. Indianapolis-style open-wheel races, midget-car races, motorcycle races, and auto thrill shows—generally called "Hell Driving" shows—were a staple of fairgrounds throughout the region. Stock car racing supplanted these other forms of motorsport in the region not only because people could identify with cars similar—at least on the surface—to the ones that they drove but also because they could identify with the drivers, who in stock car racing were much more likely to be local, or at least from somewhere else in the Piedmont. While the bootleggers did the bulk of the winning in the sport's earliest years, stock car races, particularly in the late 1930s and early 1940s, were promoted by individuals with long histories in the business of open-wheel or midget racing. Yet stock car racing, almost from its beginning, was perceived as primarily a southern sport.

Because of its roots as a Piedmont-region, working-class, moonshine-tainted, good ole boy sport, NASCAR has often struggled for respectability both in the world of motorsports and in American sports in general. Indeed, only in relatively recent years has NASCAR been covered by the major national press outlets. Much of the history of Piedmont stock car racing and NASCAR itself, like the history of the modern South, has been about joining the mainstream, transcending roots, and gaining both respectability and national recognition.

In recent years this dream of respectability and national recognition of the France family and of many in NASCAR has come true. At the same time, the sport has increasingly distanced itself from its roots. This is unfortunate, as the birth, growth, and development of NASCAR is nothing if not a great American success story. It is, finally, an intriguing and fascinating story of mechanics, mill workers, farmers, moonshiners, and bootleggers in the Piedmont South and one incredibly ambitious and creative man, William Henry Getty "Big Bill" France, who took a rough-and-tumble, red-clay-stained, white-liquor-besotted enterprise to the very pinnacle of American sport.

The Piedmont Hell of a Fellow
and the Origins of Stock Car Racing

I know exactly how racing got started. . . . In the mid-thirties, in a cow pasture in Georgia, that's where racing [of the NASCAR variety] began. We didn't have no tickets, no safety equipment, no fences, no nothing. Just a bunch of bootleggers who'd been arguing all week about who had the fastest car would get together to prove it.

. . . Thirty or forty of these bootleggers showed up in this cow pasture at Stockbridge, which is about fifteen miles outside Atlanta. They made a track by running around and digging their wheels in the ground in about a half-mile circle. These guys would run and bet against their own cars, betting who had the fastest car. That night they'd be hauling liquor in the same car. About fifty people saw this dust cloud and came up trying to see what was causing it. Next time, a hundred would show up. Then three or four hundred would show up.

. . . Pretty soon, they raced every Sunday. Five and six thousand people started showing up. Then Bill France came along and he started putting up fences, the whole bit. He made stock car racing what it is today.

—Tim Flock, in Sylvia Wilkinson, Dirt Tracks to Glory

The story of NASCAR's origins told by two-time NASCAR champion Tim Flock to journalist Sylvia Wilkinson constitutes the standard account of how the NASCAR variety of stock car racing began—although others have recounted stories placing similar events in South Carolina, North Carolina, or southern Virginia.[1] All the elements of NASCAR's founding myth are here, particularly southern liquor haulers and their souped-up cars racing on makeshift cow pasture tracks and Daytona Beach mechanic/race car driver/racing promoter and founder/owner of NASCAR Bill France.

Indeed, this standard story can be encapsulated in one sentence: In the 1930s bootleggers got together and started racing in cow pastures; people were interested and gathered to watch the spectacle; and promoters — primarily Bill France — came along, saw its potential, organized the sport, promoted it, and took it to the rest of the South and then to the nation at large.

Great story. Unfortunately, upon closer inspection, parts of this founding tale are definitely untrue, other parts may have happened but are grossly exaggerated, and all of this story oversimplifies and leaves out significant information. The first problem emerges when the sources for these "bootleggers racing in cow pastures" stories are examined. Most either have no listed source or cite Flock's early 1980s interview with Wilkinson or two similar interviews done by journalists Kim Chapin and Peter Golenbock in which Flock recounts virtually the identical story.[2] Considering that Flock was born in 1924 and these races supposedly took place when he was nine or ten years old, there is reason to question this childhood memory, especially one for which he is the only source. Although cow pasture racing similar to what Flock describes may have happened on occasion, these races definitely did not grow into the stock car racing that became NASCAR. What Flock was probably recalling were tracks cut in cow pastures with earth-moving equipment in the post–World War II era, a common occurrence. In fact, a thorough examination of the testimony and recorded history of other Atlanta-area bootleggers and moonshiners — and mill workers and farmers throughout the region — reveals no support for Flock's story of oval racing in cow pastures and indicates a strong preference for racing on highways and country roads when impromptu events were held to settle arguments over who had the fastest car.

While Flock's "racing in cow pastures" story is either untrue or greatly exaggerated, the roles played by individuals involved in the illegal liquor business as the earliest stock car racing stars and by Daytona Beach mechanic Big Bill France as the sport's promoter are undeniable. However, the real story of the beginnings of stock car racing in the South is much more complex than this simple tale would indicate and involves a number of actors and factors. Although the earliest stock car races that evolved into NASCAR were run on a combination beach/highway course near Daytona Beach, the sport took root, grew, and flourished in the red-clay soil of the South's Piedmont region and drew most of its participants, fans, and even promoters from the Piedmont's white, male, working-class inhabitants at a time when the region was being transformed by modernity, industrialization, and urbanization. Even as the region changed, however, many of its inhabitants, especially white working-class men, clung to cultural values that prized freedom, action, and even violence. For many people in the region, involvement in the illegal alcohol business allowed them to retain family farms, kept them out of the mills, and gave them the adrenaline rush they sought. Indeed, another important part of the story of NASCAR's origins is the role played by Piedmont bootleggers not only as drivers but as mechanics, car owners, track owners, and financiers. In addition, for the bootleggers but also for the mill workers and farmers of the region, in the automobile, and in the ability to modify it to go faster and race it at high speed, Piedmont men—and some women—found a pastime and a passion that helped them to express their traditional cultural values in a modern world.

Still another important factor in the sport's founding and growth is the role played by organized, professional auto racing. From its earliest beginnings, the stock car racing that evolved into NASCAR was part of the national racing scene, promoted and staged by some of its most important leaders. While many of the major promoters of American auto racing, and its fans outside the Piedmont South, often ignored, derided, or considered stock car racing an unruly, or even unwanted, stepchild, it was a child nonetheless. One of the important stories of the early history of NASCAR and its founders was the sport's struggle for acceptance first in the world of American auto racing and then in the American sporting world at large.

An interconnected factor that many histories of NASCAR ignore is the role from the beginning of American automakers. Although Detroit manufacturers did not become directly involved in the sport until the mid-1950s, stock car racing had a connection to the automakers that other forms of motorsports did not have. Since competitors raced automobiles at least similar in appearance to those sold by Detroit, if not at all similar under the hood, stock car fans formed a strong attachment to the particular make of car piloted by their favorite driver. Any study of the early history of stock car racing and NASCAR, then, would not be complete without discussion of the significance to the sport of the late 1930s Ford V-8, the Oldsmobile Rocket 88, the Hudson Hornet, the Chrysler 300, the '55 Chevy, the early 1960s Pontiacs, the Chrysler Hemi-powered cars, or the winged Dodge Daytona. While Detroit's direct involvement in the sport was sporadic and even disruptive at times, its presence was always felt.

Although the popular story of NASCAR's creation in a southern cow pasture has no apparent basis in documented fact, the story of its origins and early years *is* one of dashing bootleggers in hot cars and of one incredibly ambitious individual: Big Bill France. But a full examination of the sport's history requires an exploration of the role played by behind-the-scenes illegal liquor entrepreneurs, blue-collar Piedmonters steeped in an individualist and freedom-loving culture, professional racing promoters, and Detroit automakers.

The Piedmont Context

While NASCAR has important historical connections to other parts of the country—particularly the Daytona Beach, Florida, area—the region where it put down its deepest roots is the Piedmont South and its adjacent foothills and mountains. The sport essentially emerged from the region's red clay, and the culture of its people nurtured it in the rapidly changing world of the 1920s, '30s, and '40s. In terms of the history of NASCAR, the two most important changes were interconnected: the rise of the mills and mill towns of the region and the transformation of the manufacture and transportation of illegal alcohol into a highly organized, industrial enterprise.

The changes that created the historical context for the popularity of stock car racing in the Piedmont began in the late nineteenth century when farmers found it increasingly difficult to keep body and soul together on the small family farms that covered the region. Desperate for a way to feed their families, many sought opportunity, steady work, and a better life in the growing number of cotton, tobacco, and furniture mills of the region, a process that accelerated during and after World War I. The mills attracted poor farmers because they provided work not only for men but for all members of the family—although at lower pay. The mill village also offered low-cost housing, commissaries to supply the necessities of life, close neighbors, and improved access to health care, churches, education, and entertainment. For most families, life improved, but not as much as they had hoped.[3]

Many of these farmers turned mill workers soon came to recognize that they had traded away some very important aspects of their previous life. In the mills they faced a distinctly different lifestyle than the one they and their ancestors had developed over centuries on the farm. Instead of open spaces and independence of thought and action, they found long hours of confinement in a hot and noisy factory and close supervision by managers and owners. This supervision often continued as the workers left the factory and went to their homes, did their shopping, attended church, sent their children to school, went to the doctor, attended a movie, all in buildings owned lock, stock, and barrel by the mill owner.[4] For many men, this life proved especially demeaning and depressing as they lost a good bit of their traditional paternal role in the family. "The dependence which had been fastened upon poor whites," observed author W. J. Cash in his classic work *The Mind of the South*, "was being carried over into industry, and even extended if that were possible. Even more definitely than the tenant and the cropper, the cotton mill worker of the South would be stripped of the ancient autonomy and placed in every department of his life under the control of his employer."[5]

Piedmont mill workers also found their traditional recreational outlets severely limited. Mill management frowned on fighting, drinking, and disorderly conduct, any of which could cost a man his position in the mill and home in the mill village. Hunting became increasingly difficult as concentrations of population depleted or scared off game in areas surrounding the mill village. Besides, twelve-hour workdays and a six-day workweek in the mill left little time or energy for recreation. In addition, these time-honored pastimes—while culturally ingrained in the southern male psyche—seemed old-fashioned in this modern world. As Jacquelyn Hall has observed, "Most mill-working men had to give up their traditional sources of identity."[6]

Despite these trade-offs, most poor farmers saw few alternatives, and a steady stream headed for "public work" as the twentieth century progressed. Even with the low wages characteristic of mill work, they generally made more than the average farmworker. As historian James C. Cobb observed, "By the end of World War II, workers earning $40 per week could console themselves with the fact that such an income was far greater than what they could reasonably expect to earn on the farm."[7]

Moonshining in the Piedmont and Mountain South

Many individuals, especially in the mountains and foothills adjacent to the Piedmont, could not bear the thought of the confining life in the mill and sought ways to keep and maintain their farms and their way of life. Those who stayed on their farms had to employ what historian Crandall Shifflet has referred to as an "economic quilt" strategy, whereby they supplemented their farming income with money they made from a variety of other revenue-earning opportunities.[8] For those willing to defy the law and take a gamble—and many individuals proved willing—this meant the manufacture and transportation of illegal alcohol.

While moonshining had a long tradition in the region, the confluence of several factors—Prohibition, the persistence of "dry counties" long after its repeal, rapid increases in federal liquor taxes in the 1930s and 1940s, the growth of markets in mill towns and cities in the Piedmont, and improvements in transportation—made such activities increasingly profitable and appealing in the 1920s through the 1940s and even into the 1950s, especially given the alternatives. As NASCAR champion and racing broadcaster Benny Parsons noted, "Trust me. There was nothing to do in the mountains of North Carolina [Wilkes County for Parsons] back in the thirties, forties and fifties. . . . You either worked at a hosiery mill, a furniture factory or you made whiskey."[9] Most young men had few qualms about the illegality of the operation, especially if it meant escape from the confinement of the mills. As pioneering stock car owner Raymond Parks put it, "Back then, way back then, that's the only way . . . people up in the mountains the only way they had to make a living."[10] Wilkes County, North Carolina, moonshiner Millard Ashley spoke of the poverty of his early life: "That will put you in the liquor business. You walking around with no money in your pocket."[11] A moonshiner told journalist Joseph Earl Dabney a similar story: "Well, I tell you, you live kinda rough life up there in the mountains anyway. If you made any money at all you had to make whiskey or haul it, one or the other."[12]

In order to understand the significance of moonshining in the foot-hills and mountains adjacent to the Piedmont South from the 1920s to the 1960s—and therefore the origins of NASCAR—one must get rid of the image of the lazy, hog-rifle-toting, barefoot mountaineer minding a copper "pot tail" over an open fire. The coming of Prohibition in the 1920s and improvements in transportation dramatically changed illegal distilling in the region. The moonshiners left in the mountains during this period developed new means to rapidly distill large amounts of illegal alcohol. The 40-gallon pot tail was confined to the barn or pirated for spare parts and was replaced by the much larger, more efficient steamer still, often called a "Wilkes-type" still, which could produce hundreds of gallons at a time. Moonshiners also altered traditional recipes by adding sugar and yeast to the mix to speed up the process. Fires fueled by imported coke often replaced the traditional hardwood fire.[13]

Moonshining on such an industrial scale could provide substantial financial benefits, especially for the daring and ambitious. Journalist Vance

Revenue agents with captured steamer moonshine still in McDuffie County, Georgia, 1953 or 1954. Note canning jars and sacks of sugar on the right. (Courtesy of Vanishing Georgia Collection, Georgia Archives)

Packard noted the profitability of the industry in a 1950 article in *The American* magazine about moonshining in Wilkes County, North Carolina: "If a moonshiner can get his first run made and sold, he has gotten back his investment in the still, and everything after is gravy. If, after a couple of months, the ATU [Alcohol Tax Unit of the U.S. Treasury Department] agents discover his still and chop it up he is sad, of course, but financially he is far ahead and ready to start again."[14] Haulers, or trippers in moonshiner parlance, according to Junior Johnson, could make as much as $350 to $450 a night hauling whiskey to the cities and mill towns of the Piedmont in the 1950s.[15] In addition, profits made from the activity were free of any state or federal taxes.

Arrests and court records from the period reveal the changing nature of the illegal liquor business during the period. In 1935, the "largest inland seizure" of illegal liquor to date occurred in the Ingle Hollow section of Wilkes County, North Carolina. ATU agents seized "7100 gallons of whiskey, 9150 pounds of sugar, four copper condensers, five complete distilling plants having a combined capacity for the manufacture of 2000 gallons of liquor each week." All this equipment and product belonged to one Glen Johnson, whose son Junior would follow in his footsteps— even to incarceration in the federal penitentiary at Chillicothe, Ohio.[16] Junior, a child at the time of the raid, recalled liquor being "stacked up in our bedrooms in cases so high we had to climb over 'em to get into bed."[17] Dawson County, Georgia, moonshiners, who marketed most of their whiskey in the Atlanta area, allegedly purchased "entire boatloads of sugar from [dictator Fulgencio] Batista in Cuba."[18] A representative of Standard Brands testified in a 1935 trial in Franklin County, Virginia, that the people of the county not only purchased inordinate amounts of sugar but also bought 70,448 pounds of yeast in a four-year period, when the city of Richmond purchased only 2,000 pounds in the same period.[19]

Moonshine Capitals of America

Although moonshining was a relatively ubiquitous activity in most areas of the South, it became especially prominent in foothills counties on the edges of the Piedmont. As writer Dabney observed in his book *Mountain Spirits*, "These areas had a lot in common—a longtime liquor-making tradition, a lack of economic opportunity, and a location relatively near metropolitan centers where booze could be marketed easily and profitably. Most had two other key elements in their moonshine mix—a wild and wooly terrain, and isolation that afforded maximum security from prying federal eyes." Dabney specifically names four counties as "former moonshine capitals of America": Dawson County, Georgia; Cocke County, Tennessee; Wilkes County, North Carolina; and Franklin County, Virginia.[20] Estimates based on the number of illegal stills and alcohol seized by federal agents put the production of liquor in each of these counties at their peak in the 1930s through 1950s at better than half a million gallons per year with estimated revenues in the millions of dollars, far exceeding any other industrial or commercial enterprise in the area.[21] Not surprisingly, three of these "moonshine capitals," Dawson, Wilkes, and Franklin, played key roles in the early development of Piedmont stock car racing and NASCAR.

By the 1930s, the production of illegal alcohol permeated the economy and life of many mountain and foothill counties. As Junior Johnson observed, "If they wadn't making it, they's selling the stuff to make it with, or they's hauling it. In some kind of way about every family [in Wilkes County] was involved in the moonshine business."[22] Supplying the necessary materials for the production of whiskey tied many businesses in these counties to the moonshine industry. "Tater" Johnson, a rural Wilkes County storekeeper, kept a huge pile of coke next to his store. Writer Vance Packard queried, "Who buys the coke? Probably Tater wouldn't rightly know. He does know that there isn't any law that says you can't sell coke to anybody who wants it." Packard continued by observing that in Wilkes County "most of the county's hardware stores, garages, tinsmiths, sugar dealers, and other merchants prosper directly or indirectly from this secret wealth-producing industry. . . . North Wilkesboro, the county's No. 1 metropolis, sits in the middle of some rough country. Its mayor boasts of his 'prosperous, bustling city.' . . . In fact, you see more bustling prosperity, with fewer signs of productive capacity to account for it, than you'll find anywhere in the United States."[23] Rex White, the 1961 NASCAR Grand National champion, frequently tells a story about a visit to North Wilkesboro when he was in his teens. He asked a man on the street where he might buy some moonshine. The man pointed down the street at the local post office and replied, "That's the only place you can't buy it."[24]

Moonshiners divided labor in the business based on age and experience and kept as much of the enterprise within the family as possible. Young men did most of the heavy lifting and manual labor. As one moonshine maker related to Dabney, "Makin' likker is hard work. Don't let nobody tell you it's easy. You rawhide them 100-pound sacks of sugar and them big buckets of mash and all that stuff, and cleanin' out stills and bottling that stuff up and carryin' it miles out of the hills on your back, it's tough work. You earn every dime you make."[25] Young men with more daring than sense also did much of the hauling to market, or tripping. Middle-age and older men with knowledge and skills developed over time made the liquor, handled the marketing, and dealt with the financial transactions necessary in such a business, providing finance capital and laundering money back into the general economy, a crucial activity with the ATU and IRS closely monitoring bank activity. Little is known about the financing and laundering of money, as most research has focused on more romantic aspects of the business such as production and hauling, but these were crucial activities, ones that Piedmont stock car racing and subsequently NASCAR would benefit from tremendously. Law enforcement rarely caught the older individuals at the top, since the young men at the bottom bore the greatest risk of capture either at the still or on the highway with a load of liquor. As Vance Packard observed, "Frankly, the chances that the owner will get caught and jailed are pretty slim. Instead, he hires (or goes 50–50) with young mountain lads who do the work, and they are the ones who usually get caught."[26]

Many individuals involved in moonshining also became involved in another aspect of the illegal alcohol business: the trade in so-called red liquor. Red liquor is "federal tax–paid whiskey bottled by legal distillers." With many of the counties of the South remaining dry well after the end of Prohibition, and as people became a bit more prosperous in the region, demand for red liquor climbed, and moonshiners—already on the wrong side of the law—stepped in to meet that need, hauling the stuff in by the tractor-trailer load in many cases.[27]

Of course, moonshiners faced the risks of arrest that any illegal activity holds, although they rarely feared local or even state law enforcement. Since the local police, sheriffs, or their deputies had to live in the community and often knew or were related to many of the moonshiners, they usually limited their enforcement of alcohol violations to the occasional show bust to keep the respectable types from putting too much heat on them. As Junior Johnson observed, the "liquor business in Wilkes County [his home county in North Carolina] was more of a federal thing than it was a local sheriff thing. Most of the sheriffs was friends of everbody's. . . . We, Gwyn [Staley, fellow moonshiner and stock car driver] and myself, was basically pretty well aware they was the kind of people we was."[28] One night as Johnson and Staley hauled liquor in their cars, they came upon another car turned upside down in the ditch. Examining the wreck, Johnson and Staley discovered that the accident victims were the sheriff of Wilkes County and one of his deputies, both scratched, bleeding, and drunk. Johnson told Staley, "I'll load one of 'em on top of the cases in my car, and the other one can ride with you." They then drove the two men to the courthouse in North Wilksboro, where the officers could receive medical treatment. From then on the sheriff would greet Junior with a smile and a wink and a "You ain't been up the road lately, have you?"[29]

Enforcement fell primarily to the agents of the Alcohol Tax Unit of the U.S. Department of the Treasury—now the Bureau of Alcohol, Tobacco, Firearms, and Explosives and part of the Department of Justice—who did their best to track down stills scattered throughout the coves and hollows or catch the haulers on the road. They also attempted to monitor unusual activity, particularly sales of large amounts of sugar, yeast, or coke. In the 1930s, a major federal operation in Franklin County, Virginia, revealed that the small town of Ferrum consumed more sugar "than the entire city of Richmond." Arrested in a similar operation in Wilkes County, North Carolina, storekeeper Arvel Pruitt of the tiny crossroads community of Traphill admitted in court to selling "hundreds of thousands of pounds of sugar in a matter of weeks."[30] Convictions for the manufacture, sale, or transportation of illegal liquor usually resulted in a sentence of a year and a day in federal penitentiary, for Piedmont area moonshiners usually in Chillicothe, Ohio, or Atlanta, Georgia, and of course the forfeiture of any equipment used in illegal operations, including vehicles. Subsequent convictions drew fines and longer penitentiary stints, although rarely more than two years.[31]

Perhaps most important, at least as far as the future of stock car racing in the region was concerned, moonshining offered a level of excitement, an adrenaline rush, and a connection to traditional cultural ideals that ordinary life on the farm or life in the mill village could not match. "Moonshining is something that kind of gets under your skin, and you'd almost do it for nothin'," observed Junior Johnson. "It's a all around exciting adventure to get off in it, to tell you the honest truth."[32]

Piedmont Cultural Values and the Hell of a Fellow

The Piedmont mill worker, the farmer, and the moonshiner led distinctly different economic lives, but they shared common cultural roots in the rural South that fed directly into the development and ongoing popularity of stock car racing. As the authors of the seminal work on Piedmont mill culture *Like a Family* asserted, "Along with the belongings piled in a horse-drawn wagon in the 1880s or a Dodge truck in the 1920s, they carried the cultural baggage of the countryside."[33] This proved particularly true when it came to views on sports and leisure. In his work on sports in the antebellum South, Elliott Gorn recorded a southern, male, working-class penchant for active, violent, and intensely competitive diversions and pastimes such as hunting, horse racing, cockfighting, and rough-and-tumble brawling that often resulted in eye gouging, nose biting, and other forms of mutilation.[34] By the late nineteenth century, even as southern society became at least slightly more regulated, organized, and tamed by evangelical culture, these values remained important to southern men. Historian Ted Ownby has argued that southern men retained "a taste for recreations characterized by action—colorful, dramatic action . . . particularly those with an element of chance and the possibility of danger."[35]

Most observers agree that such pastimes and activities were very much tied up in nineteenth-century southern notions of what it meant to be a man. As Gorn and Warren Goldstein observed, "Southern sports were rituals of manhood. . . . To participate, of course, demonstrated virility, but simply being a spectator—cheering lustily, wagering wildly, losing defiantly—proved one's manhood, one's worthiness to be accepted by peers."[36] W. J. Cash pointed out that these notions of male identity were especially important to poorer whites, who could not compete economically with their wealthier neighbors. "In the South, if your neighbor overshadowed you in the number of his slaves, you could outshoot or out fiddle him, and in your eyes, and in those of many of your fellows, remain essentially as good a man as he."[37]

A popular southern male ideal, particularly among the white working class, developed out of these values. Cash called this ideal male the "hell of a fellow." "To stand on his head in a bar, to toss down a pint of raw whiskey in a gulp, to fiddle and dance all night, to bite off the nose or gouge out the eye of a favorite enemy, to fight and love harder than the next man, to be known eventually far and wide as a hell of a fellow—such would be his focus." Cash further characterized the "hell of a fellow" as "full of chip-on-the-shoulder swagger," one who would "knock hell out of whoever dared to cross him," run "spontaneous and unpremeditated footraces," "let off wild yells" for no apparent reason, "a hot, stout fellow, full of blood and reared to outdoor activity."[38]

The "hell of a fellow" figured prominently in southern folk tales and literature of the nineteenth and early twentieth centuries, including the tall tales of Daniel Boone, Davy Crockett, and Mike Fink. He was a standard character with the Old Southwest humorists, particularly George Washington Harris, whose writings featured the antics of Sut Lovingood, a "nat'ral born durn'd fool" whom the parson eulogized with the words "He had hosses, an' he run 'em; he had chickens, an' he fit 'em; he had kiards, an' he played 'em. Let us try an' ricollect his virtues—ef he had any—an' forgit his vices—ef we can. For of sich air the kingdom of heaven."[39] The writings of later southern writers, including Mark Twain and William Faulkner, often included "hell of a fellow" figures. Although the man turned out to be a coward, Twain put "hell of a fellow" words into the mouth of a character in *Life on the Mississippi* similar to ones he surely heard as a child growing up in southeastern Missouri and in his young adulthood as a pilot on the Mississippi River.

> Whoo-oop! I'm the old original, iron-jawed, brass-mounted, copper-bellied corpse-maker from the wilds of Arkansaw!—Look at me! I'm

the man they call Sudden Death and General Desolation! Sired by a hurricane; dam'd by an earthquake, half brother to the cholera; nearly related to the small-pox on the mother's side! Look at me! I take nineteen alligators and a bar'l of whiskey for breakfast when I'm in robust health, and a bushel of rattlesnakes and a dead body when I'm ailing! I split the everlasting rocks with my glance, and I squench the thunder when I speak! Whoo-oop! Stand back and give me room according to my strength! Blood's my natural drink, and the wails of the dying is music to my ear! Cast your eye on me gentlemen!—and lay low and hold your breath, for I'm about to turn myself loose.[40]

The sense of freedom and lack of dependence on anyone else that the "hell of a fellow" image idealized, a fact not always borne out in real life, made such values, and activities that expressed them, intensely important to southern men. As Gorn has noted, "Violent sports, heavy drinking, and impulsive pleasure seeking were appropriate for men whose lives were hard, whose futures were unpredictable, and whose opportunities were limited."[41] Indeed, if southern men brought anything with them to the new world of the twentieth century in the Piedmont South, it was the ongoing importance of at least preserving some of this sense of freedom and independence.

In the face of this changing world, men sought diversion from the realities of life. Hunting offered one such escape for many farmers. Ted Ownby argued that this pastime became particularly important to men during this period as "an outlet for the self-assertiveness and self-indulgence that had long constituted an important feature of male culture" and "promised excitement, freedom and an unrestrained exercise of will that characterized male values." Men in rural communities also found diversions that matched their cultural values in the small, courthouse towns on Saturdays, court days, and holidays. The congregation of men on these occasions was characterized often by "numerous fights, confrontations, and contests, the self-indulgence of the barroom, [and] easy profanity."[42]

By the late 1930s, for many young men in the Piedmont South, driving a car, racing another "hell of a fellow" on the highway, and racing a stock car on a local fairground track would provide a perfect "outlet for the self-assertiveness and self-indulgence" that had been important features of their culture since childhood. It would only take the arrival of the automobile to the region to push the process along.

The Automobile and the Piedmont Working Class

For those who stayed on the family farm, those who moved to the mills, and for the moonshiners, the arrival of the automobile took on monumental significance for both practical and symbolic reasons. In its practical aspects, the automobile—or often the truck—allowed the farmer and the moonshiner greater access to markets in the growing towns of the Piedmont. For all three groups, the benefits also proved psychological, providing them with a major form of escape from the pain, drudgery, and mind-numbing routine of daily life and connecting them with traditional southern male cultural values. Indeed, the automobile provided both means and metaphor for freedom and power for people whose daily lives often lacked both. Although observing tenant farmers in the Black Belt South, sociologist Arthur Raper noted this phenomenon: "The feel of power, even in an old automobile, is most satisfying to a man who owns nothing, directs nothing, and while producing a crop literally begs food from his landlord."[43] Historian Thomas D. Clark argued that the "automobile became actually more important to the poor southerner than either medicine or dress."[44] Jacquelyn Hall observed that for Piedmont mill workers "the automobile was irresistible. It allowed people greater choice in where to live and work; it permitted distant friends and relatives to visit more often; and it gave people fun and excitement they had never before experienced."[45] For many Piedmont residents, the automobile was their ticket out of a life that "seemed stunting and isolated." Don Faucette, who grew up in the Glencoe mill village in Alamance County, North Carolina, averred, "That's the reason I wanted to get me a car and get out, just like a bunch of us did."[46]

By the late 1920s and early 1930s, automobiles became surprisingly accessible to the Piedmont working class, especially as more and more Ford Model T's and other cheap cars found their way to the used market or to junkyards. Catawba County, North Carolina, residents Alex Mull and Gordon Boger reminisced about those days: "When the Ford Motor Company ceased manufacturing the Model T there were literally thousands still operating. Back then, kids in high school would chip in to buy a Model T for about $50. They would strip it down . . . a kid with just a little mechanical ability could keep one running with a couple of tin cans, some bailing wire, a pair of pliers, and a screwdriver."[47] Junior Johnson, one of the greatest mechanical minds in NASCAR history, has his own memories of the Model T: "Most of the time us kids, if somebody had a old T-Model or A-Model that they had kindly junked. We would pool our money and buy it and fix it up and ride and mess around on the farm with it. There was all the time something happening to it."[48]

On farms and in the mill towns of the Piedmont, the ability to drive became an important step into manhood, much like the ability to shoot a gun, ride a horse, or fight had been in an earlier era. In this society, this step was often taken at an early age. The importance of helping out on the family farm gave boys as young as nine or ten the opportunity to drive tractors and farm trucks and even, on occasions, the family car. NASCAR legend Ned Jarrett remembers growing up on his family's 300-acre Catawba County, North Carolina, farm. "That was the first thing I ever drove [a Reo farm truck] and then I was about nine years old, my dad would allow me to drive to Sunday school in the family car."[49] Even in the region's small towns where law enforcement kept a closer watch on things, young boys commonly drove. Growing up in the mill town of Belmont, North Carolina, Humpy Wheeler remembered the more personal environment of the region in the 1930s and 1940s. "The chief of police knew you and if he saw you driving about town and knew you could drive, he never said anything, particularly if you were going to get something for your daddy—which I always was. So we started driving at an early age."[50] NASCAR champion David Pearson learned to hot-wire both his dad's and his brother's cars and joyride through his Spartanburg County, South Carolina, mill-hill neighborhood by the time he was twelve.[51]

As important as the ability to drive an automobile was for men of the Piedmont, it became equally important to know how to repair them. As a result of this necessity, the "shade-tree" mechanic developed into an enduring regional icon. There was a practical side to the significance of mechanical skill, as the cheap automobiles that Piedmont mill workers and farmers could afford often required repairs. In addition, developing mechanical skill became an important way of advancement in the mill environment and even a way out of the mills or off the farm and into more interesting, less confining—if not more lucrative—work in a garage, body shop, or auto dealership. Pearson followed his brother out of the Whitney Mill in Spartanburg County and into a local body shop.[52]

Like driving, working on cars began at an early age. Jim Hunter remembered his brothers regularly dismantling their father's Model T and putting it back together at their home in North Charleston, South Carolina. Although his father allowed this activity, he was "always giving them a hard time, because he wanted them to make sure . . . there better not be any parts left over when they put it back together."[53] These skills were not limited to those who would become future skilled mechanics but became almost universal among Piedmont working-class men and a key component of coming of age for young boys. Author Rick Bragg, at the feet of his male, working-class relatives in northeastern Alabama, "learned much of what a boy should know, of cars, pistols, heavy machinery, shotguns and love, all of which, these men apparently believed, can be operated stone drunk."[54]

The automobile meshed perfectly with the cultural values Piedmont men had retained from their rural southern roots. Not only could one experience the type of freedom and self-confidence valued in the southern male world through driving around in a car, but one could tap into the wildness, the need for excess, competition, and even violence by driving that car to its very limits, often racing head to head with another "hell of a fellow." In addition, the shade tree, the garage, and the filling station soon became important male social spaces where men could bond, drink, swear, and learn from each other how to make their automobiles go even faster. Richard Petty remembered growing up in Level Cross, North Carolina: "There was always a car in the front yard or the side yard, or wherever there was a shade tree to work under. And it was always apart, in one stage or the other, being modified to make it run faster."[55]

In 1932, Henry Ford's last great invention, the first low-priced automobile with an eight-cylinder engine, greatly abetted the male ego in the Piedmont region and transformed work (especially for the whiskey tripper), leisure, and recreation and led directly to the development and popularity of stock car racing. The so-called flat-head Ford V-8 soon took on legendary status among young men wanting to go fast. Even Texas outlaw Clyde Barrows wrote to Ford in 1933 praising him for the car's speed and durability: "I have driven Fords exclusively when I could get away with one . . . the Ford has got ever other car skinned and even if my business hasn't been strictly legal it don't hurt anything to tell you what a fine car you got in the V-8."[56] Young men throughout the region quickly learned to bore the engine out, put in new rings, and make the car even faster. "The Ford automobile," Humpy Wheeler argued, "in its natural state with the flat-head V-8 became a race car in just a few days with the right hands working on it, and it was durable and fast."[57]

Of course, the automobile, especially the V-8 Ford, took on particular importance to moonshiners, as it provided them with speedier access to their markets. They became adept at modifying the flat-head Fords—the inside "hulled out" to hold up to twenty-two 6-gallon cases of whiskey—so

Fonty Flock and Red Byron power-slide through the turns in their flat-head Ford V-8s. The Ford was a favorite for both bootleggers and stock car racers from the late 1930s to the late 1940s. (Courtesy of McCaig-Welborn Research Library at the International Motorsports Hall of Fame, Talladega, Alabama)

that they could outrun law enforcement. Junior Johnson remembered the modifications trippers made to the flat-head Ford V-8: "You could take the motors and bore the cylinders out and get bigger pistons in them. The crank shaft, you could stroke it and make a longer stroke which would put more horsepower into it. You could get high performance cam shafts to go into them and cylinder heads and manifolds. You wound up with a totally different engine."[58] By the late 1930s, moonshiners also imported "hot rod" equipment from California such as Edelbrock "Slingshot" manifolds and Stromberg carburetors. Creative mechanics could further boost a car's power by adding three or four carburetors and, late in the 1940s, adding superchargers that boosted power as much as fifty horsepower or putting in a higher-powered Cadillac ambulance engine. Moonshiners also became adept at making the car handle better, even when loaded down with whiskey, by using stiffer shocks, overinflated tires, and stronger wheels.[59] One favorite chassis modification commonly used was to add additional springs from Model T's "and mount them onto the axles." With this additional support, a fully loaded car "would sink no more than an inch," thereby avoiding tipping off law enforcement with the telltale signs of a liquor car, typically a low-riding Ford V-8.[60] Souped-up, "high-tailed" V-8 Fords became ubiquitous throughout moonshine country by the late 1930s. Vance Packard observed in 1950 one "trademark of Wilkes County": "One odd thing you do see everywhere you look is high-powered cars equipped with twin exhausts and with the rear ends remarkably high in the air."[61]

The moonshiners enjoyed a major advantage over law enforcement in that they had more disposable income to make their cars ever faster. Junior Johnson asserted, "They [law enforcement] had to use what they could buy from the dealerships. We'd take the money that [we] could make in the moonshine business and fix our cars to where we didn't lose the car and didn't lose the moonshine and didn't get caught either." Even after years as a stock car driver, Johnson claimed that the fastest he ever drove was in a 1951 Ford he used to haul liquor.[62] Red Vogt developed a huge clientele and legendary status at his Spring Street Garage in Atlanta for his ability to modify the flat-head Ford V-8 engine. Vogt's clients included both trippers and law enforcement. William Thompson and Buddy Shuman also gained notoriety in the Charlotte area for their abilities in building powerful engines for running moonshine, importing speed accessories from such California companies as Edelbrock and Offenhauser.[63]

The life of the moonshiner—and that of the tripper, racing "revenuers" in a high-powered automobile down winding mountain roads—also appealed to those cultural values ingrained in the southern male psyche. The adrenaline rush of the chase and the pride of workmanship in making a vehicle superior to that produced in Detroit brought excitement and meaning to their lives. Clay Call argued, "I was anxious for the feds to get after me, to see if the car would run."[64] "It was kind of an intriguing thing to work on them and make them run," Johnson asserted; "you almost wanted the law to run you because you had such an advantage over them."[65]

Outrunning the law took more than a fast car, however; it required a strong dose of audacity as well as driving skill. Trippers employed a variety of moves to evade law enforcement, some involving trickery such as fake police lights and bumpers that easily fell off when law enforcement attempted to use a specially designed device to grab the back of a car. They also developed the power slide, a method of maintaining speed in the turns on dirt roads by causing the rear wheels to slide while turning the front wheels opposite the turn, accelerating the entire time. The bootleg turn also became a favorite tactic for evading the law. Driving at full speed, the pursued tripper would either throw "the gear into second, making a sharp turn and letting the car swing around by itself," or "put the car into a skid, pulling on the emergency brake lightly, turning the steering wheel sharply to the left, and then accelerating madly." If the maneuver was executed properly, the driver would quickly be headed in the opposite direction past his startled and angry pursuers. The move took tremendous daring, for an improperly executed bootleg turn could easily land the car on its roof and into the hands of law enforcement.[66] NASCAR legend Curtis Turner loved to demonstrate his ability to perform this maneuver, which he had perfected in his liquor-hauling days, by spinning a full-size Cadillac on a one-lane bridge.[67]

Liquor runners also took on the status of folk heroes to many children and teens in the region. Donald Johnson of Yadkin County, North Carolina, remembered listening to the sounds of the souped-up bootlegger cars as a child as they roared down the highway: "I just thought it wadn't nothing like those bootleggers . . . they were folk heroes."[68] Helen Matthews of Forsyth County, Georgia, recalled playing outside on warm summer nights and listening for the sounds of the cars of legendary Dawson County trippers Lloyd Seay and Roy Hall driving south on Highway 19, headed for their thirsty customers in Atlanta.[69] In these areas, even children's games took on a different tone. Gordon Pirkle recalled that, as a child in Dawson County, he played "trippers and revenuers" rather than "cops and robbers" or another popular game in the South, "Confederates and Yankees." Just as the one who got the short end of the stick or lost at "eeny, meeny, miny, mo" had to play the "Yankee" in most of the South, Dawson County boys who lost out had to be "revenuers." Pirkle always wanted to play his hero, tripper Gober Sosebee.[70] Young men in the Piedmont mill towns also idolized the liquor runners. If they did not have the connections or gambler's instinct to risk imprisonment for running whiskey, they could at least emulate them by purchasing a beat-up late '30s era V-8 Ford for $50 or so and modifying it with parts out of a junkyard. Often for less than $100 they could own a vehicle that would at least sound as loud as a bootlegger's car, if not run as fast.

Street Racing

Of course all this work to make cars go faster, combined with the cultural climate of the Piedmont, stimulated competitive urges among mill workers, farmers, and moonshiners. Indeed, almost as soon as the first affordable cars hit the area, racing on streets, highways, and dirt country roads became an important pastime for young men. This activity took on special meaning in a region that offered few entertainment options for young people, especially in the working class. Young men would cruise the streets of the small Piedmont towns in the evenings talking up their cars and showing them off. Talk soon turned to challenge; bets were laid, and contestants headed off to some local stretch of highway late at night to have it out. "They would go out there on the highway," Richard Petty reminisced, "lined up side by side, somebody waved a handkerchief or an oily rag or something, and it was Katie-bar-the-door!"[71] Jim Hunter remembered going out to a .75-mile straight stretch of road 15 miles outside Charleston where thirty to forty cars gathered on a weekend night. When people asked why he was racing, he responded, "I guess you'd have to say it was for the fun of it. To prove my Chevrolet is faster than your Ford."[72]

Although high school or collegiate sports were popular with the Piedmont middle class, few farm or mill children completed high school during the 1930s and 1940s, and many, because of their social status, felt unwelcome in the high school environment. Success in street racing could turn a young man with little social standing, a minimum of athletic ability, some mechanical skills, good eye-hand coordination, and a healthy dose of "hell of a fellow" ethos into a local legend. Lee Petty—Richard's father and later a three-time champion in NASCAR's top division—became such a local legend in Randolph County, North Carolina. Indeed, the elder Petty became so successful that he often had to paint his car a different color "just so the other cats would race him."[73]

Street racing competitions among bootleggers became especially intense in those communities where moonshining predominated. Participants publicized many of these late-night races and attracted hundreds of people and thousands of dollars in side bets. Max Welbourn remembered the excitement when "the first good highway was built from Yadkinville to Wilkesboro [Highway 321]." The bootleggers raced from Brooks's store in Yadkin County to Seagrave's store in Wilkes; "it was a regular Friday or Saturday night event . . . and they'd be two and three cars at a time and they'd race from one end to the other."[74]

This experience in outrunning law enforcement or in road racing primed Piedmont-area moonshiners and trippers, as well as mill workers and farmers, for success in more organized forms of auto racing. Junior Johnson observed, "It was a kind of a help to me that I had been in the moonshine business, cause I had a head start on my career. I was as good a driver as I was ever going to be."[75]

Professional Racing in the Piedmont

By the late 1930s, the Piedmont had a populace eager for thrills, hordes of young men—bootleggers, farmers, and mill workers—eager to find an outlet for their "hell of a fellow" ideals and already racing one another on the streets and highways of the region, and entrepreneurial bootleggers with interest and expertise in fast cars. However, it took a push from individuals from outside the region to jump-start stock car racing in the region. Indeed, the sport was an outgrowth of the preexisting professional racing in the region's larger cities and of the northeastern racing establishment. As strange as it may seem, stock car racing, like most forms of organized sports in the region, was essentially a Yankee import to the South. Professional promoters with experience in promoting open-wheel, Indianapolis-style racing at Piedmont fairgrounds on holidays or during the fall fair season organized and ran most early stock car racing events in the region.

Historian Randall Hall uncovered abundant evidence of a vibrant southern auto racing culture beginning as early as 1903 and sponsored by regional elites and civic boosters and often connected to the "Good Roads Movement" in the South. Between 1908 and 1911, Savannah hosted a number of prestigious road races sanctioned by the American Automobile Association and the Automobile Club of America and featuring an international cast. In 1911, the city hosted arguably the most important auto race in the nation, the Vanderbilt Cup. New Orleans, Galveston, Atlanta, and Charlotte—which constructed a 1.5-mile wooden board track banked at 40 degrees in 1924—also built racing facilities that attracted national sanctioning bodies and crowds of 30,000 to 40,000 for major events from about 1911 through the 1920s. By the late 1920s, however, and the coming of the Great Depression, much of this activity died out, with the rotting remains of board tracks providing the few reminders of a once vibrant southern auto racing scene.[76]

Perhaps the most significant, and longest-lasting, southern racing events of the first half of the twentieth century were the races and speed trials that took place on the sands of Ormond Beach and Daytona Beach from 1903 to 1935. Early events on the beach centered on the massive Hotel Ormond, an elite resort intent on attracting even more elites. In March 1903, the managers of the hotel linked up with New York promoter

William J. Morgan to organize the Winter Speed Carnival for automobile time trials and match races on the beach. Over the years the event attracted auto racing pioneers such as Ransom Olds, Alexander Winton, Willie K. Vanderbilt, Barney Oldfield, Louis Chevrolet, Vincenzo Lancia, and Victor Hemery to challenge one another and the world land speed record.[77] The Winter Speed Carnival died with the onset of World War I, but speed trials resumed after the war with record runs by Ralph De Palma in 1919 and Sig Haugdahl in 1922. In the late 1920s, the rivalry of Englishmen Henry Seagrave and Malcolm Campbell put Daytona on the international racing map, especially after Seagrave broke the 200-mph barrier on Daytona's beach in 1927. Although Seagrave died in 1929 in a speedboat accident, Campbell and his famous Bluebird returned winter after winter to attempt a new record. By 1935, Campbell made runs on the beach at well over 300 mph and attracted large crowds to Daytona Beach even in the midst of the Great Depression. However, close brushes with disaster in 1935 convinced Campbell that he needed a smoother surface for his record runs, and in 1936 he took his act to the Bonneville Salt Flats of Utah.[78]

In the 1930s Indianapolis-style racing, or "big cars" in auto racing parlance, became a common feature at fairground tracks on holidays and at fall fairs throughout the South. Auto racing at that time was, in the words of legendary racing announcer and journalist Chris Économaki, "sustained by the agricultural fair" and usually provided the feature attraction of the final day of the larger fairs in the Piedmont South.[79] Legendary promoter Ralph Hankinson organized many, if not most, of these races. Hankinson started in the business in 1910, promoting big car races and midget car racing. By the late 1930s, he was the unquestioned king of promoters of racing in the eastern United States, able to deliver the biggest stars in the sport. As one reporter put it, Hankinson "hangs up purses, pays certain guarantees and appearance monies, and the boys 'run for the dough.'"[80] In the 1930s, Hankinson regularly brought his road show to Lakewood Speedway in Atlanta—soon known as the "Indianapolis of the South"—which attracted huge crowds. In 1938, he came to Lakewood for a two-day July 4 holiday program sponsored by the most important sanctioning body in auto racing at the time, the American Automobile Association (AAA). Some 25,000 fans gathered to see Billy Winn of Detroit defeat Milwaukee star Tony Willman in the feature race.[81]

Promoters also organized big-car races in the Piedmont South in the late 1930s and early 1940s at fairground tracks in Salisbury, Greensboro,

Open-wheel, big-car race in 1947 at Atlanta's Lakewood Speedway.
(Courtesy of McCaig-Welborn Research Library at the International
Motorsports Hall of Fame, Talladega, Alabama)

Charlotte, and High Point, North Carolina, and Spartanburg, South Carolina. Such stars as Oklahoma Cherokee Indian Joie "Chief Ride-in-the-
Storm" Chitwood, Duke Nalon, Bob Sall, Tony Willman, Jimmy Wilburn,
1949 Indianapolis 500 winner Bill Holland, and Ted Horn came south
to demonstrate their dirt-track talents to large crowds. A handful of
southern drivers—such as Harley Taylor, Harry "Red" Singleton, and Tip
Lanthier from Georgia; Bob "Red" Bryon from Alabama; Al Crisler and Bill
Sockwell from North Carolina; and Johnny Grubb and Fred Bailes from
Virginia—competed in these races but rarely fared well against the AAA
stars.[82] On occasion, southern promoters held big-car races to try to boost
local drivers by holding southern-only competitions. Mike Benton, manager of Lakewood Speedway, held one such event in September 1938; eli-
gibility was limited to drivers from "the original 'Old South,'" and the race
drew competitors from thirteen states.[83] Piedmont Triad (the Winston-
Salem, Greensboro, and High Point area and adjacent southern Virginia)
promoters like Bruce Thompson held big-car races featuring local racers
on a fairly regular basis in the late 1930s and early 1940s. Despite such
attempts, however, this type of racing failed to capture the imagination
of Piedmonters, and though the competitions drew solid crowds, big-

car racing remained a novelty or a niche sport for most of the region's residents. As Chris Economaki put it: "The races in the South, . . . big car races, were very popular, huge crowds attended the events. Of course racing was a now-and-then, here-and-there thing and the cars only came to town usually once a year. . . . And those drivers all were from mysteriously distant places—Chicago and Omaha, Denver—and the minute the checkered flag waved they would disappear. That was the end of it."[84]

Midget car racing—which became wildly popular in the midwestern and northeastern states in the late 1930s and early 1940s—and motorcycle racing followed a similar track in the Piedmont, although on a much smaller scale. Promoters with their troops of drivers and riders barnstormed through the region making their appearances at fairgrounds during fall fairs or on holidays; the races drew decent crowds, but the vehicles and the competitors were soon gone until they made another appearance the next year.[85]

Although not racing per se, "Hell Driving" shows became a popular auto-related attraction in the Piedmont region by the late 1930s and helped lay the foundation for stock car racing's eventual popularity. As with the big-car and midget racing programs common in the region, rival groups of "Hell Drivers" barnstormed through the region putting on shows, generally at fall fairs. People filled the stands of fairground tracks across the Piedmont to see Jimmy Lynch's Death Dodgers, Mickey Martin—"King of the Daredevils"—and the master and alleged inventor of such shows, Lucky Teter, and his Hell Drivers. Fans thrilled at the sight of such stunts as the Return from Hell, the Double Truck Jump, Precision Driving Roman Style, the Dynamite Drive, the Suicide Leap, and the dangerous End for End Roll Over, which Mickey Martin had "so perfected" that he could pull off the stunt "without injury to himself, though seven persons fainted in the grandstand."[86] Seeing these stunts performed by standard—at least outwardly so—street vehicles heightened the appeal for many, as did the thrill and excitement of seeing these same automobiles crashed and sometimes destroyed with the knowledge that the drivers generally walked away.

Hell Driving did have its real dangers, however, which helped to maintain an edge to the performances and kept fans coming back. Atlantan Frank Mundy once accidentally released his safety belt while performing a stunt in which he drove a car around the track balanced on two wheels. As he fell out of the open window, the car toppled over on top of him, crushing his pelvis. He was in a body cast for two months.[87] Lucky Teter's

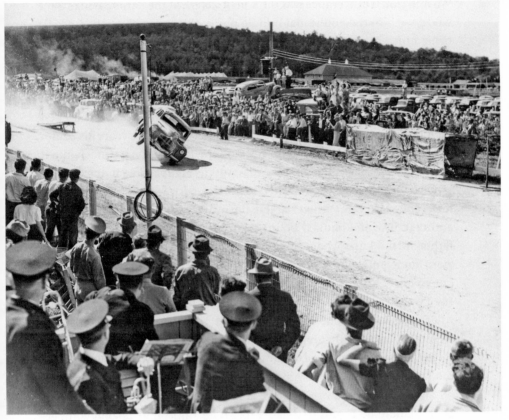

One of Jack Kochman's "Hell Drivers" performs a stunt at an unidentified fairground track. (Courtesy of McCaig-Welborn Research Library at the International Motorsports Hall of Fame, Talladega, Alabama)

luck ran out at the Indiana State Fairgrounds in July 1942 when he was killed after he crashed his 1938 Dodge into the car carrier he was trying to jump.[88]

By the late 1930s, people in the Piedmont region, especially in its growing number of towns and cities, had some exposure to a variety of auto racing. It was left to the promoters to discover what type of auto racing would truly capture their imagination.

Big Bill France

The final key factor in the origins of stock car racing in the Piedmont South was the involvement in the sport of William Henry Getty France, a Daytona Beach mechanic and erstwhile race car driver. Born in 1909 in

Washington, D.C., France was the son of a clerk at the Parks Savings Bank who gave him the additional middle name of Getty in the hope it would bring him wealth. While it did not immediately bring that result, France was imbued at an early age with an intense desire to succeed and make a name for himself. He had no interest in following in his father's footsteps in banking, however, but had a knack for auto mechanics. Ironically, he lived in a neighborhood with many young boys who were also car crazy, including a red-headed kid named Louis "Red" Vogt, five years his senior. Red later moved to Atlanta and became the first superstar mechanic in Piedmont stock car racing.[89] Like many of his compatriots in the car-mad 1920s — "everybody I knew wanted to be a race driver" — France caught the racing bug. After he turned sixteen, he would borrow his father's Model T and take it to the banked board track in nearby Laurel, Maryland. His father did not know what France was doing, but he did notice that his tires wore out awfully quickly. "Dad would complain about how his tires wore out so fast. He'd take it back to the dealer and complain, and I couldn't say a word."[90]

France dropped out of Central High School after only two years and took a job in a local garage, at the same time pursuing his passion for racing. To compete at local dirt tracks, he and his buddy Hugh Ostermeyer built a racer out of wood and canvas that France later claimed would do 90 mph. France built other cars and raced up and down the eastern seaboard, where he began to make a name for himself as a solid competitor. The experience not only provided him with valuable racing experience but also introduced him to the world of auto race promotion and its seamy underbelly. He once finished fourth in a race in Pikesville, Maryland, whose promoters announced a $500 race purse. When France went to collect his winnings, he was told that the winner would receive only $50 and he would get $10. When France complained, the promoters told him they announced the $500 purse only as a "ploy to impress the fans."[91]

In 1931, France married Anne Bledsoe, a nurse almost five years his senior who had migrated to the Washington area from Nathan's Creek, North Carolina. In another major irony of France's young life, his wife (whom he referred to as "my Annie") came from Ashe County, in the heart of North Carolina moonshining country in the mountains just west of Wilkes County. In fact, later visits to North Wilkesboro Speedway would often be occasions for Bledsoe family reunions. Perhaps most important for France's later career, Annie had a head for figures and kept a tight grip on the family's finances. She later did the same for a fledgling NASCAR as its secretary and treasurer. The couple soon added a son, William Clifton France—known throughout much of his life as Bill Jr. even though he and his father had different middle names.[92] As Bill Jr. once recalled, "While he [Big Bill] was climbing to reach lofty goals, mom firmly held the ladder and provided him a rock-solid foundation."[93]

In the early 1930s, France, dissatisfied with his life working as a mechanic on cold floors in the Washington winters, made the first of many gambles in his life when he decided to seek his fortune in Florida. "I decided I might as well go on down to Florida to work on them [cars] where it was warm and comfortable."[94] The family arrived in Daytona Beach in 1934 in a Hupmobile pulling a trailer with the family's belongings and France's mechanic's toolbox; France had $25 in his pocket—though he did have $75 in a savings account. Intending to settle in Miami, he stopped on the beach at Daytona for a swim and a view of the site where Sir Malcolm Campbell came every winter to try to break the land speed record. He liked what he saw: "When I saw Daytona Beach I thought it was the prettiest place I'd ever seen." He convinced Annie to stay, found work as a mechanic at a local auto dealership, and rented a one-bedroom house.[95]

France had found the perfect place. He soon purchased his own filling station, which enabled him to pursue his career in greater comfort, and he developed a passion for boats and fishing. In addition, he had landed in one of the hotbeds of American auto racing. France's station soon became a gathering place for local auto racing enthusiasts as they "bench raced" and worked on their cars. France's mechanic work increasingly took a back seat to his activities as a racer and as a racing promoter. By the mid-1930s France stood ready to hit the racing circuit in a big way, and he would make his name in the late 1930s and early 1940s primarily as an auto racer. Most important for the future of NASCAR, however, France found opportunities while he raced to observe the activities of promoters—especially the legendary Ralph Hankinson—and then apply those lessons to his own activities in promoting the beach/road race at Daytona, a job he inherited in 1937. France's imposing size, his natural charisma combined with an ability to intimidate when he felt it was necessary, an intense drive to succeed, and a willingness to take huge gambles in his life gave him the skills to attempt to mold a bunch of rowdy bootleggers into a professional sporting organization. As historian Pete Daniel observed, "Big Bill France brilliantly mixed the smile, the handshake, and the clenched fist."[96] In the history of American sports, no individual looms larger in the origins and early growth of one sport than he does.

Katie-Bar-the-Door!

By the late 1930s, the groundwork for the arrival and growth of organized stock car racing in the Piedmont had been laid. Hundreds of thousands of men—and some women—possessed the skills to quickly turn a late 1930s Ford V-8 into a race car. Many also possessed the driving skills, honed in street racing or running liquor, that made the transition to racing on a dirt fairground track relatively easy. Perhaps most important, their retention of traditional southern male cultural values made many young men willing and eager to prove their "hell of a fellow" bona fides—to express their freedom from societal constraints—in a public venue.

For young men of the Piedmont region, racing on a dirt track became the ultimate expression of freedom and escape from their workaday lives and linked them to their cultural roots in important ways. As Humpy Wheeler observed, "Guys might have worked in the mill. They might been an electrician. They might have been a plumber, whatever. But they had these strict rules they had to go by during the week. As soon as they walked on that race track . . . the rules disappear. Nobody's going to tell them what to do. 'Cause that's what they're getting away from."[97] "Skilled drivers," Pete Daniel asserted, "at the edge of control suggested that escape was possible for those with enough nerve."[98] The wild rough-and-tumble of racing struck a strong cultural nerve among members of the Piedmont working class who sought activities that, in the words of Ted Ownby, helped them "rise above the boredom and dissatisfactions of mundane existence and rebel against accumulated frustrations, enjoying norms of behavior that differ dramatically from everyday norms."[99] As Ownby has observed, the Piedmont stock car racer of the 1930s, '40s, and '50s almost perfectly embodied Cash's "hell of a fellow." "The sheer emphasis on speed, on barely escaping injury, on running as fast as possible, sounds as much as any modern sport like something W. J. Cash would have recognized."[100]

This expression of freedom and wildness experienced by drivers provided a vicarious experience and fulfilled some of the same psychic and cultural needs for spectators. Jim Hunter observed, "I think they [the spectators] wished they could do that. It was either, I think I could do that or I wish I could do that. . . . The fans pictured them [the drivers] as themselves."[101] "In the . . . wild and frenzied infields and grandstands at stock car races," Daniel asserted, "southerners found the space to reclaim their wildness."[102] Trips to the dirt track on the weekend played much the same role for the Piedmont working class of the 1940s and 1950s as trips to town did for their ancestors earlier in the twentieth century. Cash observed that in the drinking, fighting, and carousing that took place on Saturday nights "the old romantic-hedonistic impulses found egress . . . men and women were gratefully emptied of their irritations and repressions and left to return to their daily tasks stolid, unlonely, and tame again."[103]

Given this groundwork, it was now up to professional promoters to tap into this wellspring and offer an outlet for these deep emotions and cultural values. While open-wheel, midget racing, and Hell Driving had their enthusiasts, they did not resonate with Piedmont fans. Richard Petty commented on this phenomenon in a 1971 interview with *Sports Illustrated*: "Open-cockpit racing cars never caught on in the South, not even midget racers. I guess its just the people in the South were so poor, and those fancy race cars were so exotic that they didn't know what to make of them. People identify with stock cars."[104] Indeed, when promoters, first in Daytona Beach and then in the Piedmont itself, introduced stock car racing to the bootleggers, farmers, and mill workers of the region, folks immediately identified with the sport and the local drivers who excelled at it. By the early 1940s, stock car racing in the Piedmont took off like a bored-out, flat-head Ford V-8 in a match race on a country road, and in the words of Richard Petty, "Katie-bar-the-door!"

Home-towners Going at It Tooth and Nail
Pre–World War II Piedmont Stock Car Racing

*There was a lot of bootlegging people involved in racing when it got off the ground.
And if anything boosted it and made it successful I would think you have to give the
bootlegging people a big, big part of the credit for it.*

—*Junior Johnson, in David Padrush,*

Rumrunners, Moonshiners, and Bootleggers

*What made that [stock car racing] so popular was these were our drivers. . . . You
could see these guys downtown on the off-days. Stock car racing in the Carolinas,
Virginia, and Georgia was their sport. It wasn't outsiders coming in and then leaving.
It was home-towners going at it tooth and nail. And that's what engendered the popularity of stock car racing in the South.*

—*Chris Economaki, interview by author*

Professional stock car racing got its start in the South in 1936 at Daytona
Beach but quickly spread throughout its Piedmont region, particularly to
Georgia and the two Carolinas. Although most of the earliest participants
were experienced open-wheel racers, bootleggers—particularly from the
Atlanta area—soon came to dominate the sport as drivers, mechanics, and
car owners. In addition, while promoters from the Northeast like Ralph
Hankinson organized many of the early races, southern-based promoters
like Bruce Thompson of North Carolina's Triad area, Bill France, and his
bootlegger friend Joe Littlejohn from Spartanburg, South Carolina, made
significant inroads into the organizational end of the sport. By the start
of World War II, stock car racing had become an entertainment staple
throughout the Piedmont, with the chief attraction being its homegrown,

41

flamboyant, liquor-hauling racers like Lloyd Seay, Roy Hall, Joe Littlejohn, Sam Rice, and Buddy Shuman. Fairground tracks in Atlanta, Spartanburg, Charlotte, Greensboro, and Salisbury regularly hosted 5,000 to 15,000 fans for their stock car races. Promoters in the High Point area of North Carolina even saw enough potential in the sport to construct one of the few tracks in the country devoted purely to auto racing. The wild drivers who barnstormed the region provided Piedmont working-class fans with wonderful, cheap entertainment, spraying the stands with rooster tails of the region's signature red clay as they sped around track.

Beach Beginnings

While the stock car racing that became NASCAR put down its deepest roots in the Piedmont South, it had its origins on beach sand, not red clay, the serendipitous result of the departure of Sir Malcolm Campbell and his Bluebird from the sands of Daytona Beach in 1935. In order to continue to attract auto buffs to the area during the winter tourism lull, the city of Daytona—with the advice of Daytona Beach garage owner and former land speed record holder Sig Haughdahl—decided to sponsor a 250-mile stock car race in February 1936. The organizers created a 3.2-mile track using the beach and the adjacent U.S. Highway A1A with turns cut through the dunes to connect the two straightaways. The American Automobile Association (AAA)–sanctioned race, and its $1,700 winner's purse, attracted some stellar entries from big-car racing, many of whom spent at least part of their winters racing in Florida, including 1934 Indy 500 champ "Wild" Bill Cummings. Competitor George "Doc" Mackenzie lauded the inherent appeal of a stock car race to the press: "This event is sure to become a great speed classic for the simple reason that it is a stock car event and every car owner in the country wants to see how the automobile of his choice will stand up under competition." The race drew a total of twenty-seven entrants, including local mechanic Bill France.[1]

Although the race attracted a solid field of entries, was well promoted, and drew an estimated crowd of 20,000, serious difficulties arose almost from the start. Organizers limited the field to 1935- or 1936-model American-made cars divided into four divisions based on the manufacturer's list price. The cars started one at a time to avoid a huge pileup as cars raced into the first turn. In addition, the event was a handicap race, and so the starting order of the cars was the reverse of the order of their qualifying speed. The complicated nature of the race and the inexperience of race officials turned it into a scoring disaster, as neither officials nor

Late 1940s Daytona beach/ road race. Such races were held from 1936 to 1958, and Big Bill France played a role as driver or promoter in all of them. (Courtesy of McCaig-Welborn Research Library at the International Motorsports Hall of Fame, Talladega, Alabama)

spectators knew who led the race at any given time. Behind-the-scenes political infighting over who would hold the prize money and direct ticket sales allowed thousands of spectators to enter without paying admission before ticket sellers were in place. Others simply climbed over the dunes or strolled up the beach to watch the race.[2]

The most serious problems developed as the race progressed and the course began to deteriorate. Although the stock cars reached impressive speeds racing north on the beach and south on A1A, after a few laps the heavy racers began to bog down in the soft sand of the turns. Every car in the event had to be towed out of the deep sand at least once, leading race officials to abandon a rule that penalized drivers one lap if they required wrecker assistance. Major Goldie Gardner retired after only forty-five laps disgusted that what organizers had touted as a high-speed event had degenerated into "nothing but an obstacle race." Henry McLemore, a reporter for United Press International, asserted that the south turn "was a hog wallow. . . . Just a mess of holes that a horse would have trouble getting through." Officials finally ended the fiasco three laps short of the finish when the north turn became impassable as cars suffering mechanical failure or stuck in the soft sand blocked the track.[3]

The problems only worsened as the race ended. The lack of a proper scoring system soon came to light when apparent winner Tommy Elmore of Jacksonville pulled his Ford convertible onto the beach to accept the championship trophy and $1,700 prize. Officials, however, declared "Mad" Milt Marion the winner, Ben Shaw second, and Elmore third. Elmore filed a protest, but to no avail, and the results stood. City officials soon discovered that in addition to a chaotic and confusing end to the race, they had lost an estimated $22,000 on the venture. Big time stock car racing in the South had gotten off to a less than auspicious beginning; indeed, it appeared that it might have died aborning.[4]

Fortunately, however, the fifth-place finish of Bill France provided the one bright spot in the race. His experience in the race helped rekindle the love for auto racing he developed as a young man in Washington, D.C. After the first beach/road race, France stepped in to try to save stock car racing on the beach and, unknowingly, made his first step toward becoming the major promoter of stock car racing in the nation and the founder of NASCAR. In the aftermath of the public relations and financial fiasco of the inaugural Daytona beach/road stock car race, the city fathers wanted nothing more to do with stock cars. They were, however, interested in attracting tourists during the traditionally slow winter months. In January 1937 they agreed to a motorcycle race on the same beach/road course used the previous year. The organizers of the event made one major improvement that might have indirectly saved auto racing on the beach: they added marl—a mixture of clay, calcium carbonate, magnesium, and sea shells traditionally used as a fertilizer—to the turns, creating a much harder and more durable racing surface. The success of the motorcycle race led France and Sig Haughdahl to attempt to interest city fathers once again in a stock car race on the course. While the city offered only the use of the track and no financial support, with sponsorship from the local Elks Club the two organized a Labor Day triple-feature event that included a 75-mile motorcycle race, a short big-car race, and a 50-mile event for stock cars. The tiny purses—only $100 total prize money for the stock event—severely limited the attraction of top drivers, and only one non-Floridian—North Carolinian Bill Sockwell—showed up to compete against a field of drivers drawn primarily from the Daytona area. The race itself went off without major incident, and local bar owner, bootlegger, and gambler Smokey Purser took the checkered flag.[5]

The Original Stock Car Racing Bootlegger

Purser's victory may have been one of the most important events in the early history of stock car racing, as he helped shape the fledgling sport in important ways. He opened the door for a new type of driver—flamboyant, hard charging, full of braggadocio, often on the wrong side of the law, and ambitious—whose exploits gave working-class fans such a vicarious thrill. Smokey Purser became the first of such men who would come to dominate stock car racing in the pre–World War II era. Purser escaped the rural poverty of Lumber City, Georgia, as a teen armed only with an eighth-grade education, a wealth of native mechanical ability, and an intense drive to succeed, no matter what that took. He landed in Daytona Beach and worked at odd jobs where his mechanical abilities came in handy. The coming of Prohibition provided Purser with a chance to improve his lot in life; he jumped at the opportunity and became involved in "importing" alcohol off-loaded from boats off the Florida coast and then "distributing" it across the country. When his children asked him what he did for a living, he replied that he was a "sea lawyer" handling "cases at sea." The run from Daytona to St. Louis became a favorite of his and enabled him to polish his driving skills as he sped across the Southeast. Purser also used subtler methods to evade the law: he carried a variety of disguises to avoid being noticed—including a priest's collar—and often hauled liquor in a panel truck with "Fresh Florida Fish" written on the side. "Yeah, I had to throw a few dead fish in the back of the van to stink it up real good." With the end of Prohibition, Purser moved into more legitimate pursuits, opening the New Yorker Bar and Grill in Daytona Beach, although he became known for running illegal gambling and numbers games out of his business. Stock car racing fit his personality perfectly, since he not only became adept as a racer but knew how to put on a show for the fans with his hard-charging, hell-for-leather style. The press also loved the ever quotable Purser, who always found a way to incite fan and competitor interest.[6]

Although officials of the city of Daytona Beach remained lukewarm to stock car racing, the minor success of the 1937 event encouraged France to press on in 1938. Along with Charlie Reese, owner of Charlie's Grill and Hi-Hat Club, France formed the Daytona Beach Racing Association to promote additional beach/road stock car races. Reese came up with $1,000 in prize money, and France promised to deliver the drivers for a July 4, 150-mile race. France was as good as his word, and thirty drivers entered the event, including competitors from states other than Florida. The race even attracted the attention of Darlington, South Carolina, businessman Harold Brasington—the future builder and developer of Darlington Raceway—who finished fourth in the race. France also demonstrated a knack for promotion when he publicized Smokey Purser's pledge to defend his title as "king of the beach." Purser bragged, "If this alligator of mine will keep performing as it has in the past . . . you can bring all the drivers

Bill France in his early days as a stock car driver on Daytona Beach. He was declared the 1940 National Stock Car Racing Champion for winning an Armistice Day race at the Spartanburg, South Carolina, Fairgrounds. (Courtesy of McCaig-Welborn Research Library at the International Motorsports Hall of Fame, Talladega, Alabama)

that you want to." The race, which attracted a crowd of 4,500 who paid 50¢ admission, was an exciting one with numerous spectacular crashes as drivers rolled their cars going into the turns or lost a wheel from the stress of a 150-mile event. Purser, who had to pull into the pits early in the race to repair a fan belt that he claimed had been cut by a saboteur, put on a show for the fans as he blasted through the turns. However, he was unable to make up all the laps he lost while repairing his car and finished well back in the pack. The race came down to a battle between Ormond Beach fireman Danny Murphy and Bill France himself. Murphy won the race by thirty seconds in a 1938 Ford advertising the Hofbrau Bar-Grill ("The Best Food In Town") and collected $300. Most important, Bill France and Charlie Reese made $200 in profit.[7]

Building on their success, France and Reese quickly organized a second 1938 race in conjunction with a planned Labor Day Festival that included boxing matches, motorcycle and jalopy races, and a rodeo. The promoters also made a number of improvements to the track, built grandstands on the north turn, erected a 42-foot scoreboard so spectators could keep track of race leaders, and added a sound system. In addition, they required drivers to pay an entry fee of $10 for the first time and participate in a prerace parade thorough downtown Daytona Beach to further hype the event. As an incentive to promote aggressive racing, France rounded up lap-leader prizes from local merchants—cases of Pabst Blue Ribbon beer and Ballantine Ale, a box of Hav-A-Tampa cigars, or a small cash amount. In order to quiet concerns that some drivers competed in automobiles that were not "strictly stock," the promoters hired a technical inspector who randomly inspected a few cars before the race and then checked the cylinder size of the top five finishers after the race. France and Reese also gambled that spectators would pay more to see the race and upped the price of admission to $1.00.[8]

The race attracted only fourteen entrants, but perhaps most interesting of those entrants was the unheralded Joe Littlejohn from Spartanburg, South Carolina, who raced in a new 1938 Ford V-8. Involved in the illegal liquor business—primarily in red liquor—in upstate South Carolina, Littlejohn soon became one of the most important early figures in Piedmont stock car racing, not only as a driver but as one of the first major promoters of the sport in the region.[9] What has been lost to history is how Littlejohn and fellow Spartanburg racer Woodrow "Pig" Ridings knew about the race and what attracted them to enter. Perhaps one of the two had read about the race in some auto racing publication such as *Illustrated Speedway News*. Another possibility seems to be that an informal network of bootleggers and moonshiners existed, and perhaps they had learned of the event from Smokey Purser.[10] Whatever their reason for entering, they did well, with both finishing in the top five. Most important, Littlejohn became the first Piedmont area liquor runner to come to Daytona and began a trend of trippers from around the region making the pilgrimage to Florida's Atlantic coast to enter the Daytona races. In the years before World War II, liquor drivers like J. Sam Rice of Martinsville, Virginia; Lloyd Seay, Roy Hall, Bernard Long, and Bob and Fonty Flock from the Atlanta area; and Arvel "Red" Sluder of Asheville, North Carolina, made the trek south for the Daytona races. These bootleggers/racers not only entered, finished well, and often won those races but served as key emissaries in taking stock car racing back to the Piedmont. Indeed, Rice would join Joe Littlejohn as an important promoter and track owner in the post–World War II period.[11]

The Labor Day 1938 race itself featured a fierce battle between Smokey Purser and Lloyd Moody. While narrowly leading the race, Moody carried too much speed into the south turn on lap twenty-eight, ran off the course, and bogged down in a sand dune. He lost valuable time as a wrecker extricated him, and Purser led the final laps to win the race. The excitement of the race did not end, however, with the waving of the checkered flag. Instead of pulling into the winner's circle to accept his trophy and first-place check, Purser kept driving, left the track, and disappeared. Such an action should have ended in an automatic disqualification, but France was in the uncomfortable position of serving triple-duty as a race official, the promoter, and the second place-driver who would benefit most from Purser's disqualification. After a discussion with his partner, Charlie Reese, France decided to allow the other drivers to vote on Purser's fate, and all agreed that he should be disqualified. In order to avoid the appearance of impropriety, the promoters gave the first-place money to the third-place finisher, Lloyd Moody, and France accepted the second-place check. To complicate matters further, Purser showed up with his race car at the Seabreeze Garage ten minutes before the announced 4:00 P.M. post-race inspection. When officials informed him of his disqualification, he asserted that his car was "strictly stock" and that they had treated him unfairly. Inspectors proceeded to tear down the car and discovered that the compression ratio in the cylinders was dramatically lower than in the prerace inspection. Purser argued that this was due to the "hard grind of the race," but it was all too obvious that Purser had used the almost three hours since the end of the race to make changes to the engine, and race officials upheld the disqualification. Despite the controversy and the outlay of additional expenses, France and Reese split a profit of $2,000, and the future of stock car racing on Daytona Beach looked bright.[12]

Indeed, Bill France had almost single-handedly saved southern stock car racing from an early and untimely death. Along the way he had learned a number of valuable lessons that served him well in the future and shaped stock car racing to the present day. France learned that money could be made in the appeal of stock car racing to working-class fans, not the elite audience that had traditionally been attracted to auto racing in the South. Working-class fans identified more with the cars driven in the races, and the relative cheapness of a stock car—as opposed to big cars or even midget racers—allowed individuals of more modest means with mechanical skill and the requisite bravado to become successful drivers. He also saw that folks associated with the illegal liquor industry had the money, the mechanical skill, the cars, and the bravado to become big stars in the sport and that their wild driving style helped sell lots of tickets and turned stock car racing on the beach from a money-losing to a money-making proposition.

As valuable as these wild bootleggers were to France's promotional success, he discovered that controlling and organizing them would constitute one of his greatest professional challenges. Individuals accustomed to operating on the margins of the law and societal convention were not averse to bending the rules of stock car racing. Indeed, Purser had already done so and would constantly challenge the limits of the rules and keep rule makers and inspectors on their toes. To be sure, cheating, or at least exploiting gray areas in the rule book, would become a major feature of stock car racing from its beginnings in Daytona Beach to the present day.[13] France learned two lessons from this fact of stock car racing. First, rules were necessary in order to maintain the close competition that stock car fans came to expect. France discovered that one of his major priorities had to be to ensure that one person or automobile make did not dominate, a surefire way to alienate fans. Second, he developed great flexibility in writing and changing rules and great creative skill in interpreting them to his own advantage. He realized that sometimes you cracked down on drivers and sometimes you let things slide, especially if it meant disqualifying a particularly popular driver.

Stock Car Racing Comes to the Piedmont

As France solidified the position of stock car racing at Daytona Beach, the sport made its first major foray into the Piedmont region on Armistice Day 1938 at Atlanta's Lakewood Speedway—a one-mile, dirt fairground track on the southwestern side of Atlanta. While races at Daytona would always be important to the growth of organized stock car racing, it was in the Piedmont itself, and especially at Lakewood, that the sport began to take hold and the moonshiners and bootleggers of north Georgia transformed it into a regional working-class entertainment staple. Perhaps in response to the success of the beach races and in the aftermath of successful big-car races on July 4 and Labor Day, Mike Benton—president of Southeastern Fair, the organization that managed Lakewood Speedway—decided to hold a 150-mile world's championship stock car race on the Monday holiday (November 11). The International Stock Car Automobile Racing Association sanctioned the race, Ralph Hankinson's organization promoted it, and the event drew a distinguished field of racers, the most notable from the top ranks of big-car racing who had been barnstorming the Piedmont during the fall fair season. Chief "Ride in the Storm" Joie Chitwood headlined the event. Other notables who received early publicity included Atlanta open-wheel driver Harley Taylor; Louisville, Kentucky, ace Bert Hellmuller; Henri Guerand, the "Flying French-man," who had just won a big-car race in Spartanburg, South Carolina; and Daytona winners Danny Murphy, Smokey Purser, and Bill France. The Hankinson promotion machine further advertised the race by hyping the entry of five redheads—Red Yandle, Red Vogt, Red Singleton, Red Beal, and Red Byron. Hankinson also convinced three women to enter—stunt driver Miss Birdis V. Draper ("BVD"); Mrs. "Man Mountain" Dean, wife of a professional wrestler; and Mrs. Buddy Evans. Only two of the redheads, Singleton and Byron, and none of the women qualified for the race. The *Atlanta Constitution* reported that the race was "causing more comment among speed fans than any races since the 100-mile AAA race held on Labor Day, 1935." Montgomery Ward, which regularly used auto racing to promote its line of tires, even sent Jack Story of Oklahoma City, reportedly "the country's finest race announcer," to announce the race.[14]

Promoters and reporters, however, barely noted in prerace publicity the entry of two eighteen-year-old north Georgia boys: Lloyd Seay and Roy Hall. For the next three years the duo would do perhaps more than anyone else to popularize stock car racing among the Piedmont working class and give it its unique stamp in the world of sports. Originally from Dawsonville, Georgia, the two made their living, in the words of distant cousin Raymond Parks, "going up and down the road from Dawsonville every night"—that is, running moonshine whiskey to thirsty Atlanta mill workers.[15] While Seay and Hall escaped the notice of *Atlanta Constitution* sports writers, they had drawn considerable attention, despite their youth, from local law enforcement. Clint Chastain, a friend from Dawson-ville, remembered riding with Seay on a return trip from hauling liquor to Atlanta. As Seay sped down the road at 120 mph, "we met the state patrol coming the other way. They didn't even turn around to try to come after us. They knowed it wasn't no use. They knowed who it was."[16] Hall earned much the same grudging respect from the law, with one Atlanta police official calling him "a genius at the wheel."[17]

A huge crowd showed up for the Armistice Day festivities at Lakewood. The appearance of big-car stars Joie Chitwood, Harley Taylor, and Henri Guerand attracted many fans. Others had migrated from the failing farms of rural Georgia to find work in Atlanta and cheered for drivers with whom they could identify. Seay was their man, and he did not let his cracker fans down. As the *Atlanta Constitution* observed, Seay "was the sensation of the race." He twice recovered from flat tires to amaze the crowd as he roared past his competitors to win the "diamond trophy and world title" in a

Stock car race at Lakewood Speedway, the "Indianapolis of the South," where stock car racing first became a working-class entertainment staple in the Piedmont South. (Courtesy of McCaig-Welborn Research Library at the International Motorsports Hall of Fame, Talladega, Alabama)

race shortened 15 miles by darkness. Joie Chitwood finished second, with Danny Murphy third, Bill France fourth, and Roy Hall fifth.[18]

The race created an immediate sensation in the region. Promoters quickly followed up on the race and organized stock car events for Macon, Georgia, on the Sunday after Thanksgiving and at Lakewood a week later, on December 4. The Macon race, organized and promoted by Hell Driver Mickey Martin, drew a crowd of 4,500 despite the cold. Although the race attracted only nine entries, fans were treated to a lively show that included two "crackups" as Larry Beckett from Dayton, Ohio, won the race.[19] The Lakewood race featured a 50-mile national championship and a 10-mile state championship race and attracted drivers from Ohio, Michigan, Indiana, Minnesota, West Virginia, South Carolina, Tennessee, Alabama, Texas, and even California. Beckett once again won the feature, with Red

Byron second. Roy Hall represented the liquor drivers well for a while and led a good bit of the race but crashed into the fence when he broke a spindle. Tip Lanthier won the state championship, shortened to 6 miles when Ralph Forrester rolled his car and blocked the track. Hall was able to repair his car from his feature race crash and finish second.[20]

Big-time stock car racing had come to the Piedmont with a bang. The three Georgia races laid the foundation for the spread of the sport throughout the region as promoters recognized the possibilities for future racing programs. The notoriety and fame, not the prize money, attracted the bootlegger drivers, and working-class fans spread the news of these wild racers by word of mouth. Perhaps most important, their early experiences in organized racing hooked Lloyd Seay and Roy Hall, along with car owner Raymond Parks and mechanic Red Vogt. Seay's victory in the Armistice Day race was the thing, as Parks remembered, that "give me the fever." Parks proceeded to purchase two brand-new 1939 Ford Standard Coupes and turned them over to Vogt to prepare for the February 1939 Daytona race.[21]

In addition, the initial successes of Seay and Hall and other local bootleggers/racers hooked Lakewood Speedway and its promoters on stock car racing and on the appeal of local drivers. In a very short time, Lakewood became the center of the stock car racing universe, a universe dominated increasingly by Piedmont—mostly north Georgia—liquor drivers. By 1941, the *Atlanta Constitution* announced that officials at Lakewood Speedway had decided to focus their race promotion efforts almost entirely on stock cars and local drivers: "This event really signalizes the beginning of a new era for race drivers of Georgia and the south. Lakewood has gone off the big time [open-wheel racing] and in the future will patronize home and Dixie products. More genuinely spectacular races will result."[22]

Stock Car Racing Spreads North

Although Daytona and Lakewood remained the most important centers for stock car racing in the pre–World War II South—each holding two to four races annually over the next three years—such events became increasingly common in the Piedmont region, especially in the Carolinas. Not only did promoters have the advantage of having lots of available liquor cars and drivers to keep the racing exciting, but they had also discovered that the red-clay soil of the Piedmont made for great stock car racing, even on the fairground tracks built initially for horse racing. Driver Néil "Soapy" Castles asserted, "Everybody ran dirt tracks and your dirt tracks were horse tracks, mostly at your fairgrounds, with long straight-aways and short corners, narrow. People started running these old Fords and found they could get around these horse tracks pretty good."[23] "Red clay . . . is the greatest natural racing surface in the world," racing promoter Humpy Wheeler observed. "If it is prepared properly, it is a beautiful thing to behold." Stock cars on a red-clay track watered down appropriately created quite a spectacle for the entertainment-starved Piedmont working class. Indeed, the sight of stock cars power-sliding through the turns beating and banging on one another attracted thousands of Piedmonters to the races.[24]

In 1939, the fairground tracks at Salisbury, North Carolina, and Spartanburg, South Carolina—promoted by bootlegger Joe Littlejohn—added stock car races to the big-car and motorcycle racing they had featured in the past. Both remained major stops for stockers throughout the prewar period.[25] Greensboro came on board with a stock race promoted by Bruce Thompson at the Greensboro Fairgrounds in 1940, reportedly the first race run in the South under the lights, and held regular races throughout the prewar period.[26] Charlotte joined the club in 1941 with a Ralph Hankinson–promoted event billed as stock car racing's "world's championship"; held at the Southern States Fairgrounds, the race drew a crowd of more than 10,000, quickly making the "Queen City" a major player in the sport.[27]

High Point, North Carolina, became one of the premier venues for Piedmont stock car racing in 1941 when it drew large crowds to its new one-mile, banked, red-clay track. The High Point Speedway, one of the first tracks built in the Piedmont since the 1920s strictly for auto racing, had seating for 10,000 spectators, and its treated racing surface allowed stock cars to attain lap speeds of almost 80 mph, almost unheard of at the time. Although its inaugural race in October 1940 was a big-car race, it hosted three stock car races in 1941, including one billed as a "national championship race" in August.[28]

At the same time, stock car racing found a following outside the region with some major racing promoters organizing well-paying events in the Midwest and Northeast that attracted many of the top drivers on the Piedmont circuit. Always in the forefront in auto racing, Ralph Hankinson promoted a July 4, 200-mile "All-American Championship Stock Car Auto Race" in 1939 with a staggering purse—at least for a stock car race—of $5,500 at the legendary one-mile, circular track at Langhorne Speedway near Philadelphia. To further hype the event, Hankinson named racing legend Barney Oldfield as race director. The race attracted several big-name open-wheel drivers, including Bill Holland and Ted Nyquist, but also brought entries from Piedmont liquor drivers Roy Hall and Sam Rice. Neither Piedmont driver fared well, but a long tradition of trippers/racers going north to Langhorne and Allentown, Pennsylvania; Fort Wayne, Indiana; and other major tracks in the Northeast and Midwest to compete in, and often win, big-money events began.[29]

Like a Bomb Had Scattered the Landscape

The wildness and exuberance of the drivers and the intense competition of the stock car race made the sport appealing to Piedmont working-class crowds. Although races often ended with the winner leading by several laps, the short, narrow tracks ensured that the cars always ran close to one another. Wrecks were common, with drivers using their bumpers to get by slower cars by getting underneath them and pushing them up the track, often spinning them out—"cuttin' 'em a flip" in Piedmont stock car parlance. In addition, all of this was going on in "the same type cars Mr. and Mrs. American chauffeur on the highway."[30] Even when the cars were not beating and banging one another, the power slide used by the best drivers to negotiate the flat, red-clay turns of the fairground tracks was something to behold. "When it's right and it's not dusty and it's just got that patina on it and those cars are sliding through the corner," Humpy Wheeler asserted, "people loved it."[31]

The sheer love of racing that the drivers seemed to possess and their joy in putting on a show for the fans made the appeal of the sport even more infectious in its early years. An *Atlanta Constitution* reporter recorded one impromptu exhibition of the drivers' love for racing when a group put on an "exhibition spin" for fans after qualifying for a 1941 Lakewood race. Unfortunately for the fans, and for the owners of and mechanics on the cars, the exhibition proved short lived, as in the fourth turn of the first lap "a car bumped Harley Taylor and then with machine-like precision six others followed suit until maybe it looked like a bomb had scattered the landscape." The drivers all walked away, most laughing about the incident, and the fans had a memory that they would talk about for months and years.[32] Promoters, often at the behest of the drivers, organized special "grudge races" between rival competitors at the beginning or end of race programs simply for bragging rights—and for the proceeds of the heavy side bets on the outcome.[33]

The trippers/racers loved racing so much that they would even race each other to the races, of course accompanied by the normal side bets. As Red Vogt recalled, "The best race every year was the one *to* Daytona, and not the one *at* Daytona." In the days before the race, competitors would gather at Red's Spring Street garage and line up, and then the race began. "They raced from the front of my place to Bill France's filling station in Daytona." Some drove their race/liquor cars, while others towed them behind trucks or other vehicles. It was a sight to behold and amazing that no one was killed or injured in the process. "How all of them made it," Red asserted, "I don't know. But I guess it proved how well they could drive a car. Anywhere."[34]

As stock car racing became more common throughout the Piedmont region, the more successful drivers—most with a background in hauling illegal alcohol—became recognizable stars, and promoters touted their appearances heavily. The announcement of the appearance of Smokey Purser, Jap Brogdon, Harley Taylor, Bob and Fonty Flock, or Joe Littlejohn in a race helped bring out Piedmont crowds by the early 1940s. While Bill France made a name for himself in racing circles as the chief promoter of the Daytona races, his primary interest in the pre–World War II era was in driving. Indeed, France became the sport's first regional star in 1940 when—often billed as "Wild" Bill France—he dominated the southern tour, winning four of the nine major stock car races held in the region—Salisbury, Daytona, and Spartanburg (twice).[35] In addition, he won a major 200-mile race in Fort Wayne, Indiana, and finished second at the "All-American Championships" at Langhorne Speedway. Throughout the 1941 season, promoters often listed France as the 1940 National Stock Car Racing Champion in their advertising, a title he gained for winning the Armistice Day race at Spartanburg.[36]

Piedmont Stock Car Racing's First Superstars

The two biggest, and most marketable, headliners in Piedmont stock car racing circles before World War II, however, were Roy Hall and Lloyd Seay. Young, good-looking, brash, supremely talented, and totally fearless—the very embodiment of Cash's southern "hell of a fellow"—the pair electrified crowds wherever they went, although their frequent brushes with the law sometimes sidelined them for significant periods of time. A reporter writing a feature in the *Atlanta Constitution* after Hall's victory in a September 1939 race at Lakewood Speedway interviewed Atlanta police, who cataloged a long list of Hall's recent run-ins with local law enforcement. At the time of the race, Hall was out on a $500 federal bond for "hauling liquor," a $300 Dekalb County bond for "speeding and reckless driving," and three $500 Fulton County bonds for "running liquor, speeding and violating the state motor vehicle law." Despite his legal difficulties, Hall won the two biggest stock car races in the region back to back—the Labor Day race at Lakewood Speedway in 1939 and the March 1940 Daytona beach/road race—in spectacular fashion. The *Atlanta Constitution* called his driving "demon-like."[37] Asked if he would return to defend his Daytona crown, Hall responded, "Sure, I'll be here—that is if I'm still alive by then."[38] He did survive, but he was unable to follow up on his success, as he spent much of 1940 locked up in the Georgia State Penitentiary. After making such a spectacular debut in winning the Armistice Day race at Lakewood in 1938, Seay raced sporadically through the 1939 and 1940 seasons, dealing with his "business interests" and his own legal problems.[39]

Seay and Hall possessed two other important advantages in their dominance of Piedmont stock car racing besides their bravado and driving skills honed on north Georgia's winding roads: Raymond Parks and Red Vogt. Although stock car promoters to this day tout the daring of drivers as the key component of competitive success, since the earliest days of stock car racing, money—along with the mechanical skill it can buy—has always been a decisive factor. Indeed, there was and is a great deal of truth in the sign legendary NASCAR mechanic Banjo Matthews posted in his Asheville, North Carolina, race shop: "Banjo's, Where Money Buys Speed—How Fast Do You Want to Go?"[40] In the case of Seay and Hall, Parks provided the money and Vogt supplied the speed: Parks fielded a Red Vogt–prepared 1934 Ford V-8 Roadster for Seay for the first Lakewood stock car race and later supplied both Seay and Hall with quality race cars throughout the pre–World War II era.[41]

Parks quickly became one of the most significant figures in early stock car racing in the region as the cars he supplied dominated the sport from the late 1930s to the early 1950s. Parks joined Joe Littlejohn as one of the first of a group of entrepreneurial bootleggers who shaped Piedmont stock car racing more by their financial involvement than their bravado on the track, although both demonstrated significant skill as racers. Parks grew up poor in Dawson County, Georgia, but left home to move to Lawrenceville, where he worked making and hauling liquor for his uncle. A year later he moved to Atlanta, where he used his Dawson County connections to move into tripping full-time, hauling 60 gallons of whiskey a night in a 1926 Model T Ford Roadster and clearing 30¢ to 35¢ per gallon. Always fastidious, Parks would stop at a creek halfway between Dawson County and Atlanta, pull out a bucket and rags, and "wash that Model T up like it was new." By 1932, the hardworking and entrepreneurial Parks had become so successful in the business that he began hiring others to do the tripping, invested his profits in a service station and (legal) liquor store on Hemphill Avenue in Atlanta, and later started Parks Novelty, leasing juke boxes, pool tables, cigarette vending machines, and occasionally illegal slot machines. Once police called Parks to tell him they had fifteen of his slot machines and he could come down and claim them. Parks declined, asserting, "I'm no fool. I guess they melted them down or something." Parks also made huge profits running a numbers game in the Atlanta area known as "The Bug," which at its peak employed more than forty "pick-up men" to collect the three-digit picks (10¢ per pick) and deliver winnings ($5 for the correct pick). By the mid-1930s, Parks's enterprises hauled in thousands of dollars a day. He did serve one nine-month stint in the federal penitentiary in Chillicothe, Ohio, in 1936–37 for conspiracy, and when he got out, he decided to let associates "Legs" Law, Seay, and Hall run most of the risks of hauling moonshine while he provided the financial backing.[42]

While still in the illegal liquor business, Parks formed a key relationship with mechanic Red Vogt—Bill France's childhood friend in Washington, D.C.—who had migrated south as well and owned a garage on Spring Street in Atlanta near the Varsity Drive-In. Soon after the introduction of the flat-head Ford V-8 in 1932, the fastidious, creative, intense, and notoriously combative Vogt became the acknowledged Atlanta-area master at modifying the engine to make it go even faster. He attracted a large clientele of those who wanted, or needed, speedy automobiles, including sizable numbers of trippers and law enforcement. Red's garage was "neutral ground," in the words of reporter Ed Hinton, "sort of the Switzerland of moonshine running and moonshine chasing."[43] However, not all of Red's clients received the same treatment. As Sam Packard, who worked at Red's garage, observed, "We used to build these motors . . . and we'd give the good ones to the bootleggers because they paid cash and the police you had to wait for a check to come in." Red built a hidden, off-limits, spotlessly clean room in the back of his shop where he experimented on Ford V-8 engines to give the bootleggers more speed. He also became a master at setting the chassis up to make his cars handle better and even asked the trippers what highway they ran so that he could set their car up appropriately. Turning those same cars into race cars proved natural for Vogt.[44]

In 1941, Hall and Seay hit the road, with Parks's money and Vogt's mechanical know-how in tow, along with a pair of finely tuned, immaculate Ford coupes, and took the stock car racing world by storm, winning nine of the fifteen major races they entered—Seay won five, Hall four. Hall began the year winning Daytona for the second time; won a major race at Fort Wayne, Indiana; won the longest and richest race of the year, the 200-miler at Langhorne; and finished the season with a win in the final big race of the year at Spartanburg. Seay started the year off winning a major Ralph Hankinson–promoted race at Allentown, Pennsylvania; followed that up a month later winning at High Point; and then went on an unprecedented tear winning three major races in nine days at Daytona, High Point, and Lakewood.[45]

It was not just the fact Hall and Seay won races. It was the way they ran the race, with a level of intensity no one had ever witnessed before. The pair amazed crowds at Daytona by regularly speeding through the turns on two wheels.[46] When he won the March 2 Daytona race, the hard-charging Hall set lap-speed records on each of the first fourteen laps. In the "National Championship" race at Spartanburg, Hall set a record in qualifying and dominated the race winning by several laps.[47] At High Point in June, Seay fell behind seven laps, and his cause seemed hopeless after track dust blinded him, causing him to bounce off the fence and into the path of an on-rushing Bill France, who rear-ended him. After Vogt and his crew repaired the car, he dashed through the field in spectacular fashion, made up the lost laps, and won the 150-mile race going away.[48] In his victory at the August 1941 Daytona race, Seay started fifteenth, made an incredible sprint to the front to lead the first lap, and led every subsequent lap.[49]

The pair even lost in style. In the March 2 race at Daytona, Seay rolled his car twice and still finished seventh.[50] At Lakewood in July, he wrecked, was thrown from his car, and almost ended up in the infield lake.[51] As Hall desperately attempted to keep up with Seay in the August 24 Daytona race, his car took so much pounding from slamming back to the ground after two-wheeling through the north turn that the frame broke and he had to retire from the race.[52] Indeed, win or lose, a race that included Roy or Lloyd was an event, something you had to see to believe. When asked by a reporter in his retirement years—after having watched any number of NASCAR legends drive—who he felt was the greatest driver he had ever seen, Bill France replied: "Fella from up in Georgia. He would come through the North Turn of the old beach course on only his right-side wheels, with both left-side wheels in the air, so that the car always looked as if it was going to turn over. I've never seen anything like that, before or since. Fella by the name of Lloyd Seay."[53]

Promotion and Con: Selling Piedmont Stock Car Racing

The success and growth of stock car racing in the prewar years was a result not only of the appeal of its charismatic liquor haulers and the excitement of its races. The sport also benefited greatly from the skills of professional, experienced promoters, particularly Ralph Hankinson, Sam Nunis, Mike Benton, and Bruce Thompson. Bill France, Sam Rice, Joe Littlejohn, Alvin Hawkins—another Spartanburg racer who later became one of France's chief associates and promoter of the races at Bowman Gray Stadium in Winston-Salem—all learned important lessons in the business of auto racing promotion from these pioneers. To bring in the crowds for Piedmont stock car races, promoters used a variety of tactics, most pioneered by Ralph Hankinson and his organization. "There was a lot of con in promotion," Chris Economaki remembered, "a lot of b.s., that's what it was." The first step in promoting a race was to send in the press agent a week to ten days before the event. Economaki described the typical agent as "an imposing guy, very pompous, very loud, very boorish, pretty pushy," who usually wore spats and smoked a big cigar. He first stopped at the sports office of the local morning and afternoon newspapers, where he passed along to the sports editor an envelope from the promoter containing enough cash to ensure the paper's cooperation in hyping the event. To be sure, much of what passed for reporting in the days leading up to the big race was simply a reprinting of the press releases passed along by the press agent. The articles in the days before the race spoke of the amazing speed of the cars, the track records that would be broken, and the "fantastic . . . death-defying drivers."[54]

Promoters also thought up unique additional attractions to bring people to the race. Mike Benton of Lakewood Speedway brought in women drivers and held boxing matches and even beauty contests. Special races for local drivers only—often billed as state or city championship races "to settle the dispute as to who is the best" South Carolina, Georgia, Atlanta, or Charlotte racer—and grudge matches between rival drivers often preceded the feature races. Prior to a 1941 Armistice Day race at the half-mile Spartanburg Fairgrounds track, Joe Littlejohn organized a one-lap footrace for locally based soldiers and offered half-price admission to any military person in uniform.[55] Almost every race during the period touted itself as either a world, national, regional, or state championship event.

With no overarching sanctioning body and no points system to speak of, any race had as good a claim as another, and promoters even used titles won in races promoted by their rivals in publicizing the drivers in their own events.

Promoters invariably advertised their races as dustless and made much of the fact that they watered the track and treated it with calcium chloride. However, these measures held up only so long, and despite treatment, as an *Atlanta Constitution* reporter observed at a Labor Day 1941 Lakewood race, "the parked cars were red-topped and the dust-draped crowd was rust-colored."[56] Entertainment-starved Piedmont workers, however, seemed not to mind the covering of dust and accepted it, along with ears ringing from the thunderous sound of the unmuffled engines, as part of the fun.

As the sport grew in the Piedmont, promoters employed a tried-and-true method of race promotion by emphasizing the inherent danger of the sport. As Chris Economaki remembered his training in promotion at the feet of Sam Nunis, "That's how it was built up. Danger was part of it. Drivers facing death at every turn was part of the dialogue."[57] Stock car racing promoters emphasized the almost sure guarantee that spectators would witness at least one spectacular wreck—a tactic used in the promotion of NASCAR races to the present day. Sports writers often advertised the number of "crackups" in a particular race and referred to drivers who had spectacular wrecks as "crackup artists" or "crackup king."[58] Sports writers littered their accounts of races with descriptions of race cars "scattered over the track in torn heaps" or "blasting through the railing." Promoters also emphasized the perceived danger of racing and called drivers "daredevils," "madcaps," and "neck riskers," although they emphasized the fact that the racers generally emerged from the wrecks uninjured. In the buildup to the Armistice Day race at Lakewood in 1939, an *Atlanta Constitution* reporter informed his readers, "Three wreckers and two ambulances have been ordered out as stock car races are known for their hectic turnovers in which drivers, strapped to seats by safety belts, seem to come out unscathed."[59] An account of the wrecks in the race often took the headline of newspaper accounts or the lead in the stories. The story of the first stock car race run under the lights at the Greensboro Fairgrounds in 1940 in the *Greensboro Daily News* opened with the fairly typical headline "Johnny Grubbs Wins Auto Race As Two Cars Crash into Wall." The *Spartanburg Herald* headlined its account of the November 1941 race "Crack-Ups Enliven Show," with an additional boldfaced headline over large photos of two separate wrecks, "Crashes Thrill Racing Fans," while the *Charlotte Observer* led its article on the first stock car race in the city with a headline reading "Smashes Lend Thrills to Program." At Lakewood, in order to hype the perception of danger among fans, anyone who entered the track had "to sign a release waiving all claims for damages."[60]

Although wrecks in stock car races—unlike many of those in big-car and midget racing—generally did not involve injury, occasionally drivers suffered serious harm. E. C. Stockton "took a spectacular spill in which he sustained a broken collar bone" in a December 1939 wreck at Lakewood.[61] In May 1941, also at Lakewood, Fonty Flock suffered a dangerous concussion that required hospitalization when he wrecked his car so badly on the backstretch that rescue workers found his shoes 100 yards away. In the course of the accident his shirt was torn off, and he tore a hole in his helmet "the size of an apple." Flock left the track with wounds on his body that looked "like a razor had scraped it."[62] Five drivers received lacerations, burns, broken ribs, concussions, and knocked-out teeth when dust blinded them and they repeatedly piled into one another at a July 1941 Lakewood race.[63]

At least one driver, Eldridge Tadlock of Norfolk, Virginia, died as a result of injuries sustained racing a stock car at the new High Point Speedway. The crash actually occurred during warm-ups for the feature race. Tadlock's right front wheel came off—a common occurrence—causing the car to flip end over end several times. The unfortunate driver was thrown from the car, which then rolled on top of him, causing fatal head and chest injuries. The *High Point Enterprise* ran a picture of the demolished car above a picture of race champion Harley Taylor with the headline "Death and a Champion."[64] Surprising as it may seem to modern sensibilities, hyping these serious accidents and even the deaths of drivers was a major part of the business of early stock car racing promotion.[65]

To ensure maximum excitement at the racetrack, promoters employed talented race announcers to further excite the crowd during the race. In the late 1930s and early 1940s, the Montgomery Ward company often provided announcers free of charge as a means of promoting its line of tires, especially for big races. Experienced race promoters knew that a fan's experience could be influenced almost as much by the way the announcer described the race as by the race itself. Sam Nunis—announcer and press agent for Ralph Hankinson in the late 1930s and early 1940s—instructed his young protégé Chris Economaki to announce the race in such a way that "the people leaving the fairgrounds at the end of the day [believed] they had seen a better race than they really had." Nunis often stood at the base of the announcer's stand, especially during a boring race, shouting, "Sell it, sell it, sell it." It was all a part of the "con" that was an important part of racing promotion, and Economaki learned this lesson well. Announcing the Daytona beach/road race in the north turn for Bill France in the early 1950s, Economaki found himself in the midst of a boring race, a virtual parade with little passing. Because of the long straightaways, fans could not see the action at the far end of the track. Economaki, perched on a high tower armed with binoculars, decided the race action needed some livening up. He announced to the fans in the north turn as the leaders sped out of sight, "I've got 'em in my glasses and entering the south turn Fonty Flock is passing Curtis Turner—we have a new leader." Of course nothing had happened, but the fans didn't know that. Economaki proceeded to describe the exciting racing going on just outside the fans' field of vision—"Turner's right-hand wheels are in the Atlantic Ocean; he's regained the lead." All he had to do was "to get them back where they belong before they came into sight again." After the race, he overheard one fan telling another how much he enjoyed the race, but "next year I'm going to sit in the south turn. That's where all the passing is."[66]

Piedmont Stock Car Racing's Popularity

The excitement of the racing, the ability to identify with drivers and the cars, the hyping of promoters, and the cheap admission prices—generally from 50¢ to $1.00 for adults, with children often admitted free or charged 25¢—brought huge crowds to Piedmont-area tracks in the years just before World War II. Races nearly always attracted crowds of 5,000 or more, and the bigger races at Lakewood, Charlotte, or High Point attracted crowds of between 10,000 and 15,000. The *Spartanburg Herald* reported after a July 4, 1940, race that the 7,000-person crowd "packed the grandstand and bleachers, lined the inside of the fence, took up quite a bit of space in the infield and covered fences and housetops all around the track." Crowd management often became a problem, as did making sure that everyone paid admission. The *Herald* reported at the same race, "Despite the combined efforts of 50 national guardsmen and many law enforcement officers, non-paying customers came over and through the fence in droves, knocking big holes in the barrier at several points."[67]

For many fans, attending a race not only gave them a vicarious thrill but also made them determined to race themselves and attracted many lead-footed young men into the sport. After leaving his Dawson County farm to move to Atlanta to work for Atlantic Steel, Gober Sosebee witnessed his first race at Lakewood when he and other Dawson County expatriates went to see hometown hero Roy Hall compete. When his buddies asked him how he liked the race, he responded, "Well, that was fun but I'll never see another race 'less I'm in it." While his friends laughed at his boast, Sosebee was as good as his word. He used his steel mill earnings—supplemented by money earned from running liquor—to order a 1940 Ford directly from the Ponce de Leon Avenue Ford factory in Atlanta, took it to Lakewood, and soon became a regular at the races.[68] Bill Blair, of High Point, North Carolina, attended a few stock car races at the Greensboro Fairgrounds and got "the bug" to drive when the High Point Speedway was built not far from his family's dairy farm. Although the track hosted a big-car race first, the affordability of a stock car and his ability to practice on the huge track before the first stock race in 1941 pulled him in and started a successful driving career that lasted well into the 1960s.[69]

Only three years after professional stock car racing had come to the Piedmont region, the sport had leaped to the top of the list of entertainment options in the region, especially for men in the working class. In 1941, Piedmont tracks hosted thirteen major stock car races, almost double the previous year's total, with key venues at Charlotte, High Point, and Richmond added to the roster of stock-car-mad cities. Piedmont trippers/racers also increasingly dominated the major races outside the region and won five of the seven major stock races in the Northeast. Indeed, Piedmont stock car racing stood poised for even more explosive growth as promoters sought to emulate the success of Mike Benton, Joe Littlejohn, Bill France, and Ralph Hankinson and investors saw lucrative opportunities in the construction of purpose-built, banked racetracks—as opposed to the traditional flat fairground, tracks—such as the High Point Speedway.

Tragic Endings

Although the future looked bright for Piedmont stock car racing in the summer of 1941, the sport faced a major setback in September: the tragic death of Lloyd Seay. The Dawsonville ace had come to the Labor Day race at Lakewood Speedway on an unprecedented hot streak, having won at Daytona August 24 and then at High Point less than twenty-four hours before the Lakewood race. For some unknown reason, Seay changed his car number from his traditional "7" to "13" for the Labor Day festivities.

However, the "13" brought him luck at Lakewood, as he fought off several challengers to win one of the most prestigious races of the year against most of the top stock car racers in the region and a trophy naming him National Stock Car Champion. He also returned late that night to his Dawson County home with $150, his share of the winnings from the race.[70]

Seay's luck changed dramatically the next morning as his cousin Woodrow Anderson—well aware of Seay's winnings in the race—roused him from his sleep and demanded that the racer reimburse him for a load of sugar that Seay had charged to his account. Seay and his brother Garnett went with Anderson to a relative's house to settle the issue, but a fight broke out—accounts vary as to who instigated it and what actually happened—and Anderson shot Garnett in the neck and Lloyd through the heart, killing him instantly. Piedmont stock car racing's most attractive, charismatic, and outlandish star was gone at the age of twenty-one.[71] Indicative of his broad popularity, and notoriety, in the region, the *Atlanta Constitution* ran the following lines on its front page the day after Seay's death:

> Lloyd Seay, lanky, blond and youthful, was well known in Atlanta and all along the highways to the mountains. Federal, state, and county law officers knew him as the most daring of all the daredevil crew that hauled liquor from mountain stills to Atlanta. They had had many a wild chase when they hit his trail, but they had caught him only rarely, for he hurled his car down the twisting black-top hill-country roads at a pace few of them cared to follow. He will be missed by racetrack fans as well. Fifteen thousand people saw him hurl his souped-up Ford around the track at Lakewood Monday, running the hundred miles in 89 minutes to win more than $450 in cash.[72]

While the show did go on after Seay's death—with three more major races in the fall, including two at Lakewood—Piedmont stock car racing had lost something important. Bill France and Harley Taylor organized a memorial race for Seay, held on November 2 at Lakewood, and donated $831.32 to his family. Jap Brogden won the race, which also featured a driver no one had ever heard of before: one Ralph "Bad Eye" Shirley.[73] Actually, Shirley was none other than an on-the-lam Roy Hall, in disguise, who had come out to pay a final tribute to his old running mate. One of the most moving tributes to Seay's life and career came from Raymond Parks, who commissioned a headstone for his grave in the Dawsonville

Cemetery featuring a porcelainized photograph of Seay at the wheel of a 1939 Ford.[74]

Seay's death also brought one of Piedmont stock car racing's major liabilities to the forefront: its low-down, outlaw reputation. Auto racers in general had a major image problem during this period. As Chris Econo-maki noted, "Racing was a denigrated sport. . . . A lot of people looked upon auto racers as nuts, hot rodders trying to kill themselves, with grease under their fingernails and an oily rag in their pocket."[75] Smokey Yunick, in much more colorful language, observed that auto racers in the early 1940s "had a social status of even a leper, or a 'mon backer' on a garbage truck."[76] The bootleggers and outlaws involved in Piedmont stock car racing took the status of racing in the region to an even lower level. People of the region's growing middle class, trying to separate themselves from anything that smacked of the South's reputation and status as poverty stricken or low-down, especially frowned on the sport. "The white middle class in the South at that time, it [stock car racing] was emerging," Humpy Wheeler asserted, "did not want anything to do with the roots of the South. They didn't want their children listening to hillbilly music, going down to the dirt race track. . . . And so it made the racing business not the thing to do."[77] In addition, the fact that stock car races were held often on Sundays put racers and promoters on the outs with middle-class Baptists and Methodists, who believed strongly in the "sanctity of the Lord's day." In fact, most counties and municipalities in the region had strong blue laws that legally restricted businesses from opening on Sunday. Southern Baptists had affirmed this position by the adoption of the 1925 "Baptist Faith and Message," which asserted that the "Lord's day . . . should be employed in exercises of worship and spiritual devotion, both public and private, and by refraining from worldly amusements, and resting from secular employments, works of necessity and mercy only excepted."[78] This outlaw, low-down, working-class image that promoters exploited success-fully in the prewar era would be one that often placed substantial road-blocks in the way of Piedmont stock racing's acceptance as a mainstream sport.

Almost a month to the day after the Lloyd Seay Memorial Race, Pied-mont stock car racing received its most severe setback, at least in the short term: the Japanese attack on Pearl Harbor and the United States' entry into World War II. When it became apparent that the war would last for a long time and that the American people would need to make significant sacrifices—particularly with regard to steel, gasoline, and rubber—the auto racing world shut down. Although the process was initially a voluntary one, closures accelerated when Eddie Rickenbacker, the president of the Indianapolis Motor Speedway, canceled the 1942 Indianapolis 500 "in the interest of a full-out victory effort."[79] Most tracks followed the Indianapolis lead, but the director of the Office of Defense Transportation dashed the hopes of those who planned to continue racing when he shut down auto racing for the duration of the war in July 1942.[80]

While the initial phase of Piedmont stock car racing was now over, a solid foundation had been laid that the sport could build on in the postwar era. Stock car racing was now a well-established part of the sports and entertainment scene in most of the region's major cities. Although the sport had lost its most charismatic star in Lloyd Seay, the Piedmont had produced a number of other talented drivers—particularly from the ranks of area liquor runners—who stood poised to take his place and continue his legacy on and off the track. Talented and creative promoters like Bill France, Joe Littlejohn, Mike Benton, and Bruce Thompson stood ready to expand the sport even further in the region and beyond. Perhaps most important, those drivers and promoters had created a fan base among the mill workers and farmers of the region, who would eagerly anticipate not just the end of a terrible war but the return of the deafening roar of stock cars, with those wild liquor drivers behind the wheels, power-sliding wheel to wheel around the local red-clay fairground track.

Rough and Rowdy

Big Bill, the Atlanta Bootleggers,
and the Bootlegger Tracks

*It was rough and rowdy. It was lots of boys just getting out of the service—they had
been there four or five years in them wars—and I would say that at least 70 percent of
the men that was driving the cars in '46, '47, '48 and on up was involved, or had been
involved, in what we called trippin' whiskey, haulin' whiskey, maybe makin' a little
bit of whiskey. And not only the people that was racing, but the people that owned the
race tracks. They was just as bad as the race drivers. They had made lots of money
during the war sellin' whiskey and different things, and then they come in and build a
nice track where other people didn't have the money. Some of the best race tracks that
there is today was built with that kind of money. And some of the promoters that's
promoting today, that's how they got their money to get started in this thing. If you
found a man who was in that kind of business, he was a gambler anyhow. He didn't
mind taking a chance with his money.*

—Jack Smith, in Kim Chapin, Fast as White Lightning

Although World War II idled the cars and the tracks where stock car racing
began, the sport emerged in the immediate postwar era as one of the most
popular pastimes in the region. The success of racing during this period
was due primarily to an informal alliance formed between Bill France and
a group of individuals in the Piedmont South involved heavily in the illegal liquor business. France provided the energy, promotional skills, and
vision, while the bootleggers provided most of the marquee drivers, the
fastest cars, much of the mechanical know-how, and the financial back-

ing to promote races and construct new racetracks. Together, they tremendously boosted the sport's popularity throughout the region.

Some observers have contended that France did not like bootleggers and tried to run them out of stock car racing and that his motivation may have been due to a "puritanical" streak.[1] France himself dismissed most questions about his relationship to bootleggers, particularly later in life. As writer Sylvia Wilkinson observed after interviewing France in the 1980s, "Thunder Road [the general name for highways where trippers hauled liquor], the path that excites the legend-seekers, is a road he never drove down, and one he is tired of hearing about."[2] To be sure, while Bill France himself may never have driven down "Thunder Road," he had very close business and professional connections with lots of folks who did. If anything, Bill France knew he had a highly marketable product in the charismatic trippers/racers he had competed against and even befriended in the late 1930s and early 1940s. Indeed, he socialized with them regularly. Bill France was anything but "puritanical," as his heavy partying with bootleggers like Curtis Turner demonstrated.[3] Although France may have pleaded ignorance of the activities of these people, he unavoidably saw evidence of plenty of shady activity as he hung out with these people. As stock car racer Frank "Rebel" Mundy recalled to journalist Peter Golenbock: "I remember sometime in the mid-forties Bill France and I and a few guys were hanging around Red's [Vogt] garage, and a couple of bootleggers came in and started arguing over stealing booze or taking over territory. France and I were sitting in a car at the entrance to the garage, and they started arguing, and one of them pulled out a gun, and when France and I saw the gun, we ducked down underneath the car."[4]

The chief evidence, however, that France did not attempt to rid Piedmont stock car racing of its "unsavory" element in the 1940s, '50s, or at any time is the fact that he went into business with a number of bootleggers and maintained close business and personal relationships with them for the rest of his life. Indeed, if Bill France could trust anyone to stand beside him as he battled the odds and struggled to take Piedmont stock car racing to a national audience, it was the men like Joe Littlejohn, Enoch Staley, Charlie Combs, and H. Clay Earles—all connected to illegal liquor at least part of their lives—with whom he promoted races, built and owned racetracks, and laid the foundation for what was to become NASCAR.

World War II and the Piedmont Stock Car World

Like many of the other institutions in the region, Piedmont stock car racing was profoundly transformed by World War II. Although the legitimate threat of death or serious injury haunted many veterans, the adrenaline rush of combat produced a generation of Piedmont men who craved similar experiences, such as driving in a stock car race or just watching from the stands. A number of the sport's most important figures saw significant combat during the war and were transformed by the experience. Raymond Parks enlisted in the infantry, was promoted to sergeant, and spent much of the bitterly cold winter of 1944–45 in a foxhole on the front lines of the Battle of the Bulge. He saw half of his company killed, wounded, or captured.[5] Spartanburg, South Carolina, mechanic Bud Moore landed on Utah Beach on D-Day, served under General George Patton "for eleven months and four days," was wounded twice, and received numerous battlefield decorations.[6] Future stock car mechanic Smokey Yunick piloted a B-17 bomber on countless missions in North Africa and Europe and flew with the legendary "Flying Tigers" taking supplies from India into China over the "Hump"—the Himalaya Mountains.[7]

Perhaps the stock car racing figure most transformed by combat in World War II was Robert "Red" Byron. Byron had already experienced a great deal of excitement in his life by the time he entered the U.S. Army Air Forces during World War II. The Anniston, Alabama, native had driven open-wheel racers for a number of years and even the occasional stock car at Lakewood Speedway with a fair amount of success. In 1939, he signed on with Mickey Martin's Hell Riders; his signature feat as a Hell Rider was a "double wall-crashing turning-over stunt."[8] The excitement in Red's life continued, and undoubtedly increased, during the war when he became a tail gunner manning a .50-caliber Browning machine gun on a B-24 bomber in the Pacific theater. He flew fifty-seven successful missions—well over the normal number of missions required to complete a tour of duty—narrowly escaping death on numerous occasions. Red volunteered to fly a fifty-eighth mission for a buddy whose wife was expecting their first child at any moment. Japanese antiaircraft fire severely damaged his B-24, and the pilot had to make an emergency crash landing on Kitka in the Aleutian Islands. Miraculously, Red survived the impact, although the crash mangled his left leg. Doctors feared that he would never walk again, and he spent twenty-seven months in a VA hospital recovering.[9]

Byron left the hospital determined not only to walk but also to drive a race car again. In February 1946, he did just that, wheeling a Raymond

War hero and early stock car racing star Robert "Red" Byron after a victory at a 1949 race at Martinsville, Virginia. Raymond Parks supplied his cars, and Red Vogt kept them in top condition. (Courtesy of McCaig-Welborn Research Library at the International Motorsports Hall of Fame, Talladega, Alabama)

Parks–owned, Red Vogt–prepared Ford V-8 to victory—against the likes of Bob and Fonty Flock, Bill France, Bill Snowden, and even Roy Hall—in his first competitive postwar race at Seminole Speedway near Orlando, Florida. Red's car contained one feature not found in any production model: a stirrup, specially crafted by Red Vogt, attached to the clutch to help hold his injured leg in place. The fans loved it. Byron was not only a war hero but displayed the type of toughness, grit, and determination prized by Piedmont working-class fans. Red Byron's story was a promoter's dream, one that helped solidify the place of stock car racing on the Piedmont's cultural landscape.[10]

World War II also helped produce a new generation of mechanics who built on the legacy begun by Red Vogt and helped bring the sport to a new level of sophistication. Ray Fox gained a great deal of mechanical experience working in an army ordnance division. Especially valuable for Fox and others was the opportunity, due to the urgency of war, to experiment, use trial and error, and come up with creative solutions to mechanical problems.[11] Although he was a pilot, Smokey Yunick honed his mechanical skills working on his plane, "the only B-17 in India. Almost all through there I had to do my own maintenance on the airplane because there was no B-17 mechanics around. By that time I was pretty interested in mechanics."[12] Both Fox and Yunick set up shop in Daytona Beach after the war and, along with Bud Moore, soon became leading mechanics in Piedmont stock car racing.

Other skills, not necessarily beneficial to the sport but indicative of its outlaw image, were also honed by stock car figures in the military. Yunick became a part of a major black market operation that, according to him, involved China's president Jiang Jieshi (Chiang Kai-shek) and the boxer Jack Dempsey smuggling jade and ivory into China. Yunick contends that he pocketed more than $150,000, which he kept hidden for a number of years. When he transferred to Okinawa late in the war, Yunick also did a brisk business in war souvenirs taken off dead Japanese soldiers. He stockpiled uniforms and weapons in his tent and then smuggled them in the "backdoor" of Buckner Bay Air Base and sold them off to reporters, politicians, and other visiting dignitaries for a tidy profit.[13] Floyd, Virginia, moonshiner—and future stock car racing superstar—Curtis Turner was drafted into the navy; based in Norfolk, he spent the war patrolling the Virginia coast. Although his moonshine business took a hit, he supplemented his income by "running tires from the naval base up to friends in the hills, making a nice profit." After he was mustered out, Turner used the connections he made in the navy to smuggle moonshine into the base in exchange for sugar.[14]

The Battle of Atlanta

While the exploits of Yunick and Turner reinforced their love for being on the edge and probably benefited the sport in the long run, the wartime activities of others proved more damaging, or at the least transformative, to the future of stock car racing. Stock car racing experienced a severe setback at least partially as a result of the exploits of Roy Hall and some of his bootlegger compatriots during the war. The war years were very good for those in the illegal alcohol business. Draft boards disqualified many north Georgia bootleggers from the draft because of their criminal records, and there were lots of thirsty defense workers and enlisted men in the Atlanta area "who wanted whiskey but could hardly afford the bonded stuff."[15] Although rationing of gas, rubber, and sugar put a crimp in some of the bootleggers' activities, the skyrocketing tax on whiskey (up to $9 per gallon by 1944), the persistence of dry counties in the region, and the breakdown of traditional moral norms due to the dislocations of the war made moonshine even more popular. In addition, reductions in the numbers of agents assigned to enforce the federal liquor tax laws due to war mobilization lowered the risk of losing one's still or being arrested, further boosting liquor production. For folks already on the wrong side of the law—and not too sensitive to accusations of disloyalty to the cause of freedom—opportunities for making money in black market enterprises abounded.

The money was nice, but the absence of organized racing left an excitement void in the lives of many of those in the Atlanta underworld. In 1944, Roy Hall and others organized a series of "bootlegger sweepstakes," high-stakes races held in the dead of night over Atlanta-area highways—the Buford Highway seemed the favorite location—that drew hundreds of spectators. Organizers offered large cash prizes, and participants and spectators placed heavy side bets on the outcome.[16] In one such race in March 1945, one of Roy Hall's opponents, J. B. "Buddy" Bolling, wrecked his car and was killed. Police arrested Hall, and in July 1945 a judge sentenced him to "serve 12 months in prison, six months in jail and pay a $1000 fine" for his involvement in the fatal street race.[17]

The political and religious leaders of Atlanta—particularly at a time of major concern over the decline in morality and public order during the war and already hypersensitive about the city's public image—looked for ways of cracking down on the unsavory elements in their community. That opportunity came when Mike Benton announced that Lakewood Speedway would host a stock car race, along with the National Hillbilly Jamboree and free fireworks, on Labor Day, September 3, 1945, less than one month after V-J Day. The entry list of popular local drivers grew quickly and included Jack Cantrell, Howard Farmer, Bob Flock, Glen "Legs" Law, and an out-on-bond Roy Hall. All five had lengthy police records, mostly for traffic and liquor-law violations. While working-class fans thrilled that they could once again pack the Lakewood stands and infield to cheer for their favorite liquor haulers, influential *Atlanta Constitution* editor in chief Ralph McGill—often referred to as the "conscience of the South"—and the leaders of the Atlanta-area Baptist and Methodist ministerial associations decided it was time to draw a line in the sand.[18]

The opening salvo of the campaign began with an August 31 *Atlanta Constitution* editorial asserting that, because of the unsavory types entered in the Labor Day stock car race, the event should "be called a rat race." The editorial continued by calling the entry of these drivers with extensive criminal records in a race at a publicly owned facility "a shocking display of bad taste" and contended that Mike Benton and other officials of the Southeastern Fair Association—managers of Lakewood—needed to disallow the entry of such "notorious racketeers of the liquor running and the bootlegger races."[19] Benton and Southeastern Fair, however, declined to disqualify the offensive drivers, especially Bob Flock and Roy Hall, two of stock car racing's top draws; they argued that the men had a right to enter because no rule gave the fair board the right to refuse them entry. In response, the *Constitution* ran another editorial asking some serious questions about these "hoodlums." Why were none of these men, "all of them within draft age," in the army? The article also wondered, at a time of strict rubber rationing, "where do they get tires good enough to carry on their liquor car races and liquorruning?" The editorialist called on the "proper officers" to check their tires to "see if they are 'hot,' or illegally obtained." The article concluded by again calling on Southeastern Fair to disallow the entries of these "five rumrunning police characters." "We think it an error to permit these notorious characters to glorify their rackets in a Labor Day race—or any other." In addition, the paper contended, "the pretense that these men have a right to enter and cannot be refused is pure bunk."[20]

Behind the scenes the pressure increased on Benton and Southeastern Fair to ban the "hoodlums." Supporters of the ban contacted Chief Marion Hornsby of the Atlanta Police Department, the Georgia Highway Patrol, and Atlanta mayor William B. Hartsfield to see if they could find any legal way to prevent the bootleggers from racing. Hartsfield responded that while the city had "no direct control over the use of the race track at the fair grounds," he would consult with the city attorney "to see if there is anything the city can legally do about the matter." Louie D. Newton, influential pastor of the Druid Hills Baptist Church, opined that if Atlanta did not stop "these gangsters" from racing, then signs needed to be posted "at every entrance to the city limits, announcing that law and order in this city is henceforth abandoned."[21] In addition, both the Methodist and Baptist ministerial associations made last-minute appeals to city officials to stop the bootleggers from racing.[22]

Despite the efforts of *Constitution* editors and local ministers, on Labor Day an estimated crowd of 30,000 entertainment-starved people showed up for the race at a track that seated only 5,000. Mayor Hartsfield, facing a primary election the next day; Chief Hornsby; and a sizable contingent of Atlanta police arrived as well. The mayor presented Mike Benton with a formal protest and demanded that the five men be disqualified. Benton caved in but had to disqualify only three drivers, since Bob Flock and Jack Cantrell failed to show for the race. When Benton announced his decision, however, the other drivers in the race unanimously refused to compete unless the fair board reinstated the disqualified drivers. Negotiations continued for more than two hours, and the huge crowd began to grow restless and unruly. The fans began shouting, "We want Hall, We want Hall," and police feared a riot. Finally, one and a half hours after the announced start, Benton caved in again, this time to the demands of the drivers and fans, and the race began with all drivers, regardless of police record, allowed to compete. To the delight of the cracker crowd and the consternation of city officials and the forces of decorum, Roy Hall won the race.[23]

Hall's victory, in both winning the race and being allowed to compete, however, proved to be a hollow one as the Labor Day events unleashed a firestorm. In an editorial the next day Ralph McGill devoted his whole column—entitled "What Is Your Racket, Brother?"—to the Lakewood controversy. He compared Southeastern Fair's and the police department's caving in to the demands of drivers and fans in allowing Roy Hall and his ilk to race at Lakewood to Neville Chamberlain's appeasement of Adolf Hitler. McGill closed his editorial with an ominous warning for the future: "One of these days we will have to deal with them and their kind—or make them a part of our accepted daily society. With the inevitable results."[24]

The *Constitution* continued its campaign to clean up Lakewood for the next several weeks. Letters to the editor in support of the paper's position appeared regularly in its "Pulse of the Public" section. J. L. R. Boyd termed the Lakewood affair a "Roman Holiday," while Emma Gardner declared, "Compromise with criminals[,] appeasement[,] will bring chaos and shame." Leo P. Daly, M.D., opined, "If this is what the boys of World War I and II fought for, then God help the country."[25] Major stories also appeared in the paper highlighting the criminal element involved in stock car racing. One told the story of Ed Bagley—a stock car racer, an alleged bootlegger, and a participant in the Lakewood race—who had apparently committed suicide near his Forsyth County home. The two-column, front-page article contained little in the way of sympathy for Bagley's family and a great deal of detail of his arrest record, particularly an account of a high-speed chase with police through the streets of Atlanta that ended when he rolled his car. The paper also highlighted the trial of Glen "Legs" Law, one of the "Lakewood 5," for his alleged role in the attempted theft of six tons of sugar from Atlanta's Maryland Baking Company. Law was sentenced to one to five years in prison, but the sentence was later overturned on appeal because of insufficient evidence. To ensure that readers made the connection, the article on his conviction concluded with the words "He participated in the Labor Day automobile race at Lakewood Park."[26]

Mayor Hartsfield, the police department, and community leaders also turned up the heat on Southeastern Fair and local bootleggers. With the annual fall fair approaching, Hartsfield announced that police would inspect the midway and the shows at the fair every hour to ensure that there were no "gambling devices, games of chance, or any shows, exhibitions or other activities which may not be in accordance with the laws of the City of Atlanta or the state of Georgia." Pastor Newton called for a "full investigation of the operation of the fair and of Lakewood Park" by the Fulton County grand jury "to dismiss the concern which the regrettable incident of Labor Day has created."[27] Detective Superintendent E. I. Hilderbrand announced a crackdown on "known racketeers" and warned them to either "get honest jobs, leave town permanently or go to jail. . . . If they continue to hang around here, we will see that they work for a living or else we will lock them up for vagrancy. I have also given my men definite orders to check repeatedly at the places these men say they are working to see that they are on the job."[28]

While it is hard to say what impact the campaign had on local "racketeers," the impact on Lakewood and on Atlanta's position in the stock car racing world was dramatic. The fall fair contained harness racing and a "hell-driving" show, but not the stock car racing that had become a regular feature before the war. Indeed, Lakewood did not host another stock car race until more than a year later, in November 1946. In the meantime, Southeastern Fair announced that racers with police records could no longer compete at the city-owned speedway. In July 1946 a reporter for *National Speed Sport News* commented on the bootlegger ban and its aftermath at Lakewood: "The City Officials of Atlanta have barred most of the local drivers from competition for one reason or another. For that reason the crowd is none too good."[29] The track did eventually lift its ban on "hoodlums" and hosted eleven NASCAR Grand National races in the 1950s, but Atlanta would lose its title as the center of the Piedmont stock car racing universe.[30] That center would shift north into the Carolinas, which proved more tolerant and accepting of those wild bootlegging stock car drivers and their antics.

Big Bill Hits the Road

That shift in center was aided and abetted by Bill France—the second-place finisher at the Lakewood race—who was also transformed by his experience in World War II. France spent the war at home in Daytona Beach working as a foreman at the Daytona Beach Boat Works building submarine chasers. He evidently also spent a good deal of his time thinking about and planning his role in the future of American auto racing. After the war, France emerged with a new emphasis and a new vision. Although he continued to race stock cars on occasion, he focused on the business of promotion, on taking his experience as a driver in races all over the East and successfully promoting the Daytona beach/road race on the road. France longed to become not just any promoter but the new king of promoters; Ralph Hankinson had died during the war.

France wasted no time in gearing up his promotional activities after the end of the war. He witnessed firsthand the debacle at Lakewood on Labor Day as a competitor, but he also observed the huge crowd that came out and the intense thirst for auto racing in the post–World War II Piedmont. In addition, France paid close attention to the major auto racing trade papers, *Illustrated Speedway News* and *National Speed Sport News*, and could not help but notice the success that Sam Nunis—heir to Ralph Hankinson's empire—was having in drawing massive crowds to Piedmont fairgrounds for big-car races. Nunis-promoted races drew estimated crowds of more than 28,000 at Greensboro and 30,000 at Spartanburg.[31] While inflating the number of fans at a race is a big part of the racing promotion "con"—even to the present day—it seems likely that the crowds were indeed huge.

To capitalize on this popularity, France organized a stock car race for the Southern States Fairgrounds in Charlotte for late October. Attempting to build on the patriotism engendered by the war and draw in veterans from the area, he arranged sponsorship for the race from Tar Heels Post No. 3 of the AMVETS and used the entry of decorated veterans Red Byron and Crash Waller—also a well-known west Georgia bootlegger—to hype the event.[32] The race also featured the entry of several notable Lakewood-banned drivers including Roy Hall, Glen "Legs" Law, and Bob and Fonty Flock.[33] The race went off without any protests from civic leaders, with Roy Hall qualifying first in a Raymond Parks Ford and leading every lap except the last one. On the last lap Hall inexplicably crashed into the fence, opening the door for Bob Flock to win. Although the results did not raise the suspicion of the *Charlotte Observer*, the end was eerily reminiscent of a late August 1945 "bootlegger sweepstakes" race in Clayton County, Georgia, where a heavily favored Roy Hall lost a match race to an apparently overmatched opponent. The *Atlanta Constitution* reported that Hall had thrown the race and that he and his friends won "plenty of change collected through confederates who placed bets on the race."[34] Hall's last-lap crash also led to the cancellation of an added feature to the event, a ten-lap grudge-match race between Hall and Bill France.[35]

Although no one accused Hall of throwing the race, the suspicious circumstances of its ending do bring up one of the challenges faced by Bill

France and other promoters in the early days of stock car racing: control- ling the gambling that went hand in hand with the bootlegging. As New England auto racing promoter and later NASCAR executive Bill Tuthill ob- served, the real money in racing at this time—for the trippers/drivers and also for many of their car owners—came not from the race purse but from the side bets drivers took: "They were mostly a bunch of numbers guys and bootleggers, and most of the money involved was passed back and forth between *them*. There weren't big purses, but there were big wagers. I've seen many fellows betting a thousand dollars on a race where the offi- cial winner's purse was $50."[36] The temptation to throw a race, especially for someone as talented as Roy Hall, and make a killing betting against yourself was huge, although no direct evidence has ever been found of such things happening.

The race did not attract the type of crowds that had flocked to Lake- wood or to the Nunis-promoted big-car events, but France had made a successful initial foray into the world of stock car race promotion in the Piedmont. This move effectively launched his career as the major stock car racing promoter in the region. In 1946 France staged successful races in April and June at the Daytona beach/road course, although he had to rent portable bleachers from the Ringling Brothers because the existing ones had rotted through during the war years. Red Byron won the first race and Roy Hall the second. Hall barely made it to the track in time to qualify for the June race, as he had been arrested not long after arriving in town for announcing his arrival—at 4:00 A.M.—by speeding and doing burnouts down Daytona Beach's main street.[37]

Such antics made north Georgia trippers/racers like Roy Hall France's most important, and most marketable, assets in his early promotions. With most of these drivers now banned from Lakewood Speedway, France had an open door to take them to the rest of the Piedmont. Although he had no hold over them other than his friendship and reputation for keeping his word—particularly in actually paying the announced prize money—he regularly delivered established stars like Hall and Bob and Fonty Flock as well as promising newcomers banned from Lakewood like Ed Samples, Gober Sosebee, and Billy Carden. Wounded war hero Red Byron was another talent that drew the crowds, and although he had no record for bootlegging—and indeed defied the stock car racer stereo- type as a rather quiet, serious, and even bookish man—his car owner, Raymond Parks, was not welcome at Lakewood. France could also rely on the considerable talents of bootleggers from the Carolinas like Glenn

Dunnaway and Buddy Shuman as well as those of fellow Daytona Beach mechanic and ace stock car driver Marshall Teague.[38]

France did lose the considerable talents of Roy Hall in late 1946 when the bootlegger—who had spent so much of his life poised on the lip of a precipice, especially after the death of his friend Lloyd Seay—finally went over the edge. In August, police arrested Hall after a race in Greensboro as a suspect in a $40,000 bank robbery near Atlanta. Extradited to Georgia, Hall stood trial, was convicted for armed robbery, and sentenced to six years in the state penitentiary. His lengthy incarceration effectively ended his brilliant yet troubled career. He would attempt a comeback when authorities released him early on good behavior in 1949, but his career ended when he rolled his car at a race at Tri-City Speedway near High Point and suffered severe head injuries that put him in the hospital for a month.[39]

Another important asset that France promoted was the car owners and outstanding mechanics—most in some way connected to the illegal liquor trade—who fielded the fast cars needed to put on a good show for the fans. The most important car owner in Piedmont stock car racing up until 1950 remained Raymond Parks. Parks had come out of the war with his passion for racing intact, and his spotless Parks Novelty Fords—wrenched by V-8 Ford maestro Red Vogt and generally piloted by Red Byron and Bob Flock—were crowd and odds-on favorites wherever they showed up to race. Although Parks has never publicly stated this, several observers contend that he regularly lent Bill France money to finance his early stock car racing promotions. Parks did add some class to many of France's Daytona races by providing his current brand-new Cadillac as the pace car.[40] Bootleggers Frank Christian from Atlanta, Buddy Shuman and Hubert Westmoreland from Charlotte, and Sam Rice from Martinsville, Virginia, also fielded top-notch cars at many France-promoted races.[41] Atlanta's Bob Osiecki—who like Red Vogt made at least part of his living modifying Fords for Georgia whiskey trippers—proved to be Parks's main rival as a car owner. His cars raced by Ed Samples and Fonty Flock provided the greatest challenge to the Parks Novelty machines. Indeed, the rivalry was intense, as Osiecki and Vogt were adversaries not only on the track but in business. They often belittled each other's cars, and Osiecki poured gas on the flames when he called the Red Vogt–prepared racers "also ran" in the press. France could not ask for a much better scenario than his two top owners going at it in the newspapers and on the track, with the Flock brothers, Bob and Fonty, in the thick of it on opposite sides of the fight.[42]

Cracker stock car fans loved it, and the intense competition between drivers and between their car owners helped draw even more people to the tracks.

The National Championship Stock Car Circuit

In the late spring of 1946, France began promoting races under the banner of the National Championship Stock Car Circuit (NCSCC). He ran major ads in the racing trade papers billing himself as the "Largest Operator of Stock Car Racing Throughout the Country." He also wrote a uniform set of rules and regulations to govern the sport, proceeded to line up as many top drivers as he could for his races, and moved his operation to Greenville, South Carolina, for the summer to be closer to the Piedmont racing action. France promised track owners that if they would sign on with his organization he would "give the best Stock Car Races with name talent and CARS." Because of the lack of availability of new cars after the war, France liberalized the rules and dropped the "strictly stock" requirement common in the prewar era—"all vehicles must be 1934 models and up, with little restriction on motor make-up or additions." For creative mechanics like Red Vogt, Bob Osiecki, and Buddy Shuman, this was like throwing Br'er Rabbit into the briar patch.[43]

France's NCSCC promotions got off to a great start with the June 30, 1946, Daytona race, followed by a hugely successful July 4 race at the newly constructed Greenville-Pickens Speedway. Greenville businessman Ben Willimon built the half-mile banked track on a 37-acre tract just south of the thriving textile center and became France's first big client. The inaugural Greenville race drew a crowd estimated at more than 20,000, even though the Raymond Parks–Red Vogt cars piloted by Roy Hall, Red Byron, and Bob Flock and several other top Piedmont drivers had opted to compete in a better-paying, more visible Sam Nunis–promoted event at Allentown, Pennsylvania. Despite the absence of the sport's biggest stars, the *Greenville News* reported that police and the highway patrol turned away 5,000 fans because of a huge traffic jam. Local industrialist Harry Stephenson commented that he had never before seen "so many people and automobiles at any single event in the Greenville area." Even though victor Ed Samples, still another talented north Georgia bootlegger, did not yet have the marquee value of Hall, Byron, or Flock and the event itself had some problems—the massive traffic jam and the "dust pall" (due to a mechanical failure on the sprinkler truck) that covered the fans in red clay and obscured the vision of drivers and fans—stock car racing proved an immediate hit in the Greenville area. The *News* effusively praised France's "expert" management of the event: "The classic was pronounced an outstanding success and fans showed their appreciation with resounding cheers."[44]

What fans and the press did not know was that France had made another huge gamble, of both his reputation and his life savings, to put on the race and post an attractive purse. He was scared to death that a crowd would not show, the gate would not cover the expenses, and he would be unable to pay off the drivers and the track workers after the race was over. A low turnout would have ruined him both professionally and financially. According to some accounts, the day before the race France decided he would load his car, pack up Annie, Bill Jr., and second son Jim, and head back to Daytona Beach as fast as he could—before creditors and police could catch up with him. He almost made it to the South Carolina–Georgia line when Annie convinced him to turn around and head back to the track.[45] That fateful decision probably saved his career and his finances— he allegedly pocketed more than $3,000 in profit from the race—and boosted his prospects as a promoter tremendously.[46]

Now brimming with confidence, France and Willimon followed up their successful promotion at the track with another big race the Sunday before Labor Day. The event drew even more fans to see Charlottean Glenn Dunnaway win the race. As the *Greenville News* reported, "The multitude, estimated by highway patrolmen and track officials at 22,500, crowded the grandstand, packed 20 persons deep on the bluffs around the hills and sat in automobiles that literally covered vantage points of Willimon's 37 acres. It was a sight to behold, and not a single incident to mar the spectacle was reported." Indeed, the two France-promoted races at Greenville-Pickens had the second- and third-highest attendance of all single-day sporting events in South Carolina in 1946, surpassed only by the traditional Thanksgiving Day football game between the Clemson University Tigers and the University of South Carolina Gamecocks.[47]

In addition to the two Greenville races, France staged races in the summer and fall of 1946 at fairground tracks in Greensboro, Salisbury, and Rocky Mount, North Carolina, and Richmond, Virginia, and worked with old bootlegger friend Joe Littlejohn to promote three successful races at the Spartanburg Fairgrounds. France used the entry of established stars Hall, Byron, and Bob Flock to promote his races—although he could not bind them to his races alone, and they often raced for other promoters—and helped to promote new stars, especially Ed Samples of

Atlanta, Charlotte-area bootleggers Glenn Dunnaway and Buddy Shuman, and Daytona mechanic Marshall Teague, who all won France-promoted productions. By the end of the year, France's name and the names of his star drivers were well established in the Piedmont, and he was poised to control the bulk of stock car racing in the region.[48]

The Bootlegger Tracks

France's success in 1946 also created plenty of new opportunities for stock car racing promotion in the Piedmont as more fairground tracks started offering stock car racing and entrepreneurs constructed new tracks. The ready availability of cheap, war-surplus heavy earth-moving equipment in the postwar era created a boom in racetrack construction in the region. Anyone with a little start-up capital, a bit of skill at operating heavy equipment, a bulldozer, a motor grader, a water truck, a few acres of land, a vision, and a few friends willing to work for low or no pay could construct a track in relatively short order. Grade out the track from the red clay and slap up a board fence, a wooden grandstand, a ticket booth, a concession stand, and an outhouse and you were in business. Humpy Wheeler observed, "If you got the proper kind of red clay, you can build a race track real easy. It didn't take much money. If you got a water truck, you had a great racing surface. . . . So these little dirt tracks sprung up all over the Carolinas, Georgia, Alabama, Virginia and most of them were red clay."[49] Atlanta-area bootleggers saw an opportunity when the "outlaws" were banned from Lakewood; they carved out a track in Thomaston, 60 miles south of Atlanta, and promoted two successful races—both appropriately won by Roy Hall—in 1946.[50] Another group built a new speedway in the Greer-Landrum area of South Carolina and found a new promotional niche by holding the "South's first all-Negro stock car race," which drew entries from Georgia and North Carolina, as well as South Carolina.[51] Fairground tracks at Anderson, South Carolina, and Hendersonville, North Carolina, also hosted stock car races for the first time.

The most important development during this period in terms of race-track construction, however, was the creation of two new major tracks by bootleggers that would play key roles in NASCAR for much of the sport's history. The high profits from illegal liquor led at least indirectly to the building in 1947 of speedways in very unlikely places: North Wilkesboro, North Carolina, and Martinsville, Virginia. The North Wilkesboro track was the indirect product of France and Joe Littlejohn's successful promotions in Spartanburg, South Carolina, the previous year and perhaps of

Bill France (second from right) huddles with his key Wilkes County allies and business partners Charlie Combs (third from left) and Enoch Staley (fourth from left) at NASCAR headquarters in Daytona Beach in 1954. Combs and Staley, who built the North Wilkesboro Speedway and partnered with France on the Hillsborough Speedway, provided an important link to the illegal alcohol business in the Piedmont region. Also pictured are NASCAR field managers Bill Claggett and Johnny Bruner (on left) and Alvin Hawkins (on right), who pioneered weekly Sportsman racing and partnered with France at Bowman Gray Stadium. (Courtesy of McCaig-Welborn Research Library at the International Motorsports Hall of Fame, Talladega, Alabama)

the informal network between Piedmont area bootleggers. Enoch Staley, John Masden, and Charlie Combs — all from Wilkes County — heard about the races and attended one. After the race they sought out Bill France and talked to him about the possibility of building a track near their home and hosting France-promoted stock car races. After the near debacle at Greenville, France was eager to find investors with both a love of racing and deep pockets. In the Wilkes County bootleggers France found what he was looking for.[52]

The three went home and over the course of the next six months began one of the most successful "build it and they will come" projects in sports history, grading out a .6-mile track with seating for 7,500. Because of the terrain, the track had a unique layout. The front stretch headed downhill; an incline began between turns one and two, and the track continued uphill along the backstretch; it then headed downhill again between turns three and four.[53]

Both Staley and Combs—the two principals in the operation—had strong connections to Wilkes County's most famous product, moonshine whiskey. Staley, who eventually controlled half of the stock in the business, was the youngest son of Ranse Staley, one of the county's major illegal liquor operators. According to a number of individuals, Enoch followed in the family business, although he held down other jobs, including one driving a delivery truck for a local dairy. One source alleges that he delivered illegal liquor in his milk truck. For the most part, however, he was generally known as someone who worked in the background of the business, primarily in the financial end.[54] According to Max Welbourn, "he [Enoch] was mainly financing." Donald Johnson agreed and asserted that Staley kept a low profile in his daddy's business and was not directly involved in making moonshine or hauling it: "Enoch would not touch it." "I think my dad became part of Grandpa's operation," admitted Mike Staley—who was not born until his dad was full-time in the speedway business—in an interview with writer Peter Golenbock. "He didn't say much about it."[55] The black sheep of a family of devout churchgoers, Combs often held jobs in automobile sales but was also involved heavily in the illegal alcohol business. In 1955, he was indicted, along with his business partner in the Hickory Speedway, Grafton Burgess, for his involvement in trafficking in so-called red liquor.[56]

Both men also fit the model of the typical speedway owner Jack Smith posited; they were gamblers and "didn't mind taking a chance on [their] money."[57] Indeed, not long before the opening of the North Wilkesboro Speedway, a jury convicted Combs on an illegal gambling charge and sentenced him to one year of hard labor on the roads, although he was later acquitted on appeal. The charge was related to an armed robbery of a poker game in a private home. Two masked men armed with submachine guns broke into the home of Jim Foster—ironically, later the site of the office and ticket booth at the North Wilkesboro Speedway—and stole $11,000 from the four poker players, including Combs, and $17,000 from the owner's safe.[58] The fateful poker game is also an indication of the type of money Wilkes County moonshiners were taking in and the risks they incurred by having so much cash around. One must understand that at this time the average annual per capita income in Wilkes County was less than $2,000.[59] In another high-stakes gamble, Combs and Staley—along with their other partners Austin Ashley, Lawson Curry, and John Masden—wagered that a speedway in rural Wilkes County could be successful; with the money they could scrape together from their various business enterprises, and with lots of sweat equity, they graded out the oddly configured speedway, slapped up a board fence, and built bleachers, a concession stand, outhouses, and a ticket booth.[60]

Amazingly the North Wilkesboro track was an immediate and huge success. The owners granted Bill France an exclusive contract to promote the races at the new track and held four stock car racing events and one big-car event in 1947. Wilkes County had only a little more than 40,000 residents, the town of North Wilkesboro only 3,500, and the track was located 60 miles from the closest reasonably sized city, Winston-Salem. Still, the five events brought in an estimated 70,000 fans, "placing the track at the head of the Carolinas speedways" in one short year. As evidence of this success, North Wilkesboro offered the largest purse—$4,350, with $1,400 to the winner—for its penultimate race of the year, the Bill France–promoted Eastern Stock Car Racing Championship. Some 12,000 fans watched Daytona mechanic Marshall Teague race to victory over "Wild" Bill Snowden and Red Byron.[61] Obviously, Staley, Combs, and France had hit on a winning formula of moving the sport of stock car racing into the more rural sections of the Piedmont and its foothills. Indeed, given the lack of entertainment options as well as the cultural values of working-class people in the area—who did not perceive arrests for bootlegging as a stain on one's reputation and often considered them a badge of honor—North Wilkesboro was an ideal place for a track. To be sure, the success of the bootlegging "Mad Flock" brothers, Bob and Fonty, at the track helped attract local fans.

The success of stock car racing in general and of the North Wilkesboro track in particular attracted others with ties to illegal alcohol to the racetrack business and to partnership with Bill France. Because of the lack of available records—if there ever were any records—and the lack of detailed testimony, one can only speculate about the reasons so many bootleggers became involved in the racetrack business in the late 1940s and in the stock car racing that became NASCAR. Another complicating factor in delving into the motivations of these men is the overall secrecy surrounding such illegal activity. Individuals involved in making moonshine or tripping will often tell you about their personal involvement in the business, but if you ask them to talk about someone else's illegal activities, they will clam up, even though the statute of limitations on such crimes has long since passed. Writer W. D. Washburn discovered this fact when he interviewed a former moonshiner in Caldwell County, North Carolina, and asked if he would tell him the names of some of his former associates. The man stared at Washburn for a minute and then responded in typical fashion, "No, I don't reckon I need to give out names"[62]

Based on the solid evidence of the involvement of bootleggers in the construction and management of at least six major NASCAR tracks, we can make some educated guesses about why this phenomenon became so common in the Piedmont and surrounding foothills. Some reasons for bootlegger involvement are obvious and are similar to those of the trippers/drivers who so heavily populated the ranks of early stock car races: love for fast cars and a gambler's instincts. Other possible reasons are purely speculative but, given the nature of these men's business, make sense. First, one must realize that people involved in the illegal liquor business had a cash problem; they had too much of it. Taking large amounts of cash to the bank was not a possibility, since such deposits immediately triggered an inquiry from the IRS. Keeping large amounts of cash at home also had its risks, as the North Wilkesboro poker game robbery dramatically demonstrated. While little direct evidence exists, it seems that at least some highly entrepreneurial bootleggers, like Raymond Parks, invested part of their illegal liquor gains in legitimate enterprises—Parks in Atlanta-area liquor stores, his novelty business, and in real estate.[63] Many bootleggers, like Parks, apparently kept feet in both the illegal and legal business worlds. Investment in a speedway—Parks occasionally dabbled in the business himself—was a risky but potentially lucrative investment.

As a business investment, speedway construction also had some specific possible advantages for many bootleggers. As Humpy Wheeler has observed, constructing a speedway out of the Piedmont red clay did not require a great deal of talent or a huge capital investment—most of these speedways were probably built for less than $100,000—given the ready availability of cheap earth-moving equipment in the postwar era and the cheapness of farmland in the region. In fact, several of the bootleggers had already invested in heavy earth-moving equipment and started legitimate excavation businesses before they got involved in racetracks. In building their tracks, most of the bootleggers invested more in sweat equity—their own and that of their family and friends—than they did in cash. Owning a racetrack also provided another possible advantage for folks involved in the illegal liquor business: the opportunity to launder large amounts of cash. Again, there is no direct evidence that this occurred at these tracks, but the opportunity that these racetracks provided to move extra cash through a facility where tens of thousands of people paid huge amounts of cash for tickets and concessions and into a bank is obvious. Although ATU agents surely kept an eye on such activities, it was easy to inflate attendance numbers—something every promoter did—and who really knew how many hotdogs vendors sold in the concession stand? While cash moved through such means would have been subject to some taxes, that cost was probably worth it. Whatever their motivations, Staley, Combs, and company and their North Wilkesboro track were only the beginning of one of the most important factors in the early success of Bill France's promotions in the Piedmont: the arrival of a significant number of racetracks in the Piedmont region financed by the proceeds of the illegal liquor business, or for want of a better term, the rise of the "bootlegger track."

H. Clay Earles of Martinsville, Virginia, became the second major bootlegger to construct and open a racetrack in 1947. Earles grew up on a farm in "L.A.—Lower Axton, that is." By his own testimony, he owned several legitimate businesses, including three area service stations, and "bought and sold real estate."[64] However, Earles was also involved in the making and distribution of moonshine—in the words of Junior Johnson, "a big-time bootlegger"—and a skilled high-stakes poker player who was known for always packing a pistol.[65] Like the bootleggers/track builders in North Wilkesboro, Earles had attended several stock car races, in his case in Salisbury, North Carolina. He liked what he saw and decided he could build and manage a successful track himself. Earles partnered with 1939 Daytona winner and fellow area bootlegger J. Sam Rice, who also owned an earth-moving business, to build a dirt racetrack, shaped like a paper clip and measuring a little over half a mile, on 30 acres just south of Martinsville for a reported $60,000.[66] Bill France was again on the ground floor and secured the contract to promote the first Martinsville race on September 7, 1947, under the NCSCC banner. France delivered a top-flight field, and even with available seating space for only 750 fans, the race was a huge success and drew a crowd of more than 6,000 to see war hero Red Byron take his Parks Novelty Ford to victory.[67]

In partnering with bootleggers such as Staley, Combs, Earles, and Rice, France had hit on a business model that helped lay the foundation for the success of NASCAR. He had discovered a group of individuals with both the money and the willingness to gamble that money in the risky business of racetrack construction, ownership, and promotion. As driver Frank Mundy observed, "The bootleggers were the only ones who had any money, who were able to put up the purses."[68] In 1948, France's relationship with bootlegging became even more direct as he, Staley, and Combs entered a partnership to build a one-mile speedway just east of Hillsborough, North Carolina, which became a staple on the Piedmont tour. Other bootleggers heard—probably through the informal network of Piedmont and mountain bootleggers—about the success of North Wilkesboro and Martinsville and decided to try their hand at the racetrack business. Stokesville, North Carolina, bootleggers Harvey and Pat Charles showed up on the doorstep of the farmhouse of C. C. Allison west of Charlotte off Wilkinson Boulevard in 1947. The Charles brothers worked out a deal to partner with Allison to build a .75-mile dirt track on the property, and the first race at the Charlotte Speedway, in July 1948, promoted by Bill France, drew a huge crowd.[69] In the early 1950s, other bootleggers joined the ranks of Staley, Combs, Earles, and the Charles brothers as builders/owners of the most important tracks in Piedmont stock car racing, the most notable among them Gene Sluder of the Asheville-Weaverville Speedway and Ralph and Grafton Burgess (better known as "Puff" and "Tuff"), who partnered with Charlie Combs to build the Hickory Speedway.[70]

Aside from providing key infrastructure and financing in the sport's early years, bootleggers also proved to be key allies of Bill France. Joe Littlejohn became the top promoter of France-sanctioned races in South Carolina. Enoch Staley became France's right-hand man, not only partnering with him on the Hillsborough track but regularly serving as a troubleshooter at Daytona and even at Talladega after the France family built that track in 1969. Earles regularly helped France with the Daytona race, running the profitable concessions there for years. In addition, he served as a regional director of NASCAR in Virginia and signed up most of the state's tracks for the series. Indeed, by the end of 1947, in lining up the support of Littlejohn in South Carolina, Staley in North Carolina, and Earles in Virginia, France firmly established himself as the leading promoter of stock car racing in the Piedmont South.

As important as these "bootlegger tracks" would be to the future of stock car racing in the Piedmont region, the proliferation of smaller, less well-financed tracks proved just as essential to the sport's growth. In 1947 these tracks began to sprout across the region like mushrooms after a rainy period, holding races much more frequently than the major tracks, in some cases as often as once a week during the warmer months. Tracks were scraped out of the red clay, or in some cases fairground horse tracks were converted to auto racing, in such small towns in the region as Danville, Virginia; Mount Airy and Elkin, North Carolina; Anderson, Laurens, and Greenwood, South Carolina; and Griffin, Gainesville, and Toccoa, Georgia. By the early 1950s, almost every county in the Piedmont had at least one track, and many had two or more. While these tracks were often undercapitalized, poorly promoted, and short lived, they provided an essential training ground for new talent. Anyone who could scrape together $50 or so could find a late '30s Ford or other junk car and turn it into a race car in short order. Local liquor drivers often brought the cars in which they hauled whiskey to the tracks to test them against fellow trippers. The tracks usually created different divisions based on experience of the driver and engine size, so virtually anyone could show up and race. Although the first generation of star stock car drivers were drawn primarily from the ranks of whiskey runners, much of the second generation—with the exception of a second group of trippers led by Curtis Turner and Junior Johnson—gained their high-speed driving experience at one of these local Piedmont dirt tracks.

Piedmont Racing Fans

Thirsty for entertainment, Piedmont working-class people flocked to the track to see the races despite less-than-ideal conditions for fans at many tracks. Traffic was generally a nightmare in the early days at most tracks, as the ticket sellers stopped cars on the way into the parking lot to collect admission fees because of a lack of fences around the facilities. This meant that cars backed up generally for miles leading into the track and that many people parked elsewhere and slipped in without paying. Martinsville Speedway builder/owner H. Clay Earles remembered the first race held at his facility: "That first race we weren't organized that well. We didn't have ticket booths, just people out front collecting money. We didn't have any fences, and there were people who snuck in."[71] Restroom and concession facilities were generally primitive at best. The crowd itself could also be pretty rough, with drinking to excess and fighting among the crowd not uncommon occurrences. "It was the place your mother warned you about," Humpy Wheeler recalled.[72]

Another common inconvenience was a pall of dust that covered everyone and everything once the race began. Earles remembered that at that first Martinsville race "everyone left here looking like Red Byron—they were covered with dust all over them."[73] Frank Mundy recalled seeing one woman in the infield after a race who "was so damn dirty from sitting up in the stands, I said to her, 'What number were you driving?'" The woman, "madder'n hell anyway that she was so dirty and filthy," was not amused and "pulled back her pocketbook and was going to hit me with it."[74] In 1949, David Guthrie of Asheville, North Carolina, took his new cream-colored convertible to his first race at the Hollywood Race Track, which was carved out of a cow pasture in the nearby community of Fairview. After the race he couldn't find his car until he realized that the red convertible he kept passing was his car. He soon looked in a mirror and discovered he was covered with dirt as well.[75]

While some early spectators came to the first races because of the novelty and left turned off by the environment, a sizable number became hooked for life and helped form the foundation for the ongoing success of Piedmont racing. Humpy Wheeler observed that in those early days promoters seemed to do "everything we can to make the place inhospitable. The parking is lousy, the restrooms are terrible, the food is barely edible, and yet these people keep coming back and bring people with them."[76] Despite the covering of dirt he and his car received at his first race, David Guthrie became a lifelong fan. Gordon Pirkle of Dawson County, Georgia, got hooked on racing like many other north Georgia boys by watching the Flock brothers, Red Byron, and local favorite Gober Sosebee power-sliding through the turns at Lakewood Speedway and other area tracks. Dawson County fans would load their up cars and head off to the Sunday afternoon or holiday races in a festive caravan.[77]

Perhaps the extreme of early fandom came in the form of J. B. Day of Easley, South Carolina. As a seven-year-old in 1941, Day started slipping off to races, hitching rides to Lakewood Speedway and High Point Speedway. Even though he "got an ass whipping" from his father, he says "it was worth it." Day became a fixture at Piedmont races after the war. As a twelve-year-old elementary school dropout he helped his father pour concrete for the grandstands at Greenville-Pickens Speedway just down the road from his home and attended all the early races—often selling programs or helping out somehow at the speedway—further stoking the fires of his love for racing. Atlanta mechanic Wylie Babb took a liking to Day and made a special sprocket for his bicycle to help him produce more efficient power. The modified bike helped him win the kids' bike race, with its $5.00 prize, at the inaugural July 4, 1946, Greenville stock car race.

He also won $5.00 for winning the mule race, got a share of the prize for being the top of a human ladder that pulled a $50 bill off the top of a greased pole, and won $5.00 for catching a greased pig. He left the track with $20.00 cash and two pigs—a buddy had also caught one, but his mother would not let him keep it. Soon after, Day starting hitting the road on his bike and going to races as far away as Lakewood and even Martinsville, Virginia—he went to Martinsville only once, though, because it was uphill all the way there. He would ride by day and sleep in the woods at night. Although no one would take him to the races, Day knew that if he could get there someone from the Greenville area—or someone passing through—would give him a ride home.[78] Although Day's is an extreme example, thousands of working-class fans in the Piedmont soon developed an intense devotion to the region's dirt tracks and the wild drivers who raced on them.

The 1947 National Championship Stock Car Circuit

By the end of the 1946 season it became apparent that Piedmont stock car racing had more than regained its prewar popularity as increasing numbers of fans embraced the sport. It was also apparent that Bill France intended to control as much of this action as he could and even expand his operations throughout the East Coast. North Georgia drivers, led by the daring, dashing liquor runners Fonty Flock, Bob Flock, and war hero Red Byron in their Red Vogt–prepared Parks Novelty Fords, and Ed Samples, 1946 U.S. Stock Car Drivers Association points champion, still dominated the driving scene. Indeed, fourteen of the top twenty positions, including the top three, in the 1946 U.S. Stock Car Drivers Association Points Championship hailed from the Atlanta area.[79] While Georgia drivers dominated, however, a significant geographical shift north had occurred as Bill France promoted most of the important events in Piedmont stock car racing and the new bootlegger tracks in North Carolina and Virginia took the place of Lakewood Speedway as the focal points of the stock car racing world.

In 1947, Piedmont stock car racing exploded across the region with at least forty-one races held—and probably many more that are undocumented—the vast majority promoted by Bill France and his NCSCC.[80] After successfully promoting Daytona races in January and March and helping friend Eddie Bland promote a race at the new Jacksonville, Florida, speedway, France moved into the Piedmont in April with a major race in

Greensboro that drew a record crowd for a sporting event in the city.[81] In order to attract the top drivers and hype his events, France brought a new feature to the NCSCC, a cash-paying points championship. The points champion would receive $1,000 and a 3-foot trophy, while the second-place finisher would receive $500 and a smaller trophy. Third place would collect a "suitably engraved" Longine or Bulova watch worth $150. Not yet in a position to punish drivers for driving in other promoters' events, France tried to keep drivers in the NCSCC fold by counting points only for "races managed by Bill France." He did, however, declare that drivers would forfeit all their points if they officially entered one of his races and then raced elsewhere. He further sweetened the pot by promising to offer a minimum of $2,000 in purse money for each race.[82] France asserted, "By establishing the national point-ranking system we will be able to guarantee fans, as well as track officials, a crack field of drivers."[83]

France covered the Piedmont promoting races from Danville, Virginia, to Birmingham, Alabama, almost always drawing crowds of better than 5,000 and most of the time many more. Indeed, France became so successful by 1947 that he now flew from venue to venue in his own Ryan Navion single-engine plane. France knew his product and his audience well and became—according to the *Greensboro Daily News*—the "master of racing as the common man likes it."[84] France himself opined in May 1947, "From the success of races held during the past 12 months, the people evidently want stock car racing."[85]

The wild success of his points system also sparked interest in France's stock car racing promotions. Going into the fall of 1947, the tight points race between Bob and Fonty Flock, with war hero Red Byron not far behind, helped fill the stands. Dour, intense, and violent Bob—considered by many to be the best driver of the immediate postwar era—contrasted perfectly with the mustachioed, charismatic, and fun-loving Fonty. Both had gained their first high-speed driving experiences by hauling liquor for their uncle "Peachtree" Williams in and around Atlanta. Bob Flock and Red Byron piloted a pair of Parks Novelty Fords prepared by Red Vogt, while Fonty drove for Bob Osiecki. Although he won nine races—including the March race at Daytona and the 200-miler at Langhorne in July—Bob lost out to Fonty, Ed Samples, Red Byron, and Buddy Shuman in the points championship when he blew a right rear tire at the October 11 race at Spartanburg, crashed into the fence, and broke his back, ending his season. Ironically, Bob's accident opened the door for brother Fonty to

The "Mad Flocks," the biggest draw in stock car racing in the late 1940s.
Left to right, Bob, Tim, and Fonty Flock. (Courtesy of McCaig-Welborn Research Library at the International Motorsports Hall of Fame, Talladega, Alabama)

defect from Osiecki and drive a Parks Novelty Ford in the last few races, which helped him secure the championship.[86]

France was not content, however, with dominating the Piedmont stock car market and moved to expand his reach even as he solidified his position in the Carolinas. He particularly had his eye on expansion into the eastern market, where stock car racing's popularity boomed. France took a big step in expanding his promotional reach in July 1947 when he successfully organized a race—won by Fonty Flock and dominated by Piedmont drivers Ed Samples, Bob Flock, and Buddy Shuman—at the New Jersey State Fairgrounds in Trenton. Perhaps his most important move, however, came in the fall when he partnered with New England racing kingpin Bill Tuthill to promote an October race in Lonsdale, Rhode Island. The event drew a crowd of 12,000 fans to see Fonty Flock win the feature race—with Buddy Shuman second and Ed Samples third—and the lion's share of the $3,000 purse. Piedmont drivers dominated even though they were not power-sliding around on a red-clay track but racing on a .33-mile paved facility.[87] The success of the event also solidified the relationship between France and Tuthill, who would prove invaluable in France's future attempts to expand his empire.

Bill France's Competition

While Bill France controlled most of the largest, most profitable race-tracks in the Piedmont by 1947 and had forged formidable alliances with both Piedmont bootleggers/track owners and some prominent north-eastern racing promoters, he did face significant challenges to his self-granted title of "Largest Operator of Stock Car Racing Throughout the Country." Sam Nunis had also spent his days during the war years working in defense plants—in his case aviation plants—and planning the future of postwar auto racing, especially after the death of his mentor, Ralph Hankinson, in the summer of 1942. On the day the Japanese surrendered, Nunis wasted no time and got the jump on potential competitors as he "got on the phone and booked race meets with 16 fairs for the balance of the [1945] season."[88] Although Nunis promoted primarily big-car events, he recognized the growing popularity of stock car racing and staged three major races in the summer of 1946, two at Allentown, Pennsylvania, and one at Reading, Pennsylvania—the so-called Indianapolis of dirt tracks—which offered the "richest purse of the year" for a stock car race. Nunis also knew where the talent was, and the superior appearance and prize money he offered attracted Raymond Parks and his top team of cars and drivers as well as up-and-coming drivers such as Buddy Shuman, Glenn Dunnaway, and Ed Samples. Bill France himself even entered the second Allentown race. In a demonstration of their dominance of the sport, Piedmont drivers won all three Nunis-promoted stock races.[89]

In 1947, Nunis—who had a fifteen-year lease to promote racing at Lakewood Speedway—and Georgian Weyman Milam created the most serious and longest-lasting challenge to France's empire when they established their National Stock Car Racing Association (NSCRA), which sanctioned a number of races in Georgia in 1947 at Lakewood, Thomaston, and Macon. NSCRA competed with Bill France and his NCSCC for the talents of star drivers Bob and Fonty Flock, Red Byron, and Buddy Shuman and talented newcomers Jack Smith and Billy Carden, although Nunis's promotions at Lakewood were handicapped by the ban on convicted liquor haulers. In addition, Nunis promotions drew huge crowds for stock car races at tracks he controlled in Richmond, Virginia; Allentown and Reading, Pennsylvania; and Flemington, New Jersey, which paid hefty purses and appearance money and often attracted the top Piedmont drivers. While France did control the lion's share of stock car promotions in the Piedmont, Nunis and the NSCRA proved formidable rivals to his dominance of the Piedmont market in future years.[90]

France also faced the challenge of the ongoing popularity of big-car racing in the region. Nunis continued to stage races for Indy-style racing at Lakewood Speedway, where eight such events attracted an estimated 200,000 fans in 1946, making it one of the most popular tracks in the country for such events. In 1947, he expanded his promotions to the new track at Macon, Georgia, where he also pulled in big crowds.[91] France recognized this continued appeal and organized two successful big-car races himself—under the sanction of the traditionally midwestern Consolidated States Racing Association (CSRA)—in July at Greenville-Pickens and North Wilkesboro.[92]

Midget car racing also made major inroads into the region in 1947 to compete with the stockers. Red Crise promoted weekly midget shows in Richmond, while Jim Frattone and Jim van Cise staged them in Birmingham, Alabama.[93] Lew Franco and his National Sports Syndicate out of New York City made the greatest appeal for the hearts and minds of Piedmonters by creating the Dixie Circuit and put big-car and midget star Bob Sall in charge of southern operations. Sall promoted weekly midget races in Raleigh, Charlotte, and Winston-Salem, North Carolina; Roanoke and Norfolk, Virginia; and Columbia, South Carolina. Most of the races were held at dirt fairground tracks, but Franco and Sall brought stadium racing with them to the South. Indeed, Bowman Gray Stadium in Winston-Salem became one of the most popular venues for auto racing in the region when Franco and Stall built a .2-mile paved track around the football field used by the Wake Forest Demon Deacons. The first race at the Bowman Gray track, on June 6, 1947, attracted a crowd of 17,000.[94] Part of the appeal of midget racing was the ability to put a track almost anywhere because of the small size of the racers.

Despite these challenges, Bill France stood positioned for even bigger and better things by the end of 1947. He had secured contracts to promote stock car racing at the most important and successful tracks in the Piedmont—with the exception of Lakewood Speedway. He had discovered a lucrative source of finance capital for race purses, advertising, and the construction of new tracks in the region's bootleggers, who had the cash, the love of cars, and the willingness to gamble on a risky enterprise. He also had the loyalty and the entrepreneurial talents of these individuals, such as Joe Littlejohn, Enoch Staley, Charlie Combs, and Clay Earles, which would benefit NASCAR and the France family as long as these men lived. In addition, the proliferation of tracks and local, weekly racing in the region created the necessary minor league in small towns throughout Piedmont Georgia, South Carolina, North Carolina, and Virginia to produce new stars to stand alongside and eventually replace the established stars of the sport, the Atlanta-area liquor haulers.

Most important, for anyone trying to sell anything, France had both a wonderful product and a market of working-class Piedmonters hungry for that product. Bill Tuthill described that early racing and the drivers to author William Neely: "Those early races were heartstoppers. Nobody would give an inch, and if you didn't get out of the way, they'd run you over. When the flag dropped you'd think war was declared. They went anyplace there was an opening—down through the pits, in the grass, the infield, anywhere."[95]

A Paper Dream?

The Creation and Early Years of NASCAR

On February 21, 1948, the National Association for Stock Car Auto Racing was born. There were no champagne corks popping to celebrate the occasion. I covered the birth of NASCAR from the first meeting to the delivery on February 21, 1948. It was still a paper dream.

— Bernard Kahn, sports reporter for the Daytona Beach News Journal, *in Ben White, "NASCAR: The Beginning"*

Writing for the *Daytona Beach News Journal*, sports reporter Bernard Kahn described the birth of NASCAR as a less-than-momentous event, but his view differs greatly from the standard accounts of the organization's establishment.[1] For most observers, including NASCAR itself, the gathering at the Ebony Bar of the Streamline Hotel in Daytona Beach was the place where the leading figures of the stock car racing world recognized the need for organization and anointed Bill France to lead them into a promised land of national exposure, guaranteed purses, and better benefits for drivers. At the meeting France also proffered a vision of a series that would feature brand-new cars and new standards that would level the playing field, allow the working-class driver to compete, and produce true national champions based on NASCAR's point system. Indeed, the sessions in the smoke-filled Ebony Bar of December 1947 and the official chartering of NASCAR in February 1948 took the organization from obscurity and derision and placed it on the high road to national prominence.[2] However, this story greatly exaggerates the importance of this meeting, which only became significant many years down the road.

While the idea of creating an actual national organization was truly a "paper dream" in the late 1940s, the story of the earliest days of NASCAR is one of Bill France's drive to further solidify his position in the Piedmont—as always with considerable help from the region's bootlegger racers and financiers—and at the same time make some tentative but important moves to expand his influence into the rest of the country, especially the Northeast. Indeed, the legendary gathering in Daytona Beach was well down the list of important accomplishments for France and NASCAR during this period. One of those signal accomplishments was France's decision go back to the future and launch a "strictly stock" division in 1949. Observers often credit France with inventing the strictly stock format, but the history of stock car racing in the pre–World War II era is replete with such races. Bill France himself drove in such races throughout the Southeast and even promoted strictly stock races at Daytona Beach. While France did not originate the idea of racing new cars, the new series did quickly become the premier series in NASCAR, the one that drew the most fan attention, and the one that eventually made NASCAR a household name.

France and his associates also solidified their position in the Piedmont and greatly strengthened the sport's foundation in terms of the pool of skilled drivers and available racetracks and further expanded its fan base. Perhaps the most significant thing that France did was to partner with old friend Alvin Hawkins to start weekly racing at a failed midget car track built inside Winston-Salem's Bowman Gray Stadium. The success of the Bowman Gray races led to the spread of weekly stock car racing all over the region and to the construction of dozens of new tracks; it also created new opportunities for young men in the Piedmont to tap into deep cultural roots, to display their courage and driving talent. In a related move that proved almost as important to its future, NASCAR created its Sportsman Series in 1949 for inexperienced drivers racing older—and cheaper—cars. This series served as a development league for its Modified and Strictly Stock series. France and the promoters allied with him also showed their willingness to do almost anything to get fans in the stands. Most notable in this respect, during the late 1940s they began to encourage women drivers to compete not only in women-only "powder-puff derbies" but against the men in NASCAR's top division. Although this was, again, not an original idea of Bill France's, he used publicity generated by women drivers to help spread the word about his Strictly Stock Series. Indeed, the second strictly stock race, held at Daytona in July 1949, featured three women racers. To be sure, while the official founding of NASCAR did not change Piedmont stock car racing a great deal in and of itself, it did launch a period in which the sport shored up the foundation that had been laid in the immediate post–World War II era and even more firmly entrenched stock car racing as the region's top working-class sport and entertainment staple.

The Founding of NASCAR

In order to expand his operations outside the Piedmont and Daytona and in response to a proliferation of new stock car sanctioning bodies, including Nunis's NSCRA and Bob Streeter's American Stock Car Racing Association (ASCRA), Bill France called a meeting in Daytona for December 1947—billed in the auto racing press as the "annual convention of the National Championship Stock Car Racing Circuit"—to "set up a complete organization which will act as a guide to stock car racing throughout the United States." The call was an open one for "all those interested in stock car racing" to gather December 14–17 at the "Streamliner [*sic*] Hotel"; France set the goals of the meeting as creating standardized rules, national and sectional points systems; minimum purses for sanctioned events, and a controlled calendar to prevent conflicts of sanctioned events in the same area.[3]

Interestingly, there was little talk in the lead-up to the meeting, or in accounts of the meeting itself, of the problem of promoters absconding with purse money and not paying drivers, a problem that has been listed in most written accounts and has come down in stock car racing mythology as the primary reason for the creation of NASCAR. Enoch Staley's son Mike gave the standard account of this story in an interview with Peter Golenbock. "What NASCAR was formed to do was to make sure the competitors got paid. They used to have trouble with promoters running a race and taking the ticket money, and the end of the race when the drivers came to collect, they would be gone. Then they'd go someplace where people didn't know them, and they'd do it again. They were con men. NASCAR was started to give the drivers some protection and to make the sport legitimate."[4]

This story, however, like the story of cow pasture racing, is one that probably did happen on more than one occasion but was not a common occurrence and had little to do with the formation of NASCAR. As has been stated earlier, most races were professionally promoted. Indeed, by the time NASCAR came along, Bill France promoted the vast majority of races in the Piedmont, who for any faults he may have had—and as a former race driver who had been cheated by promoters—always made sure the purse was paid. When interviewed by Sylvia Wilkinson in the early

1980s, France made no mention of guaranteeing the payment of purses as a major reason for the creation of NASCAR.[5] Raymond Parks, the one person who was part of almost as many stock car races as Bill France in the early days of the sport, was asked point-blank by historian Pete Daniel in an interview, "Did you ever hear about promoters running off with the money?" Parks responded, "I never did know of it."[6]

The meeting itself in the Ebony Bar of the Streamline Hotel has become an important part of the NASCAR legend, and literally hundreds of accounts exist of the three-day meeting. Most observers generally agree that thirty-four to thirty-five men attended at least one of the three days of the meeting, although as journalist Ed Hinton observed, "If you counted all those who *claimed* to have been there, the number would have been in the hundreds."[7] Those present included prominent racing promoters from the Northeast Bill Tuthill and Bill Streeter; southern promoters and longtime France friends Joe Littlejohn, Alvin Hawkins, and Eddie Bland; drivers/mechanics Buddy Shuman and Marshall Teague; mechanic Red Vogt; and journalists Jim Quisenberry of *Speed Age Magazine* and Bernard Kahn of the *Daytona Beach News Journal*. In fact, the meeting at the Streamline was primarily a gathering of France cronies who came for the free liquor and the pretty models whom France brought in from a local charm school. It was a party, and part of a tradition that France had started the previous year of gathering folks together during a dead period in racing to plan for the next year and let their hair down.[8]

France and Tuthill—the driving forces in the meeting—knew from the start that many of the individuals who had gathered in the Ebony Bar had little interest in signing on to France's vision but had come for the nice weather, the booze, the pretty girls, and primarily to find out what France was up to. As Tuthill remembered years later, "That first meeting included guys from rival groups. And we knew they were there just to see what we were going to do. They never would have come with us. There was no way we could ever bring this entire group together." In addition, France and Tuthill had little interest in the input of others or in sharing power but were looking for those willing to line up under France's powerful leadership. As Tuthill recalled, "We [he and France] had made a study of every racing organization that had ever come along, so I told Bill that the democratic method, where the board voted on everything[,] had never worked."[9]

France dominated the festivities from the start, which did give those gathered an idea of what Big Bill envisioned for his organization. He opened the first meeting by speaking for more than an hour. In his talk he argued that the best way to advance the sport of stock car racing was to create an overarching body that would standardize the rules and purses and create a true national champion—at the time literally dozens of sanctioning bodies declared their champion the "national champion." He also called for the creation of a benevolence fund and insurance for drivers and mechanics, who generally had none. One of the oft quoted but misunderstood statements made by France involved the importance of stock car racing's image. "We have to think about image. If you get a junky looking old automobile, it's a jalopy to the average person's mind. Even if you get a new Cadillac and pull the fenders off and let it get real dirty, it would be a jalopy to most people."[10] While observers have interpreted this statement generally as France's call for a strictly stock series, it actually was a plea for stock car racing of any kind—modified or strictly stock—to race sharp-looking cars for a better show. France wanted to differentiate his form of stock car racing from the "jalopy racing" common in many parts of the country and generally derided by traditional racing aficionados.

France also talked openly about the core group of potential fans and drivers most attracted to stock car racing: the working class. He asserted, "Stock car racing has got distinct possibilities for Sunday shows," one of the few times working-class fans would not be working. Sunday racing would also benefit working-class drivers as it "would allow race-minded boys that work all week, who don't have the money to afford a regular racing car, to be competitive with a rich guy." France understood both the mentality of those his sport attracted and the limitations of working-class existence. Sunday races would allow them to "show their stuff, and maybe win a prize, and not make it their full-time job."[11]

Although reporters and historians have touted the historical significance of the meeting and the Ebony Bar has become a significant NASCAR pilgrimage site, the sessions themselves seem to have accomplished little of great significance other than coming up with the NASCAR name, suggested by Red Vogt, and the designation of three divisions of competition—Strictly Stock, Modified, and Roadster.[12] By the end of the three-day meeting, NASCAR was little more than a renamed NCSCC, a Bill France–dominated group with perhaps better connections to racing in the Northeast but essentially the same body. As reporter Bernard Kahn recalled, "The daylong, nightlong meetings in the bar atop the Streamline Hotel broke up without any formal action. The stock car germ had been planted, however, and two guys named Tuthill and France nourished it and kept it alive. . . . There was a shortage of money and enthusiasm."[13] Indeed, NASCAR, for several years, was essentially one among several groups seeking to dominate the stock car racing business, and one not necessarily destined for greatness or even short-term success.

In terms of the future of NASCAR, more important developments occurred in subsequent months. The group incorporated in February with the help of local lawyer Louis Ossinsky and issued stock. Although Tuthill and Ossinsky—and later promoter Ed Otto—initially owned NASCAR stock, France eventually purchased most of it for himself and his family. The appointment of auto racing legend Erwin George "Cannonball" Baker as NASCAR commissioner gave NASCAR a real boost in its drive for national credibility, particularly in the auto racing world.[14] While the sixty-six-year old Baker served primarily as a figurehead—regularly trotted out by France for major NASCAR events—his position and presence brought NASCAR a great deal of positive media exposure. Baker had become a national hero, known primarily for his record-setting, cross-country speed runs that helped advertise and popularize the automobile in its early years: driving a Stutz Bearcat from San Diego to New York City in eleven days, seven hours, fifteen minutes, he set his first cross-country record in 1915. After this first run gained so much attention, he began to market his services to auto makers with the slogan "No record, no pay." In subsequent years he lowered his record significantly, setting an official record of sixty hours, thirty-one minutes in a Stutz Versailles and claiming an unofficial record of fifty-three hours, thirty minutes in a 1933 Graham.[15] Baker's name later became well known when reporter Brock Yates of *Car and Driver* magazine christened the series of cross-country races he promoted as the "Cannonball Run," later popularized in a pair of movies starring Burt Reynolds. Baker's name regularly appeared next to France's on the NASCAR logo and in press accounts of NASCAR events. The NASCAR logo itself was also intended to further place NASCAR as part of the rich history of auto racing. The logo contained not a picture of a stock car but mirror images of Sir Malcolm Campbell's Bluebird—which had set so many land speed records at Daytona Beach—facing each other with crossed checkered flags in between.[16]

The First NASCAR Season

While NASCAR may have been, in the words of Bernard Kahn, a "paper dream"—an organization claiming national significance but based out of Bill France's house at 29 Goodall Avenue in Daytona Beach—France did have some assets that he employed to begin to make his dream of a truly national sanctioning body a reality. His primary asset was his promotion of perhaps the most popular and best-known stock car race in the nation, the Daytona beach/road race. Not surprisingly, the first NASCAR-sanctioned race was the February 15, 1948, modified race on the beach. Because of encroaching development and complaints from local home owners, France received permission from city officials to move the course south to Ponce Inlet, where he laid out a 4.4-mile course for the popular motorcycle races and within that course a 2.2-mile course for stock cars. A record number of sixty-two entries signed up for the 1948 event, with fifty-six actually taking the green flag. Once again, the Raymond Parks–owned Fords prepared by Red Vogt dominated the event, with Red Byron finishing first for the third straight time and Raymond Parks himself—relieved by Bob Flock—finishing third. Local mechanic and NASCAR secretary and treasurer Marshall Teague finished second, and the entire top ten drove 1939 Fords.[17] In order to add additional luster to the event and attract drivers from across the auto racing world, France added speed trials for modifieds, strictly stocks, motorcycles, and midget racers run "on a three-mile course on Daytona Beach with a one-mile start, one mile through the [speed] trap and one mile to stop."[18] The crowd of 14,000, who paid $2.50 apiece, gave France great hope for the future of his fledgling organization.[19]   ·

On the heels of the successful Daytona race, France moved to sign up a number of new venues for stock car racing in the Piedmont region under the NASCAR banner. The addition of races in Lexington, Wadesboro, and Reidsville, North Carolina, and Augusta and Columbus, Georgia, further strengthened France's hold on the region's stock car racing. Most important, France brought two new major tracks under the NASCAR umbrella in North Carolina: Hillsborough, known as Occoneechee Speedway, and the Charlotte Speedway. Occoneechee was a joint venture between France and Wilkes County entrepreneurs Enoch Staley, Charlie Combs, Dobe Powell, Ben Lowe, and Joe Buck Dawson, most of whom were connected to the county's bootlegging industry. The Hillsborough Speedway further strengthened France's connections to the illegal liquor business, and to Wilkes County, and led to numerous other direct business partnerships with Staley and Combs. The mile-long track—"boasting long straightaways with sharp treacherous turns" and billed as the "Langhorne of the South"—opened with a 100-mile feature offering a $4,000 purse. Fonty Flock won the race, much to the delight of local fans.[20] France's part ownership in the track began a process in which France—and later his son, Bill Jr.—gave the France family the most control over its sport of any professional sporting organization in America, its power based not only on its ownership of NASCAR but on its control of an increasing number of the venues where the sport competed. In NASCAR's early years, France gained at least part interest in several tracks and built his own palace of speed in Daytona in 1959. Two weeks after the opening of Occoneechee, the .75-mile Charlotte Speedway held its first race. The track soon became one of the premier venues in the region, even after the bootlegging Charles brothers were sent to federal penitentiary in the early 1950s for their illegal activities.[21]

NASCAR also benefited from the promotion of a points championship for its modified races. Early in the season, France announced that the points fund for NASCAR's premier races could go as high as $10,000, with $2,500 to the winner. Although the fund reached only $5,000, NASCAR, and France, benefited from another tight championship race as crippled war hero Red Byron, driving the #22 Parks Novelty Ford, edged out the flamboyant, mustachioed, charismatic Atlanta liquor runner Fonty Flock—who drove for Reading, Pennsylvania, mechanic/car owner Joe Wolf—by only thirty-two points in a fifty-four-race schedule to win the $1,250 top prize.[22] NASCAR also held a two-month-long race for the Southeastern championship, a series of double-feature races run at four North Carolina Piedmont tracks: North Wilkesboro, Charlotte, Occoneechee, and Lakeview (Lexington). The series was won by charismatic new driver, and noted bootlegger, Curtis Turner of Christiansburg, Virginia, billed as the "blonde blizzard."[23]

France's promotions also benefited from the infusion of new talent into his races. The most successful of these at both winning races and drawing fans to the track were Tim Flock—youngest brother of the "Mad Flocks," Bob and Fonty—and Curtis Turner. Both had perfect pedigrees for drivers of their era. Although Flock had not hauled liquor—his brothers insisted that he stay out of the family business and finish high school—he rode with his brothers as they tripped and was around Piedmont stock car racing almost from its beginning. In the summer of 1947, after having helped out on both his brothers' racing teams, Tim began his own career. Despite not having the liquor hauling experience of his brothers, he turned out to be a naturally gifted race driver and won a preliminary heat race in only his second organized event at the Greensboro Fairgrounds in September 1947.[24] Tim became known primarily for his smooth driving style and his ability to stay out of trouble and save the car for a final dash to the finish. Early in his racing career a reporter for *National Speed Sport News* marveled at the way he started at the rear of the field at a Greensboro NASCAR race and quickly moved up through the field to fifth. The reporter asserted that Tim Flock was "definitely the boy to watch."[25] Even though it was his first full season, Tim finished third in the final modified points standings in 1948, with one win at Greensboro and six second-place finishes, just behind his brother Fonty and two slots ahead of Bob. Tim went on to become one of NASCAR's brightest stars, winning the championship twice in its top division. In the late 1940s he helped to give Bill France his most marketable attraction, the considerable driving talents of three "Mad Flocks."[26]

Curtis Turner was in many ways the polar opposite of Flock, although he too came into stock car racing with deep roots in the moonshine business. Turner's father, Morton, was a noted and highly successful moonshiner and timber operator in Floyd County, Virginia. Curtis himself claimed that he started hauling liquor at the age of nine. By the time he reached eighteen, he ran his own logging and sawmilling operations by day and hauled liquor by night. Inducted into the navy and stationed in Norfolk in 1943, Turner supplemented his income by smuggling tires out of the base and hauling them west to sell to his moonshining friends. After he was discharged in 1946, he developed a lucrative business of trading moonshine for government sugar at the Norfolk Naval Station. In turn, he exchanged the sugar for more moonshine and cash with moonshiners back in Floyd County. When authorities arrested him with a load of government sugar in his trunk, Turner told the judge that yes, he had taken the sugar to help his family and friends back in the hills make apple butter. The judge knew that was a lie, but Turner did get off relatively easily with a $1,000 fine and two-year suspended sentence.[27]

After this incident Turner began to turn his energies more to the timber business, but he always thirsted for more excitement in his life. In 1946 and '47, he began to dabble in racing at tracks in southern Virginia and northwestern North Carolina, particularly at the new speedways in nearby Elkin and Mount Airy, North Carolina. Unlike Flock, he did not worry about saving the car for the finish and drove every lap as if it were the last, never letting anything or anyone get in the way of his winning. Early in his career, Turner earned the nickname "Pops," not because of his age but because of his tendency to "pop" people out of the way on the track. Almost everyone who drove against Turner asserted that he was the greatest dirt-track driver in history with an uncanny ability to throw the car into a power slide and maintain it longer than anyone else. At the same time, Turner cared only about winning the race, had a sizable income outside racing with his timber business, and raced for fun and by the motto "Win, wreck, or blow up." Indeed, he rarely finished a race that he didn't win. As Ned Jarrett observed, "I'd sort of write him off even before we started. He outran me more times than I ever outran him, but I'd finish three times as many races. I never expected him to be there at the end."[28] But Curtis did not care, and neither did his fans who flocked to the track to see him in action and thrilled to his high-flying lifestyle of big Cadillacs, silk suits, big airplanes, and flashy women. Turner soon came to rival Fonty Flock in the outlandish personality department and for the next twenty years would exemplify the wild, seat-of-the-pants, exuberant Piedmont stock car driver that brought working-class fans out in droves. In his first full season Turner won seven races, finished fourth in the points championship, and won the Southeastern championship. But win, lose, blow up, or crash, if Curtis Turner was in the race, there was going to be a show.[29]

France had had what most would deem a successful first season in his NASCAR series: fifty-four races; an exciting and close points championship, this time between a war hero and a mustachioed, fun-loving liquor runner; new tracks near two of the Piedmont region's most important population centers; and a stable of charismatic young drivers he could almost always deliver for promoters. The year, however, was not quite as successful as he would have hoped. NASCAR was nowhere near "national" in scope and even struggled to hold on to its dominant position in the Piedmont South. One of France's major problems was the defection of his close friend Joe Littlejohn, who in partnership with Buddy Davenport had created the South Carolina Racing Association (SCRA). With its own points championship and races rotating between the profitable Greenville-Pickens and Hub City (Spartanburg) tracks and a new track in Columbia, the SCRA had essentially locked France out of the state. Littlejohn and Davenport guaranteed a $2,000 purse for every race and a 1948 Oldsmobile to the winner of the points championship. The pair secured the services of Ed Samples, a former regular at France's races and 1946 NCSCC champion, as well as Bob Flock, who split his time between SCRA races and NASCAR races. The SCRA also boasted of new talent in Fred Mahon, Cotton Owens, and Joe Eubanks. In order to attract even more fans to their regular stock car races, Littlejohn and Davenport held powder-puff derbies—usually ten- to fifteen-lap events—as preludes to their feature events. Sara Christian, wife of Atlanta-area bootlegger Frank Christian, became as much of a draw as any driver at SCRA races, not only regularly dominating the powder-puff events but even occasionally racing in the feature races. Mildred Williams, Louise Smith, and Ruby Flock—Bob's wife—became regulars in the women's-only events. While the SCRA kept France out of the important South Carolina market, Littlejohn's series did have problems filling fields when his races went head to head with NASCAR events. Indeed, the final race of the year had a field of only twelve cars. The promoters were also unlucky in that Ed Samples ran away with the points championship, at one point in the season winning ten races in a row.[30]

The Struggle for Respectability

One of the highest hurdles France had to clear in his drive to bring NASCAR to national prominence was the lack of respect for stock car racing both among the major players in motorsports and among the more respectable classes in the Piedmont region. Even as stock car racing's reach expanded in the late 1940s, the auto racing establishment tended to see it as a southern interloper, destined to crawl back into its cave and die. As William Kay, editor of the influential *National Speed Sport News*, wrote, "Many inquiries into whether stock car racing could become a formidable intrusion on midget and big car races, we have but one answer—NO. It took 30 years to develop auto racing sport as we know it and it's hardly likely that an infant can teach its parent."[31] Even as the 1948 season progressed and stock car racing's popularity skyrocketed, Kay cast aspersions on the appeal of the sport, though he did so in a relatively diplomatic manner, making the accusation that stock car fans came out only to see the wrecks. "There are people now being attracted to stock car racing who never cared to see a midget or a big car race program who will now go out of their way to watch jalopies roll around out of curiosity to learn how much abuse a stock car can stand under the most unusual strain."[32]

Stock car racing suffered in the eyes of most key figures in auto racing in comparison with the midgets and the big cars. The midgets had the appeal of racing on short tracks, often in football stadiums, and had become weekly staples in much of the East and Midwest and even made significant incursions into the South—particularly at Bowman Gray Stadium in Winston-Salem. Matt Kleinfield in his "Speaking of Speed" column in *Illustrated Speedway News* asserted that much of the talk about stock car racing was "ballyhoo" and questioned stock car racing's staying power by

Typical scene of mayhem in the early days of NASCAR, this one at a modified race at Daytona. Such scenes attracted large crowds of working-class Piedmont fans. (Courtesy of McCaig-Welborn Research Library at the International Motorsports Hall of Fame, Talladega, Alabama)

asserting, "The Midgets have been doing their business at least once a week. Does anyone think the stocks can do that for any sustained period?" Kleinfield and Kay did credit Bill France and NASCAR with being "able to bring the sport up to a high level" but predicted that stock cars could support "no more than a few races per year on any one track."[33] Indeed, stock car racing suffered in comparison with big-car racing because it had no event remotely comparable to the venerable Indianapolis 500. Whereas premier stock car events at Daytona, Lakewood, or Langhorne posted at most a $4,500 purse and attracted 30,000 fans and little press coverage, the 1948 Indy 500 offered $160,000 in prize money, attracted more than 100,000 fans, and was covered by every major media outlet, with the winner immediately becoming a national hero.[34]

Even in its home territory, stock car racing's image as a sport for moonshiners, bootleggers, and rednecks was hard to overcome. Of course, the "respectable" folks of Atlanta had already spoken in their campaign to rid Lakewood Speedway of its bootleggers. Bob Flock did enter the Labor Day race at Lakewood in 1947, but two motorcycle cops came after him when they saw him on the track. Flock led the pair in a chase around the track—much to the delight of his cracker fans—drove through the backstretch fence, and eluded capture as he sped through the streets of Atlanta. Atlanta police accused Flock of disguising his identity and attempting to make a "sneak performance" in defiance of the bootlegger ban, and this story was passed along in most NASCAR histories. Actually, Flock turned himself in to authorities the next day and paid a $138 fine for resisting arrest, speeding, and reckless driving, but he embarrassed police officials when he produced a Lakewood program announcing his entry in the race. Despite Flock's PR victory, however, the ban on bootleggers at Lakewood remained intact until 1949, and local officials became more vigilant about whom they allowed to enter a race at the city-owned track.[35]

Despite a more hospitable environment toward NASCAR's bootleggers/racers in the Carolinas and southern Virginia, stock car racing's image left much to be desired there, particularly among the middle class. As Humpy Wheeler observed, "The country club set very definitely did not want to associate themselves with the dirt track."[36] Even in a place such as Wilkes County, where an unprecedented portion of the population turned out for the races, stock cars struggled for respectability. In an April 1948 *Wilkes Journal-Patriot* article entitled "We've Come a Long Way since 1944," sports editor Dwight Nichols highlighted positive developments on the Wilkes County sports scene since World War II. He wrote about the building of new parks and athletic facilities, new recreation, high school and professional sports teams, and the establishment of an annual horse show and agricultural fair. "If these needs had been attended to long ago we probably wouldn't have had as large a court docket as now faces the superior court sessions in Wilkesboro." However, he did not mention stock car racing, which probably attracted more fans than every other sporting event in the county combined.[37] In a September editorial, the *Journal-Patriot* lauded the successful inaugural season of the local semiprofessional baseball team. The editor asserted that the seventy-three baseball games played by the team that season represented "the many events of community recreation during which leisure time was spent by crowds in a wholesome manner."[38]

Of course Nichols never mentioned the stock car races at North Wilkesboro Speedway, by far the most popular sporting events in Wilkes County, which attracted tens of thousands of fans and competitors from all over the region and received national publicity. While the paper had given the track a good deal of publicity in its first season, by 1948 it printed only paid ads and one- or two-paragraph articles for coming races and rarely, if ever, printed the results of races. Perhaps not coincidentally, the paper and the Wilkesboro Ministerial Association launched a major campaign against bootlegging and in support of maintaining Wilkes County as dry—a move heartily supported by local moonshiners.[39] Stock car racing throughout the region generally received similar treatment in the media, with notices for races and race results, when even printed, relegated to the back pages of the sports section.

The rough nature of the tracks, the fans, and the competitors did not help in trying to attract people other than working-class fans. Not only could fans count on a coating of dust and an outhouse for a restroom at the races, but safety protections for fans were primitive or nonexistent. In a July 1948 NASCAR race at the new Columbus, Georgia track, the right front tire blew on Red Byron's Parks Novelty Ford. The car "went out of control, climbed a bank, and plunged through a guard fence into a crowd of spectators." The crash left sixteen fans injured, including a seven-year-old boy whose skull was fractured and a man "whose right leg was so badly injured it had to be amputated below the knee."[40] At Lakewood in 1949, a wheel came off Bob Flock's car and flew into a group of spectators, breaking both legs of an eleven-year-old fan.[41]

Fighting, among both drivers and fans, was also a normal part of the Piedmont stock car racing scene. Louise Smith asserted, "We'd have fights all the time. And if you was driving a car and you won a race you might as well get out with your helmet ready to fight. Because they'd jump in your car and start beating you in the face then."[42] Bob Flock especially had a reputation as a fighter but was by no means atypical. His brother Tim recalled, "If you ever walked up to Bob and put your hand on him, he'd hit you. I mean, a fan or anybody he didn't know, if you just laid your hand on his shoulder, he'd pop you—and break his wrist. . . . Bob was the most wonderful guy you'd ever meet in your life. Quiet, humble—broke his arm twenty-two times a year hittin' people."[43] Heavy drinking among both fans and drivers also shocked middle-class sensibilities. It was not uncommon even for drivers to have a few drinks before, or even during, a race.

The Strictly Stock Series

Despite his inability to make much of an inroad into northern racing and the defection of important South Carolina tracks, France and NASCAR entered 1949 optimistic about the future of the sanctioning body. That optimism was not betrayed when eighty-seven cars showed up for qualifying for the January 16 Daytona beach/road race. France attracted not only the usual contingent of Florida drivers and Piedmont liquor haulers but also some of the top drivers in the East, including New Jersey stock car ace Pepper Cunningham and midget car legend Ted Tappett, winner of twenty-nine of forty-seven races in 1948.[44] France changed the course for the race from the 2.2-mile layout that had been used in 1948 to the

4.4-mile course used in the motorcycle races. A total of seventy-five cars took the green flag, with Daytona Beach mechanic and NASCAR secretary and treasurer Marshall Teague charging to victory before an estimated crowd of 9,000. The relatively high numbers in paid attendance might have been attributed to another France innovation, signs posted in the dunes to discourage people from walking in and avoiding paying: "Beware of Rattlesnakes."[45] Despite this success, however, France knew that he had to come up with some new innovations for the season to compete with the ever increasing number of rivals.

The innovation that has received the most attention over the years was Bill France's decision to launch a strictly stock series. Strictly stock racing had been a staple of pre–World War II stock car racing, but after the war, because of the shortage of new cars, it was difficult to fill a field for such races.[46] Promoter Johnny Wohlfiel staged a July 4, 1948, strictly stock race at Oswosso (Michigan) Speedway, but few other promoters attempted to organize such races due to the shortage of suitable cars.[47] France had organized a 10-mile strictly stock preliminary race before a 100-mile modified race he promoted at Broward Speedway, a 2-mile concrete speedway at the Fort Lauderdale airport, the week after Daytona, to little fanfare.[48] In May, France announced that he would promote a 150-mile "National Championship STRICTLY Stock Car Race" at the .75-mile Charlotte Speedway. He limited entry to 1946 or newer cars "without any modification" and offered a very attractive $5,000 purse, with $2,000 going to the winner.[49]

Practically everyone who has written about the first NASCAR strictly stock event has speculated on France's reasons for holding the event even as his Modified Series drew solid crowds. Many point to the fact that prior to June 1949 it would have been difficult to get enough cars to have an attractive race. By 1949, however, Detroit's production had picked up considerably, and there were enough 1946 to 1949 cars available to fill a field with relatively recent models. Others point to the increased number of competitors, even on his home Piedmont turf, and the need to come up with something new and exciting to compete with his rivals. Indeed, young O. Bruton Smith, in his early twenties and recently off an Oakboro, North Carolina, cotton farm, presented a new and formidable challenge to France's dominance of Piedmont stock car racing. After graduation from high school, Smith worked in a cotton mill, but his love of automobiles led him into the used-car business with a sideline of promoting stock car races at Midland Speedway just north of Charlotte in Cabarrus County.[50] In the spring of 1949, Smith aligned himself with Sam Nunis and NSCRA and began attracting to his promotions some of the brightest stars in Piedmont stock car racing, including Marshall Teague, Buck Baker, Speedy Thompson, Cotton Owens, Joe Eubanks, Bill Snowden, and Buddy Shuman.[51]

At least some of these drivers came to NSCRA and Bruton Smith out of their annoyance at Bill France and NASCAR's low purses. Led by Marshall Teague, several drivers demanded that France pay out 40 percent of the gate in prize money, the standard set by big-car sanctioning body AAA. France refused and charged Teague, Jimmy and Speedy Thompson, Ed Samples, and Buddy Shuman with "conduct detrimental to the best interests of the National Association of Stock Car Racing," a catch-all charge he would later often use to discipline drivers.[52] Although several accounts of the first strictly stock NASCAR race assert that France suspended Shuman, Speedy Thompson, and Ed Samples for scattering "a few hundred thumb tacks on a track before a NASCAR Modified meet a couple of weeks earlier," their offense, and that of Teague and Jimmy Thompson, was signing an entry form for a NASCAR race, not showing up, and racing in another sanctioning body's race—in this case Bruton Smith's—at the same time.[53]

Whether it was part of France's motivation or not, the strictly stock race in Charlotte with its large purse helped bring the recalcitrant drivers in line. Before the race NASCAR commissioner Cannonball Baker held a hearing for the five charged drivers, who sought "re-admission to the good graces of the organization." Charges were dropped for Jimmy Thompson, but Baker put the other four on probation for a year and fined them— Buddy Shuman, $150; Teague and Ed Samples, $100; and Speedy Thompson, $50.[54] The following day, Speedy Thompson and Buddy Shuman came back to the track and got into an altercation with Baker and other NASCAR officials, which resulted in their being "barred from all NASCAR-sanctioned events until further notice."[55] Speedy Thompson in turn filed a police complaint against the sixty-seven-year old Baker, charging him with "assault and impersonating a police officer." Baker was later cleared on both charges.[56] Only Jimmy Thompson competed in the Charlotte race, while Teague skipped the Charlotte race but later paid his fine and raced in the second strictly stock race at Daytona. Speedy Thompson, Buddy Shuman, and Ed Samples all became regulars on the NSCRA scene and did not race in NASCAR again until 1951.[57]

France had no shortage of entries, however, for the first NASCAR strictly stock race and its $5,000 purse. Since all the drivers raced modifieds, some of them did have to find creative methods of obtaining a suitable strictly stock automobile. Lee Petty talked his friend Gilmer Goode into letting him drive his 1948 Buick Roadmaster, while Tim Flock convinced local hosiery mill owner Buddy Elliott to allow him to drive his brand-new Oldsmobile Rocket 88.[58] Glenn Dunnaway got a last-minute ride in Hubert Westmoreland's 1947 Ford, which had been used to haul liquor earlier in the week. Sara Christian's car, owned by her husband and noted bootlegger Frank Christian, was probably also a liquor car. One of the most interesting entries came from Halstead, Kansas, driver Jim Roper. Roper saw an advertisement for the race in Zack Moseley's "Smilin' Jack" comic strip—Moseley commonly advertised air shows and auto races in the strip—and talked car owner Millard Clothier into making the long trip east with two new 1949 Lincolns. Piedmont driver Bill Blair got the nod to drive Clothier's second car in the race. All in all, thirty-three drivers, driving nine different makes of automobile, took the green flag.[59]

There was also no shortage of fans who showed up for the Sunday afternoon race. Fans and their cars blocked Wilkinson Boulevard, the highway that ran near the track, with some estimates that 1,000–2,000 never made it into the race. An estimated 13,000 did make it in—according to a NASCAR press release the crowd was second only to the Indianapolis 500 crowd at that point in the season—easing Bill France's early fears that he might have to reach into his own pocket to come up with the race purse.[60]

The race itself, at least by stock car racing standards, proved to be relatively uneventful, more of a test of vehicle endurance and ability to drive through choking dust than anything else. Bob Flock started on the pole position in a Hudson and led the first five laps until Bill Blair took the lead in his borrowed Lincoln. Flock became the first victim of attrition as he knocked a hole in his oil pan on the rough track. Plenty of others joined him when their cars either overheated or lost wheels—usually the front right—from the unaccustomed punishment on stock equipment. Blair soon joined them as his car overheated as well. Dunnaway then took his Ford and moved into the lead, followed by Jim Roper. Roper's challenge faded, however, as he had to slow considerably to keep his car from overheating, and Dunnaway won over the Kansan by three laps.[61] Only one crash enlivened the festivities, when Lee Petty broke a radius rod in the third turn and rolled Gilmer Goode's new Buick four times. It took two wreckers to haul the car off, and the Petty family—who had driven to the race in the car like many other drivers—had to hitch a ride back home to Level Cross.[62]

Fans left covered in dust and thinking Dunnaway had won the race, but like Smokey Purser's 1938 Daytona win, the postrace inspection process led to the apparent winner's disqualification. Inspector Al Crisler, a well-known local race car driver and mechanic, discovered that Dunnaway's Hubert Westmoreland–owned car had illegal modifications to its suspension, "blocks welded to the crossmember . . . old buggy springs." The purpose of the blocks, as Westmoreland later admitted, was "so it would hold up on the road because we hauled liquor with it."[63] Although Westmoreland protested the decision, argued that Crisler had approved the car before the race, and even filed a $10,000 lawsuit in superior court, the decision stood, and Roper and Clothier collected their prize money and headed back to Kansas. Dunnaway did reap some benefit from the race as his competitors passed the hat for him, since he had no knowledge of the modifications made to the car. Reportedly he made more from the donations of competitors than he would have made from his 40 percent share of the first-place money.[64]

The big winner of the day, however, was Bill France, who had demonstrated that a strictly stock race could be run and be both popular and profitable. The victory by Roper, coupled with the "Smilin' Jack" story, helped generate a great deal of publicity for NASCAR. Some people actually accused France of intentionally disqualifying Dunnaway so that Roper could win.[65] Despite the controversy, France went on to promote seven more strictly stock races in 1949—including three in the North, at Langhorne; Hamburg, New York; and Pittsburgh, Pennsylvania—and held a points championship for those races, won by Red Byron. The strictly stock races outdrew the modifieds at most venues, and fans welcomed them enthusiastically everywhere but at Daytona Beach.[66] The July Daytona event, even with the strictly stock hype and the presence of three women in the race, drew only 5,000 fans, the smallest crowd for a beach race since World War II and the smallest crowd of any of the 1949 strictly stock races. The local newspapers called it "an uneventful race . . . the Strictly stocks did not hold the attention that the Modifieds do." Indeed, the strictly stocks raced a good 10 mph slower than the modifieds going down Highway A1A.[67] Despite the disappointment at Daytona, France saw enough in the strictly stocks in 1949 to dramatically expand the number of races in 1950 and make it NASCAR's premier series.

France also won a second major victory in 1949, although he had to wait until December for it, related to the first strictly stock race when the suit filed by Hubert Westmoreland—which included charges that "NASCAR had a monopoly on automobile racing in this area"—came to trial. NASCAR's lawyers Huger King and Louis Ossinsky were able to get the case moved from superior court to the federal court in Greensboro, presided over by Judge Johnson B. Hayes. Hayes, a Wilkes County native, was well known in North Carolina for his Baptist faith and hard line on moonshining but was frustrated by his lack of success in stemming the flow of white liquor in his home county. Journalist Vance Packard noted Hayes's frustration in his 1950 article on moonshining in Wilkes County in *The American* magazine: "I have tried every conceivable method to discourage this illegal commerce. I sent two carloads of liquor law violators off during one term, and the next term there were just as many cases before me."[68] Early in the trial it appeared as if Westmoreland might have a chance, until King began to repeatedly use the terms "moonshining" and "bootlegging." While Hayes could do little to stop illegal liquor in Wilkes County, this case gave him an opportunity to strike a blow against one moonshiner. He dismissed the case and ordered Westmoreland to pay all court costs.[69] France and NASCAR had won a bigger victory, however, in the right to make and enforce their rules. The lesson was not lost on drivers and car owners and gave France much greater leverage than he had before.

Like the Atom Bomb, Rum, and Home Hair Waves: NASCAR's Women Drivers

France's reintroduction of strictly stock racing was not the only major development in NASCAR in 1949. One of the more interesting directions that the series took was borrowed from France rivals Joe Littlejohn and Buddy Davenport: women race drivers. An added attraction at the first NASCAR strictly stock race was the entry of Sara Christian, by far the most successful female driver in the races held in South Carolina the previous year. She qualified thirteenth and finished a respectable fourteenth in the race, dropping out when her car overheated. For the second strictly stock race at Daytona, NASCAR heavily promoted the entry in the race of three women—Sara Christian, Ethel Flock Mobley, and Louise Smith. NASCAR publicist Houston Lawing issued a press release averring, "The woman auto racer is here to stay, like the atom bomb, rum and home hair waves." Lawing and France should not, however, be confused as budding

Louise Smith before a race. Bill France encouraged women drivers in the early years of NASCAR. (Courtesy of McCaig-Welborn Research Library at the International Motorsports Hall of Fame, Talladega, Alabama)

feminists, as the press release continued: "The ladies will get the chance to push the accelerator to the floor without needing a tearful smile for every copper who threatens to pinch 'em for speeding. Women have come a long way since suffrage. Indeed, anybody who has ever tried to pass a woman driver, with one hand clutching her cigarette and the other the wheel, knows what a futile and near fatal effort this can be. Bill France may learn that Hades hath no fury like a woman speedster."[70] It became all too apparent that France, as always, was most interested in selling tickets, and if using the gimmick of women drivers would help, so be it.

The women did have some limited success, however. Much to the chagrin of Bob and Fonty Flock and to the delight of fellow competitors—at least those who finished tenth or better—Ethel Flock Mobley finished ahead of her brothers at Daytona, in eleventh place. Sara Christian finished fifth in the Pittsburgh race and sixth in the demanding 200-mile race at Langhorne, where NASCAR officials escorted her to victory lane to stand alongside race winner Curtis Turner. Christian ended the season thirteenth in points, but her glory proved short lived as she rolled her car seven times in a late-season NSCRA race at Lakewood Speedway and broke her back.[71] The wreck scared her husband, her mother, and her young daughters as much as it did her. They all encouraged her to quit. She raced only one more time—"I just wanted to be sure I could"—in August 1950 at Hamburg, New York, and finished fourteenth.[72]

Louise Smith had the longest, and perhaps most colorful, career of any of the women who drove in NASCAR's early days. She competed in a total of eleven races in NASCAR's top division—called Grand National after 1950—three in the first season of strictly stock racing. Her best finish in one of these races was sixteenth place in the 1949 Langhorne race, and she finished generally near the bottom of the pack. One of the primary reasons she finished so poorly was that she wrecked so often. Smith herself observed, "I needed wheels on top. I'd a drove a lot better." As one writer succinctly put it, "Turning over was indeed a specialty of hers."[73] One of her most famous crashes came at Occoneechee Speedway in 1950. Smith had gotten Curtis Turner to teach her how to do the power slide. She practiced with Turner until she was confident she could pull off the maneuver. Her power slide, however, did not work as well when she tried to use it in qualifying. According to Smith, "Man, when I hit that second turn, that tire blew and that thang never did straighten up. It sailed off that bank down toward that river like a cannonball. Hit three trees. The radiator dove and I back-flopped against a tree. They had to git me out with a torch." Most of the other drivers thought she was dead, but she came back to the track in time for the race—with plenty of cuts and bruises and several broken ribs. Smith fit in well with the rough crowd at the races and could drink, cuss, and fight with the best of them. She became an attraction in her own right, and promoters all over the eastern seaboard—from the Bronx to Buffalo to Ontario, Canada—paid her appearance money to enter their races. "I made money, but I spent it all," she once recalled. "I wrecked so many cars." During her Grand National career and after it ended in 1952, Smith regularly raced in modified races until she "got saved" in 1956 and quit going to the racetrack altogether.[74]

One of the most commonly related stories about Louise Smith—one she often told herself—concerns a confrontation with her angry husband, Noah, when he found out she had not only raced in the 1949 Daytona race without his knowledge but had destroyed their brand new Ford. Like many stories from the early days of the sport, this one is probably not true.

Indeed, the *Greenville News* announced in its sports section one week before the race, "Greenville's own Miss [*sic*] Louise Smith . . . said she had
just about made her mind up to give the Daytona event a whirl."[75] The day
of the race an article appeared in the same paper with the subheadline
reading, "Mrs. Louise Smith of Greenville among Three Women in 160-
Mile Race."[76] To not know Louise was competing in the race, Noah Smith
had to have neither read the papers nor known anyone who had. In addition, accounts of the race have her driving a '47 Ford. While it may have
been a new car to Noah Smith, it was definitely not a brand-new car. To
be sure, Louise did roll the car onto its roof early in the race but with the
help of spectators turned it back onto its wheels and finished the race in
twentieth place. Smith also claimed victories in thirty-eight races during
her career, although there is only fragmentary evidence of her actually
winning races against men.[77]

Despite her exaggerated résumé as a driver, Smith helped draw the fans
and also made an impact on early racing as both a car owner and a promoter. She promoted a number of races in the Greenville area including
a "Negro Race" at Greer-Landrum Speedway in 1949. The race attracted
African American drivers from throughout the region and was won by
James Lacey of Atlanta.[78] There is very little historical information about
these kinds of races, and they were not generally publicized in the newspapers, but they seem to have been at least occasional—and of course
segregated—events at many Piedmont tracks. They appear, however, to
have died out by the mid-1950s, perhaps the result of heightened racial
tensions in the aftermath of *Brown v. Board of Education* and the need for
white patrons and promoters like Louise Smith. In 1952, Smith played
the role of car owner of a 1951 Ford—even as she drove in three races herself in a 1951 Oldsmobile 88—which was driven by E. C. Ramsey and J. O.
Staton in eleven races.[79]

In the early years of NASCAR, women drivers were a rare but not an
unusual feature at races. In addition to Ethel Mobley, Sara Christian, and
Louise Smith, other women, including Ann Slaasted, Ann Chester, and
Ann Bunselmyer, competed in races in NASCAR's top division.[80] Again,
this should not be confused as a progressive political statement on Bill
France's part. The women were there for one reason—as a gimmick to
attract fans. When the novelty wore off, the appearance money and other
forms of encouragement dried up, and NASCAR no longer welcomed the
women. Indeed, by the mid-1950s signs went up in the pit areas of most

tracks reading "No Women Allowed." The only woman one was likely to see in the infield of a racetrack—except for those occasions when promoters held powder-puff derbies—was the beauty queen who presented the victor's trophy.

Weekly Racing

While the era of women racers was relatively short lived, probably the most important and long-lived innovation of the 1949 season was the beginning of weekly stock car racing at Piedmont area tracks. Weekly midget racing had been a staple throughout much of the Northeast and Midwest at small stadium tracks since the 1930s. Promoters tried to import this pastime into the South with limited success at small venues like Bowman Gray Stadium in Winston-Salem and the Peach Bowl in Atlanta. Midget racing did not last, however, and in 1949 the promoters in Winston-Salem pulled out, leaving behind the paving bill from the previous year. Bill France and former stock car racer turned NASCAR flag man Alvin Hawkins signed a lease on the stadium in which they accepted responsibility for the paving bill and began promoting weekly Wednesday night races on May 18. The races were an immediate hit and attracted 4,500–6,000 fans for every race to see the "Mad" Flocks, Curtis Turner, Red Byron, or local favorites Billy and Bobby Myers battle it out around the tight quarter-mile paved track. In June they changed to Saturday night racing and drew even more fans.[81] Other tracks, including Royall Speedway in Richmond, Virginia, followed suit, and weekly racing soon became a staple throughout the Piedmont.[82]

A related innovation of France's in 1949, and one of his best and longest-lasting ideas, made weekly racing even more popular in the region: so-called Sportsman racing. For the August 16, 1949, race at Bowman Gray, Hawkins and France advertised two twenty-five-lap races for "amateur" drivers. Only 1932 and later model cars "that must not have a value of $600" were allowed in the races. A record crowd of more than 8,000 fans showed up to see the spectacle as thirty-seven drivers entered the race to test their mettle.[83] As Humpy Wheeler once observed, if you have local drivers, a sizable number of people they know are going to come out to see them race. "I always said that for every race car, at least thirty people were gonna come to the track to see it race. Fifteen to see it be successful 'cause they're relatives and fifteen to see the guy get beat."[84] Sportsman races became a godsend for the tracks of the Piedmont and reflected the attraction of stock car racing from its beginnings in the region. The relatives and enemies of drivers who came to the races helped keep many venues afloat and promoted the construction of dozens of new tracks.

Perhaps most important, the Sportsman Division provided a new farm system for the upper levels of professional stock car racing. While driving a liquor car had been the normal gateway to a career in stock car racing since the late 1930s and would remain an important entryway for years to come, Sportsman racing opened doors for new blood. Most of the subsequent stars of NASCAR—including Ned Jarrett, David Pearson, Bobby Allison, Cale Yarborough, and Bobby Isaac—came to the sport through racing in Sportsman events at a local track. Sportsman racing also provided an outlet for the average working-class Piedmonter to get into racing himself and perhaps become a local or even regional legend. Ned Jarrett recalled the excitement generated in his home community of Newton, North Carolina, in 1951 when construction began on the Hickory Speedway and the advent of weekly Sportsman racing neared: "You go down to the country store on a rainy day when the saw millers and farmers couldn't work and they'd be sitting around there and say boy . . . you just wait till they get the track built, I'll go up there and show them how to drive." And indeed many working-class men could scrape up enough money to put together a race car with a 1930s Ford V-8, some parts out of a junkyard, a little mechanical ability—which practically every farmer or mill worker possessed—a friend or two, a shade tree, and some sweat. Ned Jarrett purchased half interest in his first race car for $100, but a lot of young men made it to the track on much less.[85] Whether they became successful or not, Sportsman racing provided excitement in the lives of literally thousands of Piedmont working-class men who found a way to exercise the male cultural values that had been embedded in their psyche since childhood. In addition, it allowed hundreds of thousands of not-quite-so-adventurous Piedmonters the vicarious thrill of watching their friends and neighbors battle it out on the local dirt track. For many, attendance at the weekly race became as important as, or often more important than, church attendance on Sunday. Families and friends even had their seats staked out, like the family pew in church, where they sat for generations—and some still do.

The Liquor Drivers Return to Lakewood
Despite NASCAR's and Bill France's many 1949 successes, Sam Nunis gained the distinction of holding the two biggest and richest stock car races of the year: strictly stock races held in October and November at

This frightening crash at Lakewood Speedway in 1949 shortened Sara Christian's career as a stock car driver. Promoters often used crashes in previous events to hype their races. (Courtesy of McCaig-Welborn Research Library at the International Motorsports Hall of Fame, Talladega, Alabama)

Lakewood Speedway. Making the events even bigger, Nunis success-fully lobbied the Southeastern Fair Board to lift the bootlegger ban, and for the first time since 1945 Lakewood fans could watch Fonty and Bob Flock, Gober Sosebee, and other liquor-hauling racers on the track that had made them famous. Both races were 150-mile affairs and offered purses larger than the ones posted at NASCAR's richest southern races, the Charlotte and Occoneechee races. The purse for the first Lakewood race was set at $5,100, an obviously intentional move to top the $5,000 purse offered at NASCAR's first strictly stock race in Charlotte.[86] Accord-ing to NASCAR historian Greg Fielden, Bill France did offer to help Nunis stage the races, encouraged NASCAR drivers to enter, and even listed the results of the Lakewood races in the 1950 NASCAR Yearbook, though they were not sanctioned by NASCAR.[87] France received little for his efforts, however, as none of the local or national press reports about the races mentioned either France or NASCAR, and Nunis-promoted stock car races in the South continued to be sanctioned by NSCRA in 1950.

The October race attracted a huge field of 120 entries, with 40 qualifying for the race, including Sara Christian and Ethel Mobley.[88] Tim Flock won the race and $2,100 in prize money, "the largest purse ever paid a stock car winner in the South." The race drew a huge crowd, even by Atlanta standards. According to Nunis, 33,452 fans came out to see the race, "the largest crowd ever to witness a racing event in the South." *National Speed Sport News* reported that the crowd was so large that, "fifteen minutes before the start of the race, the lineup of speed fans at the ticket office stretched out for seven blocks, while the roads leading to the speedway were so thoroughly jammed that Atlanta's police force simply gave up on trying to restore order." Gober Sosebee and other drivers got caught up in the same traffic and barely made the start of the race.[89] The only thing that marred the day was when a wheel came off Bob Flock's car, flew into the stands, and struck an eleven-year-old boy. The boy's injuries were apparently not serious.[90]

The Nunis promotion proved so successful that he decided to hold another race on November 13, this time offering a $6,000 purse, tying it with Langhorne as the largest stock car racing purse ever. Nunis hyped the race by announcing the presence of all four racing Flocks, Sara Christian— who had finished a respectable eleventh in the first race—and Louise Smith, who was coming off a "stirring victory over a field of 16 men at Pensacola," Florida, the previous week.[91] The race ended up being postponed one week because of rain and despite chilly weather attracted a crowd of 22,000 to see June Cleveland of Griffin, Georgia, win the race. The big news, however, was the number of major crashes in the race. The article on the race in the *Atlanta Constitution* sports section was headed by two large pictures of the upside-down cars of Sara Christian and Olin Allen.[92] Allen's injuries were not serious, but Christian's wreck effectively ended her career.[93]

To be sure, the huge success of Nunis's Lakewood promotions in 1949 revealed that Bill France's vision of heading a national stock car sanctioning body and dominating the racing world in the manner of Ralph Hankinson in the prewar years was, at that time, only a paper dream. While France and his bootlegger allies had done much to solidify and expand NASCAR's position in the Piedmont with the Strictly Stock Series and weekly Sportsman racing at attractive venues like Bowman Gray Stadium, they still faced serious competition from Joe Littlejohn and Buddy Davenport, who had locked up the most lucrative tracks in South Carolina, and from powerful and well-funded northeastern promoters who saw no reason to sign on with France. Most important, NSCRA—headed by France's chief rivals in the business, Sam Nunis and the young, ultra-ambitious former Oakboro, North Carolina, cotton farmer O. Bruton Smith—challenged them openly in their own backyard. Nunis had battled Atlanta city authorities successfully over the bootlegger ban and returned Lakewood Speedway to its glory days and put Atlanta racing back in the center of the stock car racing world. Smith stood poised to battle Bill France head to head for the lucrative Charlotte-area market. NASCAR had considerable assets to deploy in this battle, but the question of which group would come out on top was very much open in 1949.

Darlington, Bamooda Shorts, Jocko Flocko, and the Fabulous Hudson Hornet

NASCAR Grand National, 1950–1954

Fonty Flock wheeled his Oldsmobile into the lead in the 185th lap and led the rest of the way to win the third annual Southern 500 at Darlington Raceway. . . . After the checkered flag, Flock stopped his Frank Christian–owned mount on the front chute, climbed on the hood and led the huge throng of 32,400 in the singing of "Dixie," the South's national anthem. Flock drove the 400 laps around the 1.25-mile paved track wearing Bermuda shorts.

—*Greg Fielden,* Forty Years of Stock Car Racing, *vol. 1*

One image indelibly imprinted in the minds of many traditional NASCAR fans is that of Fonty Flock—the handsome, mustachioed (the "Boston Blackie kind") former bootlegger turned biggest star in NASCAR Grand National racing—standing on the hood of his victorious Olds 88 wearing Bermuda shorts, or "Bamooda" as he pronounced it, and leading the massive crowd of over 32,000 fans in singing "Dixie." The scene reflects not only the sport's roots in the Piedmont South and the culture of the bootlegger but also its growing popularity in and out of the region.

NASCAR experienced one of its greatest periods of growth and expansion from 1950 to 1954. Its premier Strictly Stock Series—now known by the classier title of Grand National—grew from eight races in its inaugural season of 1949 to nineteen in 1950 to an average of thirty-seven per season from 1951 to 1954. The series also expanded its reach and approached its goal of becoming a truly national series, running races in twenty-two different states—including tracks at such far-flung places as California,

Fonty Flock, wearing his signature "Bamooda" shorts and argyle socks, prepares for the Daytona Beach race in 1955. (Courtesy of McCaig-Welborn Research Library at the International Motorsports Hall of Fame, Talladega, Alabama)

Arizona, South Dakota, Nebraska—and the Canadian province of Ontario. While 50 percent of Grand National races during the period were run in the Piedmont South, 39 percent were run outside the South altogether, with races in Pennsylvania, Ohio, and New York accounting for 22 percent of the total. The series also began to attract drivers from outside the Piedmont South and Florida, with Bill Rexford of New York winning the 1950 Grand National championship, Californian Dick Rathmann finishing consistently in the top five in points, and Oregonian Herschel McGriff carding a sixth-place finish in 1954 while winning four races.[1]

France also continued to build on NASCAR's strong foundation in the Piedmont South. He added two new bootlegger tracks, Asheville-Weaverville and Hickory speedways, to the NASCAR stable, which—along with North Wilkesboro, Martinsville, Charlotte, and Hillsborough—formed the core of his business. Indeed, from 1949 to 1958, these tracks hosted eighty-four Grand National races, constituting almost a quarter of all races in NASCAR's top division.[2] NASCAR also came close to matching its rivals in AAA open-wheel racing when it added a premier venue, Darlington Raceway, and a marquee event, the Labor Day Southern 500, that came closer than any other auto race in the United States to rivaling the Indianapolis 500 in prize money, popularity, and media coverage. Not only was Darlington popular, but it gave France unprecedented leverage to keep drivers from racing in rival series. Not long after the first Southern 500, NASCAR's most successful rival sanctioning body—NSCRA—folded. With France's chief rivals gone from the Piedmont racing scene, he could now add to the NASCAR fold the lucrative tracks where Sam Nunis, Weyman Milam, and Bruton Smith promoted races. NASCAR also dramatically increased it offerings of weekly racing, and the number of small, red-clay Piedmont racetracks skyrocketed. By the mid-1950s most counties in the region had at least one racetrack featuring some form of stock car racing and most of it sanctioned by NASCAR.

Another crucial development that had a dramatic impact on NASCAR's present and future during the period was the successful wooing of Detroit automakers—especially Hudson—to directly sponsor drivers. Although it was another Daytona Beach mechanic, Marshall Teague, who pioneered the Detroit connection with the "Fabulous Hudson Hornet," Bill France reaped most of the benefits. By 1954, France was as comfortable around Detroit executives as he was around Piedmont bootleggers. To be sure, by the mid-1950s, France had probably surpassed his old idol Ralph Hankinson in power and influence in auto racing and had more control over his drivers than Hankinson ever did, and NASCAR as a sanctioning body was coming to rival the mighty AAA. For the first time, the mainstream auto racing world and the American public outside the Piedmont South started to take notice of the upstart Daytona mechanic, his sanctioning body with the catchy but redundant name, and its wild crew of talented drivers and mechanics.

A Traveling Circus

In 1950, running three divisions—Grand National, Modified, and Sportsman—NASCAR attracted more than a million spectators to its 396 events and paid out $471,744 in prize money. The nineteen Grand National races averaged $6,152 in purse money per race. In addition, France could now argue that NASCAR was no longer just a southern sanctioning body because the majority of its races, in all divisions, were held in the East or

Midwest and all three of its division champions—Bill Rexford from New York, Grand National; Mike Klapak, Ohio, Sportsman; and Charles Dyer, New Jersey, Modified—were from outside the region.[3]

France and NASCAR greatly benefited from the addition of new venues outside the Piedmont, particularly in the East and Midwest. Ed Otto's decision to bring all ten of the tracks he promoted—in New Jersey, New York, Connecticut, and Pennsylvania—under the NASCAR umbrella proved to be the most important addition for the series.[4] Johnnie Marcum brought Ohio promoters Charlie Findlay, Earl Clay, and H. D. Zingleman into the NASCAR fold. A total of eighty-five NASCAR races in all divisions were held in Ohio in 1950, more than in any other state and more than all NASCAR races put together in 1949. France also signed up John Babcock and his legendary Langhorne Speedway for the year.[5]

Even with NASCAR's expansion and search for greater credibility, the sport still maintained—and even expanded—its connections to the illegal liquor industry. France welcomed his old pal Joe Littlejohn, and Spartanburg's Hub City Speedway, back into the NASCAR fold when the SCRA folded. The end of SCRA also brought lucrative South Carolina tracks, especially Greenville and Columbia, back to NASCAR. Soon after, France and Littlejohn partnered to promote racing at the new Asheville-Weaverville Speedway.[6] Indeed, Asheville-Weaverville added to the number of NASCAR's stable of bootlegger tracks. The track, located just north of Asheville, was built by one of Littlejohn's bootlegging friends, Gene Sluder, a well-known western North Carolina red liquor kingpin. He had already parlayed the proceeds from his business into a legal earth-moving business, making the addition of speedway construction and management a natural fit. Sluder cut out a half-mile, banked, red-clay track that soon became the fastest such track in the country, a favorite for drivers and fans. Sluder also regularly held weekly modified races at the tracks where local liquor haulers and would-be dirt-track heroes could display their mechanical talents and daring to working-class fans. The layout of the track enabled early arriving spectators to park their cars along a bank on the backstretch and watch the race from their cars, and Sluder advertised the track as the nation's first "drive-in racetrack."[7]

Another important bootlegger track followed on the heels of Asheville-Weaverville: the Hickory Speedway, built by Alexander County red liquor barons Ralph and Grafton Burgess in partnership with North Wilkesboro's Charlie Combs. Well known throughout the Piedmont, the flamboyant Burgess brothers—nicknamed "Puff" and "Tuff"—held court at their Highway 16 restaurant and club, the Silver Moon, a favorite hangout for liquor haulers and for the stock car racers who flocked to the Hickory track. At the Silver Moon, patrons could eat one of the best steak dinners in the area and—if they knew the right people—could head upstairs to partake of the Burgess brothers' finest imported red liquor or try their luck at a slot machine or the poker tables. The Burgess brothers and Combs made a successful gamble in building the .4-mile, red-clay Hickory Speedway, and the track soon became a breeding ground for stock car racing talent; a number of NASCAR's greatest stars—including Ned Jarrett, Bobby Isaac, Harry Gant, and Dale Jarrett—got their start there.[8]

Aggressive new methods of promotion also brought additional fans to NASCAR. In order to give the series more class—or at least the appearance thereof—France changed the name of NASCAR's premier division from Strictly Stock to Grand National.[9] Promoters also began bringing in celebrities to raise the profile of NASCAR races. As part of this campaign, France further cultivated his relationship with cartoonist Zack Mosley—of "Smilin' Jack" fame—that had begun in 1949 with the first strictly stock race. The "Tall Timber Tess" trophy, named after a character in "Smilin' Jack," was presented to race winner Curtis Turner at the Langhorne Grand National race by 6'2" Kate Murtah, star of the Broadway "Smilin' Jack"–inspired play *Texas Little Darling*. France also brought in announcer Don Stremmel—the model for "Smilin' Jack" race announcer "Flannel Mouth Don"—to emcee the festivities at several races, including the one at Langhorne.[10] Other celebrities at NASCAR races included cowboy star Lash Larue, who performed with his trademark bullwhip at a race at the Charlotte Speedway, and the famous fan dancer Sally Rand, who appeared at a NASCAR race in Ohio.[11] Other promotions included a footrace for drivers—who rolled car wheels around the .625-mile track at North Wilkesboro—won by Jim Paschal, a ten-lap collegiate stock car race for students at the University of North Carolina–Chapel Hill, North Carolina State, Duke, Wake Forest, and Elon colleges at Occoneechee Speedway, and a ten-lap race for "Wilkes Countians with 'hot' cars" at North Wilkesboro won by the brother of promoter Enoch Staley, Gwyn, a well-known local tripper. The North Wilkesboro event actually marked the racing debut of eighteen-year-old Glen "Junior" Johnson, who drove his brother L. P.'s liquor car to a second-place finish. In qualifying for the July 4, 1954, race at Asheville-Weaverville Speedway, promoter Joe Littlejohn had an extra seat belt installed in Herb Thomas's Hudson and rode with him on his qualifying run. Thomas won the pole.[12]

Our Answer to Indy: Darlington and the Southern 500

As important as these developments were to the future of NASCAR, the construction of Darlington International Raceway and the running of the first Southern 500 topped them all. The construction of the facility gave NASCAR a 1.25-mile (at the time of its construction) paved, high-banked racetrack where cars could achieve speeds second only to those at Indianapolis Speedway. In only its first year, Darlington also provided the Grand National Series with a marquee, premier, nationally recognized event. Indeed, for many years—especially before the construction of the Daytona International Speedway and the inauguration of the Daytona 500—the annual running of the Southern 500 on each Labor Day was the one NASCAR event that many Americans had actually heard of outside the Piedmont region.

The construction of Darlington International Raceway in 1950 was even more unlikely than the construction of the North Wilkesboro Speedway in 1947, the result of the vision and passion of the owner of a Darlington, South Carolina, aggregate business, Harold Brasington.[13] Darlington is a small town in northeastern South Carolina known primarily as a center for tobacco and peanut farmers. In 1950, the town itself had fewer than 10,000 people—in a county with a little more than 50,000 people—and one hotel with ten to twelve rooms. Almost half of its population consisted of African Americans, who were generally not welcome at stock car races. Brasington had raced stock cars in the prewar years, competing at Daytona in 1938, '40, and '41 and in numerous races around the Piedmont region in both Carolinas.[14]

In 1949, Brasington went to the Indianapolis 500 and returned to Darlington determined to build a world-class racing facility in the heart of the Pee Dee region. As friend Harold King remembered, "Everybody was really thinking Brasington had gone off the very deep end." Brasington poetically explained his motivation for building the track in the program of the first Darlington race: "One of the inalienable rights of every American citizen is the privilege of indulging in that delightful and inexpensive pastime—daydreaming."[15] As ridiculous as this "daydream" seemed, however, there was something in Harold Brasington's passionate conviction that he could pull it off and put Darlington on the map that convinced people to invest in the project, often against their better judgment. Brasington went "to service club after service club. He went into where anybody would listen trying to sell stock" in the enterprise and successfully sold shares to local leaders, including the owner of the local tobacco warehouse, and to Bob Colvin—who would later become president of the speedway—a local peanut broker for the Planters Company.[16] Brasington's most important investor, however, was local timber baron Sherman Ramsey, who traded 70 acres of farmland southwest of the town in exchange for stock in the enterprise. Ramsey gave Brasington the land, however, on one condition: that he not disturb a fish pond located on the property. Brasington began construction of the track in December 1949, doing most of the grading work himself with some advice from an engineer. In order to avoid Ramsey's fish pond, Brasington ended up making the track a unique pear-shaped configuration by narrowing the first and second turns and raising the banking.[17]

Surprisingly—given Brasington's experience in stock car racing and the track's proximity to the heartland of the sport—the first race scheduled for the speedway was not a stock car race but a big-car race, sanctioned not by NASCAR but by the Consolidated and Central States Racing Association (CCSRA), a group based in Columbus, Ohio. The first major notice of the track's construction came in February 1950 with an article in *National Speed Sport News* announcing the inaugural Labor Day race: "This tranquil historic southern metropolis [a misnomer if there ever was one] will become the world's focal point next Labor Day, September 3, and yearly on the same day thereafter with the running of the annual 500-mile Grand Prix automobile race at the new major super course now under construction just west of the pleasant and hospitable city." The article claimed that the big cars would reach 150 mph on the paved track's high banks and that record purses would attract not only "every ranking American speed king of note, but the best of European drivers as well with English, French, German and Italian built racing vehicles."[18] In March, Brasington announced that he had lined up a past Indianapolis 500 winner—probably Bill Holland, who was in the midst of a feud with AAA officials—who became "official entry number one."[19]

Despite the rhetoric, however, it soon became apparent to Brasington and his investors that they would not be able to attract enough quality entries for a premier big-car race. In a press release dated June 20, Darlington officials announced that their Labor Day race would be instead a strictly stock race; CCSRA would still sanction the event. Brasington also announced that he had received so many ticket requests "that I fully expect the grandstand and boxes [which seated approximately 9,000 fans] to be sold out by the middle of July."[20] Despite the change to strictly stock, however, Brasington still had few entries as July came and the race neared. One of the reasons that the race had so few entries, according to some of those involved, was that Bill France—upset that the race was sanctioned by CCSRA and not NASCAR—threatened to take away championship points from any NASCAR driver who entered and he planned to hold a Grand National race in Charlotte the same day.[21]

By the middle of July, however, Brasington and France had worked out a deal whereby CCSRA and NASCAR jointly sanctioned the race. Evidently, France had some qualms about the feasibility of running a 500-mile race for stock automobiles, particularly concerns about the durability of the cars. It would not look good to the auto manufacturers and dealers that France was trying to woo if the track were littered with broken-down cars. To be sure, France was not alone in doubting the feasibility of such a venture. Indianapolis Speedway president Wilbur Shaw scoffed at the idea, asserting, "Stock cars will never last 500 miles."[22] On seeing the track in person, however, France decided that NASCAR could not pass up this opportunity, and so he signed on. Several accounts also assert that France went to Darlington for three weeks to oversee the final construction of the speedway and assist in race preparations.[23]

NASCAR trumpeted its sanctioning of the first Darlington race in a full-page ad in the August 9 edition of *National Speed Sport News*:

> Due To The Importance And Size Of This Event C.S.R.A. And NASCAR Organizations Have Joined Hands In Sanctioning And Directing This Event—Nation's Greatest and Richest Stock Car Auto Race.

The announced prize money must have astounded potential competitors: a total purse of $25,500—in an era when a $6,000 purse for a stock car race was huge—with $7,000 going to the winner, plus lap-leader money. Equally astounding was the number of cars that the promoters allowed in the race: an unbelievable seventy-five. In order to permit this number of expected entrants from all over the country—the race did, in fact, attract drivers from as far away as California and Oregon—to attempt to make the field, promoters scheduled the beginning of qualifying trials on August 19, more than two weeks before the event. In addition, to emulate the Indianapolis 500 format, qualifying runs were 10 miles, or eight laps on the 1.25-mile course, instead of the usual one lap. An accompanying article also gave the Labor Day race a name—one that it would keep for fifty-two years—the Southern 500.[24]

Although interest was high throughout qualifying and the race attracted almost every top stock car racer in the country, Brasington and France were still nervous about the huge investment they had made in both infrastructure—according to Brasington and press reports, $250,000—and in the huge purse. They need not have worried, as 18,000–25,000 fans (press reports often estimated 35,000, but the lower figures are probably more accurate) clogged the two-lane roads leading into Darlington and swarmed over the new facility, immediately overtaxing the seating, concession, and restroom capacity. The event even overwhelmed the town itself, with thousands camping out the night before the race in the town square and all the local restaurants running out of food. In order to get people off the roads and into the track, Brasington ordered sections of the fence torn down. He later remembered, "I knew we'd draw a crowd, but I didn't know it would be that big." Harold King, who helped sell tickets to the race, recalled, "We were selling tickets for the same seats. They were piling up cash in peach baskets and buckets in the office." Clarice Sellers remembered the pandemonium in the track office: "People were running around asking this question and that, creditors were asking for their money. It was the biggest mess you've ever seen. As fast as the money came in, some creditor would take off with his and everyone was wondering whether we'd have enough left for the purse."[25] Cars backed up so far from the track that, according to *Speed Age* magazine editor Don O'Reilly, it took "three hours to travel the 12 to 14 miles to the track" from his hotel in nearby Hartsville.[26]

The beginning of the race provided an awesome spectacle for the fans. Twenty-five rows of cars lined up three abreast, another imitation of Indianapolis, and twelve different makes of automobiles—29 of the entries were Oldsmobiles—headed for the green flag. The drivers then floored it, each wanting to win such a prestigious and lucrative race. Gober Sosebee led the first four laps, then Curtis Turner forged ahead. Cotton Owens, driving a modest Plymouth, moved up from a thirty-eighth starting spot to take the lead on the twenty-seventh lap. It soon became apparent, however, that it was not the stock automobile that could not withstand a 500-mile race on asphalt but the stock tire. As reporter Don O'Reilly put it, "On the race track those tires popped just like popcorn."[27] One after the other, drivers headed for the pits to change tires only to come back in a few laps later for more. Legend has it that car owners bought tires off the cars of fans parked in the infield so they could try to finish the race. Red Byron blew twenty-five or more tires on his Raymond Parks–Red Vogt Cadillac,

The pace car leads seventy-five cars, three abreast, down the front stretch for the first Southern 500 at Darlington Raceway. (Courtesy of McCaig-Welborn Research Library at the International Motorsports Hall of Fame, Talladega, Alabama)

while Pap White wore out twenty-six tires on Sam Rice's Cadillac. Curtis Turner brought out the first yellow flag on the 275th lap when he blew a tire in the first turn and rolled his Oldsmobile.[28]

Amid all the blown tires and the wrecking, few of the fans noticed the relatively nondescript black Plymouth with the number "98 Jr." on the side: the slowest qualifying car in the race. The Plymouth steadily, but unspectacularly, moved around the track and took the lead on the fiftieth lap. Indeed, in the midst of all the confusion of the race and the myriad of pit stops, few people had any idea of who actually led the race at any given time. Even fewer fans at Darlington that day had ever heard of the Californian driving the car, Johnny Mantz. Mantz, however, was no stranger to racing and was well known in both big-car—driving for legendary owner J. C. Agajanian—and midget racing circles.[29] Bill France recruited Mantz to NASCAR when he met the Californian while both ran in the inaugural five-day Carrera Panamericana, better known as the Mexican Road Race. Mantz had a tremendous advantage over the vast majority of the field in that he had a great deal of experience driving on paved speedways, including Indianapolis. Although it had much less horsepower than the Oldsmobiles, Cadillacs, and Lincolns driven by his competitors, the lightweight Plymouth was much easier on tires than the heavier cars most drivers chose. While legend has it that Bill France purchased the car to run errands in preparation for the race and had offered it to Mantz as an afterthought, according to Bill Blair and Hubert Westmoreland—who prepped the car for the race—the Plymouth was finely tuned and well prepared to last the 500 miles. Westmoreland even admitted years later that the Plymouth had an illegal carburetor and intake manifold. France, Curtis Turner, and NASCAR starter Alvin Hawkins had purchased the car not for errands but to win the race.[30]

Mantz won the first Southern 500 by more than nine laps, with Fireball Roberts finishing second and Red Byron third, although officials scored Byron in second. The race took six hours and thirty-eight minutes to run, an exhausting experience for drivers, fans, and officials in the blazing heat and humidity of early September in the Pee Dee region. Yet, despite Mantz's dominating performance, the inconveniences of an overtaxed speedway staff and town, the long race, and the sweltering heat, the first Southern 500 became an instant classic and became both the race to win for every stock car driver and the race to attend for every stock car fan.[31]

For the top drivers—and increasingly for auto manufacturers—in the 1950s, no win was more coveted than the Southern 500. Drivers, mechanics, and manufacturers went to great lengths to win both the rich purse and the notoriety that came with victory in the race. As mechanic Smokey Yunick observed, "The first ten years of Darlington were special. To us stock car racers, it was our answer to Indy. The Darlington [Southern] 500 was hands down the most prestigious stock car race in the world. . . . I loved to race there."[32]

Darlington's success also enhanced Bill France's power over his drivers, as he was able to withhold entry in the lucrative Southern 500 as a way of keeping them in the NASCAR fold and out of races sanctioned by his rivals. After only one race at the speedway, NASCAR published a notice in an article in May 1951 in *National Speed Sport News* warning drivers that the sanctioning body might reject drivers' entries if they drove in "outlaw" events: "Although the Darlington '500' with its $25,000 purse is a long way off, many drivers and car owners are already making plans for the BIG one. NASCAR is being lenient with unsanctioned races without permission, but there are going to be some disappointed guys when their entries are turned down for the Labor Day Classic."[33]

For stock car fans, attending the Southern 500 became equally important. After the first year's difficulties with fans finding accommodations, track officials began to allow them to camp in the infield. Soon the infield scene at the Southern 500 became as legendary as the race itself for its drinking and carousing, barbecues, makeshift viewing platforms, and ever present Confederate battle flags. For the stock car racing community, especially in the Piedmont South, Labor Day and the Southern 500 became inextricably entwined.

The End of NSCRA

The success of Darlington also—at least indirectly—led to the demise of NASCAR's chief stock car sanctioning rival, the National Stock Car Racing Association. NSCRA had been a thorn in NASCAR's flesh since its creation in 1947, even taking France's preferred name for his sanctioning body—Red Vogt suggested NASCAR after he pointed out that Nunis and Weyman Milam had already appropriated NSCRA for their organization. NSCRA founder and Ralph Hankinson protégé Sam Nunis, Bill France's chief rival, had locked up the rights to promote auto racing at Lakewood Speedway and had brought a number of other promoters into the sanctioning body's fold, including Weyman Milam, who headed up promotions at Atlanta's lucrative Peach Bowl and Macon's Central City Speedway; Harold Hill of Columbus, Georgia; and Chattanooga promoters Alf Knight and Gene Wilson, who took NSCRA-sanctioned events into Tennessee and Alabama.[34]

Outside of Nunis and Lakewood Speedway, NSCRA's most important asset was young and ambitious promoter O. Bruton Smith, who challenged France in the heart of NASCAR country and promoted races in the Charlotte-Concord area. Probably no one in NASCAR history has come as close to matching the drive and ambition of Bill France as Bruton Smith— a self-made billionaire who to this day is the France family's chief rival. Smith regularly siphoned off both talent—particularly among drivers who chafed at France's increasingly dictatorial ways—and fans from NASCAR, drawing them to his promotions. In 1950, however, Uncle Sam did what Bill France was unable to do and indirectly killed NSCRA. In that year, with the Korean War under way, the U.S. Army drafted Smith, putting his career as a stock car racing promoter on a two-year hiatus. NSCRA was dead.[35]

Sam Nunis acceded to the reality of NASCAR's dominance in stock car racing and folded NSCRA in the summer of 1951. The annual Armistice Day race at Lakewood in 1951 became a sanctioned NASCAR Grand National race. Weyman Milam hosted a September Grand National race at his Macon track. The star drivers of NSCRA—Jack Smith, Billy Carden,

Gober Sosebee, Frank Mundy, Cotton Owens, and Ed Samples—had nowhere to go but back into the NASCAR fold, whether they liked it or not. "The NSCRA had a strong link in Sam Nunis, but just too many weak factions over the years wore thin," Jack Smith recalled. "Nunis was packing the house at Lakewood. Maybe we just needed more Lakewoods. But you have to remember France had some good tracks plus the backing of Raymond Parks and had the Flock brothers he could billboard. Tough combinations to beat."[36] When Bruton Smith returned from the army, he too had little choice but to join NASCAR if he wanted to continue promoting stock car races.[37]

Weekly Mayhem

The spectacular growth of weekly Sportsman and modified racing in the early 1950s also boosted NASCAR, dramatically increasing the number of races and the number of drivers. NASCAR sanctioned weekly Sportsman races during the period at Piedmont-area tracks in North Carolina, Virginia, South Carolina, and Georgia as well as in Ohio, New York, Pennsylvania, and New Jersey. Other tracks in those same states and tracks in Tennessee, Nebraska, Colorado, and Ontario ran less regular events.[38] The expansion proved to be a boon for both top drivers and those just starting out. The stars could effectively make a circuit of Sportsman races with events held in a given week in a particular region on Tuesday, Wednesday, Thursday, Friday, and Saturday nights. If they then raced on Sundays at a Grand National or major modified race, they could race six days a week. Although purse money remained relatively low at most of these races, an enterprising driver like Jimmy Lewallen, who won both North Carolina and Virginia Sportsman championships; Buck Baker; Pennsylvania champion Mike Klapak; Jack Smith; or New Jersey champion Roscoe "Pappy" Hough could make a solid, if not lavish, income strictly from their racing. For up-and-coming drivers, Sportsman racing enabled them to test themselves against the best.[39] As Carl Green commented in an editorial in *National Speed Sport News*, "While the principal purpose of Stock Car Racing is to entertain the public, it can well be classed as a driver's training school, which young and aspiring drivers may enter with minimum expense and effort."[40]

Each track in the Piedmont generally featured at least a couple of the top drivers from the Grand National ranks, a bonus to fans who could see the top stock car racing stars compete locally and at a cheaper price. Curtis Turner regularly thrilled fans at Bowman Gray Stadium and at Victory Stadium in Roanoke, Virginia, which he co-promoted with Bill France. Bob and Fonty Flock often raced at the Peach Bowl in Atlanta, while stock car fans in Charlotte could plan on seeing Lee Petty, Buck Baker, and Buddy Shuman.[41]

These races also produced intense rivalries as local drivers sought to knock off the Grand National stars and build a reputation for themselves. The competition at Bowman Gray Stadium between Curtis Turner and the Myers brothers, Bobby and Billy, proved particularly intense and helped fill the seats on many Saturday nights. The brothers, working-class mechanics, regularly clashed with the flashy playboy Turner, who always seemed to have plenty of money and generally did not care if he tore up the car he was driving—usually owned by someone else—or the cars of his competitors. The class dimension plus Turner's devil-may-care attitude only fueled the flames, and races involving the three often turned into demolition derbies. One story often told, and embellished, about the rivalry—there are varying accounts of when and where the incident took place and even some uncertainty over whether it really happened—concerns a race in which Turner forced Bobby Myers off the track and into the infield, crumpling his car and taking him out of the race. After the race, Myers headed for Turner—in the time-honored manner of stock car driver fights—with a tire iron in hand. Turner, sitting either in the back of a truck or on top of his passenger car, saw Myers headed for him, produced a .38 pistol, and asked his potential assailant, "Bobby, what are you planning on doing with that?" To which Myers responded, "Curtis, I was just looking for a place to put it down."[42] Of course promoters like Alvin Hawkins of Bowman Gray did everything they could to fan the flames of these rivalries—within certain bounds, that is—but this type of intense action became a standard part of the fare and a big part of the attraction at many weekly tracks, particularly in the Piedmont. As reporter Robert Edelstein observed, promoters generally considered "the antics of drivers the way a warden might look at a fight between convicts: Let all the conflict create a good show without thinking of breaking it up—for awhile."[43]

Weekly racing also attracted throngs of fans to see not only the Grand National and Sportsman drivers but local amateurs as well. In the short ten- to fifteen-lap races staged before the Grand National or Sportsman feature, fans were guaranteed to see plenty of action on the track. An account of a 1953 "amateur" race at the Greensboro Fairgrounds provides a vivid description of the type of on-track action one was likely to see at these tracks: "The amateur stock car drivers, always willing to oblige

with crashes, spills and thrills, held up their reputation at the Greensboro Fairgrounds third of a mile track yesterday as Robert Berrier of Wall-
burg zoomed to victory in a crash-filled 35-lap feature in which 31 cars
started and only 12 finished. The amateurs not only knocked down the
fence at several places, but they spilled the loud speakers in front of the
grandstand, skimmed the stage numerous times, rolled over their cars
and wrecked at a pace of almost one every two laps."[44] For the money, it
was hard to top the entertainment value these races provided for working-
class Piedmont fans.

Detroit Arrives in a Fabulous Hudson Hornet

Still another innovative method that France and NASCAR promoters used
to create interest in their races was a new emphasis on the make of the
automobiles in the field, particularly in Grand National events. The use
of the strictly stock format, ostensibly at least, enabled fans to gauge the
speed, durability, and overall quality of the automobiles they themselves
drove, or at least wished to drive. NASCAR picked up on the growing identification that fans made with various makes, and the potential for interesting the auto dealers and manufacturers in the sport, and began to
highlight the performance of successful makes in Grand National racing.
Beginning in early 1950, write-ups and press releases by NASCAR public
relations head Houston Lawing and secretary Bill Tuthill emphasized the
success of the Detroit models. After the February 1950 Daytona race, the
NASCAR press release read, "Whereas Oldsmobiles dominated the stock
competition last year, Lincolns earned the lion's share of the honors Sunday. Five of the 15 money winners in this 1950 classic chauffeured new Lincolns. Three Oldsmobiles, three Buicks, two Plymouths and one Ford also
finished in the money."[45] Red Byron made the headlines of *National Speed
Sport News* when he switched from Oldsmobile to Lincoln before the May
Martinsville race.[46] In the lead-up to the first race at Darlington International Raceway, "pre-race speculation ran rife" as to what make of automobile would win the grueling race. "But one and all agreed that both car
and driver will have earned his place in the racing sun at the completion
of the 500-mile grind."[47]

At the end of the 1950 season, NASCAR, for the first time, published
the number of finishes, one through five, for the top seven makes, with
Oldsmobile topping the list with ten wins and Plymouth finishing second
with four.[48] An October 1951 ad for upcoming NASCAR races in *National
Speed Sport News* asked race fans, "Have you ever wondered just how fast

your own car would really go?" The ad then offered fans the opportunity to see for themselves: "Now you can see! Here are the nation's top racing drivers speeding, roaring, racing standard make STOCK CARS of almost every manufacture . . . racing them at top speed, throttle wide open in a thrilling, daring, dangerous spectacle of endurance for both man and machine. See for yourself just how good a car you drive! See for yourself how much skill it takes to flirt with speed and danger."[49]

As a result of this interest and publicity, local car dealerships took some small strides toward direct factory involvement in NASCAR racing. The Eanes Motor Company of Christiansburg, Virginia, provided Curtis Turner with a new Olds 88 for the 1950 Grand National season, which he drove to four wins and seven other top five finishes.[50] The Edmunds Motor Company of Atlanta provided Fonty and Bob Flock with a new Lincoln, and a Nash dealer provided Bill France and Curtis Turner with a Nash Ambassador for the 1950 Carrera Panamericana.[51]

Perhaps the most important step toward involving the manufacturers, however, was taken not by Bill France or NASCAR officials but by Daytona Beach driver/mechanic Marshall Teague. Teague was a successful stock car racer and businessman, owner of a Pure Oil station in Daytona Beach. He attended the meeting at the Ebony Bar for the organization of NASCAR and served for a short while as its first secretary and treasurer until he butted heads with Bill France over the percentage of the gate paid to drivers. France suspended the independent-minded Teague from NASCAR at least twice for driving in "outlaw" races. In 1951, however, Teague performed a tremendous service for both France and NASCAR when he convinced the Hudson Motor Company to provide him with a car, spare parts, and factory technical support for the season. The Hudson Motor Company, owned by the Dutch royal family, sought a way to boost its flagging sales in an increasingly competitive automotive market and saw stock car racing as one way to do that.[52]

Fortunately for both Hudson and Teague, the Hudson Hornet was both reasonably priced and well made. As legendary mechanic Smokey Yunick observed, "The Hudson Hornet was the best buy in the United States. It had the best power, handling, safety, was cheap, and was a good looking car to boot."[53] In his first race in a Hudson, Teague won the February 1951 Daytona beach/road race in the soon-to-be-legendary #6 car emblazoned with "Fabulous Hudson Hornet" on its sides.[54] Teague went on to win five of the fifteen NASCAR Grand National races he entered in 1951 before falling out once again with Bill France over Teague's entry in a AAA stock car

Marshall Teague (left) stands next to his "Fabulous Hudson Hornet" with pioneer car owner Raymond Parks. (Courtesy of McCaig-Welborn Research Library at the International Motorsports Hall of Fame, Talladega, Alabama)

race and in the 1951 Carrera Panamericana.[55] Teague's apostasy cost him all his championship points (official NASCAR points records for 1951 completely expunged his name) and a fine of $574.50—the cost of the entry fee for the Carrera Panamericana—if he ever wished to return to NASCAR.[56]

Hudson officials were so pleased with the publicity they received from Teague's success, however, that in August 1951 they asked him to prepare two Hudson Hornets—now often referred to as "Teaguemobiles"—for the second Southern 500. The decision to run a second Hornet brought together one of the most unusual and successful pairings in NASCAR history: driver Herb Thomas and mechanic Smokey Yunick. Thomas was a struggling tobacco farmer and saw miller from Olivia, North Carolina, a loyal family man and very unsophisticated, or as Yunick put it, a "bush hillbilly—dirt poor." Yunick was his polar opposite, a fast-talking, profane, hard-drinking, carousing mechanical genius, the owner of Daytona Beach's "Smokey's—The Best Damn Garage in Town," who helped Teague prepare his Hudson. At first Yunick questioned Teague's choice of Thomas as driver, but after seeing him run practice laps at Darlington, he recognized his wisdom. "That son-of-a-bitch could flat haul ass, and you could see he was in total control."[57]

Thomas and Yunick proved their mettle, and that of the Hudson, in their first outing together, winning the Southern 500 and $8,800 in prize money. They went on to win four more races in 1951, including the important and lucrative events at Langhorne, Charlotte Speedway, and Hillsborough. With two victories in other cars and a total of sixteen top five finishes, the Olivia "'baccy farmer"—in Yunick parlance—went on to win the 1951 points championship and more than $21,000 in prize winnings.[58] Hudson was ecstatic over the minimal investment they had made and the massive amount of publicity they received.

For the next three years Hudsons dominated American stock car racing. Teague and Thomas started the 1952 season off with a bang by finishing 1–2 in the February Daytona Beach race. Thomas went on to finish second in the points championship that year to Tim Flock, who also drove a Hudson, and the make won twenty-two of thirty-four NASCAR Grand National races. Thomas and Hudson repeated as champion in 1953 and finished second in 1954, and still another Hudson pilot, Dick Rathmann, finished third in the points both years.[59] Teague had another falling out with France in 1952 and took his Hudson to the new AAA stock car series, where he won the championship in both 1952 and 1954. Teague was so dominant that in the summer of 1952 promoters launched a "Beat Marshall Teague" campaign offering special bonuses to anyone who could best him and his "Fabulous Hudson Hornet." Indeed, the only competition that Teague usually faced in the AAA was another southerner, Frank "Rebel" Mundy, who shared Hudson factory sponsorship and a distaste for Bill France's dictatorial management of NASCAR.[60]

Success on the racetrack translated into success on the showroom floor for Hudson as sales skyrocketed during the period. In its peak year of 1954, Hudson sales more than doubled, increasing from about 27,000 cars in 1953 to more than 57,000 in 1954.[61] Unfortunately for Hudson, however, the additional sales could not save the company, as the Big 3—Ford, General Motors, and Chrysler—were much better positioned to meet the demands of consumers for newer, flashier models. In May 1954, Hudson merged with Nash-Kelvinator to form American Motors, and Hudson ceased to be a distinguishable entity.[62] After the merger, Smokey Yunick, Herb Thomas, Marshall Teague, and other race car owners and drivers moved to other makes, since the Hudsons were no longer competitive.[63] In the hands of Marshall Teague and his followers, however, Hudson had made an indelible mark on NASCAR, and the lesson of "Win on Sunday, Sell on Monday" is one that resonates in the halls of both Detroit and Daytona Beach—and in recent years, Tokyo—to this day.

NASCAR was equally enthused over Hudson's success and used it to try to entice other makes into NASCAR on a more official basis. In a May 1951 article in *National Speed Sport News*, NASCAR attempted to shame General Motors—whose Oldsmobile Rocket 88 had been the dominant car in both the 1949 and '50 seasons—into becoming more openly involved in the sport by comparing Hudson's active role with GM's passive one:

> The Hudson Motor Car Co. is to be congratulated on its splendid support of stock car racing. They have really gone all-out after Marshall Teague's victories at Daytona Beach, Gardena and Phoenix and without prejudice to any other make wish them the best of luck. Unlike another make of car which capitalized on their victories through the dealers and yet gave no recognition to the sport which made this possible, Hudson realizes that racing has brought attention to their new car in a way that no other advertising medium could. This other car, which shall remain nameless, has almost been insulting in their attitude toward racing and yet engineers admit that every improvement in 1951 excepting one, has come as a result of the races on the Grand National Circuit in 1950.[64]

Unsuccessful in this tactic, Bill France and NASCAR decided that promoting a race in Detroit's backyard might be a better method of showing the manufacturers what the sport might have to offer them. France arranged for a 250-mile Grand National race to help commemorate Detroit's 250th birthday for August 1951 at the city fairgrounds. He also timed the event to coincide with the release of new Ford and Chrysler models, which gave the automakers "a chance to see how their products shape up under racing conditions."[65] France convinced the Packard Motor Company to donate a new convertible as the pace car for the event and as a prize for the winner in addition to $5,000.[66] The race itself featured fifty-nine qualifiers in fifteen different makes of car, more than 15,000 fans, and a number of Detroit executives. Tommy Thompson of Louisville, Kentucky, driving a 1951 Chrysler V-8, survived a spinout with Curtis Turner to win the race and the Packard convertible. While Detroit did not immediately jump on the NASCAR bandwagon, the event did gain the attention of the American automobile manufacturers. As an editorialist in *Illustrated Speedway News* commented: "The gigantic Detroit 250-mile race served as the impetus that cracked the Maginot line of defense thrown up by the motor industry against the sport. They know we're here."[67]

Indeed, Bill France spent an increasing percentage of his time attempting to woo other American auto manufacturers to actively support NASCAR. In racing publications NASCAR public relations personnel constantly reminded Detroit manufacturers of the value of success in the sport both "from an advertising standpoint" and "as a testing laboratory."

For most of the early 1950s, however, Hudson remained the one make fully committed to stock car racing. In December 1952, the automaker invited both Bill France and Grand National champion and Hudson driver Tim Flock to participate in the unveiling of the new Hudson Jet and Superjet at the Astor Hotel in New York City.[68]

France did begin to make some minor progress with the other automakers. In 1953, Nash gave $10,000 for the NASCAR points fund. In late 1954, France's efforts began to pay off as Chrysler held a major event to pre-show its new Dodges, Plymouths, and Chryslers at Daytona Beach for executives, dealers, and salesmen with the 1954 Grand National champion and Chrysler driver Lee Petty as "special guest of the Chrysler Division."[69] While the involvement of the Detroit manufacturers was relatively modest for the most part in the early 1950s—with the exception of Hudson—Teague's pathbreaking work and France's avid courtship of Detroit laid the groundwork for the entry of the Big 3 manufacturers in a major way in the second half of the decade.

Teague also served as a pioneer for bringing other auto-related companies into the sport. When he secured the Hudson deal, he also received financial support from Pure Oil. Mal Middlesworth, public relations director for Pure, soon became one of the most important supporters of NASCAR racing, and Pure—later Union after a merger in the 1960s—became the official fuel supplier for NASCAR's top division until 2003 and contributed significant dollars to the NASCAR points fund.[70] On the heels of Teague's work, Bill France brought in additional support for the points fund from Champion Spark Plugs, the automotive additive Miracle Power, and Wynn Oil.[71]

Even as the entry of Hudson into the sport raised NASCAR's profile, it created a problem for rule makers in 1953 when it developed the first—in the words of Smokey Yunick—"automotive manufacturer cheater racing ploy," the "Twin H Package" of options that offered dual carburetors and a dual exhaust system. Marshall Teague and Hudson engineer and racing liaison Vince Piggins convinced the manufacturer to produce the package to increase the power on the Hornet, and the make became even more dominant. NASCAR struggled from this point on with limited-edition performance packages introduced by manufacturers in just enough numbers to satisfy NASCAR as to their "stock" qualities but primarily to give them a competitive edge in racing.[72] This made France's oft stated goal of keeping the playing field level an ongoing and frustrating task.

A Deadly Game

Wooing the manufacturers brought additional challenges to NASCAR, which needed to avoid embarrassing automakers and dealers, keep the news about the various makes positive, and improve safety for drivers. Indeed, no manufacturer wanted its make associated with the death of a driver or spectator. NASCAR did have to address some problems with the ordinary stock automobile "that resulted in a number of damaging wrecks and destruction of machines in addition to threatening the lives of drivers" in the inaugural season of strictly stock racing.[73] As a result, the NASCAR rule makers allowed, and encouraged, drivers and mechanics to use heavy-duty "wheels, hubs, radius rods, steering parts and sway bars" to avoid the number of dangerous (to both drivers and spectators) and embarrassing (to automakers and dealers) accidents caused when wheels fell off cars, sending them into the stands and causing the automobiles to flip repeatedly.[74] They also allowed mechanics to cut down water pump impellers, in the hope of avoiding the buildup in pressure that caused so many cars to overheat in races, especially during the summer months. NASCAR secretary Bill Tuthill expressed his hope that these changes would prove temporary and that the series could "get back to running strictly stock with no changes at all." However, for this to happen, factory engineers needed to "get around to putting some decent wheels, hubs and steering parts on their products."[75] That never really happened, however, and NASCAR reluctantly but inexorably started down a road that gradually moved the stock car further and further from the product produced by Detroit. For the foreseeable future, however, the cars used in Grand National races were pretty close to stock, and many competitors still drove their cars to the track, taped up the headlights, strapped the doors closed with a belt, buckled up, and stomped the accelerator.

One of the major problems encountered by NASCAR in the early 1950s was that, despite some improvements in safety, stock car racing continued to be a dangerous and even deadly pastime. A basic design flaw in the Hudsons made them especially prone to end-over-end rollovers. As Smokey Yunick observed, the "Hudson's rear quarter panels were deep and strong and the rear axle shafts were weak by racing standards. So when the axle broke, rear wheel was loose, but trapped in this strong wheel housing. This caused the Hudson to bounce ass-over-head violently."[76] This type of rollover caused Jesse James Taylor serious head injuries when his Hudson flipped in the first turn of a 1951 race at Lakewood Speedway. It took rescue workers fifteen minutes to extricate him from the wreckage, a stressful situation for his pregnant wife, who subsequently miscarried.[77] Similar Hudson axle failures led to the deaths of drivers Larry Mann at Langhorne and Frank Luftoe at Lakewood, both in 1952, and Lou Figaro at North Wilkesboro in 1954.[78] The state of emergency medical care at the track did not help the situation much either, as Smokey Yunick noted: "Back then, a local doctor with a bag and an ambulance or a hearse, or maybe just a fire truck was all we had."[79]

The Hudsons were not the only makes with safety problems, as racing revealed the lack of durability—at least by racing standards—of many of the components of the stock automobile. Frank Arford was killed in his Oldsmobile in a June 1953 race at Langhorne when he was thrown from the car when it overturned after crashing through a wooden guard rail. Investigators noted that a seat brace had broken, allowing Arford to slip out from under his lap belt and be ejected from the car, landing some 30 feet away.[80] Georgian Bruce Baker died in an accident when a piece of jagged metal sliced his jugular vein, causing him to bleed to death before help arrived.[81]

The greatest safety problem with the stock automobile, however, and the source of some of the most gruesome deaths in stock car racing history was the vulnerability of the gas tank and fuel lines. The dangers of death or injury due to fire increased as NASCAR mandated that drivers fasten their doors with a belt or leather strap to keep them closed in the event of an accident. William Justice died when his car caught fire at Bowman Gray Stadium in a 1950 race. Reporters estimated that he was trapped in the car for four minutes.[82] One of the most horrific accidents in stock car racing history occurred in a NSCRA race at Lakewood Speedway in June 1950 when veteran St. Augustine, Florida, driver Skimp Hersey's car caught fire as he came out of the fourth turn. When his brakes failed and he attempted to stop the car by running into an earthen bank, it flipped over. Hersey crawled from the burning car but fell into a pool of flaming gasoline, where he sat for an estimated five minutes until rescue workers extinguished the inferno. Emergency personnel rushed him to Grady Hospital, where he died twelve hours later. Amazingly, the front page of the next day's *Atlanta Constitution* featured a graphic five-photo montage of Hersey's accident and subsequent immolation entitled "Flaming Horror at Lakewood Speedway."[83]

Problems of track management and maintenance compounded the dangers of stock car racing. The condition of most dirt tracks that NASCAR raced on was generally questionable at best. As Tim Flock recalled, "But all your half-mile tracks all over the country was turribble. You'd be right on the inside of the race track at the start, and before it was over, you'd be hangin your back wheels off the top of the track to keep from hitting them big holes. Or you'd run through the infield. You just more or less made your own race track."[84] The lack of any sort of retaining wall or fence to keep the cars inside the track at many facilities compounded the safety problems. The clouds of dust kicked up by the race cars on insufficiently watered dirt tracks often obscured the view of drivers and caused innumerable accidents. "The tracks we run were so dusty you couldn't see one car in front of the other," Flock asserted.[85] Indeed, thick clouds of dust resulted in one of the most tragic accidents of the early 1950s when Charles Parks tried to crawl away from his wrecked car and was struck and killed by another driver.[86]

Communications problems on the track resulted in other tragedies, the most notable of which was the "Black Saturday" incident at the NASCAR Sportsman and Modified series championship at the Raleigh Speedway in 1953. Rookie Bill Blevins's car stalled on the backstretch of the one-mile oval during the pace lap, and no one noticed as his car sat helpless in the middle of the track. The flagman threw the green flag, and the pack of fifty-nine cars approached 90 mph when they encountered Blevins's car. While some of the leaders swerved to avoid the car, drivers in the back of the field soon began to plow into the stalled hot rod, and it and a car driven by eighteen-year-old Jessie Midkiff burst into flames. The *Raleigh News and Observer* reported, "Flames from the two cars shot about 70 feet into the air and showered the other speeding cars." The accident demolished fifteen cars, and both Blevins and Midkiff died from the injuries they sustained. Amazingly, only three individuals required hospitalization for injuries, and one of those was a female spectator "looking through the fence on the backstretch [who] went into shock when she saw the cars explode." While the *News and Observer* did not show the bodies of either of the victims, the article did feature a large photo of the "Charred Death Car" in which Blevins died.[87]

The carnage on the race track caused NASCAR and other stock car promoters huge public relations problems as some individuals called for the banning of auto racing. In the aftermath of Skimp Hersey's gruesome death—the third racing-related death at Lakewood Speedway in three months—Atlanta city councilman Jimmy Vickers introduced a resolution to "outlaw vehicular racing at the [Lakewood] Park." Vickers argued that the track at Lakewood was inherently unsafe and characterized the auto racing there as "legalized murder." "I like to see people get a thrill, but I don't believe in allowing a man to forfeit his life that they may have it." The editors of the *Atlanta Constitution* joined Vickers citing the "large number of accidents" at the facility. "We are told the Lakewood track was never built for automobile racing in the first place. A big portion of all accidents occur at one particular turn. So certain are accidents to happen at this turn that news photographers always station themselves there." The *Constitution* further added that the unsavory nature of both fans— when police arrested a man at the speedway, an estimated fifty spectators greeted them with a "hailstorm of rocks," severely damaging their patrol car and requiring a call for reinforcements—and drivers with "long-past criminal records" provided additional reasons that "racing at the Lakewood track should be stopped."[88] While the Vickers-*Constitution* campaign was not successful and racing continued at Lakewood, it did reinforce the idea among many in the middle class that stock car races were not an appropriate venue for wholesome entertainment. In the aftermath of the "Black Saturday" incident in Raleigh, the *Raleigh News and Observer* made a similar call for the end of racing at the new Raleigh Speedway. The editors asserted, "Races of this type constitute mayhem, not sport. . . . Raleigh will be better off if this year is the last one for races of this type."[89]

Although racing continued at Raleigh, on-track deaths did create a dilemma for stock car racing promoters. On the one hand, spectacular crashes and even the deaths of drivers heightened the aura of genuine danger that helped attract many fans seeking a vicarious thrill. On the other hand, however, these types of incidents further marred the already tarnished image of stock car racing for members of "respectable" classes, limited the potential for adding additional fans, and weakened its political position when promoters tried to gain favorable legislation. Indeed, the *News and Observer* gleefully announced in September 1953 that an attempt by Bill France and other promoters to get the North Carolina General Assembly to "repeal the law which prohibits automobile races on Sunday" in certain counties had failed.[90]

In order to quiet some of the criticism, NASCAR spearheaded the organization of the Auto Racing Safety Council in 1952, a consortium of race track owners and promoters to "promote greater safety for spectators and contestants at race tracks."[91] As a result, NASCAR became more proactive in encouraging—although generally not mandating—safety improvements in cars. In 1953, NASCAR issued a bulletin in the aftermath of Frank Arford's death urging the installation of roll bars in cars and encouraging drivers and car owners to ensure that seats locked in place "so they cannot break loose or slide forward."[92] NASCAR also responded to concerns from the National Safety Council that auto racing caused the young people of the nation to drive recklessly. Cannonball Baker issued a directive designed to ensure that NASCAR drivers provided the proper example to America's youth. "Reckless driving on the highway by members of the National Association for Stock Car Auto Racing (NASCAR) will be considered a violation of racing rules and punishment will be meted out accordingly."[93] Despite these measures, however, stock car racing remained an extremely dangerous activity.

The Dictator in Daytona

In addition to the safety challenges drivers faced, they chafed at the increasingly dictatorial actions of Bill France, whose power over the drivers only increased with the growing popularity of NASCAR and the elimination of most of its viable rivals. France primarily used his powers—especially his ability to fine, take championship points away from, suspend, or ban drivers for "actions detrimental to stock car racing"—to attempt to prevent drivers from racing in competing series. Lee Petty lost the 1950 points championship when France took away all 809 of his championship points after he drove in a so-called outlaw event.[94] Other top drivers, including Marshall Teague, Frank Mundy, Gober Sosebee, Bob Flock, Jack Smith, Billy Carden, Ed Samples, and Cotton Owens, spent time in France's doghouse for driving in "unsanctioned" (non-NASCAR) events in the early 1950s.[95] By 1952, Teague and Mundy had had enough and took their act to the new AAA stock car series, racing primarily in the Midwest. While many drivers bristled at not being able to race where and when they pleased, with the death of the NSCRA there really were not many other viable options, especially if one wanted to remain in the Piedmont South.

France and NASCAR officials also made a number of controversial decisions—some of them considered highly subjective and often inconsistent—further antagonizing drivers. NASCAR used a relatively primitive scoring system, and series officials often had to reverse decisions about who had actually won a race. At a September 7, 1951, race in Columbia, South Carolina, Glen "Fireball" Roberts took the checkered flag as the winner. Tim Flock's team, however, asked for a scoring check and, after a reexamination of the scoring cards, discovered that Flock had won the race. The result so angered Ed Severance—the owner of Roberts's car—

that he refused the $700 prize money for second place. The same thing happened to Lee Petty in September 1952 at a Dayton, Ohio, race when the original decision to declare him the winner was reversed in favor of Dick Rathmann. The tables were turned on Rahtmann in April 1954 when his apparent victory was overturned in favor of Gober Sosebee at a race in Macon, Georgia.[96]

One of the most controversial finishes in NASCAR history occurred not because of scoring errors but as a result of the rule interpretations of NASCAR officials. In an extremely close race at Lakewood Speedway in March 1954, Herb Thomas, Buck Baker, and Dick Rathmann battled each other door to door, lap after lap. Officials flagged Thomas as the winner of the race, but NASCAR supervisor Johnny Bruner announced that Thomas had received a one-lap penalty for not going to the "rear of the field after making a yellow flag pit stop." They then proceeded to declare Buck Baker the winner. After a couple of more hours of deliberation, however, Bruner decided that Baker had committed the same infraction and should also be penalized one lap, now making Rathmann the winner. However, further deliberation resulted in one-lap penalties for Rathmann and fifth-place finisher Fonty Flock for receiving attention from their pit crews while their cars were still on the track. Technically this would have made the fourth-place driver, Gober Sosebee, the winner, but amid the pandemonium of screaming drivers and pit crews, NASCAR officials finally decided to ignore the infractions and let the result on the track stand. This decision was the straw that broke the camel's back for Fonty Flock. Fed up with NASCAR and Bill France's capriciousness, he quit the series and headed for the Midwest to race in the new Midwest Association for Race Cars (MARC) series.[97]

NASCAR's fickle enforcement of the rules also resulted in Tim Flock's temporary departure from NASCAR. After Flock apparently won the February 1954 Daytona beach/road race, inspectors disqualified him for illegal alterations to his carburetor. The decision infuriated Tim, whose win in the 1952 Sportsman and Modified series race at Daytona had also been taken away because the hastily installed wooden roll bars in his car did not meet competition standards. Flock accused Bill France of pandering to the Chrysler Corporation, which he was trying to woo at the time, and star Chrysler driver Lee Petty, who was declared the winner. Flock immediately quit NASCAR and began operating a service station in Atlanta, although he did join brothers Bob and Fonty in racing in some MARC races later in the year.[98]

Lord Calvert Takes Her through the Turn: The Driver's Life

Despite these frustrations and dangers, however, NASCAR drivers lived life to its fullest, and most exemplified W. J. Cash's "hell of a fellow" perhaps more than any other group of southerners. It took a great deal of physical and mental toughness to drive a stock car in the early days when racing involved not only great danger but intense physical discomfort as well. Steering wheels taped with electrician's tape tore at the hands of drivers as they forced cars without power steering into the turns lap after lap. Primitive safety belts allowed drivers to slide on the bench seats of the stock sedans they drove and caused blisters on their backside. Drivers also often left the race track with second-degree burns on their feet and legs because of a lack of heat protection, and the high temperatures inside the cars—often well in excess of 100 degrees—caused intense dehydration. Smokey Yunick summed up the situation for drivers: "Yesterday's driver ran Indy and Darlington in street shoes, slacks and a tee shirt, with a pack of cigarettes rolled up in the shirtsleeve and an open face helmet (about as protective as strapping a turtle shell to your head). They very seldom wore gloves. Nine out of ten finishing drivers had bleeding hands and some with bleeding asses . . . two out of ten with burns on throttle foot from the heat."[99]

In addition to the intense discomfort and constant threat of death or serious injury, stock car drivers in the early 1950s faced a variety of other challenges. For one thing, the amount of prize money available to racers was very limited, with the traditional winner's check only $1,000—of which the driver generally pocketed only 40 percent, unless he owned the car as well. As Tim Flock observed, "We ran for chicken feed for years."[100] Smokey Yunick observed, "In the first ten years of NASCAR, the driver's [sic] didn't make enough to hardly live on." For sustenance, "drivers ate steak and eggs and roast beef sandwiches with a half pound of gravy when they won," Yunick added, "and cold 'tube steaks' [hot dogs] the rest of the time."[101] Drivers faced two choices: either try to work a job and squeeze in racing when possible, or barnstorm the East Coast racing in every available race. If one desired to be in the top ranks of drivers in NASCAR, however, there was only one choice, and that was to hit the road.

While many fans envied the life of the racer, barnstorming could be a grueling, and even dangerous, experience. Many of the top drivers arrived at races a few days early in order to help promote the event in exchange for room and board and $100 to $200. As Tim Flock remembered, "You would do anything for a promoter."[102] There seemed to be little planning of the NASCAR Grand National schedule, and races a few days apart could be separated by hundreds of miles, forcing drivers to haul their cars overnight, make repairs and prepare the car, catch a nap, and then race. After a July 3, 1953, race at the Monroe County Fairgrounds in Rochester, New York, Herb Thomas and Tim Flock towed their Hudsons through the night so that they could drive in a July 4 race at the Piedmont Interstate Fairgrounds in Spartanburg, South Carolina. Arriving at the track in the early afternoon, the two lay down in the shade of their cars in the infield to get some sleep before the 8:00 P.M. race. A man hired by Champion Spark Plugs to post signs along the fence failed to notice the two sleeping drivers and backed his truck onto Flock's head. The driver panicked and left the truck sitting there, and Thomas and six highway patrolmen had to lift the truck off Flock. Flock was rushed to the hospital and amazingly suffered no long-term damage. The accident did keep him out of the next six races and possibly cost him that year's title.[103] Staying on the road so much was also damaging to family relationships. Fonty Flock received word that his wife had given birth to his daughter in May 1953 back in Atlanta just before he started a race in Manassas, Virginia.[104]

Life for most drivers involved a great deal of heavy drinking, carousing, and overall wildness. "Man we'd party all night before a race, get drunk, and then get in them ol' cars and put mixed drinks in a tank behind us and get drunk during the race," Tim Flock recalled. "You'd win money and then throw it away, on women. These old gals would see our cars . . . and they'd beat your door down at two o'clock in the morning."[105] Buddy Shuman once told a female reporter who asked him how he mustered the courage to go into the highly banked turns at Darlington at such high speeds, "Ma'am, I just take 'er down the straightaway. 'Lord Calvert' [whiskey] takes her through the turns."[106]

The drinking and carousing carried over to car owners, crew members, and even NASCAR officials—Bill France included—sometimes to the detriment of the overall effort. Tim Flock lost the 1951 Daytona beach/road race when his crew began celebrating prematurely, got drunk, and were unable to properly service the car when he pitted unexpectedly for gas late in the race.[107] The sexual exploits of drivers and crewmen were also legendary. As Smokey Yunick observed, "I'm not proud of what I did back then, but if a woman looked good, we didn't really abide by the Ten Commandments." Yunick also asserted, "I don't want to leave the impression that all racers were wild, drunk, womanizers—just 80 percent of us."[108]

The devil-may-care attitude of drivers that went along with the wildness made drivers increasingly popular with working-class fans; you never knew what was going to happen at a NASCAR race. Jimmy Florian won a NASCAR Grand National race at Dayton, Ohio, in June 1952 while driving without a shirt.[109] When a drunk spectator tried to drive his car across the track in the middle of a race at Columbia Speedway in April 1952 and crashed into his race car, E. C. Ramsey climbed out of his racer and "dashed over to the dazed and intoxicated spectator and proceeded to beat him to a pulp" until police arrived to haul the unfortunate drunk off.[110]

Perhaps the most outrageous stunt pulled by a NASCAR driver in the early 1950s was Tim Flock driving eight races in 1953 with a rhesus monkey—named "Jocko Flocko"—leashed to a perch in his car. The monkey, complete with driver's suit and goggles, became an immediate hit with younger fans and made Flock an even more popular figure. The fun ended for Flock, however, in Jocko's eighth race when the monkey escaped his perch, opened a trap door used by the driver to check tire wear, and was struck by a flying rock. The monkey scrambled onto Flock's shoulder in a panic, forcing the driver to pit to get him out of the car. As Flock later cracked, "It was the only time I know of in NASCAR that the official pit stop was for a monkey being put out of the car."[111]

In Herb Thomas and Lee Petty NASCAR also had top drivers who took a more serious approach and helped to provide a compelling contrast to the Flocks and Turners of the sport. Both men were hardworking family men who saw driving a race car not as a ticket to the next party but as a means to make a decent living and escape rural poverty while doing something they truly enjoyed. Both also attracted significant numbers of working-class fans who worked hard on the mill or farm and respected these men's work ethic and more sober habits and themselves dreamed of a more traditional method of moving up in the world that did not involve illegal activity or wild behavior.

Petty especially brought a new business-oriented style of driving and operating a race team to NASCAR. On the track he adopted a more conservative, stay out of trouble and make money approach. As fellow competitor Ralph Moody observed, "He had good racecars. But he didn't want to tear them up. He wanted to bring it home and make money every race he went to."[112] Petty became the master of this style of racing, hanging back, staying out of the inevitable wrecks, and, if he had the car to win, using his innate driving skill to dash to the front in the closing laps. If his car was not right, however, he held on to achieve the best possible finish and almost always finished in the top ten, collected his prize money, headed home to fix his car, and loaded up for the next race. Lee's younger son Maurice—who along with older brother Richard served as his father's pit crew—observed, "The difference between Curtis, Joe Weatherly, and the Flock boys, and my daddy was that they all drove for people. Lee owned his own deal. It was his livelihood. I mean, if he didn't finish good, we didn't eat good. . . . That makes a hell of a lot of difference how you approach racing. Lee approached it to finish. They approached it to win, but Lee was fortunate enough that he still won a bunch."[113] And that approach proved wildly successful, yielding twenty-three wins in the first half of the 1950s, top five finishes in the points championship every year, and the first of three Grand National championships in 1954; perhaps most important for Petty, it earned him more than $70,000, money that both provided his family much more than he could have earned in his previous career as a truck driver and kept him in racing.[114]

Petty's businesslike, family-oriented style and serious demeanor, combined with intense competitiveness, toughness, and unwillingness to ever back down from a challenge, also helped to create one of the first great rivalries in NASCAR history, between Petty and the happy-go-lucky, hell-raiser Curtis "Pops" Turner. While Turner cared little about what happened to the car he raced because he did not own it, Petty knew it would cost him both time and money if his car was damaged. This led to some dramatic confrontations between the two on and off the track. One of the most notable incidents occurred at a race in Virginia when Turner gave Petty one of his trademark "pops" and put him out of the race. As Ralph Moody remembered the incident, Turner sat on a fence after the race "drinking booze out of a bottle." Petty approached his rival and demanded to "talk" to Turner. "He was slapping himself in the leg with a rolled-up newspaper. He walked up to Turner, and went whack, slapped him beside the head. The son of a bitch had a torque wrench in it, and Lee knocked Turner right over the goddamn fence."[115]

Petty's methods and demeanor proved not only successful but a hit with Piedmont fans. He was twice voted most popular driver in Grand National racing in the early 1950s and became one of the first NASCAR drivers whose followers organized an official fan club. The requirements to join, according to club president Morris Metcalfe of Winston-Salem, were "an enthusiastic interest in NASCAR stock car racing and Lee Petty in particular, and that the members drive a Chrysler Corporation–made car [Petty's favored make]."[116] Bill France had to be thrilled not only with

Lee Petty became one of the most popular drivers on the NASCAR circuit in the early 1950s, winning the first of three championships in 1954. (Courtesy of McCaig-Welborn Research Library at the International Motorsports Hall of Fame, Talladega, Alabama)

Petty's popularity but with another reason for Detroit to pay attention to what was going on in the Piedmont South.

For France, NASCAR, and its hard-partying drivers, promoters, and fans, the first years of the 1950s brought unbelievable progress. The sport had grown from its roots in Piedmont red clay and spread into the Northeast, across the Midwest and Plains states, regularly traveled to the West Coast, and had even made inroads into Canada and Hawaii. The national auto racing press started to become aware of the spread of NASCAR, and the mainstream press noted the sport's growing popularity. The Southern 500 drew reporters from across the nation to tiny Darlington, South Carolina, and its victor became a nationally recognized star. Although it was a small piece and near the back of the issue, *Time* magazine even ran an enthusiastic article on Tim Flock winning the 1952 NASCAR Grand National Division title in its December 8 issue. "Stock car racing is a slam-bang sport with its own special sound effects—screeching tires, crumpling fenders and ten-car smashups. It requires nerve and verve for a driver to compete with any success."[117] Perhaps most important for an auto racing series, Detroit automakers began to take a serious interest in the sport with Hudson's success in both winning races and using the subsequent publicity to sell its "Fabulous Hornets."

Despite this national exposure, NASCAR remained close to its roots. Its most important facilities, other than Darlington, were the red-clay tracks scattered throughout the Piedmont, many built and still owned by bootleggers—most probably still involved in the business if only in the financial end. Most of its fans were still drawn from the ranks of the Piedmont working class and saw the wild races as a means of escape from the drudgery of the mill or the boredom of the farm. And finally, NASCAR's "bread and butter," its chief attraction, was still its wild drivers, who might just do anything including racing door to door, lap after lap, beating and banging on one another, wearing outlandish outfits—like "Bamooda" shorts—in a race, leading the crowd in singing "Dixie," putting beer in a douche bag to sip on during the race, and even driving with a monkey in the car.

I Would Have Been Willing to Bet . . .
We Would Never Have to Sleep in the Car Again
Feast and Famine, NASCAR, 1955–1958

Four hundred guests showed up for the big Daytona Beach Chamber of Commerce testimonial dinner on September 3, 1955. The list of invitees looked like a who's who of Daytona Beach society and the auto manufacturing world. Executives in attendance included representatives of Chevrolet, Lincoln-Mercury, and Chrysler along with associated industries such as Pure Oil, Purolator, and Air Lift shock absorbers. The honoree was an unlikely one, a man who had come to the community almost twenty years earlier virtually penniless, worked as a mechanic, journeyed throughout the Southeast pursuing a career as a race car driver, and built a racing empire with the help of some of the shadiest characters in the region. But this was Big Bill France's night—one that began with a corny poem entitled "Ode to Bill France (Plenty)!" and continued with testimonials from Detroit executives. It concluded with friends hoisting him onto their shoulders and parading him around the room.[1]

Bill France had arrived in the big time, and the sport he had helped create had arrived with him. Within a year of the 1955 dinner, Detroit automakers and other manufacturers would be pouring millions of dollars into the sport and signing star drivers and mechanics to unbelievable contracts. Instead of hauling their cars through the night, preparing them for the race in the parking lot of a seedy motel, and snacking on "tube steaks" at the track concession stand, they now flew to races, stayed in the finest hotels, and dined on prime rib. National media now covered major races, and France, NASCAR drivers, mechanics, and car owners rubbed shoulders with some of the most powerful men in the world. The parties at Daytona, Darlington, and other race venues, fueled by Detroit's deep

pockets, had more liquor (mostly of the legal variety) and more beautiful women (mostly of the legal variety) and lasted longer than ever before.

Although the success of NASCAR for a few short years matched anything Bill France could ever have imagined, that success was but a tantalizing taste of the possibilities for the sport. Indeed, almost as quickly as the party started, Detroit turned off the tap on the free liquor and all the other perks. By 1957, the sport was almost back to square one, and Bill France and NASCAR had to fall back on its fan base in the Piedmont South, on its wild, liquor-hauling drivers, and on the bootlegger tracks that formed the foundation for the sport. While it lasted, however, it was a hell of a ride.

Carl Kiekhaefer

One of the attendees at the Bill France testimonial dinner and one of the prime movers in taking NASCAR to unimagined heights in the mid-1950s was a short, balding, stocky, cigar-chomping ball of seemingly endless energy by the name of Carl Kiekhaefer. The son of a Wisconsin dairy farmer and a self-made millionaire, Kiekhaefer turned his Mercury Outboard Motor Company into the top manufacturer of boat motors in the nation. Journalist Hank Schoolfield referred to Kiekhaefer as "this hurrying man with the king-size cigar between his teeth and the problem-of-the-day whirring through his precision mind."[2] He showed up at Daytona Speed Weeks in 1955 with a new Chrysler 300 with automatic transmission, a team of white-uniformed mechanics, and an intense desire to win the legendary beach/road race. He brought his car in a new hauler with his company's name and logo on the side, had matching white uniforms for his crew, and rented out a new filling station to prepare his car for the race.

NASCAR had never seen anything quite like the man and his entourage. A young Richard Petty observed that when Kiekhaefer came to NASCAR "it was like someone had booked Ringling Brothers and Barnum and Bailey. Nobody in racing ever saw anything like it. Keep in mind, up to this point, if a whole crew had on clean jeans and shirts that even remotely resembled each other, it was considered classy. And if a guy hauled his race car to the track on the back of a flatbed truck, well, man, everybody in the place talked about it, from the pits to the grandstands."[3] As one journalist later commented, "He might just as well have been an Egyptian pharaoh arriving by barge."[4]

The one thing Kiekhaefer did not have was a driver, but he solved that problem soon when he hired Tim Flock, who had come to Daytona to see old friends after quitting NASCAR the previous year. When Kiekhaefer heard that Flock was a former Daytona winner (though he was later disqualified), he hired him on the spot. Although Flock felt some unease about the automatic transmission, and had never raced with one, he liked the power of the finely tuned Chrysler. To Kiekhaefer's delight, Flock put the car on the pole for the big race at a record speed of 130.293 mph.[5] During the race, however, Flock's fears about the ability of the automatic transmission to develop enough low-end torque coming out of the turns kept him behind Fireball Roberts in a Fish Carburetor–sponsored Buick for the entire race. Ironically, in a sort of karmic payback, officials disqualified Roberts's car for an illegal engine modification and, nearly twenty-four hours after the race, declared Flock the winner.[6]

Carl Kiekhaefer's career as a NASCAR Grand National car owner had begun with a bang, and for two years his drivers and his cars dominated the series. In that period, Kiekhaefer's cars—he entered as many as five cars in a given event—won forty-four out of eighty-six NASCAR Grand National races.[7] Along the way, he spent more than $1 million, an unheard of figure at a time when most Grand National teams had budgets—if they had a budget at all—in the low five figures. Indeed, Kiekhaefer's biographer estimated that he spent "more than 20 times [the money] his closest independent rival [spent]."[8] As Tim Flock observed, "He had the money, and he had Chrysler, and in '55 that man more or less moved into NASCAR and took over."[9]

Kiekhaefer got his first taste of auto racing—not necessarily a good one—in 1951 when he entered two Chrysler Saratogas in the Carrera Panamericana as his way of providing himself and some of his engineers with a diversion from their long hours at Mercury's Fond du Lac, Wisconsin, factory. Kiekhaefer had always loved racing and competition, but the American Power Boat Association would not allow manufacturers to compete in its sanctioned boat races.[10] He hired 1950 AAA open-wheel champ Tony Bettenhausen to drive one of his cars. Bettenhausen finished third in the race behind two factory-backed Ferraris. In 1952, Kiekhaefer hired Bettenhausen once again, but this time he finished fourth, behind three factory-backed Fords. Kiekhaefer protested that the Fords had "illegal and non-stock modifications," but his pleas fell on deaf ears.[11] While his first experience in auto racing was not as successful as Kiekhaefer hoped and expected, in the words of his biographer Jeffrey Rodengen, "The thrill of competition Carl had felt south of the border left an indelible mark on his personality. The rush he experienced in pursuit of the checkered flag was so well suited to his obsessively competitive spirit that he began to lay plans to shift his attack to the American track." His experience in the Carrera Panamericana had also intensified his hatred of unfairness and reinforced his determination to outdo the big corporations—particularly Ford—which, he believed, had cheated their way to victory.[12]

In 1954, Kiekhaefer launched his American stock car racing career in the AAA strictly stock series. Once again, he hired Tony Bettenhausen to drive a Chrysler New Yorker, although he had limited early success. When injuries sidelined Bettenhausen, veteran stock car ace Frank "Rebel" Mundy took over and won a major race at the legendary Milwaukee Mile in August.[13] With Mundy's victory, Kiekhaefer was hooked—much like Raymond Parks when Lloyd Seay won the first stock car race at Lakewood Speedway in 1938. As Rodengen put it, from "that moment, Kiekhaefer's interest in stock car racing verged on the fanatical."[14] At least part of Kiekhaefer's motivation for getting involved in stock car racing was to promote and advertise his Mercury outboard motors. He was one of the first major corporate executives to recognize the possibilities of using stock cars as rolling billboards. His primary interest, however, was in the competition, the thrill of coming out on top. "All he wanted were the trophies," asserted Mundy, who won the AAA stock car championship in 1955 and drove in NASCAR Grand National races for Kiekhaefer in 1956.[15]

Kiekhaefer's thirst for competition and desire for a wider marketing venue for his Mercury outboards brought him to Daytona Beach and into NASCAR full-time in 1955. In his obsessive pursuit of victory, he left no detail unattended. He pushed his drivers, mechanics, and himself relentlessly to constantly improve team performance; eighteen-hour days were not unusual in his shop. Kiekhaefer's formula for success was simple: "Eliminate luck, pick the best cars, the best mechanics, the most competitive drivers, and then work like hell."[16]

Before Kiekhaefer arrived at Daytona for the first time, he covered one of his most important bases, selecting the best car—the brand-new Chrysler 300. The 300 was an ideal candidate for stock car racing, as Chrysler had responded to public demand for greater power and performance by producing what some have called the "first factory-built muscle car" complete with a 331-cubic-inch engine, two four-barrel carburetors, heavy-duty suspension, and dual exhausts. Off the showroom floor, the 300 had a top speed of 130 mph and could travel from 0 to 60 mph in ten seconds.[17] Kiekhaefer also had the advantage of a direct pipeline to top engineers and executives at Chrysler. Although the corporation and he had no public relationship, the Detroit manufacturer kept an open back door to supply his needs for extra parts and engines. As Bill Newbury, president of Dodge at the time, recalled, "I smuggled him engines and parts and stuff like that, and as a matter of fact, he didn't have to go through a lot of red tape to get things done with us." Smokey Yunick, in the process of developing a relationship with General Motors at the same time, complained, "We were 14 levels below him in their [Chevrolet] organizational structure down here racing, and Kiekhaefer could go right to the top."[18]

Not content with the stock characteristics of the 300, Kiekhaefer used a team of as many as thirty crew members to put his cars in top racing condition. Initially, he took advantage of the top-flight engineers—most graduates of the leading engineering schools in the nation—and mechanics he had hired for Mercury Outboard. He also took advantage of the facilities he already had at his Fond du Lac, Wisconsin, factory, including constantly testing his engines on the factory's dynamometers, something unheard of in NASCAR circles.[19] In addition, as *Winston-Salem Journal* re-

Carl Kiekhaefer stands next to his four entries and matching car haulers and confers with a crew man before a 1956 race at Asheville-Weaverville Speedway. (Courtesy of Don Hunter Collection, Smyle Media)

porter Hank Schoolfield observed in a 1956 feature article on the obsessive outboard motor baron, "He leaves no stone unturned. Everything on his cars—tires, brakes, cooling systems, fuel systems, ignition—is the subject of constant study." Kiekhaefer even had his crew collect "dirt samples from every track his cars raced on. . . . He determines the chemical content and the size (in microns) of the dirt grains—important information, he says, when you have to know what that dirt will do to the inside of an engine and how to filter it out of the enormous quantities of air which a four-barrel carburetor consumes."[20] Indeed, Kiekhaefer's and his mechanics' intense study of racetrack dirt led to one of the most important technology transfers from NASCAR to the automotive industry in history. In conjunction with the Purolator Corporation, the Kiekhaefer team developed the vastly superior dry-paper oil filter—replacing traditional oil-bath filters—which soon became standard equipment on almost all automobiles.[21]

Although Kiekhaefer had the resources to go almost anywhere to find the type of ultracompetitive drivers to wheel his stock cars, he found what he needed among the large pool of top drivers in the Piedmont South, most with at least some experience in hauling illegal liquor. To secure their services, he gave them previously unheard-of benefits. He paid most of his drivers a monthly retainer fee—usually around $1,200, covered all their expenses, and allowed them to keep any prize money they won. Drivers normally raced in return for 40 percent of their prize winnings and any appearance money they could get out of promoters. In 1955, Tim Flock earned more than $40,000 driving for Kiekhaefer. "It was *big* money. We bought a beautiful home in Atlanta, a new car, had everything we wanted."[22] Kiekhaefer also regularly gave drivers additional rewards if they won a particularly big race or a championship. After Frank Mundy won the 1955 AAA stock car championship, Kiekhaefer gave him a $5,000 bonus and a new Chrysler.[23] In addition, Kiekhaefer's drivers only had to drive; they were no longer expected to do mechanical work or haul their car to races. Needless to say, Kiekhaefer had little trouble attracting the best. In 1955, Tim and Fonty Flock dominated the NASCAR Grand National scene in his cars, while Frank Mundy won the AAA stock championship. The following year, Kiekhaefer focused only on NASCAR and campaigned with Tim, Fonty, and Mundy as well as Buck Baker, who won the Grand National championship; Speedy Thompson; Herb Thomas; and Junior Johnson, who drove only one race for Kiekhaefer.[24] In a rather bold move, Kiekhaefer entered African American driver Charlie Scott of Forrest Park, Georgia—the first African American to race in NASCAR's top division—in the 1956 Daytona beach/road race. Scott finished nineteenth in a field of seventy-six drivers but never raced in NASCAR again.[25]

While the rewards were high for Kiekhaefer's drivers, the demands more than matched them. He drove his drivers in the same way he drove himself and his mechanics. Kiekhaefer rented out entire floors of hotels for his drivers and crews, especially before big races. Drivers had to be in bed by eleven, and he had a strict "no sex the night before a race" rule. He placed wives and girlfriends at the opposite end of the hotel and personally patrolled the halls to ensure compliance with his rules. "And he would watch all night long," Tim Flock recalled, "and if you didn't play by his rules, you were fired the next morning."[26] The days started at 6:00 A.M. for drivers, with Kiekhaefer blowing a whistle to rouse them from bed and to a day full of constant testing of his race cars. In addition, he expected his drivers to be on twenty-four-hour call, even during the winter, flying them all over the country to make promotional appearances for his Mercury outboards. According to Junior Johnson, Kiekhaefer also issued so-called team orders as to how his drivers should finish in relation to one another to prevent them from racing too aggressively and tearing up the cars, which were all, generally, near the front. Johnson recalled that in the race he drove for Kiekhaefer, at Charlotte Speedway in 1956, the owner called together the three drivers he had entered in the race and told them to select a match from his closed hand. "Whoever got the shortest match was to finish first." However, Kiekhaefer's plans for his drivers were not always followed, especially in the heat of competition. Junior got the middle-sized match, but when the driver who had the third match "blowed my doors off," he decided, "The hell with this—I'm going to race!" and took off after his teammates.[27] This life was nothing like the traditional racer's life of independent living and decision making, drinking, carousing, sleeping until an hour before a race, and getting rid of a hangover with a shot of whiskey, but again the pay was also nothing like the drivers had experienced before.[28]

Kiekhaefer's first year in NASCAR almost met his own high expectations. Tim Flock won eighteen races and the Grand National championship, while Frank Mundy dominated the AAA stock series. The team won every major race in NASCAR as well, except for the Southern 500, won by Herb Thomas in a 1955 Chevy.[29] While it was never his priority in racing, the success of his team in 1955 led to an increase in sales of Mercury outboards, especially in the South. Chris Economaki reported in *National Speed Sport News* on a January 1956 banquet he attended for 700 Mercury Outboard dealers where Tim and Fonty Flock and Frank Mundy were the featured guests. A Mercury dealer sitting at Economaki's table told him that he, and Kiekhaefer, had a "serious problem. There just aren't enough Mercury outboard motors to go around."[30] Chrysler also reaped an unexpected promotional windfall, investing practically nothing—and Kiekhaefer wanted it that way. The success of the Flocks and Mundy gave Chrysler tremendous publicity, although the relatively high cost of the 300 limited its sales appeal for the vast majority of working-class NASCAR fans.

Chevy Jumps In

While Hudson's success with the Hornet had stirred some interest in NASCAR in Detroit in the early 1950s, the manufacturers became increasingly interested in the sport because of all of the free publicity Chrysler received from the success of the Mercury Outboard team and its Chrysler

300s and Dodge D-500s. Indeed, by 1955, Detroit was already in a heated advertising and sales battle for the ever growing teenage and young adult market centered around the speed and performance capabilities of its top makes. NASCAR, with its stock requirements, core group of dedicated and avid fans in the Piedmont South with increasing amounts of disposable income due to post–World War II prosperity, and the popular Daytona Beach Speed Trials, gave manufacturers plenty of opportunities to demonstrate the superiority of their makes over those of their competitors.

Chevrolet, primarily as a result of the influence of its chief engineer, Ed Cole, and engineer Zora Duntov, became the first manufacturer after Hudson to make a major commitment to NASCAR stock car racing. Prior to 1955, Chevrolets had the reputation of being a "cheapo poor man's car" or, even worse for young people, your "grandma's car." The ultimate car for most young people was still the late 1930s flat-head Ford V-8, with a wealth of available performance parts, manuals, and hot rod magazines to help teens modify the engine and chassis to go faster. This proved especially true in the South, which was still firmly, in the words of Smokey Yunick, "Henry country." Cole and Duntov sought to drastically improve Chevrolet's image and sales position, especially with the youth market. When Duntov came to Chevrolet in 1953, Cole was already in charge of developing a new engine to replace the old Chevrolet "stove-bolt six" engine. Cole decided to create not only a new engine but an entirely new car, a "light, simple, hi-mileage, inexpensive hi-performance" machine.[31]

Not long after Duntov came to Chevrolet in 1953 and began working on this project with Cole, he wrote a now famous memo entitled "Thoughts Pertaining to Youth, Hot Rodders and Chevrolet." In his memo, Duntov pointed out the near monopoly Ford had on the youth and hot rod market and asked an important question, "Should we consider that it would be desirable to make these youths Chevrolet-minded?" With Duntov's encouragement, Chevrolet set out not only to produce the new car but to simultaneously manufacture a wide range of performance parts— "camshafts, springs, manifolds, pistons, and such"—to improve the car's speed, performance, and handling. In Duntov's rather stilted language, if Chevrolet made modification of its new automobile "easy and the very first attempts would be crowned with success the appeal of the new RPO V8 will take hold and not have the stigma of expensiveness like the Cadillac or Chrysler," as a result "a swing to Chevrolet may be anticipated."[32] The collaboration between Cole and Duntov produced the legendary 1955

Chevy with a small-block 265-cubic-inch V-8 engine, and the "swing to Chevrolet" with results that far exceeded even Cole and Duntov's wildest dreams.

The beginnings of Chevy's direct involvement with NASCAR came not as an intentional move by its top brass, however, but from a suggestion by Barney Clark, a racing fan and executive for Chevrolet's advertising agency Campbell-Ewald. Clark noticed in the results of the speed trials at Daytona Beach in the *Detroit Free Press* that Deland, Florida, highway patrolman Jack Tapscott had finished second in his class in a stock '55 Chevy at 112.113 mph. Clark immediately saw the advertising potential in Tapscott's accomplishment. "In those days you just didn't buy a low-priced car that would top 100." When Herb Thomas won a NASCAR short-track race in Fayetteville, North Carolina, in a '55 Chevy in March, followed two weeks later by a Fonty Flock victory in a Grand National race in Columbia, South Carolina, Clark—with Ed Cole's encouragement— began running ads touting Chevy's "race-proven V8" in newspapers and magazines and on the radio.[33]

Even though Cole relished the relatively free publicity generated by the success of his '55 Chevys, he believed a more intentional effort would reap even more benefits for his company. Twice in the spring of 1955, Cole tried to get Smokey Yunick—who had quit the Hudson effort in disgust—to head an experimental racing program. Yunick, however, was in a "quit racing mode" and turned him down. Bill France, eager to "get 'em [Chevy] hooked into NASCAR," convinced Yunick in April to fly to North Wilkesboro for a race and meet Cole there to talk about a possible agreement. Smokey agreed to a one-race deal to field a '55 Chevy for Darlington's Labor Day Southern 500 in exchange for $10,000 and the car. Cole assigned three-time Indianapolis 500 winner Mauri Rose to serve as a liaison between Yunick and Chevrolet engineering, and Yunick lined up his old friend and Darlington master Herb Thomas—who had raced Chevrolets on occasion—to pilot the car.[34]

Winning Darlington in 1955, however, even with Chevy's support and Herb Thomas's talent, was a tall order given the dominance of Carl Kiekhaefer's Chrysler 300s. Tim Flock, who had already won thirteen races that season, was the obvious favorite, with Lee Petty and Junior Johnson, the young bootlegger from Wilkes County, both on hot streaks coming into the big race. In addition, the small-block Chevy engine generated about 30 horsepower less than its competitors. To make matters worse, Thomas had crashed badly at Charlotte in May, and Yunick felt unsure about his fitness to race. Yunick knew he had one big advantage over his major competitors, however, and that was the overall light weight of the Chevy, especially in comparison with the heavy Chryslers. Yunick sent Rose on a mission to "travel the world and find me a good tire." Rose discovered 175 tires manufactured by Firestone for the 24 Hours of Le Mans sports car race in France but discarded as a failed experiment in an Akron, Ohio, junkyard. Rose bought all 175 tires for $1.00 a piece and hauled them to Yunick's shop in Daytona Beach. When Thomas tested and qualified the car at Darlington, it soon became apparent that, despite the long odds coming in, Yunick, Thomas, the superhard Firestone tires, and the '55 Chevy were going to be contenders.[35]

When Carl Kiekhaefer noticed the durable tires on Yunick's car, he approached Firestone officials and demanded that they sell him some. The officials did not even know the tires existed, since they were the product of a seemingly failed experiment, and the company had no more in stock. Kiekhaefer then accosted Bill France and demanded that he either make Yunick sell him tires or disallow them. When France threatened to "outlaw" the tires if Yunick did not sell some to his competitors, Yunick responded, "Bill, you're sitting here with you[r] fishing pole and the hook is in Chevy's mouth. Your [sic] waiting for them to swallow the hook. That will probably come race day. You know me well enough to know if you go through with your threat, I and the race car will be in Daytona in eight hours." France backed down.[36]

The battle with Kiekhaefer further stoked Yunick's competitive fires, and he became even more determined to win the Darlington race. Smokey already "intensely disliked" Kiekhaefer and believed the Mercury Outboard team received preferential treatment from NASCAR. "He [Kiekhaefer] drove into NASCAR with money out the ass so NASCAR was playing 'We love Chrysler' at the time." Later, to express his feelings for Kiekhaefer, Yunick placed a framed photograph of his rival in his race shop—over the toilet.[37]

The race itself proved almost anticlimactic and a virtual repeat of the first Southern 500 when Johnny Mantz won going away in a lightweight Plymouth when all his competitors repeatedly blew their tires. Thomas won the race by more than a lap and never had to push the car. While the Thomas-Yunick win thrilled Cole, Duntov, and other Chevy brass, the fact that the '55 Chevys had taken seven of the top ten positions made them even more ecstatic. The best Kiekhaefer's team could do was Tim Flock's third place. The Mercury Outboard team owner was further frustrated by the fact that Flock had consistently outrun his competitors on the track but spent considerable time in the pits replacing blown tires.[38]

The success of the Chevys had indeed "set the hook" and sparked a major investment by Ed Cole in racing and a huge jump in the number of NASCAR drivers running Chevys. Chevrolet's advertising agency immediately began aggressively promoting its "race-proven V8s." By the end of the 1955 Grand National season, fifteen drivers competed in Chevys on the circuit. Cole also signed Yunick to a $10,000 contract to prepare two cars for an attempt at the twenty-four-hour speed record and the closed-course stock car speed record at Darlington. At the start of 1956, Yunick became head of the Chevy racing effort, operating out of his Daytona Beach "Best Damn Garage in Town," for $1,000 a month plus expenses, and Chevy moved into racing in a major way.[39]

Ford, Bootleggers, and Purple "Wild Hogs"

Kiekhaefer's dominance of NASCAR—with all the free publicity going to Chrysler—and Chevy's success in both racing and cutting into the youth market also made Ford executives sit up and notice. "Ford executives—from the youngest trainees up to President Henry Ford II—were tired of seeing Chrysler Corporation bask in the glory and reap the benefits of Kiekhaefer's nearly unbeatable NASCAR teams," Tom Cotter and Al Pearce observed.[40] In addition, as historian of Ford racing Leo Levine noted, "The fact that the country's largest automaker [General Motors] was now bucking their product with a V8-engined model had been the first big shock for Ford. When Chevy started racing this car, it became too much to bear."[41] Ford general manager Robert McNamara sat down with his engineers to come up with a plan to challenge both Kiekhaefer and Chevy. They decided to place the effort "outside the company" and contracted with 1925 Indianapolis 500 winner Pete DePaolo to start a factory-backed Ford stock car team. The effort got off the ground slowly as DePaolo based his efforts in Long Beach, California, near the shop of his friend Bill Stroppe, who ran the Lincoln-Mercury team competing in the United States Automobile Club (USAC—the sanctioning body that succeeded the AAA) stock car series. Stroppe had headed the successful Lincoln effort in the Carrera Panamericana that had so angered Carl Kiekhaefer in 1952.[42] However, USAC stock car racing and the California stock scene were far too low profile for what Ford wanted for its money, and the draw of the big race at Darlington and all the attendant publicity that came with victory in the Southern 500 began to draw Ford south.

An additional push to enter Ford factory-sponsored cars at Darlington came from Bill Benton, field service manager for the Charlotte area. Benton had long believed in the sales value of supporting stock car racing in the region and secretly helped some local Ford dealers "outfit a few cars for races."[43] As Kiekhaefer dominated Grand National racing and as Chevrolet geared up its racing effort in the spring of 1955, Benton made a trip to Dearborn, Michigan, to talk to Ford engineering and marketing executives. In order to explain the technical side of stock car racing to the engineers, Benton took longtime liquor runner, racer, and master mechanic Buddy Shuman. Shuman, who strolled into the prime habitat of men in "gray flannel suit[s]" wearing a loud shirt—no suit, no tie—and talking to highly educated engineers in a Carolina Piedmont twang, made many of the Ford executives wonder what they were getting into.[44]

Despite the culture shock, Ford executives decided to field two cars for Darlington and ordered DePaolo to prepare them in the Long Beach shop and ship them to Charlotte for final tuning. DePaolo shipped the cars to Charlotte and placed them in the care of Schwam Motors—listed sponsor of the car—a local Ford dealership owned by an eccentric showman named Charlie Schwam. Schwam had the cars painted purple, added cartoon pigs to the sides, and named them "Schwam's Wild Hogs." Benton soon saw that while the cars would attract a lot of attention with their paint jobs, they trailed the Chryslers and the Chevys significantly in performance. When the Ford engineers and Schwam mechanics assigned to prepare the car couldn't get the cars up to speed, Benton brought in Shuman to get them going. Shuman overcame the skepticism of the Ford engineers and worked day and night to prepare the cars for Darlington qualifying.[45]

In addition to having the two most colorful cars in the race, Ford secured the services of the two most colorful drivers in NASCAR racing, perhaps in NASCAR history: Curtis Turner and Joe Weatherly. By 1955, Turner was already a NASCAR legend as a result of both his aggressive driving and risk taking on the track and his even more outlandish lifestyle off the track. The flamboyant Virginian flew around the Southeast in his own plane alternately making timber deals worth millions of dollars, driving in stock car races for whoever would take the risk to offer him their car, promoting stock car races, and always hosting the loudest, most liquor-soaked, lewdest, and longest-lasting parties that anyone had ever seen. In the early 1950s, Turner and Weatherly forged a firm and fast friendship based on their mutual love of immediate fun. Weatherly—often known as the "Clown Prince of Racing"—provided a sharp contrast to Turner in appearance: 5'8" to Turner's 6'4", Hawaiian shirts and saddle oxfords to Turner's silk suits and handmade shoes, round face with a pug nose to Turner's rugged good looks. But when it came to partying, they were perfectly matched, and wherever they went, there was going to be a party. The highlight of each year came with Daytona Speed Weeks, when the pair, along with Virginia racing promoter and track owner Paul Sawyer, rented out a three-bedroom house in Daytona Beach for a month and reportedly spent $1,000 a day stocking it with food, liquor, and other party supplies. Weatherly regularly used a vase for a drinking glass, entertained guests with his constant practical jokes, and was usually accompanied by his girlfriend, whom he nicknamed "Short Track."[46]

While the two had no peers when it came to partying, they were also probably the two most talented drivers in NASCAR racing. Weatherly in some ways was probably an even better driver than Turner because he knew—although he and Turner often traded "pops" on the track—how to finish a race with the car relatively intact. Indeed, Carl Kiekhaefer recognized Weatherly's talent and tried to hire him. Weatherly responded to Kiekhaefer's overture by responding, "I can't drive for you. I just can't take the bed checks."[47] But Turner and Weatherly found a great match with Ford, whose money financed an even greater level of partying, and the two wild men soon became the face of Ford racing in the Southeast driving Charlie Schwam's purple "Wild Hogs."

When Labor Day came around, Turner and Weatherly, in their Shuman-prepared "Wild Hogs," were ready to show the world what Ford had to offer. While qualifying proved a bit of a disappointment to Ford—Weatherly started seventh and Turner fifteenth, well off the pace of the top Buicks, Oldsmobiles, Chevys, and Chryslers—both drivers made their typical dash for the lead early in the race. Turner led a number of laps until he broke a tie rod and hit the wall. Weatherly put on a show for the crowd, battling Herb Thomas's Chevy door to door and leading 129 straight laps, until he also had a front suspension failure, which sent him into the wall and ended his and the "Wild Hogs'" day.[48] The finish proved a definite disappointment for Ford, but those laps in the lead, the publicity generated by Turner, Weatherly, and the "Wild Hogs," and the fanfare and sales promotion the '55 Chevys received with Thomas's victory convinced the brass at Dearborn to make an even greater commitment to NASCAR racing.

Although Ford began to invest significant dollars in racing in the

Curtis Turner takes the green flag to start a timed speed run on Daytona Beach in one of Charlie Schwam's purple Ford "Wild Hogs." (Courtesy of McCaig-Welborn Research Library at the International Motorsports Hall of Fame, Talladega, Alabama)

aftermath of Darlington, the effort got off to a somewhat shaky start. As historian Leo Levine observed, not only was Ford "involved with an entirely new form of sales promotion and image building, but they were also dealing with a totally unfamiliar type of person." Ford found out how "unfamiliar" these people were when they hired Buddy Shuman full-time and their Industrial Relations Division (IRD) ran a routine background check. IRD investigators quickly called Ford chief engineer Bill Burnett to inform him of Shuman's long police record and time spent on a chain gang—mostly for violations related to illegal liquor. Burnett "cut him off in a hurry" and responded, "As far as I know, he's doing a good job for us, we're getting along fine with him, and we don't intend to throw him out." Unfortunately, Shuman's career heading Ford's NASCAR effort—even as it began to bear fruit—ended tragically. The night before a race at the Hickory Speedway in November 1955, he fell asleep with a lit cigarette in his hand and died of smoke inhalation in the resulting fire.[49]

1956—A Battle of Titans

When the 1956 season rolled around, the intense competition between Chevy, Ford, and Carl Kiekhaefer's Chryslers sparked excitement and anticipation. All three teams invested millions of dollars in their Grand National efforts. The beginning of the NASCAR season at Daytona interested Ford and Chevy not only in the Grand National race but in gaining bragging rights through the performance of their cars in the Daytona Beach Speed Trials—now renamed the NASCAR International Safety and Speed Trials. Headlines in *National Speed Sport News* blared, "Ford-Chevrolet in Beach Battle," and the article continued, "Both groups are out to win and they mean business, because there is a great deal of product prestige at stake."[50]

Although Ford and Chevy received all the pre–Speed Weeks press, it became apparent immediately that Carl Kiekhaefer was not going away. Kiekhaefer had made his career taking on large corporations and defeating them in head-to-head competition, and Ford and Chevy's entry into NASCAR only increased his passion to win. Kiekhaefer especially thrilled at the thought of whipping Ford, whose alleged cheating in the Carrera Panamericana had cost him a victory in the prestigious race. While both Ford and Chevy claimed victory in the speed trials—as did practically every other make—the 1956 Daytona Grand National race was once again a Tim Flock–Carl Kiekhaefer show.[51]

Early in the 1956 season, the Kiekhaefer machine became even more successful, winning thirty out of fifty-six Grand National races—including an incredible sixteen straight between March 25 and June 3. Buck Baker won the second straight championship for Kiekhaefer, who hired the tough former liquor hauler/bus driver in January when he called him up and queried, "If you are as big a son-of-a-bitch as everybody says you are, I'm curious. Would you like to drive for me?"[52] Baker won fourteen races and $28,815 driving for Kiekhaefer and later fondly remembered the experience: "Mr. Kiekhaefer brought us [NASCAR] from the kitchen to the dining room."[53]

Even as Kiekhaefer's team dominated the first half of the 1956 season, however, things began to go sour for both the operation and the Mercury outboard-motor manufacturer. Indeed, even as his team wrapped up one of the closest points championships in NASCAR history, Kiekhaefer prepared to disband his team and wash his hands of the NASCAR experience. The first sign of trouble came on April 8 after Tim Flock won a Grand National race at North Wilkesboro, his third of the young season. Kiekhaefer invited Flock to come to his hotel room to celebrate with a steak dinner. Flock showed up at the door of Kiekhaefer's room but refused to go in. He told his boss, "That was the last race I'm ever going to run for you." The pressure to win combined with a history of ulcers proved just too much, and Flock—who had been discharged from the army in World War II because of a peptic ulcer—had gone down to 130 pounds and "was throwing up blood" before every race. "I won twenty-three races for that man, but he wasn't satisfied," Flock later recalled. "He wanted to win *every* race."[54]

The Mercury Outboard team's sixteen-race winning streak also began to create resentment among fans, who increasingly booed wins by Kiekhaefer's drivers. As Hank Schoolfield reported, "Fans write indignant letters to promoters such as one which said tersely: 'I'm never going to another race until something is done about Kiekhaefer.'"[55] The team's dominance proved problematic for promoters and for Bill France, who could not sell tickets to a Mercury Outboard team parade, and for Kiekhaefer and his company, since the negative publicity had an adverse affect on its bottom line.

In response to the pressure both from Kiekhaefer's competitors—who regularly claimed that NASCAR "arbitrarily modified and interpreted the rules to favor the Kiekhaefer team"—and from the fans, NASCAR put Kiekhaefer's cars under unprecedented scrutiny.[56] In fact, Kiekhaefer's success prompted the invocation of an unspoken rule still in force in NASCAR today. As author Tom Jensen observed, "Win too much, and your cars will be virtually dismantled in post-race tech inspection." NASCAR never found any evidence that Kiekhaefer or his mechanics cheated. Bill France later admitted, "Not once were we able to find any of Carl's cars illegal, and brother did we try."[57]

Kiekhaefer's frustration only increased as the factory-supported teams became better organized and the millions the manufacturers invested in racing began to pay dividends. Between June 10 and October 7, the Mercury Outboard team won only five of twenty-seven races. While such a record would have thrilled most car owners, Kiekhaefer began to look for reasons for his team's substandard performance. He soon discovered the problem in the preferential treatment he believed the factory teams received from Bill France and NASCAR. Kiekhaefer asserted that in order to bring even more Detroit money into NASCAR, officials regularly bent the rules to favor the manufacturers. He became especially incensed when NASCAR allowed the Ford teams to custom-build heavy-duty spindles, as their stock spindles regularly broke, making "flying wheels a not uncommon sight in NASCAR races." With the modification allowed—Bill France defended the move as a needed safety measure—the Fords started winning regularly. France's decision sent Kiekhaefer over the edge, reminding him of the unpleasant experience of the Carrera Panamericana, when officials turned a blind eye to modifications made by Bill Stroppe to the factory-backed Lincolns.[58] As Jeffrey Rodengen observed, "For Carl, virtually every race now entailed bitter arguments with NASCAR officials."[59] Bill France dismissed Kiekhaefer's complaints to reporter Hank Schoolfield: "Carl is a dynamic, energetic man, one who 'needs' to have problems to overcome and when problems don't exist, he'll make them."[60]

Ford products won seventeen of twenty-seven races during this period, including eight in a row. While the money pouring in from Detroit helped a great deal, DePaolo's Fords improved greatly when he hired John Holman to head Ford's Charlotte racing shop in May 1956. Ironically, the Holman hiring effectively ended the NASCAR career of the man who had probably wrenched more Fords to stock car racing victories than anyone else in history: flat-head Ford V-8 pioneer and legend Red Vogt, who had been hired to replace Shuman. Holman, who learned the ropes with such California high-performance greats as Vic Edelbrock, Dean Moon, and Bill Stroppe, was almost as intense, competitive, and detail-oriented as Carl Kiekhaefer, or Red Vogt in his prime. Howard DeHart, who worked for Holman, recalled, "Second place wasn't anything for John Holman. Most of the time he was at the shop seven days a week—more than anyone else. He'd eat twice as much as anyone else, then not eat for two days because he had something more to do." His partnering with driver/mechanic Ralph Moody—a pair of polar opposites—almost immediately put Ford in the winner's circle and began one of the most successful collaborations in NASCAR history. Ford lined up a number of talented drivers to pilot its cars, including Moody, who had four wins; Fireball Roberts, who won five times; and Californian Marvin Panch. Ford also resigned Curtis Turner and Joe Weatherly, who dominated the new NASCAR Convertible Series. Perhaps most important for both the public and Ford brass, Curtis Turner won the 1956 Southern 500 in one of Charlie Schwam's purple "Wild Hogs."[61]

Ford's success made Kiekhaefer even more blindly determined to win, and the hotly contested battle for the Grand National points champion-ship between Kiekhaefer's top driver, Buck Baker, and Chevy driver Herb Thomas further fueled Kiekhaefer's competitive fire. Thomas had driven for the Mercury Outboard team—and won three races—from late April to late July but had defected, in Kiekhaefer's view, to race a Chevrolet on his own. In perhaps his most controversial move as an owner, Kiekhaefer rented out the Cleveland County Fairgrounds near Shelby, North Caro-lina, and demanded that Bill France add an additional October race to the schedule. The new race gave Baker an opportunity to narrow the lead that Thomas held in the points race. NASCAR did not even publicize the race to drivers and teams until ten days before the race date.[62]

Kiekhaefer's move became even more controversial when Herb Thomas passed Mercury Outboard driver Speedy Thompson on lap 109 of the 200-lap event. Thompson hit Thomas in the right rear quarter panel, sending him into the fence and flipping down the track, where he was broadsided by Jack Smith. The car then came to a rest in the racing groove, where five onrushing cars, their drivers blinded by the dust stirred up by the acci-dent, demolished the Chevy. Emergency workers took Thomas from the track to the hospital in a coma with "severe head injuries which included a possible fractured skull, a badly lacerated scalp and a ruptured ear drum." People immediately assumed that Kiekhaefer had issued "team orders" to Speedy Thompson to take Thomas out of the race so Baker could win. Indeed, his seventeenth-place finish cut Thomas's points lead to ninety-eight points, and the severity of the accident meant that he would miss the last three races of the year and virtually assured that Baker would win the championship. While he announced over the public address system after the race that "he would not compete" if Herb Thomas could not race, Baker drove his Kiekhaefer Chrysler in the final three races, winning the finale at Wilson, North Carolina, and the championship by 704 points.[63]

The hostility of both fans and competitors to an effort designed—at least ostensibly—to increase sales of Mercury outboards, Kiekhaefer's frustration with NASCAR and Bill France's seemingly capricious and un-fair decisions, and Kiekhaefer's perception that, once again, the manufac-turers cheated to get ahead convinced him to shut down his racing opera-tion at the end of 1956. Kiekhaefer concluded, "We just cannot afford to have our name [both his and Mercury's] further associated with racing." He never spoke to the press but quietly dismantled his team and released his drivers even as speculation ran rampant that the Mercury Outboard Chryslers would line up for the green flag at Daytona Beach in 1957. In

May 1957, Kiekhaefer reflected on his NASCAR career in a letter to a friend that he never mailed but biographer Jeffrey Rodengen discovered in the car owner's files years later. He started off lightly dismissing his NASCAR experience: "It is a low-brow business not without its humorous aspects." But then he got to the heart of his frustration, NASCAR's capriciousness and Detroit's domination. "I believe any sport must be covered by a fixed set of rules, rules that are not constantly revised, ignored, misinterpreted and are not altered by bulletins. . . . Commercialism and sports just don't mix. I can't help but feel indignant about this sport that grew by itself to considerable proportion, only to be raped by Detroit."[64] Kiekhaefer went out as unobtrusively as he had first appeared at Daytona Beach in 1955, but he had shown NASCAR fans, drivers, and car owners a new world, one not fully realized in the sport until at least the late 1980s. For the immediate future, however, his chief legacy was the huge investment, for better or for worse, in Grand National racing made by Detroit.

The Factory Party Begins

By the time the Daytona beach/road race rolled around in February 1957, the factories had come in with a vengeance. In addition to the three factory-backed garages in the field during the 1956 season—the Pete DePaolo–John Holman Ford operation, Bill Stroppe's Mercury team, and Smokey Yunick's Chevy shop—Pontiac, Oldsmobile, and Plymouth all entered the fray. Semon E. "Bunky" Knudsen, president of Pontiac, sought to use performance to move his make from the bottom of the GM sales list and hired longtime Indiana racer Ray Nichels to head his team with drivers Cotton Owens and Banjo Matthews. Oldsmobile wooed Lee Petty and his Petty Engineering team away from Chrysler—which had given him little in the way of support, financial or otherwise—with free cars and parts support. Plymouth had a one-car operation with Ankrum "Spook" Crawford preparing the cars and Johnny Allen driving. Chevrolet also dramatically upped the ante in its effort and created Southern Engineering and Development (SEDCO), headed by Frank Del Roy and based out of Hugh Babb's Chevrolet dealership in Atlanta. Smokey Yunick still prepared all the Chevy engines in his Daytona shop but shipped them to Atlanta, where SEDCO mechanics installed them in the bodies and gave them free of charge to drivers Paul Goldsmith, Jack Smith, and Bob Welborn.[65]

The investment by the manufacturers was unprecedented, even considering Carl Kiekhaefer's sizable outlay of the previous two years, and changed the economics of the sport dramatically. *National Speed Sport News* estimated in May 1957 that Chevrolet had increased its financial commitment to racing from $385,000 in 1956 to a budget of $2.6 million in 1957.[66] In perhaps the most dramatic and unprecedented deal of the new factory era, in March 1957 Pete DePaolo wooed Smokey Yunick away from Chevy for "40 grand a year, a free million dollar life insurance policy, free medical and dental . . . and get this, they buy me an airplane, and give Thunderbirds to Paul Goldsmith and I." The deal also provided Yunick's shop with free Ford trucks and station wagons, dynamometers and other advanced shop equipment, and an expense account. "It didn't make a damn what I charged, they paid it." Ford even paid the expenses for Yunick's shapely, young "traveling secretary."[67] Except for the Kiekhaefer drivers, no one in NASCAR had seen such money, and the top racers who benefited from the factory largesse—like Goldsmith, Curtis Turner, Joe Weatherly, Jack Smith, Cotton Owens, Fonty and Tim Flock, Buck Baker, Speedy Thompson, Marvin Panch, Lee Petty, Bob Welborn, and Fireball Roberts, men who had generally lived hand to mouth to pursue their passion for racing—could not believe their luck. At Daytona during Speed Weeks the factory-backed liquor flowed like a river, and the parties seemed as if they would never end. Life changed even for the nonpartiers. As Richard Petty recalled, after his father made his deal with Oldsmobile, "I would have been willing to bet, at that stage, that we would never have to sleep in the car again."[68]

Determined to reap the benefits of their investment in racing, the Detroit manufacturers launched a frenzy of racing-related advertising. The chief initial beneficiary of all the racing publicity was Pontiac, as Cotton Owens shocked everyone by winning the Daytona beach/road race at a record pace. To show the new significance to their marketing plans, most of the chief executives at the major manufacturers—including Pontiac's Bunky Knudsen—came to Daytona to watch their cars compete in the speed trials, the Convertible Series race, and the Grand National race and to join in the partying. Interviewed after Owens's victory, Knudsen made a somewhat subdued response: "I'm happy, somewhat surprised and proud."[69] But Knudsen had to be ecstatic when, as *National Speed Sport News* reported, "sales figures for Pontiac were revised sharply upward after one of its cars won a single victory at Daytona Beach."[70] To follow up on the Owens-Pontiac victory at Daytona, the sales force unveiled a major "drive the champ" campaign in which they gave away a hundred new Pontiacs.[71]

Just because Pontiac won the first major race of the season did not mean, however, that the other manufacturers were left out in the cold. Mercury touted Tim Flock's victory in the convertible race, and almost every other manufacturer made some claim to the superiority of its marque in one of the many divisions of the speed trials. An article in *National Speed Sport News* asserted, "After the Daytona Beach stock car speed tests last winter, the claims of Ford, Mercury, Chevrolet and Pontiac made it seem they'd all won and that NASCAR, the sponsoring organization, had said so."[72] NASCAR tried to dampen some of the wilder claims of inventive advertising executives by issuing a "Pure Advertising Law" that tried to keep the manufacturers from falsely claiming "official NASCAR records" for their cars. The manufacturers virtually ignored the "law," and NASCAR could not slow the "advertising race" even when it slapped Ford on the wrist for exaggerating its cars' performance in the convertible race by taking away all its manufacturer's points won in that event.[73]

Despite the difficulties of reining in and appeasing Detroit, Bill France and NASCAR took off on an unprecedented roll in the early months of 1957. NASCAR had no significant stock car competitor sanctioning bodies challenging its dominance of the sport, and it had the relatively undivided attention of the auto manufacturers and of the racing world. Other than the Indianapolis 500, NASCAR races in the mid-1950s on the beach at Daytona, at Darlington Raceway, in Pennsylvania at Langhorne Speedway, at Martinsville Speedway, and even at the new track in Lehi, Arkansas—just across the Mississippi River from Memphis—attracted the largest auto racing crowds in the country and some of the largest crowds in the entire American sports and entertainment world. In 1956, the Southern 500 at Darlington drew an estimated crowd of 70,000 fans, placing it second only to Indianapolis in the auto racing world.[74] The attention generated by NASCAR also brought many of the best drivers in the country to the sanctioning body. While drivers born and raised in the South—most former (or in the case of Junior Johnson, current) liquor haulers—dominated the top ranks, by 1957 drivers like Marvin Panch and Eddie Pagan from California, Paul Goldsmith from Michigan, DeWayne "Tiny" Lund from Iowa, and Bill Amick from Oregon challenged the Piedmont boys for race victories and factory sponsorship.[75]

For Bill France the change was dramatic as well. Instead of cultivating financial support from illegal liquor kingpins in the Piedmont or East Coast racing promoters, he now regularly hobnobbed with chief executives in the inner sanctums of America's, and the world's, wealthiest and most powerful corporations. France flew often to Detroit to meet with top executives like Ed Cole of Chevrolet, Bunky Knudsen of Pontiac, and Jacques Passino at Ford.[76] At the 1957 Daytona Beach Grand National race, France hosted probably the most influential individual in Detroit in the 1950s—Harley Earl, the head of General Motors' Styling section and father of the tail fin and many other styling innovations. France honored Earl by naming the trophy for the February Daytona Grand National race the Harley J. Earl Perpetual Challenge Award. The trophy was a replica of one of Earl's most innovative designs, the GM Firebird I.[77] Indeed, the press attention the Daytona events garnered was unprecedented for NASCAR as reporters from the Associated Press, United Press International, *Sports Illustrated*, *Life* magazine, the *New York Times*, and *Motor Trend* flocked to the beach. France's one-time dream of gaining the power and influence over auto racing that Ralph Hankinson possessed in the 1930s and early 1940s had in many ways come true and had even been surpassed.

The Convertible Series: Gangbusters, or Davy Crockett

Further solidifying NASCAR's and France's position was the wild success of the NASCAR Convertible Series, which France acquired in 1956. Convertible racing was the brainchild of H. E. Redkey of the Midwest Association for Race Cars in 1955. Organized under the banner of the Circuit of Champions All-Stars (CCAS), the races featured 1955 convertibles and drew enthusiastic crowds to events primarily held at speedways in the Midwest. Bill France recognized the potential of such a series and promoted a CCAS event in June 1955 at Bowman Gray Stadium to popular acclaim.[78] In July, *National Speed Sport News* featured a story on the new series headlined "Convertible Rage Sweeping Country." The story enthused, "America is being treated to a new racing sport. And it's going like gangbusters . . . or Davy Crockett."[79] Bill France saw a real opportunity to further boost NASCAR and in December 1955 announced a merger with—actually a takeover of—MARC and its Circuit of Champions convertibles, renamed the Society of Auto Sports, Fellowship and Education (SAFE), in mid-1955. The beach races at Daytona now featured a NASCAR-sanctioned convertible event in addition to its usual Grand National and Modified Series races and its speed trials. The NASCAR season also included a National Convertible Championship Circuit with its own points championship.[80]

NASCAR's Convertible Circuit became an immediate hit with the fans and soon drew numbers as large as most Grand National races did.

The "Gold Dust Twins," Joe Weatherly (#12) and Curtis Turner (#26), battle it out in a NASCAR Convertible Series race at McCormick Field in Asheville, North Carolina. (Courtesy of Don Hunter Collection, Smyle Media)

The series got off to a great start at Daytona with the flamboyant Curtis Turner—"probably the most sensational performer ever to appear on the famous 4.1 mile beach and road course"—winning the first race in a Pete DePaolo Ford ragtop.[81] Regular appearances by Turner and his sidekick Joe Weatherly driving the factory Fords further boosted the popularity of the Convertible Series. The pair became so dominant, especially in the second half of the season, that many races turned into "some high speed game of tag" for the pair. Humpy Wheeler observed, "They'd let each other pass the other quite a few times, but when it came down to the last couple of laps, it was no holds barred. It was hilarious to watch them in the convertibles."[82] Although neither won a championship in the division, in the seventy-eight Convertible Series races in 1956 and 1957 they dominated the winning, with Turner taking the checkered flag in thirty-three races and Weatherly nine.[83] Members of the press soon tagged the pair with the nickname the "Gold Dust Twins."[84]

By 1957, the convertibles had become so popular that Darlington Raceway general manager Bob Colvin decided to create a spring Convertible

Series race—the Rebel 300—to complement its Southern 500. The inaugural race, despite a day's rain delay, attracted a crowd of 17,000 to see Fireball Roberts win in a factory-backed Ford. Over the next two years of the Convertible Series' existence, the Rebel 300 became one of the most popular auto races in America.[85]

Safety, Not Speed

Even as Bill France and NASCAR enjoyed its day in the sun, storm clouds gathered on the horizon. For many people, the full-scale entry of the factories into NASCAR changed the essential character of the series, making it virtually impossible for those without factory ties to succeed. At the 1957 Daytona beach/road race, Glen Wood was the first independent finisher at eleventh place, a result that became increasingly common throughout the season.[86] Even individuals who benefited from the factory system thought that it unfairly disadvantaged independents and talented, but undiscovered, young men trying to break into NASCAR's top ranks. As Smokey Yunick recalled, in his inimitable manner, "This team shit is busting up the poor racers and new comers. They ain't got a prayer. It was really wrong."[87] Even Carl Kiekhaefer, who shared a significant portion of the credit/blame for the changes in NASCAR, lamented NASCAR's transformation as the factories became ever more involved. "NASCAR stock car racing was one thing when we entered but it was something entirely different when we left."[88]

The biggest challenge for NASCAR and Bill France, however, came from mounting public concerns for safety on both the highway and the speedway. Increasingly powerful automobiles; the construction of improved highways, including the new interstate system; and a youth culture addicted to thrills dramatically increased both speeds on the highways and deaths due to auto accidents. Smokey Yunick derided the decision by General Motors to build the "Black Widow," a "street-able" version of the Chevy race cars built in his Daytona Beach shop: "This car should have been sponsored by the 'Funeral Directors of the United States.' You guessed it, the rich kid's [sic] daddies bought 'em for junior. Two in the morning, junior's had three beers, got a car full of kids, he mashes the gas and starts a demonstration of his hi-speed driving skills and thrills. We still had a wrecker service at the shop. Man, that was bad shit."[89] Statistics from the National Highway Traffic Safety Administration revealed that the death rate per 100 million vehicle miles from 1950 to 1956 averaged above six—the current average is below two.[90] A number of high-profile deaths in speeding automobiles—most notable, the death of youth icon James Dean in September 1955—increased the concerns of parents and politicians.[91]

The ongoing and highly publicized deadly crashes at speedways in the United States and abroad in the mid-1950s heightened concerns. The carnage in the first half of 1955, especially, stirred people to action. At the NASCAR Sportsman-modified race at Daytona Beach in February, driver Al Briggs lost his life in a fiery crash. *National Speed Sport News* featured a number of pictures of the accident, which involved so many cars that the wreckage blocked the whole south end of the track. The publication included one picture of Briggs's charred wreck entitled "Funeral Pyre."[92] Tragedy struck again at the Indianapolis 500 when a chain-reaction accident killed open-wheel superstar and two-time defending Indy champion Bill Vukovich when his car was struck by another car, became airborne, cleared the backstretch wall, bounced wildly several times, landed upside down, and burst into flame.[93] The American racing world had lost its most visible and popular star, but Vukovich was only one of five "top name drivers" killed in racing during the first half of 1955.[94]

The death of Bill Vukovich was enough of a blow to the racing world, but the carnage in Le Mans, France, thirteen days later dealt a much more serious setback to auto racing's reputation and potential future. In another chain-reaction accident, Pierre Levegh's Mercedes flew over a dirt embankment intended to keep cars out of the crowd, bounced wildly toward a packed grandstand, exploded on landing, and showered spectators with engine and chassis parts and flaming fuel. *National Speed Sport News* described the aftermath: "Screams of pain and terror arose as fragments of the car rained down. Smoke and flame, fed by the nearly full fuel tank of the car, spread over a wide area. Panic-stricken spectators tried to fight their way through the crowd. For 100 yards along the track pieces of clothing and parts of bodies were scattered. Blood-stained spectators wandered along the barriers." The accident killed more than eighty people and injured hundreds of others. The international reaction was almost immediate as the French cabinet placed a temporary ban on all auto racing in the country while it drafted new safety regulations.[95] In addition, Swiss authorities canceled their Grand Prix, and the Mexican government canceled the Carrera Panamericana, an event that had resulted in the deaths of eighty-seven spectators in its five-year history.[96]

In the United States, while a host of observers lamented the auto racing deaths, the greatest challenge to the future of the sport came in August

when the AAA—citing the Le Mans tragedy and the death of Bill Vukovich—announced that at the end of the 1955 season it would "dissociate
itself completely from all forms of auto racing in the United States" and
disband its Contest Board. The major reason the AAA Executive Committee gave for its decision was "that automobile racing as now conducted in
this country, with emphasis on speed, power and human endurance is not
compatible with one of the main objectives of the AAA and its affiliated
clubs in the day-to-day promotion of street and highway safety."[97]

The AAA decision shocked the American racing world. Jep Cadou,
sports editor for the *Indianapolis Star*, characterized the AAA's action as
"cowardly and unreasoning" and "a vicious and unwarranted slap at a
group of men who have given their time and energy generously to the
sport through the 54 years of the board's existence." Opinions varied as to
the potential impact of the AAA's withdrawal. Some asserted that it would
have little impact and that another body would step up and take the AAA's
place—indeed, USAC would soon take up its sanctioning mantle. Others
saw these tragedies as a serious wake-up call for auto racing to change its
approach to safety.[98] Promoter Red Crise, in an article in *National Speed
Sport News* entitled "Is Auto Racing Headed for Oblivion," called on auto
racing to clean up its act and improve its safety standards. He warned
that if the profession did not police itself and improve its safety record,
the racing fans, drivers, and promoters "should be content to sit around a
hot stove in years to come and reminisce about the great old days of automobile racing in the U.S.A. For it could very well vanish in ever-changing
times."[99]

While the AAA's move had no direct impact on NASCAR, Bill France
and other leaders became much more safety-conscious, at least from a
public relations perspective. As early as January 1955, NASCAR touted the
safety features it had mandated in its Grand National Series, including
roll bars, the bolting shut of doors, and the moving of fuel tanks and fuel
lines to lessen the likelihood of fires in rear-end collisions.[100] The biggest
change for NASCAR, however, was one of semantics, particularly the ever
evolving name given to the Daytona Beach Speed Trials. In 1956—in the
aftermath of Le Mans and the AAA's exit from racing—NASCAR changed
the name from the NASCAR Speed Trials to the NASCAR International
Safety and Speed Trials.[101] The next year, the sanctioning body took the
word "speed" out of the title altogether, and the events became known as
the International Safety and Performance Trials and Races. In his explanation, Bill France—in his own inimitable spin on the name change—

downplayed both speed and the competitive aspects of the events and highlighted them as a place that provided Detroit manufacturers with a laboratory to test and improve safety innovations: "The rather involved title means just what it implies—safety first, then performance. As every follower knows, the Daytona events are proving grounds for performance which makes the every day family car a safer and more pleasant vehicle to drive. Keen eyed technicians are not at Daytona for a certain particular glory—although all like to win—but to make a better selling product. And a better selling product means a safer and better performing car for Mr. and Mrs. America."[102]

Although France and NASCAR talked safety, serious accidents and even deaths continued to be common in NASCAR-sanctioned races. Indeed, for all the talk of safety features, unclear standards and lax enforcement led to little safety improvement on the track or even in the stands. In 1955 and 1956, in addition to Herb Thomas's serious accident at Shelby, four drivers lost their lives in NASCAR races. Al Briggs died in a fiery crash at the Daytona Beach Sportsman-modified race in February 1955, John McVitty died in April 1956 attempting to qualify for the Grand National race at Langhorne, and Clint McHugh and Cotton Priddy died in accidents at the inaugural Grand National race at the Lehi, Arkansas, track in June 1956.[103] The injuries were not limited to the track, however. In an incident that produced far too many comparisons to Le Mans, Billy Myers's car went into the stands at a Grand National race at Martinsville in May 1957, seriously injuring a number of spectators, among them an eight-year-old boy who had to be transported to Roanoke General Hospital for brain surgery.[104]

The Factory Party Ends

In 1957, at least partially as a result of these concerns over safety, even as Bill France and NASCAR rode the crest of factory support, the wave crashed down upon them, and Detroit's money and attention disappeared as quickly as they had appeared. At its June 1957 meeting the board of directors of the Automobile Manufacturers Association (AMA) shocked the NASCAR world when it issued a ban on its members—all the Detroit automakers—"participating in or engaging in any public contest, competition event or test of passenger cars involving or suggesting racing or speed." The ban, first introduced by GM president Harlow "Red" Curtice, included provisions forbidding any sort of factory financial, engineering, or public relations support for speed trials or racing and even forbade the donation of pace cars and the advertising of "the actual or comparable capabilities of passengers for speed, or the specific engine size, torque, horsepower, or ability to accelerate or perform in contest[s] that suggest speed." The AMA defended the ban based on "the growing public interest in increasing the safety of highway travel" and the automobile manufacturers' previous "unwarranted emphasis on characteristics which are associated with racing activities rather than passenger transportation."[105]

While the AMA spoke of its interest in safety, Ford racing historian Leo Levine pointed to other factors, including the growing pressure on engineers to produce high-quality, high-performance vehicles and Chevrolet, which had by far the best high-performance engine and wanted to call a "cease fire after it had won the war." Levine asserted that the engineers, who had become accustomed to their cars being "subjected to no more abuse than Aunt Mimi turning 2,300 rpm on her way to market," now had "the monkey on their backs" to produce faster, better-handling, and more durable products "and they didn't like it." At the same time, the General Motors 1955, '56, and '57 model V-8s proved wildly successful, and their modest price made them even more popular, especially with the growing youth market. If Chevy could get the other manufacturers to back out of their high-performance programs, it—like Ford in the 1930s, '40s, and early '50s—would control the market with little competition.[106]

Whatever the reasons for the ban, the move set NASCAR back years with the loss of factory money and support. While some joked about it— "What will become of the Daytona Beach social schedule? Who'll buy the booze?"—the shock waves of the AMA's decision resonated throughout stock car racing. With the ink on the contract barely dry, Smokey Yunick's unprecedented deal with Ford evaporated—no more $40,000 a year, no more staff benefits, no more free equipment, no more paid "traveling secretary."[107] Although the Holman-Moody shop in Charlotte did benefit from the cheap sale of all of Ford's racing equipment to it, the shop started producing sink units for homes and roof racks for Winnebagos.[108] Top drivers had to go back to working on the cars, towing them to race tracks, and eating hotdogs at the track concession stand. NASCAR publicist Jack Senn spoke of the changes for top drivers: "Most of these hotshots are back working on their own cars and worrying with the rest instead of being flown in, handed their gloves, stepping into a finely-tuned automobile, then flying out again as soon as the prize money was collected."[109]

Bill France and NASCAR publicists tried to put a positive spin on the withdrawal of the factories. France declared that the factory ban "occasioned no particular stir at NASCAR" and that it would have "little or no effect." Indeed, it would be healthy for the sport, level the playing field, and "give a further boost to the 'little fellows' who figured on getting back into stock car racing with a real chance of winning."[110] Senn commented that the ban even benefited the top drivers, who were never "sincerely happy despite the money which often rolled in. They felt the lack of teamwork, the lack of comradeship. They never considered themselves 'bigshots' in the first place."[111]

Despite the brave face, however, the rest of 1957 turned into a near disaster for NASCAR in almost every way. In August, sports reporter Max Muhleman of the *Charlotte News* broke a story that NASCAR's biggest star, Curtis Turner, was going to start promoting races and racing in USAC open-wheel races, including the Indianapolis 500. France had angered Turner by fining him $50 for "rough riding" and wrecking a competitor at a race in Hickory. Turner refused to race again in NASCAR until the sanctioning body revoked the fine. Muhleman also reported that Paul Goldsmith and Smokey Yunick planned to leave NASCAR as well, and rumor had it that Buck Baker would join them. The article further asserted, "The decisions of Turner and Goldsmith to run for archrival sanctioning body USAC is the worst thing that could happen to NASCAR, as far as prestige is concerned."[112]

France had already lost one of his most talented and popular, up-and-coming young drivers in NASCAR, in late 1956 when federal authorities caught Junior Johnson firing up his daddy's still, convicted him for operating an illegal distillery, and sentenced him to two years at the federal penitentiary in Chillicothe, Ohio. In order to keep the popular Wilkes County bootlegger/race driver out of prison, France telegraphed his lawyer with "assurance" that he would secure a "test driving job" for Johnson from either Ford, Chevy, or Pontiac that paid "in excess of $10,000" if the judge would grant him probation instead of an active sentence. France's plea fell on deaf ears, however, and Johnson served eleven months and three days at the federal penitentiary before he returned to racing.[113] France could ill afford to lose any more top drivers at such a crossroads in the sport's history. He repaired successfully any damaged relations with these top drivers and mechanics—and Turner, Goldsmith, and Yunick remained in the NASCAR fold—but it was plain to see that his once iron authority over his drivers was being seriously challenged.

NASCAR's Losing Battle for Respectability

In the wake of the factory withdrawal in 1957, problems for France and NASCAR worsened at NASCAR's premier event, the Southern 500—its great opportunity to reverse much of the recent negative publicity. The race attracted another record crowd of more than 70,000, but a tragic accident marred the festivities on only the twenty-seventh lap. Fonty Flock tried to squeeze between two "amateur" drivers racing side by side down the backstretch, touched bumpers with one of the cars, spun out, and stalled in the racing groove. Bobby Myers hit Flock broadside, and Paul Goldsmith plowed into Flock's Pontiac as well. The crash tore the engine out of Myers's Petty Engineering Oldsmobile and sent him flipping down the track. Doctors pronounced Myers dead on arrival at a local hospital, and the accident left Flock and Goldsmith hospitalized with multiple injuries. While officials made no announcement of Myers's death at the track, someone lowered the Confederate Battle Flag flying in the infield to half-mast not long after the accident.[114]

An ugly series of incidents involving Curtis Turner, Joe Weatherly, and Lee Petty further tarnished NASCAR's reputation. While battling for the lead in the middle of the race, Turner and Petty made contact, sending Turner into the wall and ending his chances at defending his title. Car owner Smokey Yunick and Weatherly—sitting in the pits waiting on repairs to his car, which had been damaged in an earlier accident—both believed that Petty had intentionally wrecked Turner. Yunick made quick repairs to the car, and Weatherly jumped in and rejoined the race even though the car looked "like a bow-legged, cross-eyed, flying junkyard." Weatherly, unconcerned about his finish in the race or the attractiveness of his car, carefully watched for Lee Petty to come into view. On lap 282, Weatherly got his wish and revenge for Turner when he rammed Petty into the wall and out of the race.[115]

The incident resulted in a widely circulated, and highly entertaining, letter from Yunick to Bill France that further challenged the NASCAR president's authority. The Yunick letter opened with a "request that you look into/investigate the Curtis Turner crash at the 'Cotton Picker's 500.'" The sarcastic missive continued: "I did not see the accident, but Curtis Turner and about 200 other people told me that, during and after the combination Hell Driver's Thrill Show and part-time race, it appeared as though Lee Petty, America's favorite driver, had a hell of a dislike for black and gold Fords with 31s on them, and kind of crashed it into the fence." Yunick estimated he lost $12,000 to $20,000 in potential winnings as a result of accidents not of his own drivers' making and pointed out that this was about the fourth time something similar had happened. "So Bill, you can see why I seemed a little bit upset. Of course I realize I don't have any right to, but I guess I am not quite broadminded enough. A lot of people go to races to see the wrecks, and after all, we have to keep them happy. You sure have a swell guy in Lee." Yunick also facetiously complained that he now had to walk everywhere because he drove a black and gold Ford and, since the race, "any time I drive near an Oldsmobile [the make of Petty's car] the damn Ford runs into a ditch and stops."[116]

France and NASCAR also still faced real difficulties in making stock car racing a respectable pastime in the Piedmont South. Much of the stigma of the sport's connections to the illegal liquor business still clung to it, and many decried the poor example both drivers and the rowdy fans set for young people. At a March 1956 NASCAR Late Model Short Track event at Fayetteville, North Carolina, a "minor riot" broke out when "several hundred spectators" joined in on an argument between Bob Welborn and Herb Thomas over who wrecked whom. A crew member for Welborn rushed over and broke the windows in Thomas's car after the end of the race, and both crews jumped into the fray along with hundreds of fans. Once again, events forced Bill France to walk a tightrope. Many working-class fans reveled in such incidents and talked about them for years, but the forces of propriety in the region saw racetrack rowdiness as a reason to shun and, if necessary, ban the sport. In a sign that France thoroughly understood who was buying the majority of tickets to NASCAR races, however, he "temporarily suspended" both drivers, but neither missed a race.[117]

Similar incidents at local racetracks—one partly owned by Bill France—and concerns over Sunday racing led citizens of Orange County, North Carolina, in 1956 and 1957 to organize their own Anti-Racing Association. In 1956, the Reverend C. H. Reckard, a Presbyterian minister in Hillsborough, North Carolina, wrote in the local *News of Orange County*, "We have not done right by our children, we have allowed two racetracks to be constructed in our community, the least concern of which is the disruption of our Sundays and the worst a stimulation of our young people to excessive and daring driving and the exposing of them to public drinking and gambling." The "disruption of our Sundays" also became a major issue for many in the community. The Reverend W. I. Conway of the Gospel Baptist Tabernacle organized the Orange County Anti-Racing Association in 1956 to pressure the local board of commissioners to ban Sunday racing.[118] When the board failed to respond to its demand, Conway's Anti-Racing Association allied itself with North Orange Ministerial Association to take the issue to the North Carolina General Assembly. In March 1957, the groups petitioned the legislature to help maintain "the tradition of a peaceful and restful Sunday which has its roots in our spiritual heritage." With the sponsorship of state senator Edwin S. Lanier and Representative John W. Umstead, the state senate's Committee on Cities, Counties and Towns approved a bill prohibiting Sunday racing in Orange County. When the bill looked as if it would pass, the board of commissioners approved a law on its own that banned Sunday racing, set a minimum age of eighteen for race drivers, and forced speedway owners to purchase liability insurance. Although France tried to convince the Anti-Racing Association and the board of commissioners to compromise and "limit the races to specific Sundays during the year," the ban held.[119]

While not as public a problem as the withdrawal of factory sponsorship and ongoing bad press over safety issues, the Sunday ban in Orange County seriously threatened France's Piedmont racing empire, the heart and soul of his operation. Sunday was the one guaranteed day off for working-class NASCAR fans and therefore the most profitable day for NASCAR races, particularly its premier Grand National and Convertible series. The calendar contained only so many Monday holidays that race fans had off from work—the most important of them Labor Day, the date of Darlington's Southern 500.

France lost other key battles in the second half of 1957 that seriously challenged NASCAR's future. The Grand National race at the new Memphis-Arkansas Speedway at Lehi, Arkansas, in July turned into a huge debacle. The race flagman had to throw the caution flag twice, and drivers drove slowly around the track for a total of fifty-six minutes while speedway workers watered the track to put down the choking dust. Thousands of fans left in disgust before the end of the race. The track had opened with great fanfare in October 1954 and drew huge crowds for the first few races, but ongoing problems made the 1957 race its last, and the owners never opened for the 1958 season. France had lost a potentially lucrative new market in the mid-South region.[120] Jack Smith voiced the frustration of many drivers in the postfactory era when he announced after the Memphis race that he was retiring. After losing an engine while leading the race with only nine remaining laps, Smith announced, "I can't keep buying racing engines. I quit. I have run my last race." While Smith did race again—indeed, he was back after only six days winning a race at Hickory,

North Carolina—he voiced the frustrations of many drivers who found it increasingly difficult to make a living at racing, particularly now that they were solely dependent on prize winnings for income.[121]

An additional blow came to France when three of the greatest drivers in NASCAR history—Tim and Fonty Flock and Herb Thomas—retired from racing. Unlike Smith, who obviously lashed out in frustration, they meant it. Herb and Fonty never raced again, and Tim raced only a handful of times. In the aftermath of the deadly crash at Darlington, Fonty publicly announced his disgust with the current direction of NASCAR: "I'm sick of racing as it is today. It is run by promoters who are out for the almighty dollar and they couldn't care less for the welfare of the drivers."[122] Thomas decried the aggressive driving tactics used by other drivers in announcing his retirement: "Racing is no fun any more. It used to be that you drove to beat the other fellow by driving. Now it's too rough out there. It's dog-eat-dog."[123]

Back to the Future

Despite the public relations challenges of operating in the Piedmont, however, after the factory ban France and NASCAR sought to regroup and fell back on the sport's roots in white liquor and red clay. While at the peak of factory involvement in 1956, NASCAR held 40 percent of Grand National races outside the South. During the 1958 season, the Daytona organization sanctioned only 25 percent of such races outside NASCAR's traditional stronghold in the Southeast, with the vast majority held in the Piedmont South, particularly in the heart of NASCAR country, North Carolina.[124]

Indeed, the locations of NASCAR's biggest races of the 1958 season changed little from the beginning of the decade. The Southern 500 at Darlington remained the best-attended and most important event on the schedule. The next three most important events—the Daytona beach/road race and two races at Lakewood Speedway—took NASCAR back to its roots in the late 1930s. The Daytona race, won by Paul Goldsmith in a car prepared by Smokey Yunick, was the last held on the beach/road course and proved to be one of the most memorable. The race featured a late door-to-door battle between Goldsmith and Curtis Turner, driving a Ford for Holman-Moody. With nine laps left, Turner came up too fast on a lapped car, had to slam on his brakes, and spun the car into the water's edge. It appeared as if Goldsmith had the race locked up, but he lost his windshield wipers, was blinded by a sand-blasted windshield, and sped past the entrance to the north turn and up the beach. Goldsmith realized his error, made a U-turn, and drove back onto the course in time to narrowly beat Turner to the finish.[125] The Lakewood races—the first visit to the storied track by NASCAR in more than two years—fittingly highlighted the talents of two of NASCAR's greatest bootlegger drivers, Curtis Turner, who won the April race, and Junior Johnson, who won the season finale in October. Out of the ten next best-attended races, seven were held at tracks owned and promoted by the dependable bootlegger cartel of Enoch Staley, Clay Earles, Grafton Burgess, Charlie Combs, and Gene Sluder.[126]

France could also depend on his hard-charging drivers from the region to put on a show for the fans. The Gold Dust Twins, Curtis Turner and Joe Weatherly, kept the competition lively in the Convertible Series, and Turner won three Grand National races in 1958. The old liquor hauler Buck Baker won three races; up-and-coming superstar Glen "Fireball" Roberts, from Bill France's backyard in Daytona Beach, won six races, including the prestigious Southern 500; and the pride of Level Cross, North Carolina, Lee Petty, won seven races and his second points championship.[127]

For Piedmont fans, however, the return of Junior Johnson from his stint in federal prison ignited interest and most reflected NASCAR's return to its roots. Junior won six of the twenty-seven races he entered, driving a 1957 Ford that car owner Paul Spaulding purchased from Holman-Moody. Johnson often won in spectacular fashion, perhaps most notably at North Wilkesboro in May 1958 with his first win in three years. Leading by half a lap late in the race, Junior went into the third turn of the recently paved track too fast, got into the loose asphalt—or "marbles" as racers call it—near the top of the track, and flew over a 4-foot-high earthen bank and out of the track. For most drivers this would mean a wrecked car and the end of their race, but Johnson "never touched the brakes," headed through the weeds, and sped back over the bank and onto the track never relinquishing his lead. Johnson later commented on his amazing feat in his typical matter-of-fact way, "I knew the only chance I had was to keep my speed up to get through those weeds and back over that bank, so that's what I did." The hometown crowd went wild.[128]

Johnson also won the fall North Wilkesboro race, an event as memorable for the action in the stands as it was for the on-track goings-on. Junior showed his mastery of the quirky track when he took the lead for good halfway through the race from Glen Wood. A Johnson fan in the first-turn stands, however, did not like how hard one of his competitors raced him and hurled a quart jar full of moonshine at Wood's car, which shattered on the track and brought out the caution flag. Johnson recalled the events he saw in the stands as law enforcement came after the culprit: "There was a pretty lively scuffle going on 'til deputies got him handcuffed and took him off." What Junior could not tell from his vantage point on the race track was that the culprit was his own uncle, Ernest Money. "I couldn't imagine a man getting so mad," track owner and former bootlegger Enoch Staley recalled, "he'd throw away a quart of good moonshine."[129]

While the moonshine business was never far from NASCAR racing, its proximity to Junior Johnson almost cost him another stint in the penitentiary and possibly his career in stock car racing. Junior moonlighted in the family business in 1958 even as he starred on the race track and despite his recent eleven-month hiatus in Ohio. Even though he planned to give the business up altogether and make his living entirely from racing and other legitimate businesses, Junior felt a particular obligation to his family as his father neared the end of a three-year term in prison. "I could have walked away real quick like, but what would that have meant for my family? When I made money from moonshine, it was their money too. How could I just cut off their money?" In September 1958, Johnson was arrested in a "saturation program" in which federal and state agents swept into the county and destroyed sixteen stills, including one on the Johnson property. The agents also raided the home and found illegal liquor on the premises and arrested Junior, his brothers L. P. and Fred, and their mother, Lora Belle. They later found another still on the property and added that to the list of charges.[130]

Loath to lose one of its star drivers at such a pivotal time in the sport's history, NASCAR helped Johnson and his lawyers launch a spirited defense at his trial in May 1959. Paul Spaulding testified that Johnson had been too busy testing and racing to be involved in the moonshine operation. NASCAR field manager Johnny Bruner backed up his testimony with copies of the NASCAR bulletin, and scorer Joe Epton testified that Johnson was in Raleigh on July 2, 1958, when agents busted up a still on Johnson property. While L. P. pleaded guilty and was sentenced to two years, Fred was convicted and sentenced to thirty months and fined $5,000, and Lora Belle received an eight-month suspended sentence and a $7,500 fine, the nine-person jury declared Junior innocent of all charges.[131]

Throughout the mid-1950s, Bill France and NASCAR had taken a bumpy—but often exhilarating—ride. France had gone from the heady heights of being paraded around a Daytona Beach ballroom on the shoulders of admirers, to the board rooms of Detroit auto executives and flying across the country to promote his races, back to where he started, promoting events at Piedmont racetracks owned by former bootleggers. Star drivers had to fall back on a diet of "tube steaks," sleep in their cars and trucks as they traveled to races, and work on their own cars in the parking lots of cheap motels.

Fortunately for the sport—and for Bill France—NASCAR had set deep roots in the red-clay soil of the Piedmont South that enabled it to withstand the storms of public criticism and the withdrawal of Detroit money. While Detroit CEOs might not have been answering his calls, France still had the loyalty and support of his bootlegger/track owner/promoter buddies like Enoch Staley, Joe Littlejohn, Clay Earles, Charlie Combs, the Burgess brothers, and Gene Sluder, who continued to fill the stands. He also still had his marquee event, Darlington's Southern 500, which—at least around Labor Day—drew the attention of the motorsports world and a crowd surpassed only by the Indianapolis 500. Although there may have been strong criticism of NASCAR from politicians and ministers and even attempts to shut down tracks, France also had a strong fan base among the mill workers and farmers of the Piedmont who got such a thrill from the constant action of the stock car race. Perhaps most important, France and NASCAR had its by now legendary drivers to fall back on. Detroit may not have been footing the bill any longer, but the party went on, and Curtis Turner, Joe Weatherly, Lee Petty, Fireball Roberts, Buck Baker, Junior Johnson, and all the other drivers still knew how to put on a heck of a show for their cracker fans.

Something important had changed, however, even as Bill France and NASCAR went back to their roots in tough times: they had glimpsed the possibilities of the future. That experience would create a determination to return to those days at almost any cost. Indeed, the determination to return the sport, and themselves, to the national prestige they had experienced in the mid-1950s would lead Bill France and Curtis Turner to make three of the biggest gambles in NASCAR history in the late 1950s and early 1960s. Those gambles would do much to shape the future of NASCAR to the present day.

High Stakes Poker NASCAR, 1959–1963

Saturday, August 1, 1959, proved a fateful day for Ned Jarrett of Newton, North Carolina. The twenty-six-year-old local track champion and 1957 and '58 NASCAR Sportsman Division champion made an incredible gamble to move into the top ranks of the Grand National Division. Jarrett had entered a number of Grand National races that year in his own 1957 Chevy in the hope that his driving skill would attract the attention of a top owner who would put him into a competitive car. While his Chevy won consistently in the Sportsman Division, it was no match for the majority of Grand National cars even in an era when the factories had left the sport. Jarrett knew he had the talent to make it and decided to risk his financial well-being and future in the sport on one roll of the dice to purchase a competitive car with money he did not have. Car owner Paul Spaulding had just such a car available, a 1957 Ford that Junior Johnson had raced competitively in the previous season. Jarrett wrote Spaulding a $2,000 check for the car on that fateful Saturday but made sure he gave it to the car owner late enough in the morning so that he could not get to the bank in time to deposit it—the local bank closed at noon on Saturday. Jarrett had the wild dream that he could win enough money in the two Grand National races scheduled for that weekend at Myrtle Beach, South Carolina, and the Charlotte Fairgrounds so that he could get to the bank Monday morning, deposit his winnings, and cover the check. That he would need to win both races to make the check good—each of which paid $800 for first—and that he had an average finish of seventeenth in the five Grand National races he had entered that year did not seem to phase him. What gave him some hope that he could accomplish this seemingly impossible task was that he had finished second at a Columbia, South Carolina, Grand National race in April, in the Paul Spaulding Ford he now owned, when he subbed for an absent Johnson. Jarrett loaded up the car and his dreams and headed for Myrtle Beach.[1]

Ned Jarrett risked almost everything to become a NASCAR Grand National driver in 1959. (Courtesy of McCaig-Welborn Research Library at the International Motorsports Hall of Fame, Talladega, Alabama)

Jarrett's improbable weekend began just as he had dreamed. He started ninth in the 100-mile race on the half-mile Rambi Speedway but quickly moved toward the front. Amazingly, he won the race over the likes of Grand National stars Jim Paschal, Joe Weatherly, Lee Petty, and Buck Baker. Jarrett had little opportunity to celebrate, however. He had failed to notice prior to the race that the crew member who had wrapped the steering wheel with electricians' tape—a standard practice to improve the driver's grip—had put the tape on backward. Instead of having the smooth side up as he turned the steering wheel left for 200 laps, the edge of the tape bit into his hands at every turn. By the end of the race, Jarrett's hands were a bloody mess, and he had little opportunity to celebrate his win as he headed for the emergency room at the nearby Conway, South Carolina, hospital where a doctor stitched up his wounds. Jarrett was in no shape to race the next afternoon in Charlotte, but he headed that way hoping for some sort of miracle, as it would take an act of divine intervention for him to win.[2]

Whether the intervention was divine or not is questionable, but intervention and a miracle occurred at the Charlotte Fairgrounds on August 2. Jarrett qualified the Ford tenth in a field of twenty-nine but knew he would not last long in the race with his crippled hands. He pulled into the pits early in the race, and Joe Weatherly—on hand as an observer—jumped into the car to relieve Jarrett and quickly moved it up through the field. Weatherly came into the pits after fifty laps, and Junior Johnson—who had wrecked his Wood brothers Ford earlier in the race—took the wheel of his old racer. Johnson soon wheeled Jarrett's car to the lead and held on to win by more than one lap. If it was divine intervention, it was definitely a case of the "Lord working in mysterious ways," as two unlikely angels—both former bootleggers—came to Jarrett's aid. Both men knew of Jarrett's predicament with the check written to Spaulding and refused to take a share of the prize money. The next morning, Jarrett arrived at his bank when the doors opened, deposited his winnings, and covered his check. His gamble paid off not only in the immediate sense but in the long term as well, since the two wins helped launch a career that resulted in two Grand National championships (1961 and 1965) and successful stints after his retirement from driving as a racing promoter and radio and television broadcaster.[3]

The history of the late 1950s and early 1960s would be characterized by such outlandish, high-stakes gambles, some successful and some disastrous. NASCAR as a sport had been built by gamblers from its early days. Gambling was everywhere, from the bootleggers and their huge bets on the "Bootlegger Sweepstakes" run on the streets of Atlanta during World War II and on the racing on the highways in every community in the Piedmont and mountain South, to the track owners and promoters who gambled that construction of a speedway would pay off, to the drivers who gambled their very lives in the racing game, and to those who participated in the high-stakes poker games that seemed to pop up everywhere around the sport. The gambles, however, made by Bill France, Curtis Turner, and Bruton Smith would prove to be some of the most extreme and would have the highest stakes in the sport's history.

Bill France's Daytona Dream

While France and NASCAR had plenty of tracks to race on and plenty of drivers and cars to fill the fields, the exposure to the national spotlight during the factory era of the mid-1950s left many in the sport longing for something that would return it to national prominence. Accomplishing this goal would require France, like Jarrett, to commit all of his resources in a colossal gamble that risked not only his own economic future but the very future of NASCAR itself. France's gamble was the construction of the 2.5-mile, high-banked Daytona International Speedway, and in this gamble France was even more amazingly successful than Ned Jarrett.

France had long dreamed of constructing a huge new speedway in Daytona Beach, one that would rival and surpass any such facility not only in the United States but in the world. At least part of the reasoning behind construction of a Daytona speedway was practical; by the early 1950s, the South Peninsula area of Daytona Beach had attracted development in the postwar boom times. The annual beach/road races and speed trials on the beach led residents of the area to complain increasingly of the noise, litter, congestion, and the blocking of Highway A1A that lasted nearly a month during Speed Weeks. On several occasions France threatened to move the beach races to more hospitable surroundings, but Daytona Beach authorities had an interest in keeping winter racing in the area— a staple of the local tourism industry since the early years of the twentieth century—and began looking for ways to construct a speedway. In 1954, local officials created the Daytona Beach Racing and Recreational Facility District, headed by local auto dealer Saxton Lloyd, Bill France's first Daytona Beach employer, and gave the special district the power to sell tax-free bonds to finance the construction of a speedway. In 1955, the City of Daytona Beach approved a ninety-nine-year lease on a 377-acre tract near the airport, and news of construction of a $3 million high-banked facility spread throughout the racing world. At the same time, Bill France created the Daytona Beach Motor Speedway Corporation to construct and operate the facility, leasing it from the special district. The early plans, however, fell apart when, after the collapse of the bond market in 1957, it became apparent that the needed money could not be raised through the sale of bonds.[4]

With the speedway project near collapse, France took over the project himself. In October 1957, he signed a fifty-year lease with the special district and issued 300,000 shares of stock in the Daytona Beach International Speedway Corporation at $1.00 per share. In November 1957, he made the bold announcement that the 1958 beach/road races would be the last and that the new speedway would open for the 1959 winter races. At the time he had little money and only an incredible drive to see the project through. By March 1958, it became apparent how much France had put on the line when *National Speed Sport News* reported that in order to economize France had rented a trailer to haul his furniture from Winston-Salem, where he traditionally spent most of his summer, to Daytona instead of hiring movers. On the way to Daytona, a lighted cigarette set fire to the trailer and burned it and the contents, with an estimated loss of $700.[5] Many thought France's plans were simply a "pipe dream" and gave the project little chance for success. Years later France recalled that Harley Earl had told him the only way he "got the whole thing completed" was that he was "too dumb to know it couldn't be done."[6]

The project was indeed ambitious, with plans for a 2.5-mile track banked at 31 degrees. In order to create the banking and help drain the swampy land, a 45-acre lake—later named Lake Lloyd after Saxton Lloyd—was dug out of the infield. France and engineer Charles Money-penny designed the track as a unique tri-oval design so that fans seated on the front stretch would have a better viewing angle of the action on the track than at traditional tracks. France hoped that the shape would also allow stock cars to travel as fast as open-wheel racers and that the curves, which were designed in "flat planes, instead of the bowl-shaped designs they had in Europe," would allow cars to "pass in the turns as easy as on the straightaway." France—who became increasingly obsessed with high speeds and ever escalating speed records as a means of marketing NASCAR—clearly dreamed of having a speedway where the closed-course speed records being currently set at the high-banked Autodromo Nazio-nale in Monza, Italy, would soon be broken.[7]

Seeing his dream come to fruition, however, proved to be one of the great challenges of France's life as he struggled to find the resources to keep the construction machinery running and get the track completed. Harley Earl allowed France and Moneypenny to tap into GM's computer expertise to design the unique turns of the track. France secured a loan from the Lamar Life Insurance Company, and longtime friend Harry Moir of the Pure Oil Company helped him obtain a $35,000 line of credit for fuel to keep the heavy equipment rolling. When France needed $30,000 within four or five days to keep the earth moving going, he called a friend at Coca-Cola and offered to sell Coke products exclusively at the speedway and to provide a full-page ad in every NASCAR program for the next ten years. When Coke turned him down, France made the same offer to Pepsi, which immediately accepted. Daytona Speedway and its parent company, International Speedway Corporation, maintained an exclusive relation-ship with Pepsi into the early years of the twenty-first century.[8]

The most important help for France came through a chance encounter at an air show with oil and construction millionaire—and future owner of the Dallas Cowboys—Clint Murchison. When France learned that Murchison needed to get to Miami quickly because of a business emer-gency, France flew the millionaire there in his private plane. In the pro-cess of their meeting, Murchison learned of the challenges France faced in the construction of his ambitious speedway project and recommended he talk to Murchison's financial adviser, Howard Sluyter. Sluyter came to Daytona to see the progress on the project, became convinced it provided a wonderful business opportunity, wrote France a personal check for $20,000 so that work could continue, and helped arrange a $600,000 loan. As France later recalled, "If it had not been for Clint Murchison and Howard Sluyter we never would have accomplished the job of building the speedway as it is today."[9]

Even with the $600,000 loan, France still barely had the track ready for the first scheduled race. As he later remembered, "We had spent two million dollars between the time the first tree was knocked down and we had the speedway completed. Which I didn't have the year before. I borrowed $600,000, ordered four steel and wood grandstands from Reeves Steel in Tampa and started selling tickets. And we used the ticket money for construction just as fast as it came in."[10]

While evidence of ongoing construction abounded as the first drivers came in to test the new track in early February 1959, the Daytona International Speedway was unlike anything any of them had ever seen. Curtis Turner and Fireball Roberts ran the first laps on the track, and even though they had to stay in the lower groove because of sand at the top of the track, they soon turned laps at over 140 mph. Indeed, early practice speeds were near the speeds open-wheel racers ran in qualifying for the Indianapolis 500.[11] For a stock car, the speeds were unprecedented, awe inspiring, and scary. "I'll tell you what," Lee Petty recalled, "there wasn't a man there who wasn't scared to death of the place."[12]

Although the track had already attracted a huge amount of national publicity, France wanted more and lined up local millionaire and sports car enthusiast Chapman Root to provide his "Sumar Special" with local driver Marshall Teague at the wheel to make a run at the world speed record for a closed course—177 mph set by Tony Bettenhausen at Monza in 1957. Teague had long been on the outs with France and spent most of the 1950s driving stock cars in the rival AAA/USAC series. With NASCAR now such a dominant force in stock car racing, Teague sought a way to get back into France's good graces and into the more lucrative—especially with the new Daytona Speedway—NASCAR ranks. On his first day on the track in the powerful, streamlined, and lightweight racer, Teague turned a lap at 171.82 as he "played around."[13] Smokey Yunick, however, warned his friend that the car was too unstable at such high speeds and too susceptible to gusts of wind coming off the ocean and refused to help Teague set up the car for a record run.[14]

Undeterred by Yunick's warning, Teague boldly asserted that Daytona International Speedway was "safer than U.S. [highway] 92," and he pushed ahead for an attempt at the record, to tragic results. On February 11, Teague took the car out once again, and after three laps he began to push the car to try to break the record. Heading into the first turn, the Sumar Special lifted off the ground slightly, slid to the bottom of the track, and began flipping wildly. The car rolled five times, covering an estimated 500 yards from the first roll until it finally came to rest. The violent accident ejected Teague, still strapped into his seat, from the car as it rolled, and he landed 150 feet farther down the track than the car itself. Before the first race at the track was even held, Daytona had its first fatality.[15]

France, fearful that the tragic accident would spark concerns about the track's safety and foster a public backlash similar to the one that produced the withdrawal of factory support in 1957, immediately tried to deflect criticism of the track and imply that Teague was to blame for the accident. "There is no indication of tire or mechanical failure," he asserted. "It could have been physical failure or something like that."[16] Mel Larson, in his "Convertible Comments" column in *National Speed Sport News*, challenged France's implication that Teague was at fault. "I am sure and am certain that thousands of other race drivers, mechanics, officials, and fans know that Marshall Teague didn't know how to lose control of a race car. Certainly there has to be some cause for an accident such as this, whether it was noticed or not; but one thing I'm certain—the trouble didn't originate in the driver's compartment."[17] While the news of Teague's tragic accident occupied the news media for a few days, the excitement building for the first Daytona 500 soon moved safety concerns into the background.

The First Daytona 500

It was in the events of the first Daytona 500 that Bill France's gamble paid huge dividends that would put NASCAR on the front pages of newspapers all over the country and secure France's position as the unquestioned leader in American stock car racing. Indeed, Hollywood could not have scripted a more unbelievable finish to the race, which immediately made the Daytona 500 the second most important auto race in the United States. Fifty-nine cars, both sedans and convertibles, started the February 22 race as, appropriately, Clint Murchison drove the pace car.[18]

The race itself featured thirty-five passes for the lead, but Johnny Beauchamp in a Ford Thunderbird and Lee Petty in an Oldsmobile saved the best for last as they repeatedly swapped the lead in the final fifteen laps and battled door to door all the way to the checkered flag. A factor that

Bill France had not anticipated when he designed the track made all this passing possible—although it took the drivers a while before they fully understood what was going on. What Beauchamp and Petty took advantage of was an aerodynamic feature known now as the draft and the "slingshot" effect whereby a car in the draft is able to shoot past the car ahead of it. This effect is much more dramatic in stock cars, which are bulkier and less aerodynamic than open-wheel racers and punch a much larger "hole" in the air. As the cars flashed to the finish, it was difficult to tell who had actually won. The task was made even more difficult in that Joe Weatherly—who was actually a lap down—made it a three-wide finish, a fact that made the photos of the race's end even more dramatic. Unfortunately, Bill France and NASCAR had not planned on the possibility of such a close finish in a 500-mile race and had no official cameras at the finish line. France and flagman Johnny Bruner declared Beauchamp the winner, but Lee Petty drove to victory lane and claimed that he had nosed out his challenger. Most members of the press agreed that Petty had won, but again there was no definitive proof either way. France quickly announced that he would seek photographic evidence to determine who had actually won the race, and the crowd left the track still debating the outcome. Chris Economaki reported on the front page of *National Speed Sport News*, "The Daytona International Speedway has a champion for its first major event, but nobody was quite sure today who he is."[19]

Bill France knew a media opportunity when he saw one. He allowed the cantankerous Lee Petty to defend his case vocally to the media and let the media speculate and argue about the finish for several days, even though the vast majority of the early photographic evidence—including the famous photo of the three-abreast finish taken by NASCAR photographer T. Taylor Warren—showed Petty clearly crossing the line first. Finally, on the Wednesday after the Sunday race at 6:00 P.M.—in time to make the first edition of the next day's newspapers—France announced that he had seen conclusive evidence in newsreel footage taken by "Hearst Metrotone News of the Week," flown to NASCAR headquarters from New York, that Lee Petty had indeed won the race. France had effectively manipulated the media and the American public and kept the race in the national limelight for four straight days and permanently stamped an image of the dramatic finish in the American psyche. In addition, the race attracted a crowd of better than 41,000 fans, made $500,000 in profit—which France quickly used to satisfy his many creditors—and lasted only eight seconds longer than the fastest Indianapolis 500 on record. The results of the race and the consequent media exposure offered proof positive of France's, and NASCAR's, incredible luck and his talents as a promoter in taking advantage of the situation.[20]

The new Daytona Speedway was the boost that NASCAR needed after the factory withdrawal, although it did not fulfill all France's dreams, particularly his dream to be the unquestioned leader of not just American stock car racing but auto racing in general. Despite what should have been warning signs from Marshall Teague's fatal accident in the Sumar Special, France and USAC scheduled an open-wheel race for the track in April 1959. In qualifying, George Amick almost broke Tony Bettenhausen's closed-course record with a lap of 176.88, and many, including Bill France, anticipated that the race itself might rival the Daytona 500 for the publicity and excitement generated. The event, however, proved to be a near disaster. First, it attracted a crowd of only 7,500 paying fans, a crowd that appeared even smaller when placed in such a huge facility. Second, the last lap of the 100-mile race produced another Daytona tragedy when Amick crashed in the third turn at 170 mph. The impact was so severe that "the car's front end was sheared off and . . . tore out eight of the posts which supported the outer guard rail." The driver died on impact, the second fatality in an open-wheel car at Daytona in less than two months.[21] Other drivers struggled for control throughout the race and had nothing but scathing criticism for the track afterward. Rodger Ward asserted, "They can give it back to the Indians. . . . At Daytona, I'm breezing along, leading the race under perfect control, when WHAM, I'm in a real rough one. For no reason. I want no more of that speedway." Tony Bettenhausen flatly stated, "I don't think much of it. You don't have a chance at those speeds," and Tony Hinnershitz admitted the track scared him to death, a rarity for a race car driver: "I wouldn't even take a warm-up lap ride on it. I'm chicken. It's too fast with no room or time left in case of error." Mechanic Clint Brawner echoed these concerns: "I'll never go back there. It's too fast for safety. The tire experts claim there is absolutely no weight on the tires when the cars slap level as they leave the banked turns."[22]

As a result of the disastrous race, USAC moved its July 4 race scheduled for Daytona to the France-owned Raleigh Speedway. USAC racing director Henry Banks tried to sound diplomatic when he made the announcement, calling the track "basically well designed," but asserted that "the plant is not suitable for speeds attained by USAC's present speedway cars." NASCAR publicist Brad Wilson put a positive spin on USAC's cancellation and held out hope that the open-wheel cars would return to the track in the future: "Primarily, NASCAR officials and aerodynamics experts concluded that the Speedway is ahead of modern race cars in construction."[23] Since the 1959 debacle, there have been no further attempts to hold Indianapolis-style, open-wheel races at the track.

NASCAR and Bill France, despite the problems with open-wheel cars, had an amazing run of good luck at Daytona with stock car racing over the next several years. When USAC moved the July 4, 1959, race, France quickly scheduled the Firecracker 250 for stock cars—changed in 1963 to 400 miles, the race's current length—and Daytona now hosted two major Grand National races each year. While none were as thrilling as the first Daytona 500, nearly all the finishes from 1959 to 1964 were dramatic, with the races won generally by the biggest names in the sport. Daytona native Fireball Roberts became the sport's first nationally known superstar at least partly as a result of his three wins in the July 4 Firecracker races— including another thrilling finish in the 1963 races where he won by a car length over Fred Lorenzen and Marvin Panch—and his victory in the Daytona 500 in 1962.[24] Junior Johnson pulled a huge upset in the 1960 Daytona 500 when he took an underpowered Chevy to victory lane by taking advantage of the draft. Whether Johnson was the one who "discovered" the draft at Daytona—any number of others make the same claim—is a question that probably cannot be answered, but he did understand it earlier and better than most drivers. As his crew chief, Ray Fox, remembered, "I knew that while our Chevrolet wouldn't run all that fast by itself on the track, the car would draft like Jack the Bear. And Junior had found out how to do that better than anyone." Indeed, Johnson's victory was virtually sealed when the rear window of Bobby Johns's Pontiac blew out as a result of the high speeds, Johnson's close drafting, and the air turbulence caused by traffic on the speedway.[25] Other popular finishes in Daytona races came with the victories of California transplant and now Daytona resident Marvin Panch in the 1961 Daytona 500, Spartanburg mill-hill native David Pearson in the 1961 Firecracker, Richard Petty's first of seven Daytona 500 wins in 1964, and USAC superstar A. J. Foyt's last-lap pass of Bobby Isaac in the 1964 Firecracker.[26]

Perhaps the most dramatic and definitely the most heartwarming Daytona 500 victory came in 1963 when 6'6", 250-pound Dwayne "Tiny" Lund edged Fred Lorenzen for the win. The popular journeyman Lund had come to the track without a ride and was standing in the infield when Marvin Panch took a Ford-powered Masserati out for a test drive, another near tragic attempt at a land speed record. When Panch crashed near where Lund was standing and the car caught fire, Lund and four other men rushed to pull him from the car—Lund would later win a Carnegie Medal of Honor for his actions. Legend has it that from his hospital bed Panch asked car owners Glen and Leonard Wood to allow Lund to drive the Ford that Panch was scheduled to pilot in the 500. Glen Wood, however, later recalled that he and Leonard made the decision simply "because Tiny Lund was the best driver available." However, France and NASCAR officials played up the "reward for heroism" angle, and a record crowd of 71,000 fans sat on the edge of their seats as the race featured thirty lead changes and ultimate victory by Lund in the Wood brothers Ford. Again, France and NASCAR could not have scripted a more dramatic finish, and Daytona began to develop an incredible mystique and became further ingrained in the national consciousness as one of the top sporting venues in the nation.[27]

The Factory Back Door Reopens

The popularity of Daytona and NASCAR's increased exposure to the nation had another important effect, the reentry of manufacturers, if only through the back door. Actually, Pontiac's Semon "Bunky" Knudsen, determined to transform the make's image from an "old maid's" car to a high-performance juggernaut, blazed the trail to NASCAR's back door in 1958. Despite the AMA ban, Knudsen secretly hired mechanic Smokey Yunick and driver Paul Goldsmith for a one-race deal to run for the win at the final Daytona beach/road race. Goldsmith won the race in a Yunick-prepared Pontiac, and Knudsen hired the mechanic as head of a not-so-secret Pontiac racing program for $10,000 plus expenses. In 1959, Knudsen and Pontiac found the perfect means to promote its autos when Fireball Roberts began driving for Yunick. From 1959 to 1963—when he defected to the Holman-Moody Ford team—Pontiac and Roberts became linked inextricably in the minds of NASCAR fans. In order to keep up the illusion that Pontiac honored the AMA ban, however, Pontiac dealers sponsored ostensibly the racers. "Knudsen is pissing all over the AMA ban on racing so he needed a dealer's name on the side of the car," Yunick recalled. "The idea being, to the public, the dealer was paying for the race teams. As a result, Stevens [Stephens] Pontiac of Daytona Beach got a three-year free ride from me."[28] Other manufacturers followed suit, with Ford slipping parts through the back door of Holman-Moody and other manufacturers using the "dealer sponsorship" ploy to hide their involvement. In 1961, Ned Jarrett made a deal with Chevrolet to pick up new cars from the B. G. Holloway dealership in Melbourne, Florida.[29] While the factory help did not remotely match Detroit's spending frenzy of 1956 and 1957, it did help many drivers stay afloat and pumped much-needed funds into the sport.

The Superspeedway Boom

The success of France's Daytona enterprise also sparked similar gambles by others who decided to construct new superspeedways—generally defined as racetracks larger than one mile. Even before the opening of Daytona, the Georgia Securities Corporation announced construction plans for a $1 million, banked, 1.5-mile track seating 50,000 just south of Atlanta near Hampton, Georgia.[30] Construction problems and cash shortages delayed the opening well past the planned debut of November 1959. Even though the crowd of 25,000 for the first race at the new track on July 31, 1960, proved a bit of a disappointment to the organizers, the two annual races at Atlanta International Raceway soon became fixtures on the NASCAR Grand National schedule.[31]

While the builders of Daytona and Atlanta made significant gambles to see their projects come to fruition and experienced their share of delays and shortfalls, these paled in comparison with the outlandish risks and the obstacles faced by Curtis Turner and Bruton Smith in constructing the Charlotte Motor Speedway. The chaotic process started in April 1959, when Smith and Turner called press conferences on the same day to announce competing speedway projects for the Charlotte area. Both men had huge ambitions for their projects; Turner planned a 1.5-mile track, and Smith envisioned a 2-mile track with a football field in the infield.[32] Both also possessed huge aspirations in terms of their position within NASCAR and sought to challenge Bill France's dominance of the sport. Turner and France were old friends going back to the earliest days of NASCAR. The two had raced a Nash together in the first Carrera Panamericana and partied and fished together, and the flamboyant Turner had long been one of France's and NASCAR's greatest human assets. However, by the late 1950s Turner searched for his niche in racing beyond his career as a driver. He had cut back significantly on racing and in 1959 entered only ten Grand National events. Turner was also a successful (sometimes) timber baron who flew around the Southeast making, and losing, millions of dollars in land and timber deals. In many ways, he saw himself as an equal to France and began to look for ways to put himself into a position of power in the sport.[33]

Smith had similar dreams. Even as a very young man, he successfully challenged Bill France's domination of stock car racing in the region through his Charlotte-area promotions under the rival NSCRA umbrella. The NSCRA gave NASCAR and France serious competition—especially in Georgia, South Carolina, and the Charlotte area—in the late 1940s and early 1950s until the army drafted Smith during the Korean War. By the time Smith returned from the service, France had effectively broken the NSCRA, and the competing series had gone out of business with the tracks that hosted its races and the vast majority of its star drivers now in the NASCAR camp. Instead of trying to compete once again with France, Smith began promoting races in the Charlotte area under the NASCAR umbrella with a good bit of success. However, Smith also saw himself as a peer of France's, and the construction of a major speedway in Charlotte would prove his bona fides as a major player in the sport.

Although Turner and Smith had grandiose visions for what their projects could do for their sport, for the Charlotte area, and for themselves, they had much more in the way of dreams and pure chutzpah than they had in capital and other resources required to complete such a project. As Turner biographer Robert Edelstein observed, both Turner and Smith were "playing poker with less-than-stellar hands."[34] Both soon realized that the odds of success for their individual projects were much lower than if they partnered. While neither cared to share the limelight with the other—and accusations continue to fly today as to which of the two was more unethical, deceitful, or downright criminal—they decided to pair up and focus their efforts on a tract of land to the northeast of Charlotte just over the line in Cabarrus County.[35]

Turner and Smith began a frantic chase for money to finance the project in the summer and fall of 1959 as the pair announced that they would hold the first race at the track—an unprecedented 600-miler—on the same day as the Indianapolis 500 in 1960: Sunday, May 29. Both hit the road selling stock in their speedway corporation, "literally," as Humpy Wheeler recalled, "out of the trunks of their cars for $1 each." The corporation also made commercials and sent out mailings advertising its stock. The mailings in particular drew the attention of the Securities and Exchange Commission because they violated rules on the interstate marketing of stock.[36] Turner also sold several tracts of timber to finance construction and, ever the creative and outlandish businessman, even pursued schemes to commercially produce rockets to send satellites into space and explored the possibility of selling advertising on the margins of U.S. currency.[37]

The Charlotte Speedway

Serious problems arose almost as soon as construction of the track began in late 1959. One of the wettest on record, the winter of 1959–60 turned the site into a sea of mud and considerably slowed construction. The biggest setback came, however, when what the core-drill report termed as scattered "boulders" turned out to be "half a million yards of solid granite." Immediately, the cost of excavating the site rose from 18¢ a yard to $1.00 a yard, "TNT not included." "If they'd searched North Carolina for the worst possible place to build a racetrack," Smokey Yunick later recalled, "that's where they built it."[38]

At this point, however, Turner and Smith had put too much money and prestige on the line and could not afford to turn back. While Smith tried to keep the contractors moving—often with empty promises that they would be paid soon—Turner flew around the country calling in favors, selling stock and timberland, and trying to get loans. As Edelstein observed, Turner began "a unique practice of exhausting desperation: he'll write paychecks on a Friday evening and then spend the weekend in a mad flying rush around the country, collecting money to cover checks and be at the bank the moment it opens Monday morning."[39] At one point as the race date approached, contractors threatened to cease work until Turner and Smith paid their debts. Turner flew to Memphis, where he got a "Mafia guy" to give him a "phony cashier's check" made out to Turner for $250,000 and drawn on the fictitious "Bank of New York." "It was a nice lookin' check," Turner recalled. Turner took the check to a meeting with contractors, allowed them to examine it, but told them that he would not pay them until they completed their work. The ruse worked, and the contractors resumed operations. The delays did force Turner and Smith to ask NASCAR to move the date of the race to June 19, but it looked as if their gambles might pay off.[40]

However, one week before scheduled qualifying runs—when Turner and Smith thought they were going to make it to the first race and their potential financial salvation with a big gate—excavation contractor Owen Flowe threatened to shut down the entire operation. Flowe had his men move heavy equipment onto the track, blocking the paving of the last section, and refused to move it unless Turner and Smith paid $600,000 owed to his company. A phony cashier's check would not do the trick this time, and Turner and Smith did not have the money to pay him; they had even struggled to come up with the money to place in escrow to guarantee the $106,775 purse, a NASCAR requirement. In the most audacious, and most dangerous, of their gambles yet—one right out of Piedmont stock car racing's wild and woolly bootlegger past—Turner, his brother Darnell, Smith, Acey Janey, and driver Bob Welborn confronted Flowe and his workers armed with shotguns. While Turner and Smith held the men at bay, Darnell and Janey hot-wired a huge Caterpillar tractor, and Welborn used it to push the other equipment off the track. They then set up lights and an armed guard for the night to prevent further sabotage, and the next morning contractors completed the paving.[41]

While the track was ready for racing, Bill France threatened to pull the plug on the first race unless Turner and Smith came up with the remaining $75,000 in prize money for the escrow account. Turner flew to Lynchburg, Virginia, where he convinced a banker friend to loan him the money on a three-day note "guaranteed against gate receipts," and Turner and Smith turned over a check for the NASCAR-record purse to Pat Purcell on the Thursday before the Sunday race. To be sure, NASCAR officials rushed the check to the bank to make sure it cleared before the race.[42]

The First World 600

Unfortunately, troubles were not over for Turner and Smith as race day approached. As drivers began to test their cars on the track in preparation for the Thursday, June 16, qualifying runs, the track began to come up in large chunks—particularly in the 24-degree banked turns—a result of both the haste in finishing the track and attempts at cutting costs. Reporter George Cunningham of the *Charlotte Observer* argued that after Wednesday practice the track "looked like a post-invasion Okinawa." Turner's buddy Joe Weatherly even weighed in with his tongue-in-cheek assessment that the track was "just like the guy who built it [Turner], rough as hell."[43] After qualifying, driver Tom Pistone observed cynically, "The people want blood, and I'm afraid we'll give it to them on Sunday." The pole-winning qualifying run by Fireball Roberts at better than 134 mph, however, dampened some to the criticism of the track and helped build excitement for the coming race. Curtis Turner himself qualified third in a Holman-Moody Ford and desperately hoped to win the race, not only for the publicity it would generate but also for the prize money he could recoup and pay to creditors.[44] More bad news for Turner and Smith came on Friday's second round of qualifying when "at least 20 cars had windshields shattered by flying rock from holes in the track." Drivers and reporters speculated that the race would never go the announced 600 miles. Cunningham led his story on the qualifying runs averring, "There will be a race Sunday at Charlotte Motor Speedway. The duration is questionable." Buck Baker observed, "The places that have been weak are getting worse. I think we'll be real lucky to get in 300 miles Sunday." Possum Jones—who hit one of the track's holes and bent a sway bar designed for a 2-ton truck—predicted that if the race did go 600 miles "the winning speed won't be 100 miles an hour. They'll be plenty of action, though, with 55 cars trying to dodge holes and win a race at the same time. Gosh, if I'd known all this I'd built my car for dirt instead of asphalt."[45]

Amazingly, despite all the obstacles, the race went on as scheduled. In preparation for the track conditions, drivers tried to do whatever they could to protect their windshields and radiators from flying debris. Cunningham reported, "Mechanics were busy installing added safety precautions on all cars to guard against the expected flying rocks which are anticipated from track holes. Shields were mounted on the hoods to deflect rocks from the windshields, fender flaps were installed behind rear wheels and wire screens were put over the grill work to protect the radiator and motor."[46] Lee Petty cracked, "Most of the cars looked like army tanks."[47] On another front, Turner had to post a $20,000 bond in a local court in order to hold off an attachment order placed on the property two days before the race by an advertising agency that claimed the speedway owed it $10,000. On the day of the race, the headline of the lead story in the *Charlotte Observer* sports section read, "600 Reality Today, If Track Holds." The article proceeded to give the litany of "rain, snow, postponement, shot guns, law suits, and a multitude of other deterrents" that had threatened to derail the project.[48]

The adverse publicity, however, did not seem to deter the Piedmont fans as they jammed Highway 29 in both directions Sunday morning. Although the numbers did not reach the predictions of promoters—80,000–100,000—or even the announced numbers of 78,000 by one account and 60,000 in another given out by Turner and Smith, a crowd of probably 35,000 fans showed up for the race, enough paying customers to at least satisfy the most immediate demands of the speedway's creditors.[49] Turner stuffed $75,000 in cash from the gate receipts into a milk can and had an aide fly it to Lynchburg, Virginia, the next morning to pay off the bank loan he had secured for the purse escrow account.[50]

The race itself was not the classic—à la the first Daytona 500—that Turner and Smith hoped would secure their and the track's future, although fans who loved to see crashes had their fill. As many had predicted, the race turned into a virtual "demolition derby" or "obstacle course race"—both descriptions used by the *Charlotte Observer* in headlines about the race.[51] Fortunately, none of the accidents involved serious injury, and the race did not turn into the bloodbath predicted by Tom Pistone. Fans did not have to wait long for an accident, as Johnny Wolford lost control of his car on the tenth lap and caused a three-car pileup involving Cotton Owens and Johnny Allen. Polesitter Fireball Roberts led much of the early going but lost a wheel, hit the fourth-turn guardrail, and slid into the infield. Tom Pistone led a number of laps but retired with a broken axle. It looked as if veteran driver Jack Smith would cruise to victory, as he held a lead of five laps with only forty-eight to go. However, a large chunk of pavement knocked a hole in his gas tank, handing the lead to journeyman Chattanooga, Tennessee, driver Joe Lee Johnson, who won the race by four laps. Only twenty-three of the sixty cars that started the race made it to the finish line.[52]

The aftermath of the race proved almost as ugly as the race itself. In a bizarre move even for NASCAR, officials disqualified Richard and Lee Petty, Bob Welborn, Junior Johnson, Paul Lewis, and Al White after the race was over for making "an illegal pit entry" by cutting across the infield. The disqualification cost the Pettys more than $6,000 and dropped them from first and second in the point standings to fourth and fifth. Bruton Smith decried NASCAR's decision, particularly since the infractions occurred early in the race and NASCAR had black-flagged none of the alleged violators. "We at the Speedway think it is ridiculous to disqualify a man for such a minor thing. We disagree with the NASCAR decision wholeheartedly."[53]

Press reports of a "near-riot involving an estimated 6,000 surging, yelling spectators" at 3:00 A.M. in the speedway infield the night before the race did not help with Turner and Smith's public relations problems, especially when the incident involved the arrest of two teenage girls, a "negro band," rocks thrown through a police cruiser's windshield, and threats by police to use tear gas bombs. The news of the goings-on at the speedway seemed especially ironic at a time when the *Charlotte Observer* featured daily front-page accounts of local evangelist Billy Graham's Washington, D.C., crusade, where he preached on the topic the "Sins of America." "We Americans have committed every sin in the book and broken every commandment of God." Indeed, if Charlotte's respectable sorts were not con-vinced of the truth of Graham's statement, they only had to look to their new local speedway to witness the breaking of probably nine of ten of those commandments—there were no reported murders.[54]

Turner and Smith's Dilemma

The Turner-Smith era at the speedway lasted for only two more races, the National 400 held in October 1960 and the second World 600 in May 1961. Both races were a relative "parade of blowouts and crack-ups," with only twenty-five of fifty cars finishing the October race and twenty-five of fifty-five finishing in May. The National 400 featured a near fatal accident when Don O'Dell suffered a puncture wound in the neck when his Pontiac hit the spinning Ford of Lennie Page. Fortunately for O'Dell, Chris Econo-maki was taking pictures for *National Speed Sport News* near the scene of the accident; he rushed to the car and used his shirt to apply direct pressure to the wound until an ambulance arrived. Richard "Reds" Kagle was not so fortunate in the World 600. His car hit a guardrail that had been improperly installed. When the guardrail sheared off, it cut into the car, causing severe damage to Kagle's left leg, which surgeons later ampu-tated.[55]

Even though the track earned close to $400,000 with the second World 600 and its preliminary events, the speedway still owed more than $800,000 to creditors, who became increasingly impatient. Businessmen James McIlvaine and Henry Morgan, who held a second mortgage on the property, became especially troublesome. They threatened to foreclose on the track and put it up for auction unless Turner and Smith resigned and the board of directors put new management in place. After several days of behind-the-scenes wheeling and dealing—with differing accounts and competing allegations from Turner and Smith allies still flying around—the board fired Turner as president of the speedway in a 4–3 vote. It re-tained Smith as director of promotions, but he later lost his position and seat on the board when the track filed Chapter 10 bankruptcy.[56]

NASCAR and the Teamsters Union

Determined to regain control of the speedway at all costs, however, Turner made his riskiest gamble yet: he attempted to organize NASCAR drivers under the Teamsters Union. William Rabin, an accountant and attor-ney hired to handle financial affairs for the speedway, first introduced

Big Bill France (left) and Curtis Turner, with daredevil aviatrix and test driver Betty Skelton, in more congenial times during the mid-1950s before Turner tried to unionize NASCAR drivers in 1961. (Courtesy of McCaig-Welborn Research Library at the International Motorsports Hall of Fame, Talladega, Alabama)

Turner to Teamsters officials. Rabin not only was a savvy finance officer but had a number of wealthy and influential friends and clients, including Teamsters president Jimmy Hoffa.[57] Prior to Turner's ouster, Rabin and Teamsters vice president Harold Gibbons offered him an $800,000 loan if Turner agreed to lead an effort to unionize drivers. Turner refused the offer, but after losing his position as speedway president, he called Gibbons to see if the deal was still good. Gibbons put Turner together with Teamsters organizer Nick Torzeski, who headed an effort to organize professional athletes under affiliate union the Federation of Professional Athletes (FPA). NASCAR drivers would be the first major group brought under their umbrella, or so the Teamsters hoped.[58]

Turner did have a fertile field in which to sow the union idea, as NASCAR drivers had plenty of complaints. Bill France's dictatorial powers and the seeming capriciousness of many of his decisions topped the list. Few drivers had not experienced some sort of penalty from NASCAR, with the catch-all charge of "actions detrimental to auto racing" frequently coming into play to cover any penalty NASCAR and France wanted to assess. In a 1959 *Charlotte News* article on France's unquestioned power within NASCAR, reporter Max Muhleman quipped that since deposed Cuban dictator Fulgencio Batista had moved to the Daytona area, "now there are two dictators in Daytona Beach." France seemed intent on demonstrating the accuracy of Muhleman's assessment when he flew his airplane to Charlotte and unsuccessfully attempted to convince the editor of the

News to fire the reporter.[59] The recent events of the first World 600 and the seemingly capricious disqualification of six drivers there did nothing to dampen the criticism.

The rising expenses of racing and the lack of correlation between gate receipts and race purses also drew the ire of most drivers. As NASCAR Grand National racing grew in popularity through the 1950s and early 1960s, and with the withdrawal of the factories—at least from open sponsorship—racing became more competitive and more expensive for drivers and owners. "Ten years ago NASCAR was paying $4,000 purses for 100-mile races," Turner complained. "Then it cost $3,000 to build an automobile. Today, NASCAR is still paying $4,000 purses for 100-mile races. But it costs $6,000 or $7,000 to build a first-class automobile." *Charlotte Observer* reporter George Cunningham estimated that a 1961 race at Bristol, Tennessee, attracted 25,000 fans who paid on average $8 a ticket to produce gross revenues of $200,000. "Forty-two drivers divided a purse of $15,000 which included about $4,000 put up by manufacturers."[60] The industry standard in auto racing—first set by the AAA and then followed by its successor, USAC—had long been that the purse should comprise 40 percent of the gate. NASCAR had never met this standard, and when Marshall Teague as NASCAR's first secretary and treasurer tried to get the sanctioning body to meet the standard, Bill France both suspended him from racing and relieved him of his position.[61] "We weren't making no money," observed Tim Flock. "We were only getting a thousand dollars for first place in most races. They were probably paying about 7 percent of the gross."[62]

Drivers also became increasingly troubled about inadequate insurance coverage, especially given the inherent danger of the sport. When Bobby Myers died after he crashed head-on into Fonty Flock's stalled car at the Southern 500 at Darlington in 1957, he had little to show for his long career as a NASCAR driver. "When my dad died, he didn't have any insurance, didn't have anything," recalled Myers's son, Danny "Chocolate" Myers. "I can remember someone bringing a bucket of change into the house. NASCAR gave us whatever they could collect in a five-gallon bucket. So the day after my dad got killed, we moved in with my grandmother and lived there."[63]

Poor track conditions concerned many drivers. Ned Jarrett noted that "the promoters made very little effort towards the care of the tracks." Dirt tracks often had huge holes, mud, and blinding dust. "Dust . . . was our worst problem, in one form or another."[64] Richard Petty recalled, "When a race started, there was always mud, because they had just watered the track down. You'd have to reach outside the car and try to wipe it off the windshield. Then by the time you'd run fifty laps, it got so dusty you couldn't see a thing. There was as much dust on the inside of the windshield as there was the outside, so you had to wipe off on both sides. You finally just had to take your goggles off, because the dust would get on the inside, and you'd sweat and that turned it to mud. My eyes were as red as the clay for two days after a race."[65] Drivers fared little better on many of the paved tracks, as the first World 600 and the ongoing problems with the Charlotte track proved, although Curtis Turner could not exactly complain about that.

When Turner first began approaching drivers about joining the Federation of Professional Athletes in August 1961, he found an eager and willing audience. He told his fellow competitors that union membership would bring them higher purses, "a pension plan, death benefits, health and welfare benefits, a scholarship fund for children of deceased members, strong and meaningful complaint procedures, and assurance of adequate safety conditions."[66] Within weeks the top drivers in NASCAR—including Fireball Roberts, Tim Flock, Ned Jarrett, Junior Johnson, Glen Wood, and Rex White—signed union cards. "The way Turner explained it to me, it sounds like a good deal for drivers, car owners and racing in general," Glen Wood told a reporter as he signed his card. "It will only cost me $10 to find out. I have been at races before when drivers would want to strike because of a low purse and a large crowd."[67] The only major holdouts were three-time Grand National champion Lee Petty and his son, rising NASCAR star Richard, primarily because of their personal antipathy for Turner, Lee Petty's bitterest racetrack rival. Despite the unwillingness of the Pettys to join, the union movement in NASCAR appeared unstoppable.[68]

Turner and the Teamsters, however, had underestimated greatly the determination and force of personality that Bill France would bring to opposing the union movement and protecting the sanctioning body he had birthed, nurtured, and owned. The Glen Woods of racing soon found out that union membership would cost them much more than $10. Although France had grown up in the Washington, D.C., suburbs and lived in Daytona Beach, Florida, much of his life, in his years promoting races in the Piedmont South he had obviously learned a great deal about the control of labor from the region's textile, furniture, and tobacco mill owners. Indeed, the NASCAR boss employed practically every tried and tested method of keeping unions out, from threats and intimidation, to "yellow dog" contracts, to accusations of communism, to propaganda, to blacklisting.

When Turner went public with the union, France immediately flew to Winston-Salem to confront the Grand National drivers before the August 9 race at Bowman Gray Stadium. In an hour-long meeting with drivers he announced, "Gentlemen, I won't be dictated to by the union." Before he had "this union stuffed down [his] throat," he swore he would shut down all the tracks in which he had a direct interest, plow them up, and plant corn. France also pledged that no known union member could work in his organization. "And if that isn't tough enough," he vowed, "I'll use a pistol to enforce it. I have a pistol, and I know how to use it. I've used it before."[69]

France also immediately banned all union members from competing in the next scheduled Grand National race at Asheville-Weaverville Speedway. He then proceeded to point out the problems unionization would produce: "If you unionize, any support from the factories will be withdrawn. And all of you car owners if you hire a mechanic, as you will, then you'll have to pay him time and a half on Saturday and double time on Sunday." He also argued that drivers were not employees of NASCAR. They were "independent contractors" and therefore responsible for their own insurance and pension. France defended his actions by arguing that banning the union was a "safety measure." He pointed out that union drivers might threaten nonunion drivers during a race, coercing them to join. "A Fireball Roberts or a Curtis Turner will drive alongside you on the track and say, 'Hey you signed up yet?' I'm not going to allow that to happen. I'm protecting NASCAR drivers by not letting union members compete." Finally, France dropped a bombshell on the group when he revealed that Turner and the Teamsters planned to bring pari-mutuel betting to NASCAR racing. "As far as pari-mutuel betting is concerned, we know it won't work with auto racing. Auto racing is a clean sport. We've never had a scandal. And I will fight any pari-mutuel attempt to the last tilt."[70]

According to Turner biographer Robert Edelstein, Turner and Tim Flock stood listening to France's tirade outside an open window. At one point France averred that if a union was such a good thing then he'd join himself. Turner reportedly slid a union card through the window and said, "Here's your application." France shut and locked the window.[71]

France offered drivers a chance to sign cards nullifying their union membership and proceeded to set up a special grievance board of drivers, promoters, and car owners to deal with complaints. Almost all the drivers who had joined the union immediately pledged their allegiance to NASCAR and dropped out of the FPA. "I joined this union. And I've been thinking about it ever since," mused 1960 Grand National champion Rex White at the time. "Drivers have legitimate beefs. And the drivers want a fair deal and more money. But let's let this board France has appointed decide what's good for racing, not some union. . . . I'll admit the union offer of a retirement plan sold me. But from now on, I'll think for a while before I sign anything else." When asked if his offer of amnesty applied to union officers Curtis Turner, Fireball Roberts, and Tim Flock, France replied, "Maybe. Just maybe. If they make an affidavit and swear on the Bible."[72]

France also launched a public offensive and issued a prepared statement that characterized his fight against the union as a defense of the nation and the Constitution. "A recent newspaper story suggests that I might be some rootin', hootin', shootin' cuss, waving a pistol and itching to shoot up anyone who might disagree with me. Honest, I'm nothing like that. But I am an American who believes our constitution and our laws— and that bearing arms to repel invasion is a part of our great American Heritage." In a statement to reporters, France clarified what he meant by his reference to repelling invasion: "I don't think people realize the seriousness of this Teamsters move. There is only one promise I'll make. And that is that I will always do everything I can to keep them from taking over the country. The ultimate aim of that man that's heading the Teamsters [Jimmy Hoffa] is to control the country."[73]

In defense of the union movement, Roberts fired back: "Curtis and I fully realize just how far we have our necks stuck out. We know our careers in auto racing are at stake, but we're not backing down. We've made no demands, made no moves other than to try and sign up drivers for the union. We must have grabbed Mr. France where it hurts, though, from all the things he's said in the papers." If drivers looked at how France tried to strong-arm the union leaders, Roberts continued, they would realize that their best interests lay in supporting the union. He argued further that affiliation with the Teamsters Union would give the FPA the leverage and backing needed to gain the concessions from NASCAR that all the drivers agreed they needed.[74]

France, however, marshaled his forces and overwhelmed the already weakened opposition. His longtime close relationships with track owners—particularly those former bootleggers with whom he had built the sport—paid off as most jumped to his, and NASCAR's, defense, both literally and figuratively. Clay Earles recalled a particularly tense period: "I went to every race . . . the Frances were afraid to go to the races. Back in that day the Teamsters Union had a real bad name. They had some rough people. And so I went to every race fully dressed [packing a gun] though they never did confront me." Perhaps most important, Earles spoke on behalf of his fellow promoters to the drivers: "We cannot afford to run under a union. We can't afford to have a race scheduled and have you people strike on us. That's going to put us out of business. And if it puts me out of business, it puts you out of business."[75] Gene Sluder, owner of the Asheville-Weaverville Speedway, agreed: "I think it would be the devil for that outfit union [the Teamsters] to get in. I believe all the promoters are going to stick with Bill [France]."[76]

France also traveled to Washington, D.C., with Darlington track owner Bob Colvin and allegedly received assurances from an assistant attorney general that NASCAR was on solid legal footing. "Drivers are individual contractors according to the entry blanks they sign," Colvin told reporters. "There is no form of union for individual contractors. We will have the F.B.I. at Darlington for the Labor Day Southern 500. The law states that pickets, etc., for independent contractors are illegal and anyone participating in such or trying to stop the race will be liable for prosecution." Colvin noted no irony in his and France's desire to prevent union organizing at a Labor Day race.[77]

The death knell for the union movement sounded when Fireball Roberts succumbed to pressure, resigned as FPA president, and severed his ties with the union. The day after publicly defying Bill France, Roberts took a slow drive from Charlotte to Asheville, the site of the next race. On the drive he made his decision: "My motives in the FPA were quite clear. I simply wanted to better the positions of race drivers, car owners, myself and racing in general. I can see now that by affiliating the FPA with the Teamsters that we could possibly accomplish more harm than good for racing. I feel if I do anything to hurt the least man in racing, I will be doing a disservice to my fellow drivers who have been my friends for fifteen years. And I'll have no part of it." France quickly welcomed his most popular star back into the fold: "I think in future years Fireball will regard this move as the best thing he ever did for sports in America."[78]

With Roberts's defection, Curtis Turner and Tim Flock stood alone against France. Turner's gamble had failed, and as his biographer Robert Edelstein observed, he and Flock were "like the last two players in a round of poker that has become too rich for everybody else's blood."[79] The

Junior Johnson stands shirtless after the Grand National race at Asheville-Weaverville Speedway in August 1961. Johnson won despite the hole in his windshield caused by flying debris when the track began to come apart. NASCAR shortened the race because of the conditions, and fans rioted and kept the drivers from leaving the track for four hours. (Courtesy of Don Hunter Collection, Smyle Media)

NASCAR president banned both drivers from NASCAR racing "for life." The two tried to hold out and even filed a number of lawsuits against the organization, seeking injunctions to prevent NASCAR from blackballing them for their attempt at unionization. The courts dismissed all their petitions, and the ban on both drivers stood. Bill France had won. Any factory owner in the Piedmont South could look with pride at the manner in which France defeated the union effort.[80]

Ironically, the race held at the Asheville-Weaverville Speedway in the midst of the union controversy aptly demonstrated many of the problems faced by NASCAR drivers. Word of a possible confrontation between France and Turner attracted an unusually large crowd of more than 10,000. Though neither showed, the race generated a major confrontation of its own. About 60 laps into the scheduled 500-lap race, holes began to appear in turn four of the recently paved racetrack. "The holes soon became gaping monsters," observed *Asheville Citizen-Times* reporter Bob Terrell.

When driver Bunk Moore hit one of the holes on lap 208, bounced off the outside wall, careened into a temporary pit area, smashed through the pit wall, hit a pickup truck, and injured a spectator in the process, officials threw the red flag, temporarily stopping the event. While track workers tried to sweep up debris and make track repairs, Pat Purcell, executive manager of NASCAR, called all the drivers together. He informed them that because of track conditions the drivers would run only fifty more laps and left the drivers with the reassuring thought: "I hope you can make it." Race officials failed to tell the spectators that they had shortened the race.[81]

When the flagman threw the checkered flag at lap 258, abbreviating the race by 242 laps, pandemonium broke out. Four thousand enraged fans blocked the exits to the track to prevent the drivers from leaving. "I paid five bucks to see a 500 lap race. Somebody owes me some laps or some money," one member of the mob demanded. "Fist fights broke out in the crowd," Terrell observed. "Someone was thrown in the lake at the western end of the infield and two persons who attempted to quiet the crowd were heaved bodily from the track over the pit wall." Part of the mob hoisted a pickup truck and placed it across the exit road, trapping the drivers and crews inside the track for three and a half hours. Sheriff's deputies called to the scene failed to disperse the crowd. Finally, 6′6″, 285-pound Pop Eargle, a crew member for car owner Bud Moore, approached the mob's ringleaders to convince them to let the drivers go. When one of the leaders jabbed Eargle in the stomach with a two-by-four, "Eargle grabbed the big piece of wood and whacked the mobster in the head." Shortly after this incident, the crowd allowed the drivers to leave. Local hospitals treated four individuals for injuries incurred in fights, and sheriff's deputies arrested three members of the mob. As they finally headed for their homes, the drivers had to wonder whether they had not made a big mistake in failing to back the FPA.[82]

France did make some concessions in light of the union movement, particularly the formation of a special advisory committee to oversee Grand National racing. He took no chances, however, that the committee would threaten his status as undisputed ruler of NASCAR and stacked the deck in his own favor. He appointed a respected driver, but one unlikely to cause trouble, Ned Jarrett; driver/car owner Lee Petty, who loathed Curtis Turner; car owner Rex Lovette; his longtime bootlegger/track owner/promoter friends Clay Earles and Enoch Staley; and two of his own employees and loyalists, NASCAR officials Ed Otto and Pat Purcell. NASCAR instituted some minor changes as a result of committee activity—primarily increases in prize money and insurance benefits, and improved track conditions. As Ned Jarrett recalled, however, the committee met "off and on for a couple of years and then it just sort of died out."[83]

Aces in the Hole

Despite the loss of Curtis Turner to the "lifetime ban" for union organizing and lingering tensions from his crushing of the FPA, Bill France still held plenty of face cards in his hand, and in 1962 and 1963 NASCAR experienced one of its greatest periods of growth. The new superspeedways at Daytona, Atlanta, and Charlotte, in combination with the races already held at Darlington, began to form a new foundation for the sport. While the beating and banging on the short tracks that made racing so appealing to working-class Piedmont fans would remain an important part of the sport for years to come, Bill France's gamble on speed and the setting of ever escalating speed records captured fan imagination and drew record crowds to the superspeedways. Speed even became the major selling point at some of the shorter tracks, especially with the construction of the new high-banked half-mile speedway in Bristol, Tennessee, in 1961. Indeed, the Asheville-Weaverville Speedway and Bristol regularly swapped the distinction as the "world's fastest half-mile track."

The construction of one-mile or larger tracks also changed the fan experience. Races at these larger tracks became weekend pilgrimages, not just pop-in-for-the-evening type of events. Now more and more fans could camp in the infield and cook out, drink, and party with friends. Technology, particularly the development of camper trailers and pickup truck covers and campers, and increasing disposable income for working-class fans helped crowd the infield for such major events as the Daytona 500, the Atlanta 500, the Rebel 300, the World 600, the Firecracker 400, and the American 500. Don Good from Hickory, North Carolina, remembers going to his first race in 1964 at the World 600 at Charlotte. His truck driver dad, Wayne, spent much of the weekend drinking and playing cards with buddies while seven-year-old Don roamed the infield and then slept in the back of their pickup truck. Don was hooked on NASCAR for life. Monica Jernigan's father, a foreman at a factory near Asheville, North Carolina, purchased a used bread truck and used his handyman skills to convert it into a camper. The family traveled to many races, and Monica has fond memories of close encounters with both cars and drivers—particularly her favorite, Richard Petty—through the close accessibility the infield experience provided. Although more fans did bring family, the infield was still a pretty rough place. Like track owner Clay Earles, Wayne Good always went to the track "fully dressed" just in case.[84]

The NASCAR fan experience also changed in 1963 with the creation by Hank Schoolfield and Bob Montgomery of a forty-station network of radio stations—Universal Racing Network—to broadcast the major weekend Grand National races. While Daytona and Darlington had contracted with a handful of stations in the 1950s to broadcast their races, fans across the Piedmont region could now tune in to the big races at Charlotte, Atlanta, Bristol, North Wilkesboro, and Martinsville. The voices of Bob Montgomery and Hal Hamrick—with his trademark "man, oh man, oh man" when a wreck or significant event occurred on the track—calling the race soon became an important component of Sunday afternoon life for area fans as they listened to the races and lounged on their porches or worked on a car in the yard. Given the fact that most area newspapers and television stations provided little coverage of NASCAR, the broadcasts allowed them not only to keep up with the current race but to stay up to date with the latest news in the sport.[85]

In 1962, NASCAR increased its driver appeal even more when an agreement was made through the Automobile Competition Committee for the United States (ACCUS), the American arm of the Federation Internationale de L'Automobile (FIA), to allow USAC drivers to compete in a few selected NASCAR races annually.[86] Throughout the rest of the 1960s, the biggest stars of open-wheel racing, including Dan Gurney, A. J. Foyt, Rodger Ward, Parnelli Jones, Johnny Rutherford, Mario Andretti, Gordon Johncock, Gary Bettenhausen, and Al Unser, competed in NASCAR races at Riverside, California; Daytona; Atlanta; and Rockingham and Charlotte, North Carolina.[87] Some NASCAR drivers complained that the policy created a "possible rich windfall [for the USAC drivers] at the expense of NASCAR drivers," especially Fireball Roberts.[88] The attitude of most drivers, however, echoed that of Junior Johnson, who challenged the USAC drivers: "Let 'em all come down here. I can outrun all of 'em as easy as I can outrun one."[89]

The head of USAC, Henry Banks, poured fuel on the fire when he asserted that USAC drivers were superior to those in NASCAR and predicted "a sweep in the win, place, show, positions" at the 1963 Daytona 500. Generally speaking, the USAC hotdogs fared poorly in NASCAR trying to manhandle the much heavier, less aerodynamic, and less powerful stock cars.[90] However, the open-wheel pilots excelled at the 2.7-mile road course at Riverside, California, with Dan Gurney winning four NASCAR Grand National Motor Trend 500s in a row from 1963 to 1966. His lock on winning Riverside was broken only when fellow open-wheeler Parnelli Jones won in 1967. Gurney won again in 1968. Back-to-back wins by A. J. Foyt in the Daytona Firecracker 400 in 1964 and 1965 and Mario Andretti's victory in the 1967 Daytona 500 kept the rivalry interesting, however, and only expanded the national exposure that NASCAR received as a result of the ACCUS agreement.[91]

With the new tracks—some of them in previously untapped markets—a large stable of star drivers, and fans now able to keep up with the sport better over the Universal Racing Network radio broadcasts, attendance began to increase dramatically during the period. Superspeedways Darlington, Daytona, Charlotte, and Atlanta consistently drew crowds of well over 50,000 for their two annual major races. Charlotte—sans Curtis Turner and Bruton Smith—emerged from Chapter 10 bankruptcy protection and issued a 10 percent stock dividend to investors in 1963 and a 25 percent dividend in 1964. A. C. Goines, speedway president, asserted that Charlotte "has emerged as a strong, financially sound organization and the stockholders who stuck with the track through the thin years are now finding their confidence in racing and Charlotte Motor Speedway amply justified."[92] NASCAR's popularity benefited tracks across the board, large and small, and helped create new hotbeds for the sport, especially in southern California and middle and eastern Tennessee.[93]

Detroit's Front Door Reopens

Still another benefit of Bill France's successful gambles during the early 1960s was the open reentry of auto manufacturers Ford and Chrysler into the sport. In June 1962, Henry Ford II announced that the 1957 agreement of the Automobile Manufacturers Association banning the advertising of speed and power and of supporting racing as a means of advertising had "neither purpose nor effect" and therefore Ford was abandoning it "to establish our own standards of conduct." On the heels of Ford's announcement, a Chrysler executive declared that corporation's view that the AMA ban was "non-operative" and therefore they would no longer abide by the restrictions. While Ford and Chrysler immediately jumped in and factory support poured in from Ford for Holman-Moody, the Wood brothers, and Bill Stroppe and Chrysler support came to Petty Engineering and Ray Nichels, General Motors—which had flaunted the AMA agreement with its Pontiac support for Smokey Yunick in 1961 and 1962—and American Motors pledged that they would maintain the ban.[94]

Fords dominated the biggest, richest, and best publicized races of the 1963 season at Daytona, Atlanta, Darlington, Charlotte, and the new half-mile track at Bristol, winning seven of the ten races held at these tracks. Fred Lorenzen, driving for Holman-Moody, was Ford's big star of 1963, entering only twenty-nine of the fifty-five Grand National events that year but winning six and finishing in the top ten an amazing twenty-three times. Most startling, however, was the fact that Lorenzen smashed previous records for race winnings by taking in $122,587, almost $50,000 more than the race winnings of runner-up Richard Petty, who entered fifty-four Grand National races. In late March, Holman-Moody's money and Ford's factory support helped steal Fireball Roberts away from Banjo Matthews and his Pontiacs. Roberts, entering only twenty races, won four major races and $73,059—third on the money list.[95]

Ford regularly trumpeted its racing success in an aggressive advertising campaign. When Fords took the first five places in the 1963 Daytona 500, an unprecedented feat, Ford ads crowed: "In the open test that tears 'em apart . . . the Daytona 500—Ford durability conquered the field." Ford ads also taunted rivals at General Motors and American Motors, without naming them, who criticized the make's embrace of stock car racing. "Daytona is no 'private' test arranged by a manufacturer to favor his cars' strong points. It is open competition—anyone can enter—and the one thing that is proved by its searing 500 miles is just exactly how well a car hangs together."[96] Ford Division general manager Lee Iacocca also defended the make's decision to go racing: "Why shouldn't we if it improves the breed of the car?"[97]

Joe Weatherly, the 1962 points champion who drove mostly Pontiacs for nine different owners; Richard Petty driving a Plymouth; and Junior Johnson's campaigning in a Chevrolet did keep things interesting in the manufacturers' battle, winning many of the short-track races that still dominated the fifty-five-race Grand National schedule. Weatherly was an early victim of GM's decision to close its back door through which money, parts, and knowledge had flowed to Smokey Yunick, Banjo Matthews, and Bud Moore in previous years. Moore told Weatherly early on that he would take his Pontiac only to the biggest, best-paying races. Weatherly, however, wanted to defend his title and had to beg car owners to let him drive in their cars in races that Moore did not attend. His diligence paid off when he edged Richard Petty for the championship in the final race, the Golden State 400 at Riverside.[98] Petty kept Chrysler Corporation's name in the racing news by winning fourteen races, and Junior Johnson teamed up with legendary Daytona Beach mechanic Ray Fox to successfully campaign a Chevrolet to seven wins, including big wins against Ford in the Atlanta 500 and the National 400 at Charlotte. Fox had been able to hold on to some factory support, and Johnson delivered additional financing from sponsor Holly Farms Poultry—one of the first nonautomotive companies to offer significant sponsorship dollars in the sport's history—of his home Wilkes County. After winning the National 400, Johnson taunted the rival Fords and their star Lorenzen, "I don't guess Freddy will be doing any more of his bragging about him outrunning me. He had his chance today and he didn't do it."[99] However, as it turned out, Chevy would not return to victory lane in a Grand National race until 1966.

Given the huge odds against success that NASCAR and Bill France faced in the late 1950s, their gambles paid off in spectacular fashion. With the construction of his wildly successful Daytona track and the crushing of Curtis Turner and the Teamsters' attempt to unionize his drivers, France had emerged even more firmly in charge of stock car racing and the sanctioning body he had founded. The ancillary effects of Daytona's success—particularly the construction of new superspeedways at Atlanta and Charlotte and the high-banked short track at Bristol—brought in new fans and a renewed emphasis on raw power and speed. Detroit's reentry into the sport once again put steaks on star drivers' dinner tables and fueled their partying. While Curtis Turner—whose gambles proved disastrous—was no longer welcome at the parties or on the track, NASCAR had a strong stable of established stars in Turner's buddy Joe Weatherly, Junior Johnson, Marvin Panch, Ned Jarrett, Rex White, and Jack Smith as well as a group of rising talents in Richard Petty, Fred Lorenzen, and David Pearson. The sport also had a new leader in Fireball Roberts, who possessed the same aggressive style on the track as Turner and who was fast becoming NASCAR's first nationally recognizable star. By 1963, then, NASCAR seemed poised to move beyond its humble Piedmont, bootlegging, dirt-track roots and into the top ranks of American professional sports.

Give 'Em All a Shot of Whiskey and Drop the Flag
NASCAR's Danger Years, 1964–1967

The stock car racing world—gathered in Daytona for the 1964 Firecracker 400—reacted in shock to the news: its biggest star, Fireball Roberts, had died, a result of the severe burns he incurred in a wreck on the seventh lap of Charlotte's World 600 a month earlier. Reporter Max Muhleman, a close friend of Roberts's, asserted he was the "Mickey Mantle, the Johnny Unitas, the Bob Cousy of stock car racing" and that hearing the news of his death was "like awakening to find a mountain suddenly gone."[1] Former Roberts crew chief Smokey Yunick remembered the star driver as being "about as complicated as the cars he raced" but hailed him as one of the great competitors in stock car racing history. "Finishing second or third was of absolutely no interest to him. He always aimed for the front, and that is the mark of a great driver."[2] Ned Jarrett put it simply: "He was the ideal. A lot of drivers copied him but few had his ability." For Fred Lorenzen, hearing the news of Fireball's death "was like finding out Santa Claus didn't exist. . . . It just killed racing for me."[3]

Roberts's death presaged one of the most difficult and challenging eras in NASCAR history. While the sport had seemed poised to storm the towers and challenge the dominance of America's professional stick-and-ball sports in early 1964, it was not to be so. In a scenario eerily similar to the mid-1950s when NASCAR rode the crest of the first wave of the auto makers' entry into the sport, once again the sport faced near collapse over safety concerns, the deaths of star drivers, and Detroit-induced chaos.

The Stars of NASCAR
In 1964, practically anyone trying to assess the future of NASCAR would have predicted that the series was destined for the top levels of the American sports and entertainment world. One of NASCAR's greatest strengths

Fireball Roberts became the first NASCAR driver with national celebrity. (Courtesy of McCaig-Welborn Research Library at the International Motorsports Hall of Fame, Talladega, Alabama)

was its deep stable of talented, charismatic, and marketable drivers. Although NASCAR had banned its most popular driver, Curtis Turner, "for life," the sport had a number of drivers who kept up the tradition of hard-charging, seat-of-their-pants racers. Turner's cohort in fast living and former bootlegger Joe Weatherly emerged from his fellow Gold Dust Twin's shadow and had his best years in the early 1960s. He won the Grand National points championship in 1962 and 1963, at the same time keeping fans and fellow competitors alike entertained by his constant practical joking and high-flying lifestyle. Weatherly never showed up at a race or party without a joy buzzer, rubber snake, or, his favorite, a spring-loaded "mongoose in a box" that he used to scare the wits out of unsuspecting victims. The only effective revenge his competitors could exact on Joe was to take advantage of Weatherly's equally outrageous superstitions concerning peanuts at the racetrack, the color green, and black cats.[4]

Former bootlegger (at least allegedly at this time) Junior Johnson reached his peak of popularity as a driver during the period with his win-or-blow-up style of driving. Reporter Dick Thompson of the *Roanoke Times* averred that the 225-pound Johnson "looks like a wrestler and drives like a maniac."[5] His victory in the Daytona 500 in 1960 and his successful campaigning of a Chevrolet—the only really competitive Chevy at the time in Grand National racing—to seven wins in the 1963 season made him a legend in the region and began to attract national attention. In one of the strangest pairings in history, the overalls-wearing Johnson, the epitome of the rural South in many ways, encountered international fame in 1965 when journalist Tom Wolfe, the epitome of urbane sophistication, traveled to Wilkes County to interview him—wearing spats and seersucker suit. Wolfe wrote a breathless article for *Esquire* magazine, one of the classics of the New Journalism style, entitled "The Last American Hero Is Junior Johnson. Yes!" Johnson later recalled his encounter with Wolfe: "That Wolfe guy was something else. He showed up down here in Wilkes County talkin' funny, with a New York accent, and wearin' fancy clothes, including spats. Spats! I doubt anybody in Wilkes County ever had seen spats, at least not in recent times. I didn't have much time to spend with him. I didn't figure he'd get much of a story. But somehow he got local people to talk to him and his story turned out to be pretty doggone good and accurate."[6] Wolfe in turn described the Wilkes County driver as "a coon hunter, an ex–whiskey runner, a good old boy who hard-charges stock cars 175 m.p.h. Mother dog! He is the lead-footed chicken farmer, the true vision of the New South."[7]

Junior's success also represented a transition in both NASCAR and the broader Piedmont world as an individual who had moved from the shadowy world of the bootlegger into the mainstream as a popular and successful sports star and businessman. While he became the most notable case in the sport, others had already made that transition to middle-class (or even upper-class) respectability. Raymond Parks, Enoch Staley, Charlie Combs, and Clay Earles were now respected businessmen in their communities, welcomed into the ranks of the local chamber of commerce and service clubs. Many locals may have known about their past "enterprises," but few, if any, spoke about it publicly.

The early 1960s also produced a new generation of Piedmont drivers who came not out of the rural, moonshine, liquor-hauling tradition but out of the mill towns of the region. While they shared much in common culturally with their bootlegger compatriots, the boys from the mill hill possessed more reserve and a hard edge to their character that reflected their roots in the gray life of the mill and the company-owned town. Writer Ron Rash spoke of this edge possessed by many working-class southerners who had achieved some success in life in his novel *The World Made Straight*: "They were always friendly enough but there was a certain hardness in the eyes, as if believing what they'd worked so hard to have could be snatched away in an instant."[8] The most important and successful of these drivers was David Pearson, who grew up on the mill hill of Whitney, just outside Spartanburg, South Carolina. Pearson learned to drive and work on cars at an early age and saw the automobile—in one form or another—as the ticket out of the dreary mill existence of his parents. He also was steeped in stock car racing, having attended many of Joe Littlejohn's promotions at the Spartanburg Fairgrounds and coming of age in one of the hotbeds of NASCAR, with the race shops of Bud Moore and Cotton Owens serving as anchors for a thriving stock car racing community.

Like most young men in his home community, Pearson dropped out of school after the ninth grade and followed his parents into the Whitney Mill. His career as a mill hand, however, was to be a short one, as he shared with Peter Golenbock: "I'd be in there working, and I'd look out the windows and saw all my buddies working at the little service station/hot dog joint we always hung around at, and I just couldn't stand it, seeing all them out there. So I didn't last very long at the cotton mill. I had to quit and find something else." He joined his brother working in a local body shop and began wrenching on his own cars in his spare time. Pearson debuted as a stock car racer in 1952 at the age of eighteen and soon became one of the top local Sportsman drivers in the Upstate region of South Carolina. After he won the track championship at Greenville-Pickens Speedway in 1959, local fans collected money to help him buy a car and head for the Grand National circuit. When Pearson won Rookie of the Year honors in 1960, he began to attract the attention of top car owners and became one of the smartest, and most creative, drivers—nicknamed the "Silver Fox"— in NASCAR's top ranks. Perhaps most important, NASCAR's core fans in the Piedmont South could see one of their own in David Pearson and hope that with some luck they too could escape the drudgery of the mill.[9]

The most popular partying, hard-drinking, womanizing, hard-charger of the early 1960s was Fireball Roberts. His dominance on the fastest tracks—particularly Daytona—in the #22 black and gold Smokey Yunick Pontiac made him the first NASCAR driver whose popularity transcended the Piedmont South to make him a nationally known figure. Fireball's only problem was that the tire technology was far behind engine technology, but the spectacular crashes he often had only endeared him further to fans. As Yunick observed, "Fireball ran a live tire test every race. You just run behind him till he blew, and then went on at a slower pace. It happened so often, Fireball's official hillbilly song was [Faron Young's] 'Hello Walls.'"[10] In an unprecedented move for a NASCAR driver, in May 1964 Roberts signed a personal services contract with Falstaff Brewing Company that placed him in print and television ads alongside baseball legends Dizzy Dean and Pee Wee Reese and football stars Johnny Lujak and Red Grange.[11] He was also the first NASCAR driver to have a feature story written about him in *Sports Illustrated*, in February 1964.[12]

A new breed of driver also began to emerge in the early 1960s—a clean-cut, clean-living, more media-conscious type of driver—and soon entered the limelight. The arrival of these drivers on the scene produced an interesting contrast to the traditional rough-as-a-cob, hard-partying drivers and helped make each NASCAR race into a sort of morality play in which good battled evil, propriety struggled with impropriety, and liquor drinkers vied with milk drinkers. In many ways, young Richard Petty embodied this new breed. Petty started racing in NASCAR's top division in 1959 but became the top driver in the Petty Engineering shop when his father, Lee, had a career-ending wreck in a qualifying race at Daytona in 1961 that hospitalized him for four months. In sharp contrast to his dour, combative father, Richard smiled constantly, stayed at the track for hours after races signing autographs in an elaborate Spencerian-script—"like one of those cats who signed the Declaration of Independence"—learned at King's Business College in Greensboro, and openly talked about his Methodist faith and his loyalty to family. Indeed, the fact that Petty was a high school graduate and had attended business school separated him from most of his competitors. Petty's winning smile, clean-cut image, and winning ways soon made him a fan favorite.[13] Petty also continued and solidified the important place of family connections in NASCAR racing—going back to the sport's origins with cousins Roy Hall and Lloyd Seay and all the "Mad Flocks"—as he took up his father's mantle with brother Maurice and distant cousin Dale Inman working on his crew.

Another driver of the new breed was the pride of Newton, North Carolina, Ned Jarrett. When he won the 1961 Grand National points championship and was called on by local civic groups to speak, Jarrett realized that he needed more than a lead foot to properly represent NASCAR and himself. He enrolled in a Dale Carnegie speech class (Carnegie was the author of *How to Win Friends and Influence People*) to improve his public speaking and social skills and became a sophisticated—at least compared with most of his competitors—spokesperson, a fact that endeared him to NASCAR and Bill France, to auto manufacturers, and to a growing number of more family-oriented fans.[14] Jarrett solidified his good guy bona fides in 1965 when he addressed a Christian youth rally on the night before Darlington's Southern 500. Jarrett asked the youths to pray for him the next day as he raced. When he won the race by a record fourteen laps, he told reporters in victory lane, "I was saying a prayer every lap for the last 20 laps. Don't underestimate the power of prayer."[15] When Jarrett accepted the Grand National points championship trophy and check for his 1965 championship, he, car owner Bondy Long, and members of his crew wore "pale blue dinner jackets, dress trousers and sported a red carnation in their lapels." Evidently such dress was becoming more common but was less than universal, as the *National Speed Sport News* reporter covering the event observed: "It was nice to see that most banqueters have learned that sports shirts and sweaters are out of place at such functions."[16]

In early 1963, *National Speed Sport News* commented on the arrival of this new type of driver in an article entitled "New Breed of Racing Man": "There was a time when the Superstar of the Southern stock car circuit was of questionable character. The most successful race drivers were those who drove fast and lived fast. Now that the sport has grown into the South's top year-around spectator attraction a heavy foot is not the only requisite for stardom. It takes money to keep a race car going and the men who sponsor the machines are looking for skilled leaders mechanically and clean men competitively and personally." As an example of the type of "racing man" they were talking about, they pointed to Cotton Owens of Spartanburg, South Carolina, a former successful driver—victor in the 1957 Daytona beach/road race—turned car owner. The reporter lauded Owens as one who "doesn't drink or use profanity" and as an "active member" of a local Baptist church who regularly gave "10 percent of his race winnings" to his church.[17]

Even with the appealing contrasts and skills of these star drivers, other than Floridian Fireball Roberts, they did not draw much attention outside the Piedmont South. That changed in 1961 when Chicagoan Fred Lorenzen burst onto the Grand National scene and signed on to drive for the Holman-Moody Ford team. Lorenzen was the fulfillment of Bill France's dreams of expanding the appeal of NASCAR beyond the Southeast. While quiet and reserved, Lorenzen was a gutsy and skilled driver who had learned the stock car racing craft well and dominated the stock car races promoted by impresario Andy Granatelli at Soldier Field in the late 1950s. Perhaps his greatest asset, however, was his movie-star good looks, combined with what in the 1960s was referred to as a "Pepsodent smile," which attracted female fans by the droves.[18] He first drew acclaim in the stock car racing world when he battled Curtis Turner in a legendary fender-rattling duel over the closing laps of the May 1961 Rebel 300 at Darlington. "He bumped me 50 times and I bumped him 50 times in the last 20 laps," Lorenzen recalled after the race. Although Turner effectively blocked every attempt by Lorenzen to pass him, the Chicagoan faked high coming out of turn four on the next-to-last lap and then dove under the legendary bootlegger as they took the white flag beating and banging down the front stretch. Lorenzen then blew by Turner, winning by six car lengths in one of the most exciting finishes in NASCAR history.[19] "Fast Freddie," as he came to be called, skyrocketed to the top in popularity and brought hordes of new fans to the sport, particularly in the Midwest. In 1964, Lorenzen became the first NASCAR driver to sign with a major sports management company when he inked a contract with Sports Headliners, an agency that managed the careers of USAC stars A. J. Foyt, Rodger Ward, and Parnelli Jones.[20]

The Hemi

Another asset NASCAR had going for it in the mid-1960s was the strong backing of, and intense competition between, Ford and Chrysler. In 1964, tired of losing out in big races to its rival, Chrysler turned the tables on Ford when it went back to the future, bringing the hemispherical combustion chamber engine—better known as the "hemi"—that it had first introduced in 1951 "out of mothballs" to dominate the season. Richard Petty knew Chrysler was on to something special when early in 1964 the manufacturer brought him to Goodyear's 5-mile test track in Texas to test the "426-cubic inch bomb." Chrysler paid Junior Johnson to bring along his 1963 Chevrolet, which had the most powerful engine during the previous season. "I went past Junior like a rocket," Petty later recalled.[21] After the experience in Texas, Johnson and owner/crew chief Ray Fox, who had planned to campaign a Mercury with factory support in 1964, immediately switched to Dodge to take advantage of "hemi" power. Chrysler stood prepared for a February surprise when the 1964 season kicked off at Daytona with Petty Engineering fielding two factory-supported Plymouths and Ray Nichels, Ray Fox, and Cotton Owens campaigning Dodges, all powered by new hemis.[22] In order to comply with NASCAR rules, Chrysler "did some modifications and stuffed it back in a few street cars" so that the engine would be "legal for racing," but the car—in reality, a purpose-built racer—pushed the definition of "stock" to its extremes, launched a war between Ford and Chrysler, and caused Bill France and NASCAR no end of headaches.[23]

When Speed Weeks arrived at Daytona in 1964, the Chrysler forces and their hemis were ready to take the stock car racing world by storm.

When they hit the track for qualifying runs, they astounded onlookers and drove their Ford rivals to distraction. "If there were any doubts about the 1964 Plymouth being the hottest monoxide snorters at the Daytona International Speedway," *National Speed Sport News* trumpeted, "Richard Petty and Paul Goldsmith dispelled them all here Saturday." Both drivers smashed the world closed-course stock car speed record in qualifying with Goldsmith taking the pole at 174.910 mph—easily bettering Junior Johnson's record from the previous year of 166.005 mph—and Petty in the second qualifying spot with a run of 174.418 mph.[24] Racing reporter Bob Maginley announced the news to the auto racing world: "The biggest revolution in the stock car speed record department is taking place here [Daytona]." In addition to Goldsmith's and Petty's record-setting qualifying runs, Chrysler hemis took the next three positions and the eighth position, giving them six of the top ten starting spots.[25]

The hemis backed up their qualifying runs and "KO'd much of the opposition" in the Daytona 500 with Petty leading a 1–2–3 Plymouth sweep, almost matching Ford's unprecedented finish in 1963.[26] The ads—with the headlines "High Speed" and "Your Speed"—from Chrysler soon followed touting the power of the hemis. "Plymouth rocks racing world with 1–2–3 sweep in Daytona 500. According to the record book for stock cars in competition, there is no higher average speed for 500 miles than the 154.334 m.p.h. set by a competition equipped Plymouth in winning last month's Daytona 500."[27]

Daytona set off a season of almost frenetic battle between Ford and Chrysler. Richard Petty, entering sixty-one of the sixty-two Grand National races, followed up his victory in the Daytona 500 with eight additional victories in his Plymouth Hemi Super-Commando, won his first of seven points championships going away, and became only the second driver in NASCAR history to break $100,000 in winnings. In addition to their victory in the Daytona 500, the Chrysler forces won three more of the eight major superspeedway races, with Jim Paschal winning the World 600 at Charlotte in a Petty Engineering Plymouth, A. J. Foyt winning the Firecracker 400 at Daytona in a Ray Nichels Dodge, and Buck Baker winning his third Southern 500 in a Ray Fox Dodge at the age of forty-five. David Pearson also made a big splash in Cotton Owens's Dodge, winning eight races and finishing third in the points.[28]

The Ford folks, however, also had plenty to brag about in 1964. Ned Jarrett won fifteen races driving for owner Bondy Long, including the Dixie 400 in Atlanta, and finished second in the points. Once again, though,

Fred Lorenzen had the most outstanding year of any driver in Grand National racing piloting the Holman-Moody Ford. Holman-Moody entered Lorenzen in only sixteen races, but he won eight of them, including three of the eight superspeedway contests—the Atlanta 500, the Rebel 300 at Darlington, and Charlotte's National 400. Lorenzen also finished second on the money list, with more than $72,000 in race winnings.[29]

The attractiveness of its drivers and the Ford-Chrysler rivalry—which effectively divided much of the Piedmont South into Ford, Plymouth, or Dodge camps, with a few Chevy or Pontiac holdouts—drew huge crowds to NASCAR races. The superspeedway races at Daytona, Atlanta, Charlotte, and Darlington drew anywhere from 40,000 to 70,000 fans, and the road course at Riverside, California, brought in more than 50,000 fans. The midsize "bootlegger" tracks at North Wilkesboro, Martinsville, Asheville-Weaverville, and Hickory raked in large profits for their owners by drawing between 10,000 and 20,000 to their Grand National races, and the new half-mile track at Bristol packed more than 20,000 fans into its stands. Small weekday races at the old dirt tracks in Columbia, Spartanburg, and Myrtle Beach, South Carolina, and Concord, North Carolina, and small paved tracks like Bowman Gray Stadium in Winston-Salem and those at Roanoke, Virginia; Huntington, West Virginia; and Old Bridge, New Jersey, drew 3,000 to 5000 fans for the show.[30] With sixty-one races on the schedule, NASCAR, Bill France, drivers, track owners, and promoters basked in the glow of the sport's fan popularity—especially in the Piedmont South and adjacent areas, where two-thirds of all Grand National races were held—and in the attention and money of Detroit bigwigs like Ronnie Householder of Chrysler and Jacques Passino of Ford.[31]

The Factory Support "Catch"

While NASCAR may have seemed more solid than ever in 1964, the influx of factory technical and financial support created significant problems for Bill France and for the long-term health of the sport. Indeed, factory support very quickly created a two-tiered system of both races and drivers. Most of the factory-backed teams eschewed the weekday races and even Saturday or Sunday shows at the short tracks with small purses. As Bobby Allison explained, for most of the top teams short-track racing did not make much economic sense: "If you went to Winston-Salem [Bowman Gray Stadium], it took four or five employees, an engine that cost $750 from Holman and Moody, and at least twelve to sixteen tires that were $40 each at the time, but then you talk about $800 or $1000 first-place money, you were a loser before you showed up, and if you came in second, you were really, really a loser."[32] A few factory-backed teams—Petty Engineering, Bondy Long, and Cotton Owens in particular—tried to run all or nearly all the races in the season and competed for championships. But though the reward of $10,000 or so that the points championship paid in the mid-1960s may have motivated individual drivers, it did not create much of an inducement for car owners with factory deals.[33]

The small number of teams that actually ran for the championship brings to the forefront another major myth of NASCAR history: that the most talented drivers were the ones who won points championships. Winning at least one championship has often served as the major criterion for judging the greatness of a driver's career. In fact, NASCAR itself and many of the writers who have written its history have promoted this idea. The fact of the matter is that until the arrival of R. J. Reynolds Tobacco and the Winston Cup in 1972, the points championship meant little to many of NASCAR's most skilled drivers in terms of either monetary rewards or prestige. Obviously, it was always worth a lot to both Lee and Richard Petty, but most of the greatest drivers of the 1940s, '50s, and '60s never won a championship. Fonty Flock heads the list of early drivers who never finished first in points in NASCAR's top division, but any perusal of the racing news of the late 1940s and early 1950s reveals he was by far the biggest draw in NASCAR. Curtis Turner, perhaps NASCAR's greatest driver of the 1950s and called the "Babe Ruth of Stock Car Racing" in a 1965 *Sports Illustrated* article, never finished higher than fifth in a points championship.[34] In the 1960s, Junior Johnson, Fireball Roberts, and Fred Lorenzen never came close to winning a championship, but few other drivers—and, generally speaking, only those who raced in most of the races—could approach their wins, their qualifying victories, prize money, popularity and, perhaps most important, their winning percentage.[35]

The Independents

Factory backing also created a system of haves and have-nots in Grand National racing whereby so-called independents filled out the fields at races but had little chance of finishing at or near the top. Drivers such as Roy Tyner, Neil "Soapy" Castles, J. T. Putney, Herman "The Turtle" Beam, Larry Frank, G. C. Spencer, Bunkie Blackburn, Wendell Scott, Buddy Arrington, Earl Brooks, Elmo Langely, Paul Lewis, Henley Gray, John Sears, J. D. McDuffie, Friday Hassler, James Hylton, and, in the early days of his career, Bobby Allison showed up for Grand National races week after week with little to show for their efforts other than an occasional short-track win paying $800 to $1,000. Many of the drivers held day jobs that allowed them to get away for races, although several tried to make it full-time and hoped a factory team noticed their talent and offered them a slot, which occasionally did happen.[36]

Even the most successful of the independents often existed on the ragged edge of destitution. In 1966, James Hylton won the Grand National Division Rookie of the Year award and finished second in the points to David Pearson. However, it took a win in the Sportsman Division Cracker 250 at Atlanta Speedway—along with the $4,050 in prize money—in early November to keep him in the racing game for another year. "I'm telling you, if I hadn't won today I really don't know what we'd done this winter. . . . If I hadn't won I'd have to get out and hunt up a job or we wouldn't have nothing to eat."[37]

As the factories openly reentered racing, the inequities between the factory-backed teams and the independents began to disturb some observers. NASCAR began to have a problem filling some fields as more and more drivers realized that, while the financial and physical risks were high, the chances for reward in terms of prize money or the ultimate of being selected for a factory team were very low. In 1964, NASCAR executive director Pat Purcell publicly noted the problems encountered by independents, who could generally afford to spend about $15,000 a year on their cars at a time when the factory teams spent that much for each of the big races at Daytona, Atlanta, Darlington, and Charlotte. "We've gotten into a situation where no one but the factory backed teams have a chance," Purcell observed.[38]

Chicago insurance agent Perry Luster, who sold high-risk insurance policies to race drivers and tracks, even launched a campaign in the racing press to ban factory-backed teams from NASCAR: "Imagine what an independent operator thinks when a factory team pulls into the pits with a machine shop on wheels and equipment the independent can't buy. They're being forced to quit."[39] Luster also bought full-page ads in *National Speed Sport News* with the bold-print headline in all capital letters: "FACTORY TEAMS ARE DESTROYING LATE MODEL STOCK CAR RACING."[40]

Despite the long odds, many independents persevered, saving money by traveling together to many races (in the words of Bobby Allison, "We gypsied up and down the road"), sharing whatever they had with each other. As Eddie Allison—Bobby's brother and chief mechanic—recalled,

"We had a good camaraderie. No one had any money. . . . If we needed to, we borrowed trailers, borrowed trucks. We did everything to get to the race." The independents shared parts and knowledge with one another, but perhaps most important, they shared their labor, working on each other's cars whenever they found an opportunity. The Allisons even put together a makeshift pit crew to try to compete with the factory teams. "We needed a jack man, a gas man, a tire man, and none of the independents had much help, so a group of independent owners—James Hylton, Richard Childress, John Sears, Roy Tyner—pooled their help to form one pit crew. . . . The one pit crew pitted all our cars. The way we did it, the driver who was highest in the standings in the race got to pit first."[41]

Although all the independents had been successful—generally champions—at their local short tracks, in order to stay in the big time they were forced to stroke, or stay low on the track, trying to complete as many laps as they could without getting involved in a wreck or damaging the engine and hoping that attrition in the race would leave them with enough prize winnings to cover their expenses and allow them to race another day. Perhaps the pioneer of "stroking" was Herman "The Turtle" Beam, who raced as an independent from 1957 to 1963 and then put a series of drivers in his car for part of the 1963 and the 1964 seasons. Beam's "stay out of trouble and finish" style earned him $12,571 in winnings in his best year of 1962 and career winnings as a driver—all of which he kept because he was also the owner—of $42,163.[42] Although he was much more averse to "stroking," Wendell Scott generally stayed out of the way as well, especially when he knew he did not have a competitive car. Scott's daughter Deborah Scott Davis, who served as her dad's scorekeeper at most races and worked on the car as well, recalled her dad's racing philosophy, one common to most independents: "He didn't race as hard as some would have thought he should have and that was because he had to preserve what he had to make sure he'd make it to the next race."[43]

Wendell Scott

Of all the independents who traveled around to NASCAR Grand National races in the mid-1960s, none was more unique, or more unexpected, than Wendell Oliver Scott of Danville, Virginia. Scott possessed a pedigree and résumé that were similar to those of most independents of his era. He grew up in southern Virginia, got his first high-speed driving experience hauling liquor, was a natural mechanic who gained additional mechanical training in the army during World War II, and owned his own garage,

Wendell Scott, the ultimate "independent" driver in NASCAR, stands next to his #34 Ford before a race at North Wilkesboro in April 1966. (Courtesy of McCaig-Welborn Research Library at the International Motorsports Hall of Fame, Talladega, Alabama)

contracting with funeral homes and taxi companies as part of his business. He also started racing at local dirt tracks in the early 1950s and soon became consumed with a passion for racing. By the late 1950s Scott accumulated almost 200 wins at tracks in the region, and in 1959 he won the Virginia State Championship. In 1961, he decided to make an attempt at the Grand National big time. Wendell Scott was, however, very different from his competitors; he was an African American in a sport populated and dominated by white, working-class, southern Piedmont good ole boys.[44]

Scott's racing career began when the promoter at the Danville Fairgrounds, in search of some gimmick to put fans in the seats, contacted him about entering a race. As Scott recalled, "I didn't go after the promoters; they come to me, looking for somebody to race the white boys, trying to get people in the stands."[45] The promoter had gone to the police to find out about local African Americans with extensive speeding records.

"They thought they'd get a hold of some of these wild speeders in the streets, you know," Scott told reporter Jerry Bledsoe. Local law enforcement told the promoter, "You want somebody to drive a car, you want Wendell Scott."[46] The promoters probably did not expect Scott to be so good or to have such a long and successful career. But despite the extreme odds against an underfunded, African American driver succeeding in racing, Scott made it happen as an independent among independents, doing almost all the mechanical work himself with the sometime help of his two sons, Wendell Jr. and Frank, and daughter Deborah. On the side of his race car Scott painted the words, "Mechanic—Me."[47]

As difficult as racing as an independent driver was during the 1960s, Scott faced additional challenges because of his race. He attempted to keep as low a profile as possible and never made a major issue of his race in public. As his son and pit crew member Wendell Jr. recalled, "We weren't blacks in racing, we were in racing and happened to be black." It probably helped that Scott was relatively light skinned—"half the time the spectators didn't know I was black"—and had features that testified to his Native American heritage.[48] Wearing a hat, he could often pass as white and eat in restaurants with his independent racer friends such as Earl Brooks or Jabe Thomas, although Brooks remembered, "If he took the cap off his head, all hell broke loose."[49] Scott knew the potential danger of the situation he was in and sought to avoid open conflict with drivers and fans, although the rough-and-tumble nature of racing sometimes made that difficult: "I've never really got involved in too many fights. I've always tried to figure out a way not to have to do that, 'cause I knew that one black with thousands of white people, I wouldn't have too much chance. But I have been involved in some right stiff arguments."[50] On one occasion, however, while racing on the old Dixie Circuit in Virginia, conflict became unavoidable. A tire flew off Scott's car and into the grandstands, injuring five fans. An ugly situation soon developed as an angry crowd gathered to go after Scott. Fortunately, Earl Brooks stepped in between Scott and his potential attackers, iron pipe in hand, and soon dispersed the crowd.[51]

Try as he might to avoid it, however, race was an issue and a major one that Scott had to contend with every day. On some occasions promoters flat-out refused his entries to races. Once a Birmingham, Alabama, promoter sent his entry form back "because he didn't want trouble."[52] Although he became a Grand National regular in 1961, officials at Darlington Raceway refused Scott's entries until the May 1965 Rebel 300.[53] On other occasions track officials placed special stipulations on Scott's racing. In one race in Atlanta, Scott had to wait until a "colored ambulance" arrived before he could take the track. When a serious wreck occurred in the race, the "white ambulance" wouldn't start, and rescue workers took the injured white racer to the hospital in the "colored ambulance." In talking about the incident with reporter Sylvia Wilkinson, Scott asked, "I often wondered, if I had a wreck and the black ambulance wouldn't start, would they have taken me in the white ambulance?"[54]

Although Scott had praise for most of his competitors—he had, and his family has, especially fond memories of the help and kind treatment of Earl Brooks, Jabe Thomas, Tiny Lund, Richard Petty, Junior Johnson, and Ned Jarrett—some drivers remained intent on keeping Wendell in his place. In an interview with Sylvia Wilkinson, Neil "Soapy" Castles recalled one particular incident in which he and other drivers reminded Scott of his position in the NASCAR world. "He stayed in his place. If he got out of his place, somebody put him back in his place. We were in upper state New York racing and the NAACP took Wendell to New York City and made a big deal out of him, the only black racer and everything. Brought him into the race track in a big Cadillac convertible, with a half dozen gals. Started the race that night and Wendell made it to the first corner and somebody shot him right out of the ballpark. Wendell quit riding in that damn Cadillac with those damn women, and that was the end of that. He went back to riding his goddamn pickup truck and he didn't have no more trouble."[55] While Richard Petty asserted in his autobiography that "there never was a hint of racial prejudice," he admitted that the tolerance of Scott and his racing in a "white man's sport" had its limits. "I'll tell you something I always figured: Those cats helped Wendell and said they weren't worried about the color of his skin because he wasn't competitive—they weren't threatened by him. But if Wendell had found, say, 50 more horsepower, the help would have come to a screeching halt."[56]

Besides his race, however, Scott's longevity and relative success as an independent driver separated him from most of his colleagues. Between 1962 and 1971, Scott on average entered forty-six races per year, an incredible show of determination to succeed.[57] As his son Wendell Jr. observed, "I've seen him get frustrated, but quitting wasn't in the plan."[58] Four of those ten years he finished in the top ten in points, and he narrowly missed the top ten in 1964 and 1965. Scott's best earnings year was 1969, when he won more than $47,000, but like most independents he seemed content to just break even. The naturally optimistic Scott also kept at it because, as son Frank put it, "He always felt he was going to get a big break." However, the automobile manufacturers never came knocking at the door, and as Scott himself observed, "I think I was good enough to get some help, but I never did."[59]

On one day—December 1, 1963—Scott was definitely "good enough" when he won the Jake 200 at the Jacksonville (Florida) Speedway, although the outcome was shaped by Scott's race. On the 176th lap of the 200-lap race, Scott passed Richard Petty for the lead and kept that lead for the rest of the event. However, when Scott completed his 200th lap, the flagman did not wave the checkered flag. Scott completed two more laps, and after he passed the flag stand for the 202nd time, officials flagged Buck Baker with the victory, credited Jack Smith with second, and scored Scott in third place. Scott knew he had lapped Baker three times in the race and immediately filed a protest. Meanwhile, the promoters escorted Baker to the winner's circle, where he received the trophy and the traditional kiss from the beauty queen. It took four hours of wrangling and rechecking the score cards before they finally declared Scott the winner of the race. By way of explanation NASCAR spokesmen declared, "The lengthy delay in posting the official results was caused by a scorer missing two of Scott's laps." By the time NASCAR announced the official results, the crowd of 5,000 fans, the beauty queen, Buck Baker, and the trophy had left the premises. Scott did receive the $1,000 winner's check at least.[60]

None of the NASCAR officials present at the race have ever explained the "lengthy delay" in declaring Scott the winner on that day, but Wendell always felt he knew why—the age-old southern taboos concerning white women and black men: "They had Miss Florida there that day to kiss the winner. While all the pictures were being taken, they said Buck Baker won. Then, after they got her away from there, they saw where they had made a mistake in the scoring. I think that was why it happened." Scott did not receive a trophy from NASCAR until almost six months later—Buck Baker never returned the original one—and it was, in Scott's words, "a joke," a cheaply made award without Scott's name on it, just the words "The Jake 200, Jacksonville, Florida." Despite the bittersweet nature of the experience, Scott had done something that very few independents ever accomplished: he had won a race.[61]

It's Become a Pretty Jumpy Game

Although the plight of independents and the relatively small number of competitive cars created a problem for NASCAR, a much more serious one came with the increasing speeds made possible by the new superspeedways and the massive engines in the cars: safety. In 1964 and 1965, a rising toll of serious injuries and deaths on the track caused many drivers to question their future in the sport.

Drivers and mechanics had complained since the superspeedway era took off in the early 1960s about safety problems connected to the high speeds generated on the new tracks, the inability of tires to handle the stresses of those speeds, and NASCAR's inattention to safety concerns. Jack Smith recalled later in life that the rapidly escalating speeds on the superspeedways in the early 1960s made them "the danger years."[62] In 1961, Smokey Yunick sounded the alarm about the failure of the tire companies to keep pace with the high speeds and high stresses created by the new tracks and more powerful cars when he asserted, "Man we are 15 m.p.h. ahead of the available tires."[63] In 1964, Junior Johnson made a similar observation about the deadly combination of speed, high stresses, and inadequate tires: "The cars are going too fast for the tracks. We haven't learned enough to keep the cars handling safely at the speeds we can now travel. And the tire companies are having trouble developing compounds that will give adequate tire wear."[64]

By 1964, even the toughest drivers in NASCAR complained about safety. "It's reached the point at the superspeedways where it's a big relief when a race ends and you're okay, no matter where you finished. It's become a pretty jumpy game," noted driver Buck Baker, by anyone's estimation one of the toughest drivers in the sport.[65] "We've reached the ragged edge . . . it's time for a cutback," Junior Johnson declared. He then frankly admitted, "I'm driving scared for the first time in my life."[66]

Drivers began to call on NASCAR to take action to make the sport safer. The laxity of NASCAR's safety rules, particularly in allowing inexperienced drivers to compete at superspeedways in order to have a full field, prompted Baker to comment, "The safety rules are worthless. They might as well just give 'em all a shot of whiskey and drop the flag."[67] In the summer of 1964, Fred Lorenzen called on NASCAR to take measures to cut speeds for safety reasons: "There's a borderline . . . we're going too fast. I'm sure the fans couldn't tell the difference if the speeds were cut 10 or 15 m.p.h. If the power isn't reduced some way, I'm afraid a lot of guys aren't going to be there for the fans to watch race."[68]

Drivers had good reason to complain, as NASCAR lost some of its most experienced and marketable stars and some of its up-and-coming young drivers in 1964 and 1965. The carnage began with the death of Joe Weatherly at the Motor Trend 500 at Riverside International Speedway in California in January 1964. The colorful Weatherly—wearing his trademark "bright sport shirt, saddle shoes, and golf gloves"—died when his engine blew and his car hit the wall on its left side. The impact caused his unrestrained head to slam through the window opening, striking the retaining wall and killing him instantly.[69] Weatherly had once commented, "I move around so much, I'd rather have the freedom of a seat belt." Ironically, it was his belief that just a lap belt provided more safety and comfort than the shoulder harness worn by most drivers that probably caused his death. While his fans and fellow competitors mourned his passing, most believed the accident unavoidable and asserted, as one friend did, "This is a great loss to the sport. But Joe Weatherly died doing what he liked best—racing stock cars."[70]

The second fatal accident of 1964 sent much greater shock waves through the sport. Only seven minutes into the Memorial Day weekend World 600 at Charlotte, a three-car accident involving Junior Johnson, Ned Jarrett, and Fireball Roberts sent Jarrett's and Roberts's cars into the wall, causing both gas tanks to explode. Jarrett jumped to safety, but Roberts—whose car overturned—lay trapped inside his flaming car. Jarrett rushed to Roberts's car as the driver screamed, "Help me, Ned. I'm on fire." Jarrett eventually pulled Roberts from the inferno, but by the time he freed him, Roberts had suffered third-degree burns over 65 percent of his body. Reporters for *National Speed Sport News* estimated that Roberts "was enveloped in flames for more than 90 seconds."[71] The driver lingered near death for over a month in a Charlotte hospital until he finally succumbed to sepsis and pneumonia on July 2.[72]

Unfortunately, Weatherly's and Roberts' deaths ushered in a deadly period for NASCAR's top drivers that lasted twenty-two months, casting a pall over the sport. In September 1964, Jimmy Pardue of North Wilkesboro, North Carolina, died from massive head and internal injuries during an accident tire testing for Goodyear at Charlotte. While he was racing along at over 140 mph, the right front tire on his car blew, and "the car sailed through the guard rail . . . traveled 300 yards through the air and down a 75-foot embankment before coming to rest."[73] A similar accident claimed the life of rising Houston, Texas, star Billy Wade—who won four straight races in 1964. At tire testing at Daytona in January 1965, Wade's right front tire blew, sending him repeatedly into the outside wall. The cause of death was the same as Pardue's.[74] In September and October 1965, two more drivers—Buren Skeen and Harold Kite—died in accidents in Grand National races. Both drivers sustained massive injuries when their cars spun out on the track and competitors hit their cars broadside in the driver's door.[75] Richard Petty later referred to the 1964 and 1965 Grand National seasons as the "bloodiest period in racing history. . . . Everybody got paranoid."[76]

The rash of deadly and near deadly accidents on the track did lead to some safety improvements. In response to Fireball Roberts's horrifying death—fire generally tops the list of driver fears—both Firestone and Goodyear began applying military technology to the development of rubber fuel bladders to prevent gas from leaking into the driver's compartment after accidents.[77] In 1965, Firestone introduced the "Racesafe" fuel cell at the first race of the year at Riverside, California, and from that point on its use became increasingly common until mandated by NASCAR in September 1966.[78] The deaths of Pardue and Wade sped up the development by Goodyear and Firestone of inner liners on racing tires that prevented the tire from going completely flat when it was punctured. By the spring of 1965, Goodyear introduced such a tire and even used its success in preventing driver accidents in its ads. After the Atlanta 500, a Goodyear ad in *National Speed Sport News* touted Marvin Panch's victory in the race on Goodyear tires but also declared that the company was "just as elated about the guy who finished fourth." The testimonial of the fourth-place finisher, Dick Hutcherson, who had blown a tire in the race, followed: "But that Goodyear Inner Tire took over. Kept me safe. Out of trouble. I was able to make the pits for a tire change. Those Goodyear tires let me finish the race. But more than that, the LifeGuard Inner Tire saved my neck."[79] In May 1965, NASCAR mandated that the drivers use inner liners at Daytona, Charlotte, Darlington, and Atlanta.[80] After the deaths of Skeen and Kite, crew chiefs also began strengthening the welds on roll cages to withstand the harder crashes that came with greater speed. They also added additional bars to the roll cages, particularly on the vulnerable driver-side door. Car owner Cotton Owens responded by adding a third "crash bar" to the car raced by David Pearson to give his driver that "added measure of safety."[81]

Factory Feuds

In the midst of this rash of fatal accidents, feuds between Bill France and the two main automakers supporting the sport—Chrysler and Ford—further depressed fans and drivers and threatened NASCAR's very existence. The source of the controversy came from France's desire to maintain a relatively level playing field between the two manufacturers so that neither make dominated competition. By the mid-1960s fan brand identification made France fear losing fans if a rival make won too many races. With the Detroit manufacturers, however, the rivalry became so intense, with reputations, careers, and millions of dollars on the line, that the desire to crush the competition ruled. France was guaranteed to hear loud complaining, accompanied by threats to pull out of racing, if either Ford or Chrysler felt it was getting the short end of the stick. At the heart of the problem was the whole shifting definition of what constituted "stock" for the National Association for Stock Car Auto Racing.

Serious trouble began late in the 1964 season when France announced NASCAR's rules on specifications for the 1965 season. In formulating the new rules, France was addressing in particular the runaway points championship by Richard Petty and the domination of the Chrysler hemi engines on the series' four superspeedways. The sanctioning body outlawed "special high-performance engines" like the Chrysler hemis and the Ford "hi-riser" overhead cam engine not readily available to the American public. In addition, it mandated that competitors' race cars have a longer wheel base—119 inches as opposed to 116—on the four NASCAR superspeedways. Chrysler head Ronnie Householder immediately protested the new rules and asserted that they gave Ford a competitive advantage. "Aerodynamically, we'll be dead. . . . The new rules NASCAR announced put us out of business down South." He also threatened, "There is a definite possibility that factory sponsored Dodges and Plymouths will be withdrawn from NASCAR competition in 1965."[82] Ford brass, however, welcomed the new rules, as the make had a distinct horsepower and aerodynamic advantage in its regular production cars. "We believe that automobiles in stock car events should be as representative as possible of regular production models," puffed Leo Beebee, Ford manager of special vehicles. He further claimed that the new rules would result "in NASCAR stock car races in 1965 that are even more closely contested by more cars than this year's competition."[83] France shot back sarcastically at Chrysler, evidently believing that the manufacturer would not follow through on its threat and also believing the new rules would bring General Motors back into the sport: "If Chrysler Corp. feels that its standard 426 cubic inch automobiles are not competitive with comparable sized cars of other American makers, then I would be the last to criticize Chrysler on its withdrawal from NASCAR racing."[84]

In early November 1964 Householder announced that, unless NASCAR changed its mind and gave Chrysler twelve months' notice on changes to the rules, it was pulling its cars from the sanctioning body's races. "The effect of the new NASCAR rules will be to arbitrarily eliminate from NASCAR competition the finest performance cars on the 1964 circuit, including the car of the Grand National champion [Richard Petty]."[85] When NASCAR failed to change the rules, Chrysler boycotted and focused its efforts on stock car racing in the USAC series—which allowed its hemi engines—and on drag racing. Richard Petty started racing a factory-backed, 426-cubic-inch, hemi-powered Plymouth Barracuda with the number "43/Jr." and the word "OUTLAWED" emblazoned in its side on drag strips throughout the South.[86] The banning of the hemis outraged Dodge and Plymouth fans throughout the region. Indeed, Hayes Plymouth in Sanford, Florida, did a brisk business in distributing bumper stickers reading "Plymouth—If You Can't Outrun 'Em, Outlaw 'Em!"[87]

The Chrysler boycott did not work out particularly well for Chrysler, Richard Petty, Bill France and NASCAR, or even Ford. Chrysler officials and Petty had to stand by and watch a Ford parade dominate the 1965 Daytona 500; Fords or Mercurys took the top thirteen spots in the race. Fallout from the lack of competition between makes became immediately apparent as announced attendance for the race dropped more than 10,000 from 69,738 in 1964 to 58,682.[88]

For Richard Petty, the Chrysler boycott turned from irritation at his inability to defend his title to horrific tragedy. Petty drew large crowds to drag strips throughout the South to see his 43/Jr. Barracuda race. In early March, a crowd of 10,000 gathered at the Southeastern International Dragway in Dallas, Georgia, to see the popular Grand National champion race over the quarter mile. In the feature match race with Arnie Beswick, Petty's car swerved off the starting line, "slammed into an embankment, jumped a fence, and fell onto spectators." The flying dragster injured eight people in the crowd, including eight-year-old Wayne Dye, who died at the scene.[89] Petty, thrown from the car but uninjured, watched in shock as rescue workers treated his fans. He later recalled: "Seeing a race driver get killed is one thing, but that little boy was something else. I couldn't stand to think about it. I've never had anything in my life get to me like that." Petty honored a few more commitments for races but soon gave up drag racing: "My heart wasn't in it."[90]

The boycott soon became problematic for Bill France as well. Attendance lagged at all NASCAR tracks, and France had to fight near mutiny from track owners and promoters. "I've got to think that racing is suffering because of the Chrysler pull out," Carl Moore, vice president at Bristol

International Speedway, asserted. "We've been selling out our track in past years, but our advance sales are way down."[91] Although he denied that the track owners of Atlanta, Charlotte, and Darlington were putting pressure on France to settle the dispute with Chrysler, Darlington owner Bob Colvin admitted that with the Ford monopoly NASCAR track owners would "suffer until other companies get into production with cars to race."[92] While Atlanta track president Nelson Weaver declared himself "neutral" on the NASCAR-Chrysler dispute, he held out the possibility that the track might not renew its contract with NASCAR for the 1966 season. "If our evaluation of the current situation indicates we might better serve our fans by making changes, then we shall give serious consideration to making changes after the June 13 race."[93]

Problems continued to mount for France as the crucial summer NASCAR season approached. Chrysler factory drivers, many of whom had sat idle unhappily for much of the 1965 season, began to defect to other stock car series. Three of NASCAR's biggest stars, Richard Petty, Bobby Isaac, and David Pearson, announced that they were going to start racing in the rival USAC series—which allowed the hemi engine in cars with a short wheel base—if they could not race their factory rides in NASCAR.[94] Perhaps most threatening to France and NASCAR was word floating out of Sumter, South Carolina, of the organization of a rival sanctioning body, the Grand American Racing Association (GARA), which signed up tracks in the Piedmont region for races, would not allow factory teams, and drew interest from some of NASCAR's top talent. Rumor had it that the "banned for life" Curtis Turner had signed with GARA and that he would headline its first races.[95]

France and promoters Richard Howard of Charlotte and Bob Colvin of Darlington attempted to hold the line against Chrysler by helping car owners who could challenge Ford dominance on the track. According to Chris Economaki, the three "spent much moola" in helping car owner Ray Fox prepare a competitive Chevy for the World 600.[96] Howard also aided Buck Baker with financing to try to put a hemi engine into a NASCAR-legal Plymouth Fury and, when that project failed, to field a Chevy for the 600.[97] None of these attempts, however, succeeded in the least in breaking up the Ford gridlock at the top of the pack, and fans stayed away in droves.

Finally, under increasing pressure from promoters, France had to take some drastic measures to salvage the 1965 season. In late June he crafted an accord with Henry Banks of USAC to create a standard set of specifications for both series. The most important aspect of the pact allowed the hemi engine in the shorter cars at NASCAR tracks of "one mile or less and on road courses." This allowed the factory Chryslers—and most important, Richard Petty, Bobby Isaac, and David Pearson—into all NASCAR events except for the ones at Daytona, Charlotte, Darlington, and Atlanta. While Chrysler initially played coy with France and special car manager Robert Rodger asserted that Chrysler "had not planned at all to compete in NASCAR this year," Petty and his Chrysler-backed compatriots returned to NASCAR tracks by late July, winning a few races and providing at least a little manufacturers' variety in the top ranks.[98]

Howard, Charlotte Speedway president A. C. Goines, and Colvin also came up with a creative plan to boost flagging fan interest in NASCAR and deal with the threat of GARA: lift the "lifetime ban" on Curtis Turner. Although France initially resisted reinstating Turner, he knew he had to take some drastic action, and Turner, even at age forty-one, still drew the fans.[99] Turner sat in the infield of the Concord Speedway preparing for a GARA race when the car phone in his Cadillac rang and Colvin gave him the news of his reinstatement. He jumped at the chance to return to NASCAR and immediately told reporters, "This is the best news I've had in ... four years. You can bet money that I'll be back—and back winning."[100] France justified his decision to rescind Turner's "lifetime ban" to reporters—well accustomed to his repeated reversals: "We feel Curtis Turner has paid the penalty for his actions by sitting out four years of NASCAR racing."[101] After he drove borrowed, underpowered Plymouths for his first few races, Ford racing director Jacques Passino stepped in and secured a top ride for the rest of the season for Turner with the factory-backed Wood brothers team.[102] Although the first few months of racing drew lots of press attention and little in the way of results—Chris Economaki reported that Turner was "commanding more ink than his finishing positions deserve"—Turner broke through in a major way at the next-to-last race of the year, the inaugural event at the new one-mile North Carolina Motor Speedway at Rockingham.[103] The race took on even more significance as the only race of 1965 with all of NASCAR's top drivers—and Curtis Turner to boot—and attracted a sellout crowd. Bill France himself could not have written a better script for the race. Driving with a broken rib incurred two weeks earlier at a race at Charlotte, Turner battled Cale Yarborough, scorching heat, and an overheating car that smacked the wall twice in the closing laps to win the five-hour marathon of a race. After the race, in characteristic style, Turner announced to the press, "We're gonna go home after this, and we're gonna start a brand new party every fifteen minutes. I think Little Joe [Weatherly] would like that."[104]

Even though the charismatic Turner was back, his presence could not salvage the 1965 season. Fords won fifty of the fifty-five races contested in the Grand National Series, including the first thirty-six. Ned Jarrett, driving a factory ride for Bondy Long, ran away with the points championship with Holman-Moody driver Dick Hutcherson finishing second. Seven of the top ten drivers, including the top six, drove Fords.[105]

Ford's Turn to Boycott

After the disaster of the 1965 season, NASCAR looked ahead to fans flocking back into the stands with a renewal of the intense Ford-Chrysler competition of earlier years. Indeed, going into the Daytona 500, it looked as if 1966 would be a banner year for the sport. The event featured strong contentions of factory-backed Fords, Plymouths, and Dodges, as well as a handful of independent Chevys. All of NASCAR's star drivers were there as well, including Curtis Turner. The presence of Indy stars A. J. Foyt and Mario Andretti added competitive spice to the mix. Holman-Moody Ford driver Dick Hutcherson crowed, "The field is tremendous, the best I've ever seen in NASCAR." A reporter for *National Speed Sport News* asserted that the 1966 race "should go down in the history books as the race that dawned a new era for stock car racing."[106] A record crowd of more than 90,000 fans came to see Richard Petty and Chrysler's hemi-powered Plymouths and Dodges dominate the race and seven of the top ten spots.[107]

Unfortunately, a season that began with such optimism soon degenerated into a sad parody of 1965. This time Ford boycotted, while Chrysler dominated the season. Only five days after Chrysler-backed cars whipped Ford-backed cars in the Daytona 500, Ford announced the availability to the public of a street version of its powerful 427-cubic-inch single overhead cam engine (SOHC). Ford execs then argued that NASCAR should legalize the engine for NASCAR racing. Ford ran ads announcing that astronaut Gordon Cooper purchased the first commercially available 1966 SOHC Galaxie 500, and it distributed photos of Cooper and Ford racing head Jacques Passino looking over the car's engine.[108] NASCAR and USAC soon came to a decision about the legality of the SOHC, and while they approved use of the engine, they "slapped a weight penalty on the car" of one pound per cubic inch of engine capacity. In the case of the SOHC, this meant the Fords would carry 427 more pounds than their competitors. At the same time, the sanctioning bodies liberalized the rules for Chrysler and GM products.[109]

In April, Ford chairman Henry Ford II himself announced Ford's boycott of stock car racing. One unnamed Ford official justified the company's withdrawal on the basis of fairness and safety and claimed, "We can't be competitive under these rules. We are giving away too much to the Chryslers. And besides that, the safety factor in this is quite important. We couldn't keep wheels on the car at this weight." As one author observed, France and Banks "didn't ban the engine, they merely handicapped it out of business."[110] Overnight, the announcement sidelined established stars Fred Lorenzen, Dick Hutcherson, Curtis Turner, Marvin Panch, and Ned Jarrett as well as talented newcomers Bobby Isaac and Cale Yarborough. Jarrett lamented the possible damage the Ford walkout might cause: "We just can't keep treating the spectators the way we have the last couple of seasons."[111]

Fans responded negatively almost immediately to the news of the Ford boycott, as demonstrated by plummeting attendance.[112] The Gwyn Staley Memorial race at North Wilkesboro on April 17 drew only 6,000 fans, "less than half the normal attendance." The "Rebel 400" had the worst crowd in Darlington history when only 12,000 fans showed up, with 5,000 of those Boy Scouts given complimentary tickets. The defections of Ford drivers Marvin Panch, who went to drive for Petty Engineering, and Ned Jarrett, who boycotted the boycott and fielded an independent Ford, helped attendance some, but overall NASCAR limped through spring and summer with growing numbers of alienated fans and promoters.[113]

The Yellow Banana

Under pressure from track owners and promoters, Bill France had to take drastic action this time to break up the Chrysler parade and bring in more competitive Fords and Chevys. In the process he reinforced his reputation as a capricious dictator. Events came to a head around the August 7 Dixie 400 at Atlanta. Ford was already making plans for a "limited return" to the sport in 1966 and a full-force reentry in 1967, as France had announced that he would drop the weight penalty for the SOHC engine for the '67 season. John Holman asked Junior Johnson—who had cut back on his race driving to become a full-time car owner—to prepare a competitive Ford Galaxie for the Atlanta race. Junior put all his creative energies to work to build a Ford to challenge the hemi-powered Plymouths and Dodges on a superspeedway. The result was an aerodynamic gem, a car with a severely sloped front end, a raised rear end, and a cut-down roof line. Driver Fred Lorenzen actually had to have his seat lowered so that he could fit into the car's cockpit. Wags around the track soon christened the car the "yellow banana" because of its unusual shape and its pale yellow color—the color of the car's sponsor, Holly Farms Chicken.[114] According to *Southern MotoRacing* editor Hank Schoolfield, "The car looked weird enough to be put together by committee."[115]

Johnson's "supposed to be Ford" prompted quick reaction from his competitors, especially when it passed inspection and qualified third. Driver Bobby Johns complained loudly, "If Freddy and that Ford win this race, then it will be the biggest injustice in the history of NASCAR. . . . That Ford is strictly illegal and everybody knows it." He equated the entry of the "yellow banana" with a boxer being allowed to have "a glove filled with lead." Johnson simply responded, "All I can say is that Johns has an awfully big mouth."[116]

To make matters even worse for many, NASCAR allowed Smokey Yunick to enter a '66 Chevy Chevelle that was almost as creatively designed as the "yellow banana." "Bunky" Knudsen, now head of Chevrolet, had secretly paid Yunick to build a Chevelle earlier in the season.[117] He had run it at a few major races without much success with drivers Mario Andretti and Bobby Allison. In July, Yunick paired with Curtis Turner—who had jumped the Ford ship—and qualified third and finished fourth at Daytona's Firecracker 400. For the Atlanta race, Yunick added some handcrafted touches to the front end and a lip on the rear of the roof that acted as a spoiler—all illegal modifications—to the Chevelle, and Turner qualified it on the poll.[118]

While France allowed the obviously illegal cars fielded by Johnson and Yunick into the field—primarily to get drivers Lorenzen and Turner in the race—NASCAR disqualified three other cars after inspection. Inspectors disqualified immediately LeeRoy Yarbrough's car, owned by Jon Thorne, when they discovered wooden blocks—designed to fall out once the race began and lower the front end to provide an aerodynamic advantage—inserted in the front springs. NASCAR gave owner Bernard Alvarez a long list of things to fix on Ned Jarrett's Ford Fairlane, and the owner withdrew the car rather than go to the extra time and expense. Cotton Owens also withdrew the David Pearson–piloted Dodge in protest—despite the fact Pearson was leading the points race—when inspectors told him to remove a cable that could be pulled to illegally lower the front end. "I refused to change my car for reasons of principle. The principle involved was

NASCAR allowing two cars to flaunt the rules while blowing the whistle on others. I realize that Lorenzen and Turner are valuable as drawing cards, but that didn't make what happened right."[119]

As luck would have it, neither Johnson's or Yunick's cars fared very well in the race, a subpar crowd of only 25,000 fans showed up, and Bill France was left to come up with a creative explanation as to why he allowed the two cars to race. France's "clarification" of the situation was a classic case of the reasonably sounding, contradictory double-talk for which he had become the master: "I admit the rules were bent at Atlanta. After Fred Lorenzen drove Johnson's car in Atlanta, it sort of opened the door for any of the other Ford drivers to return to racing if they wanted to. The entire deal happened at the last minute and there was not time to prepare another body for the car. We are going to make every effort to stick to the rule book and everybody knows it. Junior knows it. He is rebuilding the Ford and putting a new body on it."[120] NASCAR also "grounded" Yunick's Chevelle. Asked if he was going to compete at Darlington's Southern 500, Yunick replied, "I haven't got the racing good seal of approval from NASCAR."[121]

Driver Defections

While attendance improved for the rest of the year as Ford reentered the fray, safety issues and the constant wrangling with the auto manufacturers led four of NASCAR's most prominent drivers to hang up their helmets. As Richard Petty summed up the mid-1960s in NASCAR: "Not only [was it] a brutal period [referring to driver deaths], but it marked the first mass exodus of top drivers in NASCAR history."[122]

Marvin Panch's retirement did not come as a great surprise to many people, as he had just turned forty and had planned all along to quit at that age. At the same time, the Ford boycott and his boycott of the boycott when he defected to Plymouth and Petty Engineering in the 1966 season probably shortened his career. As he later put it in an interview, "When they [Ford] came back, they sure didn't come running to ask me to drive one of their cars," despite the fact he had "been with them for so long over a 10-year span."[123]

Junior Johnson cited both the uncertainty over manufacture involvement and safety issues when he retired. "The situation with the manufacturers being in and out and then in and out again was gettin' aggravating."[124] When he first announced he was stepping down as a driver in November 1965, Johnson—whose bravery no one questioned—asserted,

"I've taken enough chances on those superspeedways. I know I can run them good but why take any more chances?"[125] Johnson did decide to stay in the sport as a car owner/crew chief, although he did get back in the driver's seat for eight races in 1966. In October of that year, his driving career ended with a blown engine while he was leading the race at North Wilkesboro Speedway, the same place his career had begun. In reflecting on the end of his driving days, Junior was not sentimental: "I didn't feel sad. I had held a notion for some time that I'd accomplished practically everything I set out to accomplish. I didn't have anything to prove to anybody, including myself. On top of this driving wasn't fun anymore. The thrill was gone, even the excitement of the speed had gradually wore off. Like I said, I'd run faster in a liquor car than I ever did on racetracks, including Daytona, Charlotte, and Atlanta. I was quitting, and this time I stuck to it."[126]

In the midst of the Ford boycott, Ned Jarrett announced his retirement to take a position with a Greenville, South Carolina, marketing firm. In speaking of his decision, Jarrett observed, "I got to looking at the security, or the lack of security really, that this sport offered and I wanted to spend more time with the family, the kids were growing up, and so I made my decision to retire then at the end of the 1966 season."[127]

Perhaps the most shocking retirement for NASCAR was that of Fred Lorenzen at the age of thirty-two. Losing good friend Fireball Roberts; his own devastating accident at Daytona in 1964, in which he severed arteries in his hand, almost lost a foot, and cracked three vertebrae; the confusion over Ford's boycott; and the stress of a naturally shy person constantly being in the limelight caused him to develop painful ulcers. Finally, early in the 1967 season, Lorenzen gave it up: "I was losing interest. I had won everything, and it just wasn't fun anymore, and all my buddies were getting killed. I just wasn't into it, and when you're not into it, it makes a difference how you'd drive. You don't drive as hard."[128]

Back to the Roots

While the driver deaths, the manufacturer boycotts, and the retirements of four of its top drivers made the mid-1960s one of the low points in NASCAR history, the sport still held some considerable assets. First, despite the dangers and uncertainties of the sport, the retirements of top drivers were more than offset by the arrival at the top of probably the greatest group of drivers in NASCAR history, drivers who not only could handle the close, door-to-door beating and banging of the short tracks but who

Leonard Wood flies around the car while pitting David Pearson. Car owners/mechanics Glen and Leonard Wood revolutionized the NASCAR pit stop, turning it into an athletic ballet. (Courtesy of Don Hunter Collection, Smyle Media)

had no fear of the high banks and harrowing speeds of the new super-speedways. Rising stars Richard Petty and David Pearson had already won points championships and were threats to win in every race, and a new group of drivers steeped in traditional Piedmont male culture but shaped by newer economic and social realities stood ready to challenge them.

Two of the new stars were out of the David Pearson school, guys who came to the sport as an escape from a life in the mill. LeeRoy Yarbrough came to NASCAR from the tough working-class neighborhood on the west side of Jacksonville, Florida, that produced Ronnie Van Zant and other founding members of pioneering southern rock band Lynyrd Skynyrd. As a teen, Van Zant told friends his chief goal in life was "to be the most famous person to come out of Jacksonville since LeeRoy Yarbrough." Yarbrough was cut from the same cloth as early star Bob Flock—dour, moody, and shaped by dire poverty as a child to fight for every scrap. As fellow driver "Little Bud" Moore recalled, "Like most people in racing, he was poor, low-class who had to pull himself up from that. And he was violent. He would fist fight in two seconds." While Yarbrough came of age on the dirt tracks in the Sportsman ranks like almost every driver of his era, he thrived on the new superspeedways, never shied from the escalating speeds, and was at his best in the big races.[129]

Bobby Isaac grew up in similar poverty after his father died. He dropped out of school in sixth grade and came to NASCAR after teen years spent working in the saw mills and cotton mills of the North Carolina Piedmont in the community of Catawba near Hickory. Isaac was desperate to escape the environment of his youth and testified that he "hated working in that cotton mill." Friend Humpy Wheeler asserted that Isaac's youth spent in poverty gave him an intense drive to make it in NASCAR: "He was so afraid that he would have to go back to that environment he had been in, that terrible poverty environment, that he would do anything to keep from it. For a person who had been dirt poor, that is a fear like no other fear." Like Pearson and Yarbrough, Isaac was not comfortable in the limelight and was self-conscious about his hardscrabble background, poor grammar, and lack of education—although stories of his inability to read and write are untrue. Like Ned Jarrett, Isaac discovered stock car racing at the nearby Hickory Speedway, threw together a makeshift '37 Ford racer, and headed for the local dirt tracks. Although he built his early reputation for success on the short tracks, by the late 1960s—when he secured a ride in Nord Krauskopf's K&K Insurance Dodge crew-chiefed by Harry Hyde—he began to develop a name as one unafraid to push the powerful automobiles coming out of Detroit to their limits on the high banked superspeedways.[130]

As successful as Yarbrough and Isaac became, their accomplishments pale next to those of two others who came on the scene in the mid-1960s: Cale Yarborough and Bobby Allison. Yarborough was straight out of the pages of W. J. Cash's *Mind of the South*. He grew up on a tobacco farm in the Pee Dee region of South Carolina not far from Darlington. Steeped in the "hell of a fellow" ethos from an early age—his daredevil father died in a plane crash when Cale was eleven—by the time he was twenty he had been bitten by a rattlesnake, dived out of an 80-foot-tall cypress tree into 5 feet of water, wrestled an alligator, survived a parachute jump when his chute only partially deployed (the soft, newly plowed field he landed in probably saved his life), ridden bulls in a rodeo, and started his own auto and airplane thrill show. He was, if ever one existed, a natural-born stock car racer and brought a love for thrills and speed and an intense competitiveness to the sport.[131]

While born and raised in Miami, Florida, well outside NASCAR's Piedmont heartland, Bobby Allison brought a new level of intensity to the sport in the mid-1960s. He moved to Alabama with brothers Eddie and Donnie to pursue his interest in stock car racing, and his driving skill, mechanical ability, toughness, intelligence, and incredible competitive drive made him the most successful independent driver on the circuit. He soon drew the attention of factory teams, but his unwillingness to kowtow to anyone often made his stints with factory teams he did not himself control short lived. Despite this, he began in the mid-1960s crafting one of the great careers in NASCAR history, and his late 1960s rivalry/feud with Richard Petty would help fill the stands with eager fans.[132]

France had also been able to maintain the loyalty of many of his top promoters/track owners, especially the core group that had created the infrastructural foundation of NASCAR with the "bootlegger tracks" of the late 1940s and early 1950s, even as he courted the attentions of Detroit CEOs Ronnie Householder, Henry Ford II, and "Bunky" Knudsen. When France needed their assistance, he knew he could count on Enoch Staley, Clay Earles, and Joe Littlejohn for help. In 1966, in a little-noted move, France partnered with Staley, Earles, Littlejohn—who quit his job as promoter at Atlanta to head the operation—Raymond Parks, and Grafton Burgess to purchase the Asheville-Weaverville Speedway from Gene Sluder, who was on the verge of bankruptcy. The list of partners reads like a who's who of early NASCAR pioneers/bootleggers from the 1940s and 1950s and was indicative of the continued reliance of France on these key men. While not noting the background of most of the principals in the deal, *National Speed Sport News* reported that Asheville-Weaverville "has, in its operating corporation, more promotional brains than any other track in the world."[133] With Parks and Burgess as the promoters of record, the track held a successful inaugural race—the Fireball 300—in June 1966 in honor of Fireball Roberts.[134]

Perhaps most important, even as NASCAR began moving increasingly to the superspeedways that would dominate its future, it still had the unmatched attraction of its short tracks and drivers who knew how to put on a show for the fans. As Chris Economaki observed in 1966, "If you want to see great racing, catch a NASCAR Grand National on a half-mile dirt track." One example of this "great racing" came at the Fonda (New York) Speedway in July of that year. The excitement started even before the race began when Tiny Lund took too much speed into the third turn, ran onto "what appeared to be an escape road," and ended up driving through a neighboring cemetery before heading back into the track "through the sign-in gate." The race itself turned into a "ding-dong duel" as Richard Petty and David Pearson battled over the last fifty laps, with Pearson edging out his rival. For many fans, however, the highlight of the race came on lap thirty-one when independent driver J. T. Putney went over the bank in turn two, drove up a service road that paralleled the backstretch, made a "270-degree left turn" back onto the track, and in the process took out the cars of Tiny Lund, Bobby Allison, and Lyle Stelter. Angered by Putney's recklessness, Lund—one of the biggest drivers in NASCAR history at 6'4", 250 pounds—"charged down the pit lane and landed a 'haymaker' on Putney, kayoing him." Putney later came to in an ambulance on the way to the hospital.[135] NASCAR fined both drivers $100, and fans had memories to last a lifetime.[136]

The entertainment value at any short track doubled with the presence of Curtis Turner, and the veteran bootlegger/timberman put on two unforgettable shows in 1966 that only increased his already considerable legend. At a race in Columbia, South Carolina, immediately after the "yellow banana" fiasco, Turner once again piloted a Junior Johnson Ford. Holly Farms executives had told him they wanted him to look professional and wear a "driver's suit" when he competed in their car. Turner arrived "half-juiced" right before the end of qualifying and decided to take the Holly Farms directive literally. He "figured what the hell, I'll drive in what I got on": a brown silk business suit.[137] He did take the jacket and vest off but left his tie on as he qualified the car second and led 134 of the 200 laps to finish third in the race behind Pearson and Petty. After the race Turner told reporters, "They wanted me to be a gentleman driver and I figure this is the first step. You've gotta look good you know."[138]

At Turner's next appearance in Johnson's Ford, the driver again wore a business suit—this time pale yellow to match the Holly Farms colors on the car—but his behavior was anything but "gentlemanly." The race was at the quarter-mile Bowman Gray Stadium in Winston-Salem, North Carolina, where much of the Turner legend began with his epic battles with Billy and Bobby Myers. Ironically, the race was the "Myers Brothers Memorial" to honor the two deceased local racing legends. The event drew a capacity crowd of more than 15,000, most there to see Turner once again. "Pops" started in the fourth spot but soon became impatient to get up to leaders Pearson and Petty. Young Bobby Allison, making a splash in

Grand National racing with three wins in only his first full season, was in the way, however. Turner took his usual approach to such impediments, lived up to his nickname, and spun Allison out on lap eight and headed after the leaders. Now down a lap, Allison took almost a hundred laps to catch up and came up on the now-leading Turner's bumper to try to get his lap back and vie for the win. At the same time that Tom Pistone battled Turner on the outside for the lead, Allison tried to take him on the inside. At Bowman Gray two-wide is a stretch, and three-wide is nigh on impossible. Pistone hit the wall and Turner and Allison came together, with Curtis getting the worst of the contact and spinning out. Richard Petty took the lead in the midst of the mayhem as the caution flag came out.[139]

The action, however, did not stop with the caution. Turner had to pit for repairs and new tires, and when he came back onto the track, he slowed considerably and lay in wait for Allison. Allison anticipated that Turner was going to ram him, so he took matters into his own hands, slammed into the side of the yellow Ford, and pinned Turner against the wall, allowing the field to pass. This set off a ten-lap demolition derby as each driver repeatedly crashed into the other until both their cars died on the front stretch. It was a return to the old days of the bitter Myers brothers–Turner rivalry at the stadium. A near riot ensued as fans of both drivers climbed the fence and rushed the track. Police intervened before anyone was hurt, and wreckers cleared the cars from the track so that the race could proceed. Pearson won yet another battle with Petty, but few fans would remember the race winner. Once again, NASCAR fined both drivers $100, less than a third of the cost of a Curtis Turner "driving suit."[140]

Junior Johnson was not quite so sanguine about the incident, however. He told Turner "next time I'll pay the fine and you'll pay to fix the car." After thinking about what had happened, he changed his mind and told reporter Hank Schoolfield, "This will be the last time Curtis Turner will ever drive a car of mine." In a later comment, Johnson also presaged the coming modern era of NASCAR when ties to sponsors would end most of such behavior. He declared the incident "really embarrassing for Holly Farms. It wasn't the image they wanted."[141]

By 1967 NASCAR was at a crossroads in its history. It had one foot solidly in its past of white liquor and red clay as it depended on the close racing of the short tracks and the antics of its star drivers to stabilize its base in an uncertain era. At the same time, it had made important steps, albeit unsteady, into a future characterized by high-speed superspeedways and heavy—and often heavy-handed—involvement from Detroit automakers Ford and Chrysler. Somehow, Bill France had reached at least a détente with the automakers, kept the organization from splitting apart in the process, and stood poised to fulfill the bright promise of nationwide legitimacy and exposure he and others had seen in NASCAR as far back as the mid-1950s.

The Dirt Tracks Are
Rapidly Becoming a Thing of the Past
The End of the Beginning, 1968–1972

"It is one of the most well-wired, well-built stills I have ever seen in operation," observed Peach County, Georgia, sheriff Reggie Mullis of a newly busted illegal distillery operation near Macon in October 1967. In addition to the uniqueness of the still's construction, its location in a 125-foot tunnel on the property of the Middle Georgia Raceway with access through a "dummy ticket booth" on the north side of the property proved even more startling.[1] While many observers may have been unsurprised by the discovery of the still—indeed, the Macon operation was probably not the first on a speedway property given the provenance of many of the early NASCAR tracks—the Georgia still was in reality a vestige of a bygone era as NASCAR moved rapidly into its modern age.

Within a few short years, most of the evidence of the sport's founding era in the Piedmont South had disappeared. With but a few exceptions, the bootleggers who had created the sport were gone from the scene. In the late 1960s, NASCAR would hold its last dirt-track race in its top division, and short-track races would become an increasing rarity. By the early 1970s, even Big Bill France himself stepped out of the limelight and gave up control of the sport. In the place of dirt tracks, liquor barons, and Big Bill France, NASCAR would have even more, and faster, superspeedways, corporate sponsorship of both cars and the series itself, a lucrative television contract that began to showcase the sport to more and more people outside the Piedmont region, and new leadership in Bill France Jr.

The Coronation of the King
In 1967, however, the future success of NASCAR was anything but clear, and the sport desperately needed something to keep its old fans and bring

in new ones after the deaths and retirements of star drivers, two years of manufacturers' boycotts, and turmoil at all levels of the sport. Although Bill France had tried to manipulate things to create a stir in the sport and maintain a viable presence of representatives of each of the "Big 3" auto makers, it was a good, old-fashioned, unmanufactured winning streak that brought the fans back in droves and elevated a thirty-year-old Richard Petty from star status to legend in one season. Petty's performance in 1967 was so incredible that it transfixed Piedmont fans and brought national media attention. During the season, he won twenty-seven out of forty-nine races, shattering Tim Flock's record of eighteen wins in a season; topped his own father's record for career victories; and from Bowman Gray Stadium on August 12 to North Wilkesboro on October 1 went on an unbelievable ten-race win streak—including his first win in one of NASCAR's most prestigious races, the Southern 500.[2] "Everything we did was like magic. . . . I got to thinking I could win every race," Petty later recalled.[3] While some observers contend that Petty faced little competition at this time—especially on the short tracks that most owners of factory-backed cars shunned—the streak included the Southern 500 and races at Martinsville and North Wilkesboro against the top factory-backed Fords (Ford brass became obsessed with ending the streak), Plymouths, and Dodges. In addition, the odds of going through such a stretch of races without a wreck, mechanical failure, or human error of some kind are tremendously long.[4]

Petty's popularity skyrocketed after the 1967 season. Even as early as September 1967, in the midst of his streak, bumper stickers touting "Richard Petty for President" popped up all over the Piedmont South.[5] During the presidential election year of 1968, the numbers of these bumper stickers only increased. At about this time Petty started to become known in racing circles as simply "The King," a moniker even his own son Kyle often uses to refer to his father. Petty poured much of his 1967 winnings into expanding and modernizing the Petty Engineering facilities at Level Cross, North Carolina. When he held an open house after the renovation, more than 20,000 people showed up. In characteristic style, Petty sat at a workbench and signed his elaborate autograph for hours. "I mean, people came from all over the country, and it took a whole bunch of the North Carolina Highway Patrol to control traffic."[6]

Richard Petty takes a victory lap complete with rebel mascot and Confederate battle flag at Darlington's 1967 Southern 500. The win in one of NASCAR's premier events was his fourth in a row on his way to a record ten straight victories and his second Grand National championship. (Courtesy of Don Hunter Collection, Smyle Media)

The Feud

In addition to Petty's rising superstardom, NASCAR benefited from something every sport needs: an intense and even bitter rivalry. The arrival of upstart independent driver Bobby Allison from Hueytown, Alabama, provided a perfect working-class foil for NASCAR's "King." Their rivalry would prove as bitter, as long-lasting, and as attractive to fans as any in NASCAR history.

The unheralded Allison burst onto the NASCAR scene in 1966, winning three short-track races in a lightweight Chevrolet Chevelle. His win at Oxford, Maine, in July was the first win for a Chevy product since 1963 and sparked a renewed interest among "bowtie" fans at a time of Chrysler dominance. His lack of factory sponsorship in an era when fans became increasingly fed up with Detroit's meddling in the sport, his dogged determination, and his unwillingness to back down from anyone, including the sport's biggest stars—evidenced in his Bowman Gray demolition derby with Curtis Turner—also captured the imagination of working-class fans.

As Bobby's brother Eddie—who worked with his brother on the car—recalled, "To take a car out of the backyard in Hueytown, Alabama, and go beat that [Petty] Plymouth was unreal. It was so neat, because Bobby scared them hot-dog racers to death. This hick from Alabama . . . could come out and beat them with this race car that they thought couldn't outrun a kiddie car."[7]

Allison's connection to the working-class suburb of Hueytown near Birmingham also helped make Alabama a new hotbed of NASCAR fandom. Although he migrated to central Alabama from Miami, Florida—and was a Catholic to boot—he was embraced by his adopted state and became the patriarch of the legendary Hueytown-based "Alabama Gang," which included such NASCAR luminaries as Bobby's brother Donnie, Sportsman Division star Red Farmer, Neil Bonnett, Hut Stricklin, and Bobby's son Davey.[8]

The Allison-Petty rivalry/feud started in November 1967 in the last race of the season at Asheville-Weaverville Speedway. Allison had recently moved into a factory Ford ride with Holman-Moody crew-chiefed by Fred Lorenzen and was anxious to prove his worth to his new team. Twenty-two laps from the end of the race, Petty bumped Allison out of the way and up the track to take the lead. Only a few laps from the end of the race, Allison caught "the King" and returned the favor, moved him up the track, and passed him to take the lead and finish first. After the race, the pit crews rushed together and "nearly came to blows" until NASCAR officials separated them. Petty later told the press, "I guess when you've won as much as I have, everyone takes pot shots at you." Allison characterized the event as just normal racing: "Things like that happen on short tracks when you have two cars that are equal and two drivers who are racing for the win." While Allison downplayed it, the incident marked the beginning of a rivalry that carried over from the drivers, to their crews, to their fans and would last well into the 1970s and even beyond.[9]

The spark struck at the Asheville-Weaverville race fanned into flame in July 1968 at the tiny, .2-mile Islip (New York) Speedway. Allison was back in his independent Chevelle after quitting Bondy Long's factory Ford team. Petty was running away from the field and, in trying to move Allison out of the way and put him a lap down, damaged his own front fender, necessitating a pit stop for repairs. Allison, undamaged in the incident, sped away and took the win. The Petty crew cried foul and accused Allison of ignoring the "move over" flag and blocking his rival. Allison defended his actions and asserted that Bobby Isaac blocked him, preventing him from getting out of Petty's way. Richard's brother, engine builder/crewman Maurice, and crew chief Dale Inman did not wait for an explanation of the incident and took off after Allison as soon as the race ended. Maurice got there first and knocked Bobby down, and both Maurice and Dale then piled on the driver until bystanders pulled them off.[10] To compound the tension, Allison's Aunt Myrtle went after Petty's crew and "whacked Maurice with her pocketbook."[11]

Later, both Maurice—who was fined $250 by NASCAR—and Bobby gave their versions of the incident to the press. "I guess it was a blowoff of one of those things that build up over a period of time," Maurice asserted. "It started last year at Asheville-Weaverville when Bobby roughed up Richard real bad and got away with it. You might say we settled an old score." Allison accused Inman of being an "agitator" who incited Maurice to go after him. He explained further, "I was going to call the police and have Maurice and Dale arrested. Lin Kuchler [NASCAR official] was there and talked me out of it."[12]

While Allison biographer Peter Golenbock referred to the rivalry as the closest thing "to motorized ballet as NASCAR ever presented," it was the intense competitiveness of both drivers and the possibility of the two roughing each other up, or their pit crews duking it out—a staple of short-track racing everywhere—that captured the fans' imagination and brought them back time after time to see the two go at it. As Eddie Allison recalled, "Bobby just loved to beat Richard." For Bobby that meant beating him not only on the track but at anything, including signing the most autographs. He recalled, "I could write fast, so I would get rid of my autograph seekers faster than he could his. I can say I signed as many or more autographs than he did, because I got done quicker. . . . Even if it's signing names. Everything's competitive."[13]

The Grand Touring Series and New Tracks

The institution of the companion Grand Touring Series helped boost further NASCAR's popularity in 1968. The series—designed to highlight the new breed of popular "sports sedans" produced by Detroit, such as the Ford Mustang, Mercury Cougar, Plymouth Barracuda, Chevrolet Camaro, Pontiac Firebird, and AMC Javelin—played much the same role as the Convertible Series did in the late 1950s. Races were 250 miles in length and run the day before many of the major Grand National races and occasionally as stand-alone events.[14] NASCAR designed the series as a sort of minor league for individuals desiring to move up to the Grand National ranks. As *National Speed Sport News* observed, "The new Grand Touring Division of NASCAR has stirred a lot of interest among Dixie Sportsman and modified drivers. They look upon it as an opportunity to get in the big leagues at a minimum of cost."[15] The series featured primarily such drivers but also included Grand National drivers without factory rides. One such driver, popular journeyman and 1963 Daytona 500 winner De-Wayne "Tiny" Lund, dominated the series for much of its history, winning three of its four championships.[16]

In addition to Petty's rise to superstardom, the Allison-Petty rivalry, and the new Grand Touring Series, NASCAR benefited from the construction of new tracks and the expansion of the sport into new territories well beyond its Piedmont, dirt-track roots. Promoters announced the beginning of construction for the Dover Downs (Delaware) International Speedway—a unique combination of facilities: a thoroughbred horse track inside a one-mile, high-banked speedway—in November 1967. The track hosted its first race in July 1969 and attracted a crowd of more than 20,000.[17]

The entrance of Michigan entrepreneur Larry LoPatin, his publicly traded American Raceways, Inc. (ARI), and the concept of "franchise racing" further boosted the sport. Even though LoPatin knew little about the sport, he took the NASCAR world by storm when he announced in January 1968 that he would build a 2-mile speedway in the Irish Hills near Detroit and that this would be only the beginning of a racetrack franchise that would host "20–25 major races by 1971."[18] Michigan International Speedway hosted its first race on June 15, 1969, and drew a crowd of nearly 50,000. At that point LoPatin and ARI had almost completed a twin track at Bryan, Texas—near College Station—and hosted the 1969 season-ending race there in early December. ARI also gained control of the financially troubled Atlanta International Raceway in 1969 and purchased 48 percent of the stock of the Riverside, California, road course.[19]

Talladega

The biggest, most important speedway project of the era, however, came out of a collaboration of two of the South's most iconic figures: Big Bill France and Alabama governor George Corley Wallace. France discovered the perfect site for a new superfast speedway in or around 1965 at an abandoned World War II airstrip near the mill town of Talladega, Alabama.[20] In conducting a demographic survey, France discovered that 15 million people lived within a 300-mile radius of the tiny town, 50 miles east of Birmingham and 100 miles west of Atlanta. The property became even more attractive when France developed a close relationship with Alabama's demagogic but development-minded governor. The two exchanged letters and met face to face in Montgomery in August 1965. They formed a close personal friendship, and Wallace agreed to speed up construction of the Alabama portion of I-20, which ran by the site; facilitate water and sewerage improvements; aid in the condemnation of land; and build new access roads to the track.[21] In 1966, Wallace wrote to France, "We stand ready to do anything that we can to help make this project possible in Alabama."[22]

Later France returned the favor by becoming a vocal supporter of and financial contributor to Wallace's presidential campaigns. When Wallace first ran in 1968, France asserted, "George Washington founded this country and George Wallace will save it." In 1972, France served as campaign manager for the "Wallace for President" effort in Florida, allowed the governor to use Daytona Speedway as a backdrop for advertising, and helped deliver every county in the state in the Democratic Party primary.[23]

In May 1968 France broke ground for the massive 2.66-mile Alabama International Motor Speedway, with 33-degree banking. The *Birmingham News* reported: "Here friends is the kind of BIG money for Alabama that usually has Chamber of Commerce folks doing handstands in the streets. My hats are off to the Talladegans who were willing to dream along with NASCAR's Bill France, and whose efforts are about to bring tourists and dollars into here in bunches like bananas."[24] Some Talladegans must have wondered what they were getting, however, when France used strong-arm tactics to oppose incorporation of the speedway into the city and quiet talk among county commissioners of a 50¢ per ticket tax. In an interview with the *Talladega Daily Home*, France told a chilling parable that gave the local folks a clear idea that Bill France did business on his own terms and would brook no interference from the locals: "It reminds me of the story of the dog coming home with the bone. He was passing over a little bridge when he saw his reflection in the water. He leaned over and opened his mouth to grab the other bone from the dog in the water. When he did, the bone in his mouth dropped out and he had nothing."[25]

Anxious to recoup his investment in the track, France scheduled the first race for September 14, 1969, and anticipation grew as to what speeds the Grand National cars could attain on the high-banked superspeedway. Alabama congressman Bill Nichols asserted that the first Talladega race would be "by far the biggest sporting event in the State of Alabama," a huge claim in a state that was obsessed with college football and home of the annual Iron Bowl between Auburn University and the University of Alabama.[26] France obviously had two dreams for the race, or at least for Talladega's near future—the breaking of the world closed-course speed record and topping the 200-mph barrier. Advertising for the race played on the potential spectacle: "Think about it. Fifty rumbling, roaring NASCAR Grand National stockers blasting down the longest straights in stock car racing . . . then dipping three abreast into the steepest banks in the business at better than 180 miles per hour! The toughest, bravest, and fastest drivers in the world battling each other for 500 miles . . . fighting heat and fatigue . . . pushing their machines to the limit and sometimes beyond."[27] The announcement by Chrysler that it would field several of its new Dodge Daytonas for the race—a car test driven by Charlie Glotzbach at Michigan at over 193 mph—only heightened the anticipation of fans.[28]

But natural and human forces seemed to conspire against France and his 200-mph dreams in Alabama. Delays caused by the inauspicious arrival of Hurricane Camille in August led contractors to rush the paving job, and the results proved less than satisfactory to drivers who tested the new track. After making a lap at over 193 mph, Bobby Allison sounded an alarm: "This place is rough as a cob. It would be a beautiful speedway if it was smooth. The roughness bounces the car around so much it feels like it's tearing the wheels off in the corners. . . . The only way they're going to fix it is to repave it." After taking practice laps on the track, other drivers expressed their concerns that tires lasted for only a few laps with the combination of unprecedented speeds and rough track conditions.[29]

The Professional Drivers Association

Unfortunately for France, the speedway's inaugural race also coincided with growing driver unrest and the formation of a new drivers' union. This time around the organizers proved more effective in maintaining secrecy and the loyalty of top drivers. On August 14, 1969, eleven drivers met in Ann Arbor, Michigan, and organized the Professional Drivers Association (PDA). The group elected the sport's reigning superstar Richard Petty as president of the organization, Cale Yarborough and Elmo Langely as vice presidents, and a board of directors composed of Bobby Allison, Buddy Baker, LeeRoy Yarbrough, David Pearson, Pete Hamilton, Charlie Glotzbach, Donnie Allison, and James Hylton. The success of organization efforts in the National Basketball Association (NBA), Major League

Baseball, and the National Football League encouraged the drivers. The PDA hired Lawrence Fleischer, who had spearheaded the organization of NBA players, as general counsel.[30]

The goals of the organization differed little from those of Curtis Turner and the Teamsters' 1961 organization of the Federation of Professional Athletes: retirement and insurance plans, improved facilities for driver convenience, driver safety, and higher purses. Richard Petty remembered the reasons he became involved in the PDA: "All of a sudden the cars started running 190, 195 mile-an-hour. We was running on some of these race tracks that it wasn't safe to really be in the pace car. Also, the guys was getting concerned about, hey man, there's more people coming but the purses ain't going up."[31] NASCAR's apparent concern that the "show must go on" despite safety concerns also brought driver complaints. Lee-Roy Yarbrough asserted after the 1968 World 600 at Charlotte, "If I had a rock, I'd throw it at him," when flagman Johnny Bruner failed to throw a caution flag despite pouring rain. Yarbrough further complained that Bill France and NASCAR officials "sit up there in their glass tower and talk about safety and then act like they want to kill us."[32] Charlie Glotzbach complained that France ran NASCAR "like a Communist organization. Drivers are afraid to say anything bad about the way they are treated." He pointed to a breach of safety protocol when NASCAR went ahead with a Sportsman Division race at Daytona in 1969 despite a wet track. Driver Don McTavish was killed in an accident that resulted from the poor racing conditions. "I don't know how those NASCAR officials can sleep at night," Glotzbach averred.[33]

The need for the PDA was at least one thing that Richard Petty and Bobby Allison could agree on. Allison defended the organization of the PDA: "We formed an organization because we felt foolish in not forming one. Every other major sport has its players' organization. . . . A guy devotes his life to racing, and he gets only $7,500 if he gets an arm torn off. If he gets killed, his wife gets $15,000."[34] Allison added that many drivers could not afford the high insurance rates for individuals in such a risky enterprise. He also talked about the need for retirement benefits so that when drivers "got out of the cars we wouldn't be working in a gas station for $1.19 an hour."[35] NASCAR's lack of concern for driver convenience and expense when it scheduled races further drew his ire. "We've never had a voice in planning or scheduling. They might have a 500-mile race and two days later, a 100-miler a thousand miles away."[36]

Initially, the PDA proved content to just talk about the problems it saw in NASCAR, although a few "wildcat" actions in August 1969 occurred among a handful of independent drivers. At short-track races at South Boston, Virginia; Bowman Gray Stadium; and Asheville-Weaverville Speedway, drivers started races and then quit after a few laps to protest the lack of prize money for individuals running outside the top few spots; a tenth-place finish paid only $60 more than last in the race. As driver Neil "Soapy" Castles observed, "There's only three drivers who make any money. The guy who wins, the guy who finishes second, and the man who runs dead last. The last place finisher never uses up any tires. Everybody else loses money."[37] PDA officers, however, met and told the independents to "knock off the protests" for fear of weakening the overall effort.[38]

Big Bill Strikes Back

France was not one to sit idly by and watch his drivers organize a union, however, as he had demonstrated in 1961. He denied the validity of the drivers' claims and asserted that they had never had it so good: "NASCAR has been pretty great to this bunch. I drove in a day when there was zero prize money posted and the track operators were rinky dink guys who were not responsible people. . . . I can't see why LeeRoy Yarbrough, for instance, would want such a group. He's won $150,000 this year alone. That's not too bad."[39] France then tried to quell any potential uprising among his Grand National drivers. To demonstrate that the Talladega track was safe and perhaps embarrass the drivers into silence on the safety issues, he got behind the wheel of a Holman-Moody Ford Grand National car and turned a lap at 175 mph hour on the high-banked track. After this lap, France proudly announced to the press: "It's a world record for a 59 year-old man." France then applied for membership in the PDA when he filed an entry for the Talladega 500 eight days before the race. When asked about France's request, Allison replied: "I'd say he would be a foolish old man. He wants to get into the PDA any way he can."[40]

As more drivers arrived in Talladega for race practice and qualification, safety concerns mounted. In many cases tires blistered and cracked after only two laps at 190-plus mph. After representing Dodge in a controlled tire test on the Friday before the Sunday race, driver Charlie Glotzbach — who had qualified on the pole with a world closed-course land speed record of 199.466 mph — argued: "They ought to call this race. Nobody has tires any good for more than 15 laps." Donnie Allison, who drove a Ford in the test, asserted, "My heart was in my mouth through the whole test. That was the most scared I have ever been in my life."[41] Talk among the drivers in the garage area—where traditionally there was "never any talk of danger and the risk, as if people were making believe it didn't exist"— changed dramatically as the race neared. Reporter Bob Carey of *Stock Car Racing* magazine observed that for the first time in his experience, "the words 'widow' and 'funeral' were spoken in clear pear-shaped tones" by the drivers.[42] LeeRoy Yarbrough asserted: "There is no way you can drive a car at speed under those conditions. I don't want to make my wife a widow this early in life."[43] Driver Buddy Baker spoke out: "Every man down there wants to race, this track is so exciting. But we don't want to race under these conditions. I'll be tickled to come back here and race when the various things are all straightened out. Not now, though. I like me. I've grown accustomed to living. And I'm not sure I would be living if I went out there and raced the way the track and the tires are now."[44]

Car owners and tire company representatives joined in and asserted that neither the track nor the tire companies were ready for this race. Owner Mario Rossi, a former driver himself, claimed, "The tire problem seems to stem from a combination of G forces, lateral load, speed and the rough condition of the speedway surface. I wouldn't run the race and I wouldn't expect a driver to run it at a competitive speed."[45] On Friday evening before the Sunday race Firestone officials, fearing a disaster, withdrew their company's tires. One unnamed tire manufacturer's representative defended the drivers: "The drivers' concern for their safety is legitimate. As much as I hate to admit it, the tires just won't withstand the pressure of running 200 miles-per-hour. This is a whole new realm for us and it shows. The right side tires are virtually falling apart after only five or six laps."[46]

Bill France dismissed these concerns and fired back that a "foreign substance" on the track cut the tires and ordered his crews to sweep the track to remove the problem. A Goodyear spokesman countered France's assertions and argued: "The reason the tires are lasting only four or six laps is because of high speed, the poor condition of the track surface and tires. There's no such thing as a foreign substance. We didn't have enough time to test here. This was a rush-rush race." France refused to budge and had too much tied up in the race to cancel or postpone it. "We will have a race here. Right now I don't think we have a major problem."[47] As journalist Gene Granger later observed, "The bottom line was that Alabama

International Motor Speedway was not ready for 200 m.p.h. speeds. Everyone knew it but one stubborn man—Bill France—whose obsession with speeds of 200 m.p.h. is still not understood today."[48]

The PDA Boycott

After the dismaying news from the Glotzbach and Donnie Allison tire test, Petty met with PDA members individually, polling them about boycotting the race. The next morning Petty informed France that the PDA drivers would not run and likened running in the race to playing "Russian roulette." France shot back: "There will be a race tomorrow. If you don't want to be in it, pack up and leave." Petty proceeded to load his car on his trailer, and several other drivers followed suit. A few hours later, France confronted Petty and a group of PDA drivers. When Petty tried to convince France that the only thing to do was to postpone the race, France shouted: "What you hot-dogs do is your business. But quit threatening the boys that want to race. If you want to go home, then go." The NASCAR boss then tried to convince the drivers to stay around and observe what happened in that day's Grand Touring race: "I tell you the wear isn't going to be as bad as you say." Bobby Allison responded to France by arguing that comparing tire wear on the smaller and lighter Camaros, Mustangs, Javelins, and Cougars run in Grand Touring races would be like comparing apples to oranges. Allison demonstrated his distrust of France when he sneered, "Don't try to fool us."[49]

France then advised the drivers that if they were so concerned about tire wear and safety they could just run at slower speeds. LeeRoy Yarbrough jumped in: "Bill, we can't put on a decent show the way things are now. Sure we can go out and run 175 and not wear any tires, but is this fair to the guy that's paying $25 for his seat?" Petty countered: "We don't want to run. We want to race." Bobby Allison then launched into sarcasm: "Can we start on foot and get paid by position? Wait, I take that back, the track is so rough we'd probably trip and fall before we got to the first turn."[50] PDA organizer and lawyer Larry Fleischer offered a criticism still leveled at NASCAR on occasions: "Any event held where cars are not run at their full potential would be like staging a 'wrestling match.'"[51] The meeting almost came to violence when Petty called drivers together for a meeting and Bill France tried to follow. Cale Yarborough blocked his way and angrily asked: "Where do you think you're going?" This is a "drivers' meeting and only drivers are coming in." France backed down from the former Golden Gloves boxer, but it was soon obvious that he was

Bill France (taller man in striped cap) confronts Richard Petty and other drivers over the Professional Drivers' Association decision to boycott the first Talladega race. (Courtesy of Don Hunter Collection, Smyle Media)

not to be deterred in running the race.[52] But for the top Grand National drivers, however, the confrontation simply confirmed that they would not drive in the race. "The end came abruptly," Gene Granger observed, "when France denied emphatically the track was unsafe, then asked the drivers, in essence, to run a 'controlled race.'"[53]

France scrambled to fill the field with the departure of his top drivers. He had no trouble convincing factory driver Bobby Isaac, shunned by the PDA because of his independent streak, to stick around for the race. Isaac was no fool, however, and announced before the race that he would not run at full speed. "I'm going to run. You can bet on it. But I'm not going to run 190. I'm smart enough to know what speed to run when the tires won't stay together."[54]

Nine journeyman, independent drivers joined Isaac as the only Grand National drivers in the field. The independent drivers were torn between the PDA boycott and the opportunity for an unusually high finish in a high-prestige, big-money race. Roy Tyner compared the experience to being "caught in a vise. I've made a deal and it's too late to get out of it."

For Richard Brickhouse the opportunity to drive the factory Dodge Daytona vacated when Charlie Glotzbach left was too tempting to pass up, even though he had joined the PDA. "This is the chance of a lifetime for me. I may never have another opportunity to drive a factory car. It's what I wanted all my life." Coo Coo Marlin loaded his Chevy on the trailer to join the boycott, changed his mind, unloaded it and headed for the garage entrance, changed his mind again and loaded it back up, and finally unloaded for the last time and entered the race.[55]

Even as the top Grand National drivers pulled out and headed for home, France employed another common union-busting tactic to fill the field for the Sunday race: the hiring of replacement workers, or scabs. His power as both head of NASCAR and speedway owner/promoter gave him a tremendous advantage in combating the union as he once again threw out the rulebook in order to hold a semblance of an official race. France filled the rest of the field by allowing twenty-five Grand Touring drivers with their smaller cars—in clear violation of NASCAR rules—to enter the headline event. The NASCAR boss also provided Grand Touring driver Tiny Lund with the Holman-Moody Ford that France had driven previously around the track. The Ford never went through official NASCAR inspection, another blatant violation of the rules.[56]

As the race approached, France demonstrated not only his toughness and determination but also his mastery of public relations. France knew his core customers, the Piedmont working class, and like many southern union busters before him, he played their distrust and suspicion of unions masterfully. As spectators arrived, track ushers handed them a statement from France, who laid all the blame for the boycott at the foot of an irresponsible PDA, credited his determination to hold the race to his obligation to the fans, and offered them an incentive to come back:

> I am very much surprised that some of our drivers and car owners would wait until the last day prior to a major race and withdraw their automobiles from a race. Track officials and NASCAR officials worked until the last moment to get the drivers to fulfill their obligations to the fans who traveled some distance to see the event. Everyone expected they would race.
>
> It would be unfair to the spectators who traveled to Talladega to see a race to postpone it. It would also be unfair to drivers and car owners who wish to compete.
>
> Therefore, we will start the first annual Talladega 500 at 1:00 p.m.

Sunday as scheduled, lining up the Grand National cars in the order they qualified. We will allow the Grand Touring cars to start in the back of this field in the order that they finished the 'Bama 400. We will pay the purse of $120,000 as advertised.

Persons who attend the race, and those holding reserved seat tickets who do not attend, will be allowed to exchange them for tickets for a future race at Daytona Speedway or for a future race at Alabama International Motor Speedway.

They can see two races for the price of one.

This does not apply to press tickets, complimentary tickets or credentials.

Sincerely, Bill France.

To France's great relief, more than 62,000 fans showed up for the race, many attracted by the controversy of the previous weeks. After the race, France told reporters that, while he feared a negative reaction from fans, "with what we planned—the ticket arrangement—I felt sure that fans wouldn't be mad at the speedway or NASCAR, and they weren't."[57]

In order to avoid a race marred by tragedy, as the PDA drivers feared, France and race officials took some special measures. France quietly directed NASCAR's control tower to tell "some teams to slow down when they went too fast," brought out the yellow caution flag every twenty-five laps so that drivers could pit and change tires, and told teams ahead of time when they would throw cautions. Flagman Johnny Bruner also warned the drivers piloting the smaller, slower Grand Touring cars in the race to stay low on the track and out of the racing groove, or "we're going to have the damnedest wreck in history." The drivers themselves kept their speeds down until late in the race to prevent blowouts. The winning car averaged only 153 mph, almost 3 mph slower than the winner in the previous day's Grand Touring race.[58] Despite the slower speeds, tires still came apart on the heavy Grand National cars. In order to hide this from the press, "as quickly as they came off the cars, they were covered up." Photographers still recorded plenty of evidence of extreme tire wear due to the rough track, high speeds, and heavy cars. Despite the dangers, however, France dodged a bullet, and there were no accidents or even spinouts by drivers.[59]

Independent driver Richard Brickhouse won the race driving the factory-backed Dodge Daytona originally intended for Charlie Glotzbach, one of only three cars running on the lead lap. Brickhouse had resigned from the organization over the public address system prior to the race. In presenting the winner's check and trophy to Brickhouse, an overjoyed Bill France took a jab at the PDA when he announced to the cheering crowd: "Winners never quit, and quitters never win." Later, France gave Bobby Isaac a Rolex watch with those words inscribed on its back.[60] In the next day's *Charlotte Observer* reporter Tom Higgins captured the essence of the previous day's proceedings: "Bill France, who has survived some harrowing crises in 20 years as head of the NASCAR organization he created, pulled a rabbit out of the hat again Sunday."[61]

The Demise of the PDA

NASCAR's top drivers now knew they had little leverage left to gain any concessions from France. Although France had told drivers that "any driver who pulls out won't be penalized," technical inspector Bill Gazaway allegedly told one driver that if he boycotted the race "you might as well turn your car into a farm tractor, 'cause it won't ever get through inspection again." France himself gave the PDA drivers cause for worry when he told the press: "As far as I'm concerned, the boys that raced today saved this track, and they saved NASCAR racing. . . . The boys who pulled out owe their future to the drivers who ran today—if they have a future."[62]

Although the PDA issued a public statement defending its boycott, the teeth were gone from its attempt at organizing, and Bill France knew it. France took advantage of the situation by adding a new clause to future Grand National entry forms creating, in effect, a "yellow-dog" contract for NASCAR drivers and ensuring that there would be no repeat of the Talladega boycott. "In signing this blank, both driver and car owner recognize their obligation to the public and race promoters or speedway corporation posting the prize money and conducting the event. Therefore, we agree to compete in the event if humanly possible unless the event is postponed, canceled or if the car fails to qualify for the starting field."[63] In a nod to driver complaints, France also created a committee of drivers, owners, promoters, manufacturers' representatives, and NASCAR officials to look into the possibility of providing pensions and other retirement benefits to drivers. The committee, like the one France created in 1961 in the aftermath of the first union movement, met sporadically and soon disappeared with little changing for the drivers.[64] Although Petty and the PDA initially resisted signing the new entry forms, after a union meeting at Charlotte on September 24—especially when both factories and promoters backed France—the drivers backed down from almost all their

The shy and intense Bobby Isaac (left) with legendary crew chief Harry Hyde. Isaac was the only factory-backed driver who did not boycott the 1969 Talladega 500, which only increased his popularity with many working-class fans. (Courtesy of McCaig-Welborn Research Library at the International Motorsports Hall of Fame, Talladega, Alabama)

demands. In explaining the purpose of the meeting, Petty explained: "We wanted to assure the motor companies, the promoters, the fans and everybody concerned that we are going to race the rest of the races this year and next." He concluded by asserting that drivers had just wanted "someone to talk to" about their problems.[65]

Negative fan reaction to the Talladega boycott further weakened the union effort and gave the drivers additional motivation to back down. In the first race after the boycott, at Columbia, South Carolina, Bobby Isaac—the only top driver who had not participated in the driver boycott—received the loudest applause of any competitor during driver introductions. When he passed PDA leader Richard Petty to win the race, fans cheered even louder. At the next two races—at Martinsville and North Wilkesboro—fans threw beer cans and bottles onto the track, most apparently aimed at Petty. At Martinsville a beer can hit Petty's car directly in the windshield, bringing out the caution flag which, ironically, allowed Petty to close up behind David Pearson and eventually pass him for the win. After the race Petty commented: "Today was the worst I've seen for beer cans on the track. I don't know if the Talladega deal had anything to do with that or not." A beer bottle thrown onto the track the next week at North Wilkesboro brought out a caution with four laps left, reversed Petty's fortunes, and erased his huge lead over Pearson, who passed him for the win.[66]

A three-year $1,365,000 contract with ABC Sports to televise selected NASCAR events provided France with additional leverage against the drivers' union. The contract called for the broadcast of nine races at some of NASCAR's biggest tracks—Charlotte, Daytona, Rockingham, Darlington, and Talladega—in 1970, five broadcast on the day of the race, which would include a half-hour recap of the race with the last hour live, and four shown at later dates on tape delay. ABC aired most of the races on the popular *Wide World of Sports* program. While NASCAR had had some races televised on tape delay in the past and a successful contract with a company to broadcast the Daytona 500 on closed-circuit television in theaters, this was the first time a major broadcaster televised races live across the country. The money from the contract helped to buy the loyalty of promoters and track owners, even those whose races were not televised, as France provided them with a share of the rights money. *National Speed Sport News* reported that, after a meeting of promoters in February 1970, most of them pronounced their share of the television package as "more than fair."[67]

The Rise and Fall of Larry LoPatin

France also used the leverage of the television deal to strike a blow against his chief rival in the business, Larry LoPatin. France and LoPatin had clashed soon after American Raceways Inc. began to become such an important player in the sport. LoPatin first alienated France when he broke ranks with his fellow promoters and publicly criticized the NASCAR boss's handling of the PDA boycott at Talladega. The ARI president particularly pointed out France's conflict of interest as the head of NASCAR and the owner of two of the sport's most important speedways—a charge still leveled today. "This may be the end of an era," LoPatin asserted. "You can't run an organization without order. The Ford Tiny Lund drove at Talladega was illegal. The GT cars aren't eligible in Grand National racing. Would the same decision have been made if the NASCAR president was not president of the track?"[68]

From this point on France and LoPatin's relationship deteriorated rapidly. First, France "temporarily" took the inaugural race at ARI's new Texas track "off the Grand National schedule" because the purse announced for the race was too low—although NASCAR had no published standards. LoPatin boosted the purse and France put the Texas race back on the schedule, but their relationship began to worsen seriously. In November 1969 the two became involved in a "face-to-face confrontation" at the Ford Motorsports Banquet, and France stormed out. In December, France delivered a major blow to LoPatin and ARI's stockholders when the television contract came out with none of the ARI tracks listed on the schedule, despite the fact they hosted some of the best-attended races.[69]

In the aftermath of his falling out with France, LoPatin's empire collapsed. In December, three of ARI's key employees resigned—Michigan general manager Hank Lowdenbach, Riverside general manager Les Richter, and Jim Hunter, the popular public relations head at Atlanta. In the aftermath of Richter's resignation, ARI also became embroiled in a lawsuit for control of Riverside Speedway. Nature also conspired against LoPatin, as bad weather plagued his races in late 1969 and early 1970 and attendance and revenues suffered. By August 1970 and the arrival of one of its top races—the Dixie 500 at Atlanta—ARI was in dire straits, and LoPatin fought to maintain control of the company. Once again, ARI had trouble posting the purse money, and NASCAR and Richard Howard had to step in to guarantee the payout to drivers. On the day of the race, fewer than 20,000 people showed up, a problem compounded when a lien holder with a court order temporarily suspended ticket sales in order to get ARI to pay its bill. In the aftermath of the Atlanta debacle, ARI was unable to come up with a scheduled payment of $100,000 to its creditors for the Michigan track, Investors Diversified Services. The board of directors ousted LoPatin and named Les Richter as the new president.[70] France ally and Daytona Beach sportswriter Bernard Kahn asserted, "His fall was long overdue. The Detroit promoter came in racing as a fast mouth looking for a fast buck."[71] LoPatin defended his tenure and his vision of "franchise racing" to the press. "I know my concept was right. The question is: Was Larry LoPatin's personality right for it?" He then blamed his ouster on the "stranglehold" Bill France had on the sport: "I know as a native Detroiter that I would never have believed that man or his sanctioning body could push around the automotive companies the way they do."[72] Like another visionary in the sport, Carl Kiekhaefer and his team concept, LoPatin was simply a man before his time.

The money from the television contract also allowed France to "sweeten the pot" for car owners—and indirectly, their drivers—by creating the Automotive Research Bureau (ARB), a "wholly owned subsidiary of NASCAR," which paid $500 to the top owners in selected major races. Charlotte promoter and head of the NASCAR television committee Richard Howard asserted that the ARB was not about "deal money" but designed to provide "post-race information" to NASCAR to improve safety and the sport itself. However, everyone in racing knew the money helped both to guarantee the presence of top drivers at major races and to keep them in line. The television contract—which required that at least ten of the top twenty drivers be entered in a broadcast race—at least partially necessitated this move, but damage to the PDA was an added benefit for France.[73] While Richard Petty knew the deal would help him personally, he did not "think this is intended to help the PDA." Indeed, this action virtually killed it. By the early 1970s as even more money came into the sport, drivers like Petty could make more than $100,000 in appearance money alone.[74] In noting France's skillful use of the carrot and the stick, Pete Daniel observed: "He [France] brought undreamed-of prosperity to stock car racing. With the help of sponsors, France hammered at drivers' rough edges, discouraged public fighting, and generally kept them on a short leash. Whatever political notions, if any, these wild men had in the early days of racing, prosperity made them Republicans."[75]

The End of an Era

The 1970 season marked the end of an era in many ways for NASCAR as the sport became increasingly distanced from its roots. When NASCAR announced its Grand National schedule in February, it contained only four dirt-track races.[76] Only three of these—two at Columbia and one at Raleigh—were actually run because Bill France closed down the Hillsborough, North Carolina, track that he had built and co-owned with Enoch Staley in 1947 and shifted the planned spring race date to Talladega. The last dirt-track race in NASCAR's top division came on September 30, with Richard Petty winning the Home State 200 by two laps in front of a crowd of 6,000. Petty seemed to sense this might be the end of NASCAR's dirt-track era and mused after the race, "The dirt tracks are rapidly becoming a thing of the past. I hope a few dirt tracks are kept on the schedule. This is where our brand of racing started."[77]

Bootleggers also became a disappearing breed in the sport. By the early 1970s, few of the top drivers, car owners, or track owners in the sport had had even a historical connection to the business. Curtis Turner—perhaps the greatest bootlegger/driver in NASCAR history—lost his life at the age of forty-six when his twin-engine Aero Commander airplane went down in Pennsylvania in June 1970. Turner had just announced his entry in the National 500 in Rockingham, the track where he had won his last race right after Bill France reinstated him in 1967.[78] Junior Johnson was still around the sport, but as a car owner, although his propensity to skirt the edges of NASCAR's law and exploit the gray areas of the rule book kept inspectors on their toes. While NASCAR legend generally presents Johnson as the beginning of the moonshine/race driver era in the sport, he was in actuality one of the last. When North Carolina governor Bob Scott asserted that the approval of "liquor by the drink" sales in many of the state's municipalities would "put a gradual end to moonshining," promoter Joe Littlejohn—one of the first bootleggers/racers in the sport's history—quipped, "Where will our race drivers get their early training?"[79] Though Littlejohn made this comment in jest, it did reflect the changes that had taken place in the economy of the Piedmont and neighboring foothills and mountains during the 1960s. Expansion of industrial opportunity and improved working conditions and pay in the region combined with new opportunities on the farm—especially chicken raising and processing—created many new legal alternatives for making a living. Improvement of law enforcement and harsher penalties for liquor law violations also changed the landscape in places like Wilkes County, North Carolina, and made the production of illegal alcohol even less attractive to young men.

The early 1970s also marked the end of most of the tracks built by bootleggers that had formed the infrastructural foundation for NASCAR. Charlotte had closed in the early 1960s because of construction of I-85 and the crosstown Charlotte Motor Speedway. Occoneechee in Hillsborough had its last race in 1968. The consortium of former bootleggers who ran Asheville-Weaverville had failed to make a go of it, and Gene Sluder's track held its last race in 1969. Hickory and Middle Georgia hosted their last Grand National races in 1971, although Hickory remains a staple of weekly racing to this day. Two of the bootlegger tracks—North Wilkesboro and Martinsville—remained viable venues in NASCAR's top division as Enoch Staley and Clay Earles skillfully ushered their tracks—both built in 1946—into the modern era of NASCAR and continued as trusted aides to Big Bill France and his son and successor Bill Jr. Few people in or around the sport knew much of the men's—and their tracks'—early history.[80]

Along with the exit of dirt tracks and bootleggers, some observers complained that the very essence of the sport had changed. Smokey Yunick, whose association with NASCAR went back to the early 1950s, wrenched a car in his last Grand National race in 1970. As he left the sport, he lamented the loss of the seat-of-the-pants informality of NASCAR racing that had endeared the sport to many. "I don't like what has happened to racing. I'm not knocking it, but the kind of racing I knew, I'd go home and build a race car and you go home and build a race car, and we'll unload our cars at Daytona, and then we'll walk down the track, and I'll pull my pants up, look around, and say, 'sons of bitches, let's have a race.'"[81]

The Factories Exit

The exit of the factories in the early 1970s changed the sport further. As early as the late 1960s—in the aftermath of Chrysler, then Ford boycotts— the factories began to decrease their direct involvement. Both manufacturers sharply curtailed their racing budgets—Ford had cut its budget from a high of $12 million in 1967 to $2 million by 1970—and the number of cars they supported as the 1970 season began. They were, in many ways, victims of their own arms race, which had resulted in what were essentially limited-production race cars like the Ford Talladegas and the Dodge Daytonas. *National Speed Sport News* complained about this lack of "stock" in stock car racing: "One of the big reasons for a motor company falling out of love with racing is the necessity for special cars that are unlike those sold—the long-nosed Ford Talladega and the winged Dodge Daytonas being cases in point. These are out and out racers and the knowledgeable public (including the kids) know this. . . . The sooner the stock gets back into stock car racing; the better things will be."[82]

But instead of making their race cars more stock, the manufacturers decided to end their direct involvement. In November 1970, Ford announced it was disbanding its factory-sponsored teams, while Chrysler reduced its factory support to one Dodge and one Plymouth, both fielded by Petty Engineering.[83] Chrysler ended its sponsorship of the Petty cars at the end of the 1971 season, and the era of direct sponsorship was over. Reaction to the factory departure was mixed. Jacques Passino, who had headed Ford's racing effort since 1962, resigned from the company in protest: "I still feel the race track, which has proven to be the real test track for automobile production, will be the same—even more so in the future." Junior Johnson declared that he was cutting back his involvement and was probably on the way out of the sport altogether. "I can't race without a sponsor. I've sold one car, in the process of selling another and hope to sell the third car. After that, I'm out of racing."[84] Bill France, however, was uncharacteristically quiet and even seemed relieved by the factory exodus.

The end of factory support also led to the demise of still another NASCAR legend, Charlotte's Holman-Moody Racing. Holman-Moody, the very symbol and center of Ford's factory effort, had always been the product of an uneasy alliance between two brilliant mechanical minds: the prickly John Holman, who focused on the business end of the enterprise, and the gregarious and beloved Ralph Moody, who ran the day-to-day racing operations. The partnership had launched the careers of Fred Lorenzen and a number of other top drivers; dominated the series in 1965—the Chrysler boycott year—winning forty-eight of fifty-five Grand National races; and won Grand National championships with David Pearson in 1968 and 1969. By 1971, Holman and Moody's relationship was well frayed at the edges, and the end of Ford's direct support caused it to fall apart all together. As Ralph Moody later recalled, "We were barking at each other about this, that, and the other thing. . . . Why fight it? We had fought all of '71, and I had enough. I wanted out of it."[85] Mechanic Waddell Wilson remembered one incident in which tensions were at their greatest when Moody fired up a race car in the garage not knowing Holman was on the phone. Holman got so angry that he went down to the shop floor, took a forklift, and proceeded to lift the car off the ground and deposit it in the parking lot outside.[86] While Holman would continue with the company, have success as an engine builder, and retain the company name, the departure of Ford and Ralph Moody ended their iconic status in the sport.

Respectable NASCAR

While NASCAR changed as a result of the departure of dirt tracks, bootleggers, and Detroit manufacturers, it also entered a new era of respectability. The growing popularity of NASCAR did not go unnoticed by politicians, who began to use the sport for their own publicity purposes. Perhaps the first politician to publicly declare himself a NASCAR fan was Georgia governor Jimmy Carter. Named grand marshal for the April 1971 Atlanta 500 at the Atlanta International Raceway—a facility still reeling from the financial troubles of American Raceways, Inc.—Carter helped boost attendance at the race by hosting a highly publicized dinner at the governor's mansion for more than 300 NASCAR drivers, crews, and officials before the race. Car owner Glen Wood asserted to reporter Bob Myers, "This is a first for racing. I've never seen anything like it and I really have a lot of respect for that man."[87] Carter backed up the publicity with action when he publicly pledged, "We'll keep this place open—somehow," and vetoed a bill from the state legislature that allowed Henry County to charge an amusement tax for the raceway's tickets.[88] NASCAR races also drew the attention of politicians in North Carolina in the early 1970s. Chris Econo-maki noted the presence "in the pits with racing types" of North Carolina gubernatorial candidates Harlan "Skipper" Bowles and Hugh Morton at an October 1971 race at Charlotte.[89]

In the 1972 presidential election, NASCAR gained even greater exposure and recognition as a political player. George Wallace asked Bill France to chair his Florida campaign in the Democratic Party primary, and France delivered not only the state but every one of its counties. The biggest boon to NASCAR, however, came in October when President Richard Nixon in-vited 168 "racing figures from across the nation"—which included Indy racing and drag racing—to the White House. The invitees included Richard Petty (and one of his race cars), Bobby and Donnie Allison, Bobby Isaac, Pete Hamilton, Tiny Lund, and Bill France. Nixon had effectively wooed post–civil rights–era white southern voters in 1968, and this was obviously an expansion—an effective one—of that strategy in his campaign against George McGovern. At the gathering Nixon declared, "The reason racers command respect in this country is that you're competitive. You represent something America admires. We are a competitive people. That's why we are where we are. When American loses its competitive spirit, we're in trouble."[90] Nixon's move paid off very quickly as France—after an assas-sination attempt left his preferred candidate, George Wallace, paralyzed from the waist down and led to the Alabama governor's withdrawal from the race—created "The Motorsports Committee for the Re-Election of President Nixon" and lined up Petty, Isaac, David Pearson, James Hylton, Bobby Allison, Cale Yarborough, and LeeRoy Yarbrough to offer their pub-lic support for the effort.[91]

Despite its still running the majority of its races on Sunday, NASCAR also made inroads into respectability among evangelical Christians in the Piedmont region. Change began in 1970 when a former alcoholic and hell-raiser turned preacher from Gadsden, Alabama—Brother Bill Frazier—showed up at Talladega with a makeshift pulpit in the back of a pickup truck and a gospel quartet. Frazier figured that in drivers, crews, and fans he had a ready-made congregation. As he told a reporter from *Sports Illus-trated*, "You see Goodyear, Prestone, Grey-Rock, and just about everything else you can think at these races. I figured it was time the Lord got a little representation. I'm going to promote God just like the other guys pro-mote STP." Rainy weather kept him from preaching at his first race, but he came back to the next Talladega race better prepared. In the interim he had built a small chapel on a trailer—complete with a pulpit and six two-person pews—which he parked in the infield next to the garage area; he posted a sign that he would hold a worship service at 11:00. Maurice Petty was the first to show up, and Brother Bill had his first racetrack service with Petty, driver "Soapy" Castles and three of his crew members, and two teenage boys who followed them in.[92] Richard Petty recalled when Frazier first showed up with his chapel on wheels: "We went to Talladega one day and here Bill had him a little rig-a-ma-roo out there in the infield and done decided he was going to save everybody. . . . Right out of the blue, here he come. He and my brother hit it off real good."[93]

Although his chapel on wheels survived only six races—and was abandoned on the side of I-85 after a race at Rockingham—Brother Bill soon became a fixture at NASCAR races, trusted increasingly by drivers and NASCAR officials. His style of preaching, which focused on love rather than judgment, won a ready audience at the track. "I don't preach against racin' on Sunday, or wearing miniskirts, or long hair on kids. They's just as many bald-headed folks going to hell as they are long hairs. I preach to a man's heart." He also gained the trust of racing people by never taking up an offering. Donations began to come in, however, and he received more than $14,000 in 1972 alone, with Richard Petty and Bobby Allison serving on an advisory board and contributing financially to the ministry. By 1971, NASCAR officials asked him to close driver meetings with prayer, allowed him to use the scoring stands for his chapel services, and even broadcast his sermons over the public address system. Most drivers also displayed on their dashboard a sticker of Brother Bill's "The Racer's Prayer":

> Lord I pray as I race today,
> Keep me safe along the way,
> Not only me but others too
> As they perform the jobs they do.
> I know God that in a race
> I, the driver, must set the pace.
> But in this race of life I pray
> Help me Lord along the way.
> Although I know I am a sinner,
> Help me believe that with
> God you're always a winner.[94]

While Bill Frazier did not realize it, he had created one of the first Christian chapel programs for professional athletes in the United States. Richard Petty observed, "Being we were southern-oriented operations . . .

the people went ahead and accepted it. . . . I think in other sports and in other parts of the country, they wouldn't have even let them in the gate to begin with."[95] Although his tenure as NASCAR's chaplain would be relatively short lived, others would come along to fill his shoes, and NASCAR today has one of the largest, most influential professional sports ministries in the Charlotte-based Motor Racing Outreach.[96] But at the height of his ministry in the early 1970s, Brother Bill both influenced and reflected the changing world of NASCAR racing. As he told author Jerry Bledsoe, "Racin' itself has took a different image in the past few years. . . . It's not just git out here and run on a weekend, raise hell, drink likker, and like you used to read about. It's become very refined, and we just happened to come along at the same time. Any other time, it might not have worked, see."[97]

Corporate Sponsorship

NASCAR's newfound respectability also helped it fill the void left by the auto manufacturers' exit and attract significant new sponsorship dollars to the sport. Prior to the early 1970s the bodies of the cars displayed the make of the automobile and had decals on the front quarter panels of auto parts companies that paid into the points fund—a requirement to qualify for the money. The car might also display the name of an auto dealership. Junior Johnson, a creative trailblazer in every area of the sport, was one of the first in the sport to see the possibilities for advertising something other than automotive products on the side of a stock car. In 1961, he lined up a small sponsorship deal with the Wilkes County–based Holly Farms Chicken, and he raced throughout most of the 1960s with Holly Farms Chicken emblazoned on the side of his cars. He even adopted a "racing chicken" logo for his race team.[98]

By the early 1970s, however, national nonautomotive corporations started advertising in the sport. As writer Peter Golenbock observed, "By 1972, the superspeedways were drawing upward of 100,000 fans, big enough crowds for a few companies to consider spending close to six figures to become sponsors."[99] Even earlier, in 1970, the Falstaff Brewing Corporation provided $50,000 in incentives, with $25,000 going to the points champion. "We are positive that we are wisely moving into America's soon to be most widely attended professional sport," asserted Falstaff president Joseph "Papa Joe" Griesedieck. As welcome as Falstaff's money was in NASCAR, the company also provided invaluable promotional assistance to most of the major tracks in the sport.[100]

Beer was not the only beverage of interest in NASCAR, as the major soft drink companies jumped in as well. Coca-Cola sponsored Bobby Allison for part of the 1969 and all of the 1970 season. The Coke sponsorship paid car owner Mario Rossi $50,000 in 1970.[101] Other soft drink companies sponsored cars in 1970, and *National Speed Sport News* commented on their intense interest in the outcome of the Daytona 500 with the Coke-sponsored Allison car, Jim Hurtubise in a Pepsi-sponsored Ford, and Pete Hamilton with the 7-Up logo emblazoned on the rear quarter panels of his Petty Engineering Plymouth Superbird. "Sunday's Daytona 500 may be worth $200,000 and of great interest to the Detroit automakers, but the soft drink industry is watching closely as well."[102]

The advertising of auto-related products was still a natural for NASCAR, however, and in 1972 two giants in the sport of auto racing set the NASCAR world on its ear with one of the most lucrative and long-lasting sponsorship deals in sports history when Richard Petty signed an agreement with Andy Granatelli of STP. While Granatelli had some familiarity with stock cars as a promoter at Chicago's Soldier Field and other midwestern tracks, most of his experience was with Indy racing, where he had competed as a driver and owner. Throughout the 1960s he effectively used his Indy cars to advertise his STP oil and gas additives. The NASCAR television contract, combined with Petty's popularity, made a deal with a NASCAR team especially attractive for Granatelli as a method of increasing his products' popularity in the Southeast. Indeed, it was not long before STP stickers became standard issue on the automobile of any Petty fan, or even on the bicycles of young fans, throughout the region. The only sticking point in the deal came when Granatelli wanted Petty to paint his race cars red to match the STP logo. Petty refused and even turned down $50,000 to do so, but he did create a paint scheme for his cars that combined the STP red with the legendary Petty blue. Most important, however, the STP deal greatly upped the ante for potential sponsors throughout the sport and created a financial environment that enabled race teams to weather the departure of the manufacturers.[103]

The Winston Deal

The biggest sponsorship news, news that would change NASCAR for generations to come and usher in its "modern era," came as a result of the confluence of the growing popularity of the sport, its national television contract, the federal ban on advertising cigarettes on television and radio, and the creative mind of Junior Johnson. Johnson had curtailed his racing operation in April 1970, as the sport had gotten "just too expensive" since the factories had withdrawn. "I'm not racing for glory, I'm racing for money and I don't mind admitting it. I ain't gonna spend money outta my pocket. I never had to depend on what I won racing and I'm not going to start now." Although Johnson threatened to quit racing altogether and "devote all his time to his poultry business," he decided to see if he could not find a sponsor with deep pockets with the $50,000 to $75,000 needed to operate a successful Grand National team.[104] When Johnson heard that the federal government had banned cigarette advertising on television and radio as of January 1, 1971, with the Public Health Cigarette Smoking Act, he decided to take the short trip down Highway 421 from Wilkes County to the Winston-Salem headquarters of R. J. Reynolds Tobacco.[105] In preparation for his visit with RJR executives, Johnson called *National Speed Sport News* editor Chris Economaki—who also worked as a color commentator for the ABC NASCAR broadcasts—and asked him if television producers could "erase the name of a company when it's on the side of a car, or on banners and signs at the track."[106]

While Johnson—and many other moonshiners/stock car drivers—had made countless trips down 421 to the Piedmont of North Carolina, none proved as important to the history of NASCAR as this one.[107] When Johnson arrived at RJR headquarters looking for tens of thousands of dollars to fund his team, he discovered that the corporation had tens of millions of dollars in its advertising budget and desperately needed to find new media to push its products. When Johnson realized that RJR was not interested in sponsoring a single car, he referred it to Bill France to discuss the possibilities of sponsoring races or even the series itself.[108]

Given both Bill France's and the tobacco industry's penchant for secrecy, little is known about those negotiations, but in December 1970 NASCAR and R. J. Reynolds announced a historic deal. The May 1971 Talladega race would be renamed the Winston 500 and offer a $165,000 purse, second highest in NASCAR behind the Daytona 500. RJR would also provide $100,000 for a Winston Cup points fund distributed incrementally at three points during the season, with $25,000 divided between the top ten drivers after the Charlotte World 600 in May, $25,000 more after the September Southern 500 at Darlington, and the final $50,000 distributed among the top twenty drivers at the end of the season. Although only races of 250 miles or more would be part of the Winston Cup, the final point payoff would be for points earned in all races.[109] Lawyers for NASCAR and RJR had evidently discovered that nothing in the federal law prevented them from prominently displaying cigarette companies' names on racetrack walls even if they were seen on television broadcasts or were announced by broadcasters as the title sponsors of events or the series itself.

The impact of Winston's entry into the sport became immediately apparent to the drivers in the substantially higher payouts from Winston Cup races and in the points money. In 1971, Richard Petty smashed David Pearson's 1969 winnings record of $229,760 by winning more than $350,000. Bobby Allison, second in prize winnings, topped Pearson's record, and Buddy Baker and Bobby Isaac both topped the $100,000 mark.[110] In 1972, R. J. Reynolds sponsored the entire season, which it would do up until 2004. Despite the fact that NASCAR eliminated from the series all races of under 250 miles—at RJR's request—reducing the schedule from forty-eight to thirty-two races and removing all the tracks that seated fewer than 15,000 fans, prize money skyrocketed to more than $2 million.[111] Although Petty did not break his record in 1972, he once again topped $300,000, as did Bobby Allison. Five other drivers brought in more than $100,000, and ten more netted over $40,000.[112]

One detail not announced initially but one of the most important aspects of the Winston-NASCAR deal was that the tobacco company virtually became the promotion arm of the sport. RJR immediately began to spend money on billboards and full-page newspaper ads advertising Winston Cup races. In addition, its ad people worked with individual speedways to improve race promotion and even painted the walls of speedways with the characteristic Winston red and white colors and prominently plastered "Winston Cup" every few feet.[113]

In 1972, R. J. Reynolds increased its marketing role in the sport when it created its Special Events Operations (later known as Sports Marketing Enterprises—SME). Under the leadership of talented admen Ralph Seagraves and T. Wayne Robertson, Winston and its red and white colors became the face not only of NASCAR's top division but of NASCAR short tracks as the company sent out teams of painters and financed building projects to upgrade facilities at many local tracks. Seagraves and Robertson also funded the Winston Racing Series to provide points money for regional and national champions at local tracks all over the country. The two even helped team owners find corporate sponsors for their cars, most famously in the case of a young Richard Childress, who secured sponsorship from Piedmont Airlines with SME's help in 1982. Indeed, SME became so influential through its sports promotion in NASCAR, National Hot Rod Association drag racing, and professional golf that T. Wayne Robertson was named one of the "50 most powerful people in sports" by *Sporting News* in 1991.[114]

The impact of the Winston deal on NASCAR is incalculable. The alliance gave the sport new credibility with corporate America outside Detroit and greatly expanded its horizons. Chris Economaki noted in his autobiography, "Winston, and parent R. J. Reynolds, was an American business at the highest level, and it was endorsing auto racing. Somewhere down the line, auto racing had finally become fully accepted. Up to that point the perception of racing had been a bunch of hot rodders trying to kill each other on the track, wearing overalls, with an oily rag in their pocket. The presence of Winston helped change that. To me, that was one of the key benefits of Winston's involvement. Suddenly racing became okay in the eyes of corporate America."[115] Humpy Wheeler later observed: "They rescued us in a dire time of need, dressed us up, and took us to town. They cared, and they nurtured us. They put their money where their mouth is and served as the lubricant for our red-hot growth."[116]

Big Bill Retires

The biggest change in the sport, however, came in January 1972, just as the first full season of Winston Cup racing geared up: Big Bill France announced that he was stepping down, "effective immediately," as the head of NASCAR. While he retained his position as chairman of the board of International Speedway Corporation with its prime Daytona and Talladega properties and served in an "advisory capacity" with NASCAR, he turned over day-to-day operations to his oldest son, William Clifton France, better known as Bill Jr.[117]

Bill France and the sport of stock car racing had come a long way since that first southern stock car race on Daytona Beach in 1936. The man who had started out as a dirt-poor mechanic looking for a place to ply his trade in warmer temperatures had built—often with great struggle—a firm foundation for NASCAR that his son could build upon. He had gone from driving a stock car as "Wild" Bill France, to wooing illegal liquor kingpins in the Piedmont region to drive in his races, sponsor cars, and even construct tracks, to near dictatorial power in his sport, to the boardrooms of America's most powerful corporations and the inner sanctums of its most powerful political offices. Along the way he battled competitor sanctioning bodies like the NSCRA that cut into his business; the forces of decorum and respectability that threatened to shut down tracks; his own drivers, who often resisted his attempts at organization and tried to challenge his authority twice by attempting to unionize, and Detroit CEOs, who tried to run his sport on their own terms. While France had taken his lumps along the way, he had built an empire on his personal ownership of NASCAR and control of two of the most lucrative speedway properties—Daytona and Talladgea—in the world, and that empire formed the foundation for perhaps the greatest family fortune in world history based strictly on sports management. Indeed, his rags-to-riches success story is one that few in sports history, or even in the broader business world, can match.

The sport he helped create had experienced as great a transformation as France himself. Although NASCAR still earned most of its bread and butter off the talents and daring of its rough-around-the-edges drivers, ticket sales to Piedmont working-class men still footed most of the bill, and most middle-class fathers in the region still did not want their daughters going to the race track, NASCAR was making serious strides away from its white liquor and red-clay roots. By 1973 and its silver anniversary as an organization, NASCAR stood at the top of American motorsports. The sanctioning body had more than 16,000 members, racing at eighty different tracks across the nation, in six divisions, competing for over $6 million in prize money. Its drivers and car owners in its top Winston Cup Division now raced primarily in weekend 500-mile races on superspeedways and claimed half of that prize money, and money pumped into its points fund by American corporations—primarily R. J. Reynolds—made the championship something most drivers now wanted to pursue.[118] Indeed, the drivers who made it to the top levels of the sport made a better living and had to race in many fewer races than ever before.

Progress had its price, however, and NASCAR had lost some of its working-class charm and some of its edge. For a number of years to come, most drivers would still work on their own cars, break into the sport by hauling the cars that had made them stars on a local short track to Winston Cup races on an open trailer, and vent their anger with the occasional fistfight, although these became less and less common at the track itself. Bill France Jr. would use some of his father's tactics for running the sport based on personal relationships with drivers and crewmen. But the days of drivers hauling liquor at night and racing in the same car the next day; "Lord Calvert taking her through the turns"; the proceeds of illegal liquor fueling the sport; racing in "Bamooda" shorts, without a shirt, or with a monkey in the car; Curtis Turner's and Joe Weatherly's seemingly endless parties; rooster tails of dirt flying through the air and covering competitors and fans; and Smokey Yunick shouting out, "All right you sons-a-bitches, let's have a race" as he strutted through the pits were gone forever.

Conclusion Back to Bristol

In August 2008, as I neared completion of this book, I once again made the pilgrimage from my home in Asheville, North Carolina, across Sam's Gap, to the Bristol Motor Speedway. As usual, my friend Don Good was with me. Although I had been to races there more than a dozen times since my first trip, I looked at Bristol a little differently this time, as my graduate school mentor, and all-around southern-history guru, Jim Cobb accompanied us. While he had attended a number of short-track races in his younger days in north Georgia, Cobb too was interested to see what the attraction of a big-time NASCAR race was and asked me to take him.

As we parked and began the hike to the track, I immediately began to think about my own first experience at Bristol and how much things had changed in that fourteen-year period. The first change you could not help but notice was the change in the price of a ticket. Fourteen years ago, we paid about $50 for tickets on the backstretch. This time our tickets cost more than double that—around $130—for seats between the first and second turns, but since Dr. Cobb was footing the bill, I did not mind. As we topped the hill and got our first glance at the speedway proper, another change from 1994 was obvious in the sheer size of the facility. Since my first trip to Bristol, its seating capacity had also more than doubled, from 70,000 or so to more than 160,000, and it continues to sell out every race. A huge Canadian flag flying from a pole attached to the top of a tour bus full of fans from Ontario helped to provide a nice visual frame to the panoramic view of the speedway and pointed to still further changes in the clientele. Even for someone who attends every home football game at the University of Georgia's Sanford Stadium as if it were a religious rite, Jim was impressed with the whole scene.

Since the start of the race was a couple of hours away, we sat on the side of a hill to people-watch. Nearby was an outdoor mall of souvenir trailers, venues for corporate sponsors, and the stage for the prerace show

293

broadcast on the SpeedTV Channel—a subsidiary of Fox Sports. The presence and footprint of television are ubiquitous, with a major network contract—currently with Fox and ESPN/ABC—worth billions of dollars to broadcast nationally all the races in NASCAR's top three divisions and literally dozens of NASCAR-related shows airing during the week. While we sat, a steady parade of well-dressed men and women driving by in golf carts headed probably from a corporate tent—where they were plied with food and drink and regaled by some NASCAR driver or television personality—to one of the fifty or so corporate suites (which were not there in 1994) overlooking the track. We also noted that NASCAR races definitely attract more women than they used to, but I would argue—based on my unscientific observation—that the percentage of women fans would be closer to 30 peercent than NASCAR's oft quoted figure of 40 percent.

A quick scan of the program and the listing of the drivers, pictures of the cars, their teams, and the car sponsors pointed to still other changes. Of the top twenty-five drivers in Sprint Cup (current name of NASCAR's top series) points at the time, only seven hailed from the states that had formed the Confederate States of America, and only five came from NASCAR's historic heartland in the Piedmont South. Ten of the top drivers came from the Far West—six from California and two each from Washington and Nevada. One driver, Juan Pablo Montoya, even came from Colombia, as in South America, not South Carolina; there are no longer any drivers in NASCAR's top ranks from the homeland of Joe Littlejohn, David Pearson, Cotton Owens, Bud Moore, and Cale Yarborough. Not only are most drivers no longer from the South, but most of them grew up in solidly middle-class suburban homes and got their first high-speed driving experience not in a liquor car or a '55 Chevy on a local dirt track but in a high-powered go-kart as a child. Their demeanor is decidedly different from that of the NASCAR driver of the past as well, with a prime qualification being ability as a corporate spokesperson, a skill almost as important as driving skill. Indeed, it is hard to imagine most of these guys being called a "good ole boy," much less a "hell of a fellow."

Another dramatic change has come in the shape of the cars. In 1994, while practically every fan knew that underneath the hood the "stock car" of NASCAR had no resemblance to a production car, at least the cars were outwardly identifiable as Ford Thunderbirds, Chevy Luminas, or Pontiac Grand Prixs. In the name of keeping the competition between the manufacturers close, two years ago NASCAR mandated that all makes adopt the "car of tomorrow" template. Today, the only difference one can tell between a Ford Fusion, a Dodge Intrepid, a Chevy Impala, and a Toyota Camry is in the brand decals the teams stick on the cars. Distinctions between makes may be unimportant to newer fans, but for traditional fans who made an identification with an auto brand at an early age—and often followed in their father's footsteps as Chevy, Ford, Dodge, or Plymouth "men"—the loss of brand identity changes an important dynamic in the sport's appeal. Some traditional fans also grew concerned that NASCAR had veered too far from its roots when it allowed Toyota into the sport a few years ago. Even though most Camrys sold in the United States are made here, some fans argued that NASCAR should not allow a "foreign" manufacturer—Toyotas have traditionally been referred to by working-class Piedmonters as "rice burners"—into the sport especially at a time when America's Big 3 automakers struggled to compete.

While corporate America had discovered NASCAR when I went to my first race in 1994, by 2008 the list of major corporations sponsoring race teams had expanded from Budweiser, Dupont, McDonald's, Caterpillar, General Mills, and Proctor and Gamble to include Lowe's, Home Depot, Federal Express, UPS, NAPA, 3M, M&M's, Hershey, Best Buy, Target, Aflac, and Subway. In addition, the amount of money these corporations paid to have the race cars emblazoned with their logos annually had gone from a few million to upwards of $20 million. In 1994, most of the race teams were one-car affairs with many people considering Rick Hendricks's two-car team a wasteful vanity project. By 2008—after Hendrick proved the naysayers wrong and organized his multicar team with corporate efficiency, and after his drivers won seven championships—the sport was dominated by multicar teams; only a handful of single-car teams attempted to make the race, and none of them were anywhere near the top rankings.

To be sure, the evidence is everywhere at a major NASCAR race of the success of Bill France Jr., who passed away in 2007, and the current head of NASCAR, his son Brian, in selling American corporations, the middle class, and even many elites on the joys of NASCAR. Indeed, NASCAR management—particularly under the leadership of Bill France Jr.—has drawn wide acclaim as a major key to the sport's success. While many observers doubted Bill Jr.'s ability to do the job—Smokey Yunick told France Sr. that his son "didn't have enough sense to pour piss out of a boot"—he proved an able replacement. Years later Yunick asserted, "Billy's probably out-did the old man three to one in profit and status."[1] Bill Jr. brought new talents to NASCAR in a new era. As business writer Robert Hagstrom observed,

"What was needed was not a sheriff but an ambassador, someone who knew stock car racing and could communicate its attributes to an increasingly sophisticated audience."[2]

Under France Jr.'s leadership, NASCAR became one of the most successful sports businesses in the world. In a 1989 *60 Minutes* profile of Richard Petty, CBS reporter Harry Reasoner asserted, "If the aim of a professional sport . . . is to operate as a successful business, the most successful business in American sports is stock car racing."[3] Hagstrom in his 1998 book *The NASCAR Way* argues that NASCAR's success is an "example of the capitalist model at its best. It is a sport that is still built on opportunities, not guarantees."[4] In their 2008 Stanford University Press book *Fans of the World Unite: A (Capitalist) Manifesto for Sports Consumers*, law professor Stephen Ross and economist Stefan Szymanski attribute NASCAR's growth to the sport's centralized structures of authority by which "an independent entrepreneur was able to identify the best locations for racing, establish complex rules designed to produce close racing with cars perceived to be similar to those driven by fans, and determine the appropriate economic rewards that would attract the best drivers, engineers, and crews." The two scholars go so far as to hold up NASCAR's corporate organization as a model for other professional sports whose organizations with strong players' unions, competing team owners, and relatively weak centralized authority "encourage mediocrity."[5]

While many have praised NASCAR for its successful embrace of corporate America and respectability, many traditional fans—particularly in the Piedmont South—have complained that the folks in Daytona Beach are running from their roots and have alienated their core fans and that the NASCAR of today is but a pale, overly scripted imitation of its much more colorful and spontaneous past. Those fans point to the tragic death of Dale Earnhardt, perhaps the last true "hell of a fellow" in NASCAR, on the last lap of the 2001 Daytona 500 and NASCAR's decision in 2004 to move its Labor Day weekend race (which had been Darlington's Southern 500 since 1950) to the Fontana, California, facility—a move characterized by NASCAR officials as "modernizing tradition"—as points when they became increasingly alienated from the sport.

A Whiff of White Liquor and the Slight Stain of Red Clay
As Don, Jim, and I took in the scene at Bristol, however, I was heartened to note that, while NASCAR has become more mainstream, more corporate, and much more respectably family oriented, there are still things about

attending a race—particularly at Bristol—that reflect the sport's white-liquor and red-clay roots. There may not be many (or any) "hell of a fellow" drivers anymore, but there sure are still plenty of "hell of a fellow"—and even "hell of a gal"—fans. Although corporate types roamed about, there were also fans strolling the grounds who looked like they might have sacrificed meal money—or pawned something—to purchase a ticket. Don took us to an area populated by fans in relatively modest campers and pop-up trailers where some of his friends hung out. There we saw a side of NASCAR—a veritable "hell of a fellow" heaven—that the folks in Daytona Beach do not depict generally, complete with Confederate flags, the consumption of large amounts of alcohol, including moonshine, and women in revealing bikinis, in some cases revealing much more than most people would want to see. As we walked on, we came back into NASCAR's present as we passed by a makeshift track where fans could test-drive brand-new Toyota Tundra trucks. But we were quickly back into an area representative of NASCAR's rough-and-tumble roots, with trailers selling T-shirts and other souvenirs related to breast or penis size, pubic hair (hard to tell if these were references to the president of the United States at the time or the current loud-mouthed points leader with the last name Busch), the glories of the Confederacy, and other things that would get any one of us brought up on racial or sexual harassment charges on our respective campuses. This was definitely a scene reminiscent of Humpy Wheeler's "place you didn't want your daughter to go."

We made our way into the track itself in time for the opening festivities. These had changed little as well and reflected the working-class, red-state conservatism often on parade at NASCAR races—lots of McCain-Palin shirts but nary an Obama one in sight. The air force jets did their obligatory flyover (for some odd reason, several times), and a group of parachutists sailed over the edge of the skyboxes—one trailing a huge American flag—and landed on the track. The public address announcer then asked all veterans and current service people to stand and be recognized. While this was going on, a color guard marched out to the start/finish line accompanied by representatives of each armed service, a group of New York City policemen and firemen—a bit curious almost seven years after 9/11—and a contingent of drivers' children wearing Uncle Sam outfits. A pastor led an invocation, and although it was pretty clear where he stood theologically, it was the first one I've ever heard at a NASCAR race that did not end with "in Jesus' name." Some country music singer I had never heard of sang the national anthem, and a representative of some corporate sponsor gave the "Gentlemen, start your engines" command (there still are no regular female competitors at the sport's top level) and the traditional assault on the eardrums began.

NASCAR has received a good deal of criticism for its boring races in recent years—particularly on the 1.5- and 2-mile tracks constructed in the 1990s and early 2000s by the France family–controlled International Speedway Corporation and Bruton Smith's Speedway Motorsports Inc. Yet one big reason Bristol had sold out its 160,000 seats in the midst of a recession and $4 a gallon gasoline is that it is hard not to have an exciting race when you put forty-three stock cars on a half-mile track. Bristol did not disappoint, and there were several early crashes, including one that took out nine cars right in front of us. I was also excited that one of the few drivers still left from NASCAR's Piedmont South past, fifty-three-year old Bill "Awesome Bill from Dawsonville" Elliott, had not only made the race in the legendary #21 Wood brothers car but qualified first and spent much of the first half of the race in the top ten. However, the third quarter of the race—dominated by twenty-three-year-old Kyle Busch—began to look as if even Bristol had succumbed to the NASCAR malaise of follow-the-leader racing.

In the last quarter of the race, though, things began to pick up once again as several cautions tightened the field and brought Carl Edwards up on Busch's rear bumper. With thirty laps to go, Edwards executed a classic Bristol "bump and run" maneuver to "rattle" Busch's "cage"—in Dale Earnhardt–speak—push him up the track, and take the lead for good. Busch could never catch up to him and had to settle for second. After Edwards took the checkered flag, I told Cobb to keep watching, since often at Bristol someone will "send a message" to another driver by running into him, and I knew Busch was angry about the Edwards pass (I had tuned in to his scanner frequency to hear a flood of profanity). Busch did not disappoint and gave Edwards a retaliatory shot in the rear bumper, "rattling his cage" a bit as they entered the backstretch. However, Edwards was not through either; he got behind Busch and spun him out. The crowd went crazy and cheered even louder as Edwards stopped his car on the start/finish and perfectly executed his signature victory backflip from the window sill of his car. It was a great race, one that many fans thought might bring back the days of the intense and bitter rivalries that fueled so much fan interest in the sport's early days. I was thrilled Dr. Cobb got to see what the excitement is all about.

Alongside the great racing, however, I was also heartened to see that while most of the crowd seemed to be similar to that seen at any major American professional sporting event these days, there were still plenty of holdovers from NASCAR's working-class past. When we first got to our seats, we were soon joined by a couple of shirtless, already inebriated, and highly entertaining good ole boys, although they were evicted from their seats before the race by the people who actually held the tickets for them. Several rows down to our right, a woman wearing her baseball cap backward held a can of beer in her left hand while she stood and wagged an encouraging right index finger at Dale Earnhardt Jr. and gave Kyle Busch the middle finger on almost every lap. After the race as we climbed down the innumerable stairs to get out of the speedway, we encountered a number of instances of the drunk leading the drunk and hoped that these folks were camped nearby, able to sleep it off, and that we would not encounter them again on the drive home. We had a great time, and as I've told many people who just do not "get" NASCAR, you have got to experience a race firsthand to fully appreciate the sport.

My goal in doing this book from the start has been relatively simple: to offer my narrative of NASCAR's history from the earliest days of stock car racing up to the retirement of Big Bill France. I have sought to do that in a way that relied on the best possible source material, with facts double-checked for validity, and that helped to dispel many of the myths that have passed for NASCAR history. To me, the story is one of the great American success stories, a story of people creatively struggling to overcome their own backgrounds in poverty and desperation to bring entertainment and even hope to people from the same background. Along the way, they discovered that the sport had potential for even broader appeal and used those same creative energies to build one of the top professional sporting enterprises in history.

A great temptation for the historian is to try to write "prescriptive history" and assume to advise people in the present how they should live and act based on that historian's version of the past. Indeed, NASCAR has done pretty well without my advice and made incredible strides in the world of professional sports in its more than sixty years of existence. However, at the risk of being prescriptive, I would encourage NASCAR officials, drivers, corporate sponsors, and fans to look to the sport's past not as a source of embarrassment to be ignored or whitewashed but as a source of pride to be appreciated, welcomed, and even honored. I would humbly suggest that it is time for NASCAR to stop "modernizing tradition" and start embracing its tradition.

Notes

ABBREVIATIONS

AC   *Atlanta Constitution*
ACT   *Asheville Citizen-Times*
CO   *Charlotte Observer*
GDN   *Greensboro Daily News*
GNI   *Grand National Illustrated*
HPE   *High Point Enterprise*
ISN   *Illustrated Speedway News*
NSSN *National Speed Sport News*
PP   *Pioneer Pages*
RNO   *Raleigh News and Observer*
SH   *Spartanburg Herald*
WJP   *Wilkes Journal-Patriot*
WSJ   *Winston-Salem Journal*

INTRODUCTION

1. Susan Reinhardt, "Racing Fan's First Lap His Last," *ACT*, May 20, 1999.

2. *ACT*, December 8, 2005.

3. My inspiration for this approach in many ways comes from the early work of Bill Malone, who pioneered historical research on country music. Prior to Malone, few professional historians considered country music a topic worthy of serious academic study. Malone changed that with the publication in 1968 of *Country Music, U.S.A.*, and hundreds of books and journal articles by professional historians have followed, greatly enriching our understanding of the genre itself and of southern and American culture.

4. Although the two terms are often used interchangeably, in this study I stick to exact meanings; moonshiners are people who manufacture illicit alcohol, while the bootlegger is a person who sells illegal alcohol—alcohol that either has been manufactured illegally or is of a variety that is illegal in a particular county, state, or even country (as was the case in the United States during the days of Prohibition). People who transport illegal alcohol are bootleggers but may also be referred to as "trippers" or "blockaders." Many individuals involved in the early days of southern stock car racing also became involved in the trade in "red liquor," or legally manufactured liquor illegally brought into a dry county or state.

5. Wheeler, interview by Daniel.

6. Wilkinson, *Dirt Tracks to Glory*, 150.

7. Pillsbury, "Carolina Thunder," 43.

8. Wright, *Fixin' to Git*, 72.

9. Wilkinson, *Dirt Tracks to Glory*, 18–20.

10. Daniel, *Lost Revolutions*, 91–120.

CHAPTER 1

1. Flock's story in Wilkinson, *Dirt Tracks to Glory*.

2. Chapin, *Fast as White Lightning*, 46; Golenbock, *Last Lap*, 15. Most recently this story is repeated in Thompson, *Driving with the Devil*, 88–89.

3. Accounts of this transition from farm to mill life can be found in Hall et al., *Like a Family*, and Tullos, *Habits of Industry*.

4. Hall et al., *Like a Family*; Tullos, *Habits of Industry*.

5. Cash, *Mind of the South*, 201.

6. Hall et al., *Like a Family*, 154.

7. Cobb, *Industrialization and Southern Society*, 77.

8. Shifflet, *Coal Towns*, 16–26.

9. *The Fifty* (video).

10. Parks, interview by Daniel.

11. Ashley, interview by Daniel.

12. Dabney, *Mountain Spirits*, 162.

13. Dabney, *Mountain Spirits*.

14. Packard, "Millions in Moonshine," 103.

15. Johnson, interview by Daniel.

16. Gabbard, *Return to Thunder Road*, 49.

17. Higgins and Waid, *Junior Johnson*, 19.

18. Dabney, *Mountain Spirits*, 132.

19. Carr, *Second Oldest Profession*, 115.

20. Dabney, *Mountain Spirits*, 131.

21. Packard, "Millions in Moonshine," 47; Dabney, *Mountain Spirits*, 132.

22. Yanacsek, *North Carolina Moonshiners* (video).

23. Packard, "Millions in Moonshine," 102, 47.

24. White, *Gold Thunder*, 26.

25. Dabney, *Mountain Spirits*, 162.

26. Packard, "Millions in Moonshine," 103.

27. Ibid., 105.

28. Yanacsek, *North Carolina Moonshiners* (video).

29. Higgins and Waid, *Junior Johnson*, 29.

30. Packard, "Millions in Moonshine," 47, 100.

31. Dabney, *Mountain Spirits*, 149.

32. Padrush, *Rumrunners, Moonshiners, and Bootleggers* (video).

33. Hall et al., *Like a Family*, 43.

34. Gorn, "Gouge and Bite."

35. Ownby, *Subduing Satan*, 13.

36. Gorn and Goldstein, *Brief History of American Sports*, 25.

37. Cash, *Mind of the South*, 50.

38. Ibid., 50, 30, 42–43.

39. Blount, *Roy Blount's Book of Southern Humor*, 235.

40. Ibid., 547–48.

41. Gorn, "Gouge and Bite," 19.

42. Ownby, *Subduing Satan*, 27–28, 39.

43. Raper, *Preface to Peasantry*, 174.

44. Clark, *Emerging South*, 127.

45. Hall et al., *Like a Family*, 253.

46. Quoted in Tullos, *Habits of Industry*, 22.

47. Mull and Boger, *Recollections of the Catawba Valley*, 116.

48. Johnson, interview by Daniel.

49. Jarrett, interview by Daniel.

50. Wheeler, interview by Daniel.

51. Pearson, interview by author.

52. Ibid.

53. Hunter, interview by Daniel.

54. Bragg, *All Over but the Shoutin'*, 58.

55. Petty, *King Richard I*, 18.

56. Quoted in Flink, *Automobile Age*, 230–31.

57. Wilkinson, *Dirt Tracks to Glory*, 54.

58. Johnson, interview by Daniel.

59. Ibid.

60. Dabney, *Mountain Spirits*, 111.

61. Packard, "Millions in Moonshine," 47.

62. Johnson, interview by Daniel.

63. Packard, interview by Daniel; Thompson, *Driving with the Devil*, 76–78; Wilkinson, *Dirt Tracks to Glory*, 83.

64. Call, interview by Daniel.

65. Johnson, interview by Daniel.

66. Dabney, *Mountain Spirits*, 155.

67. Yates, "Who the Hell Do You Think You Are?"

68. Johnson, interview by Wise.

69. Williams, *Appalachia*, 309–10.

70. Pirkle, interview by author.

71. Petty, *King Richard I*, 43.

72. Hunter, interview by Daniel.

73. Petty, *King Richard I*, 43.

74. Welbourn, interview by Wise.

75. Johnson, interview by Daniel.

76. Hall, "Before NASCAR."

77. Punnett, *Racing on the Rim*.

78. Hinton, *Daytona*, 32–59; Fielden, *High Speed at Low Tide*, 9–10.

79. Economaki, interview by author.

80. *GDN*, September 30, 1941.

81. *AC*, July 1, 4, 5, 1938.

82. *AC*, September 11, 1938; July 5, 1939; October 30, 1939; *GDN*, September 5, 1939;

September 30, 1941; *HPE*, October 21, 1940; *CO*, July 3, 1938; August 2, 1938; October 26, 1939.

83. *AC*, September 11, 1938.

84. Economaki, interview by author.

85. *CO*, October 22, 1939; *AC*, June 2, 1940; *GDN*, June 2, 1940.

86. Golenbock, *NASCAR Confidential*, 21; *AC*, October 2, 1938; *CO*, October 15, 1939.

87. Golenbock, *NASCAR Confidential*, 24.

88. "Teeter Tots," <http://freepages.genealogy.rootsweb.ancestry.com/~teeter kinmy/teetertot.html>.

89. Thompson, *Driving with the Devil*, 72–73.

90. Wilkinson, *Dirt Tracks to Glory*, 20.

91. Golenbock, *American Zoom*, 69.

92. Wilkinson, *Dirt Tracks to Glory*, 20.

93. "Anne France," <www.nascar.com/2002/kyn/women/02/02/France/>.

94. Wilkinson, *Dirt Tracks to Glory*, 20.

95. Ibid.; Golenbock, *American Zoom*, 74.

96. Daniel, *Lost Revolutions*, 99.

97. Wheeler, interview by Daniel.

98. Daniel, *Lost Revolutions*, 96.

99. Ownby, *Subduing Satan*, 3.

100. Ownby, "Manhood, Memory and White Men's Sports," 335.

101. Hunter, interview by Daniel.

102. Daniel, *Lost Revolutions*, 93.

103. Cash, *Mind of the South*, 289.

104. Blount, "Million-Dollar Sunday Driver."

CHAPTER 2

1. Hinton, *Daytona*, 64–65; Fielden, *High Speed at Low Tide*, 11–13.

2. Fielden, *High Speed at Low Tide*, 16–20.

3. Ibid., 19–20.

4. Ibid.

5. Ibid., 21–24.

6. Ibid., 33–35.

7. Ibid., 24–28.

8. Ibid., 29–30.

9. Testimony on Joe Littlejohn's involvement with illegal alcohol comes from Golenbock, *Last Lap*, 9, and Johnson, interview by author.

10. Conversations with people involved in illegal alcohol during this period provide evidence of such networks. See Johnson, interview by author.

11. Fielden, *High Speed at Low Tide*, 30–32.

12. Ibid.

13. Jensen, *Cheating*.

14. *AC*, October 27, 30, 1938; November 1, 2, 6, 7, 8, 10, 11, 1938.

15. Parks, interview by Daniel.

16. Quoted in Hinton, *Daytona*, 73.

17. *AC*, September 10, 1939.

18. *AC*, November 12, 1938.

19. *ISN*, December 2, 1938.

20. *AC*, December 5, 1938.

21. Parks, interview by Daniel.

22. *AC*, May 24, 1941.

23. Wilkinson, *Dirt Tracks to Glory*, 60.

24. Ibid., 54.

25. *CO*, June 26, 1939; *SH*, November 12, 1939.

26. *GDN*, September 7, 1940.

27. *CO*, July 5, 1941.

28. *HPE*, October 3, 1940; May 12, June 30, September 1, 1941.

29. *ISN*, June 30, July 7, 1939; February 28, August 2, August 9, 1940; May 30, 1941.

30. *CO*, July 4, 1941.

31. Wheeler, interview by Daniel.

32. *AC*, May 19, 1941.

33. *AC*, November 30, 1939.

34. Neely, *Daytona, U.S.A.*, 59–60.

35. Results for most major stock car races in 1940 can be found in the issues of *ISN*.

36. *HPE*, May 4, 1941.

37. *AC*, September 10, 1939.

38. Quoted in Fielden, *High Speed at Low Tide*, 48.

39. Hinton, *Daytona*, 72–76.

40. "Edwin Keith 'Banjo' Matthews," <http://www.legendsofnascar.com/Banjo_Matthews.htm>.

41. Parks, interview by Daniel.

42. Ibid.; Hemphill, *Wheels*, 88; Thompson, *Driving with the Devil*, 41–42, 47–49.

43. Hinton, *Daytona*, 65.

44. Packard, interview by Daniel; Pirkle, interview by author; Thompson, *Driving with the Devil*, 72–78.

45. See *ISN* for 1941.

46. A photo of Seay performing this amazing feat can be found in Fielden, *High Speed at Low Tide*, 71.

47. *SH*, November 12, 1941.

48. *HPE*, June 30, 1941.

49. Fielden, *High Speed at Low Tide*, 70–74.

50. Ibid.

51. *AC*, July 14, 1941.

52. Fielden, *High Speed at Low Tide*, 73–74.

53. Hinton, *Daytona*, 70.

54. Economaki, interview by author.

55. *SH*, November 8, 1941.

56. *AC*, September 21, 1941.

57. Economaki, interview by author.

58. *AC*, September 21, 1941.

59. *AC*, November 23, 1939.

60. *GDN*, September 7, 1940; *SH*, November 12, 1941; *CO*, July 5, 1941; *AC*, November 23, 1939.

61. *AC*, December 4, 1939.

62. *AC*, May 26, 1941.

63. *AC*, July 14, 1941.

64. *HPE*, May 12, 1941.

65. Economaki, interview by author.

66. Ibid.

67. *SH*, July 5, 1940.

68. Hemphill, *Wheels*, 94.

69. *HPE*, May 6, 1941.

70. *AC*, September 3, 1941.

71. Ibid.

72. Ibid.

73. *AC*, November 2, 3, 1941.

74. Thompson, *Driving with the Devil*, 148, 131; Hinton, *Daytona*, 79–80.

75. Economaki, interview by author.

76. Yunick, *All Right You Sons-a-Bitches*, 22.

77. Wheeler, interview by Daniel.

78. "Baptist Faith and Message," 1925, <http://www.sbc.net/bfm/bfmcomparison.asp>.

79. *ISN*, January 2, 1942.

80. *NSSN*, August 1945.

CHAPTER 3

1. Thompson, *Driving with the Devil*. This is a major theme throughout this book.

2. Wilkinson, *Dirt Tracks to Glory*, 20.

3. For more about Bill France's social life than you want to know, see Yunick, *All Right You Sons-a-Bitches*, 105–9.

4. Golenbock, *NASCAR Confidential*, 25.

5. Parks, interview by Daniel.

6. Golenbock, *American Zoom*, 150–52.

7. Yunick, interview by Shackleford.

8. *AC*, July 8, 1939.

9. "Robert 'Red' Byron," <http://www.livinglegendsofautoracing.com/drivers_pages/drivers_red_by.html>; Thompson, *Driving with the Devil*, 164–67.

10. Thompson, *Driving with the Devil*, 179–82.

11. Fox, interview by Daniel.

12. Yunick, interview by Shackleford.

13. Yunick, interview by Daniel.

14. Edelstein, *Full Throttle*, 30.

15. Hinton, *Daytona*, 78.

16. *AC*, September 2, 1945; January 25, 1948.

17. *AC*, August 31, 1945.

18. Ibid.

19. Ibid.

20. *AC*, September 2, 3, 1945.

21. *AC*, September 3, 1945.

22. *AC*, September 4, 1945.

23. Ibid.

24. *AC*, September 5, 1945.

25. *AC*, September 8, 14, 1945.

26. *AC*, September 11, 1945.

27. *AC*, September 16, 1945.

28. *AC*, September 21, 1945.

29. *NSSN*, July 18, 1946.

30. Golenbock and Fielden, *Stock Car Racing Encyclopedia*, 749–50.

31. *CO*, October 18, 1945.

32. *CO*, October 23, 1945.

33. *CO*, October 27, 28, 1945.

34. *AC*, September 2, 1945.

35. *CO*, October 28, 1945.

36. Neely, *Daytona, U.S.A.*, 51.

37. Fielden, *High Speed at Low Tide*, 85.

38. See *ISN* and *NSSN* for 1946 and 1947; Byron's personality discussed in Thompson, *Driving with the Devil*, 198, 222.

39. Thompson, *Driving with the Devil*, 190–91, 306–7.

40. Ibid., 168–225.

41. Golenbock, *NASCAR Confidential*, 28–30; Golenbock, *American Zoom*, 17; Neely, *Daytona, U.S.A.*, 52.

42. Thompson, *Driving with the Devil*, 219–20.

43. *GNI*, June 23, 1946.

44. *GNI*, July 5, 7, 1946.

45. Day, interview by author; also recounted in Thompson, *Driving with the Devil*, 187–88, based on a J. B. Day interview.

46. Thompson, *Driving with the Devil*, 188.

47. *GNI*, September 2, 1946; April 13, 1946.

48. See *ISN* and *NSSN* for summer and fall 1946.

49. Wheeler, interview by Daniel.

50. *NSSN*, September 25, 1946; November 6, 1946.

51. *SH*, October 1, 1946.

52. *WJP*, April 14, 1947; Golenbock, *NASCAR Confidential*, 40.

53. *WJP*, April 14, 1947; May 15, 19, 1947.

54. Golenbock, *NASCAR Confidential*, 40; delivering liquor in a milk truck story told by an anonymous source, witnessed by Don Good and Suzanne Wise on May 24, 2008.

55. Welbourn, interview by Wise; Johnson, interview by Wise; Golenbock, *NASCAR Confidential*, 46.

56. Testimony on Staley's and Combs's connections to the illegal liquor business comes from Junior Johnson in Golenbock, *American Zoom*, 20; Johnson, interview by author; Frank Mundy in Golenbock, *NASCAR Confidential*, 31; Enoch Staley's son Mike Staley in Golenbock, *NASCAR Confidential*, 40; Welbourn and Johnson, interviews by Wise; and Washburn, *Hickory Motor Speedway*, 14–20.

57. Chapin, *Fast as White Lightning*, 49.

58. *WJP*, March 10, 1947.

59. *WJP*, September 11, 1947.

60. *WJP*, April 14, 1947.

61. *NSSN*, September 3, 1947.

62. Washburn, *Secrets on the Mountain*, 41.

63. Thompson, *Driving with the Devil*, 35–49, 275–76.

64. Golenbock, *NASCAR Confidential*, 4.

65. Testimony on Earles's involvement in bootlegging comes from Johnson, interview by author; Golenbock, *American Zoom*, 20; Waid and Thompson, "Martinsville Speedway," 113–14; and, most important, an interview of Earles by Steve Waid in *GNI*, September 1982, 11, in which Earles directly admitted that he used money from "other businesses," "a pretty lucrative one" to build and make improvements to Martinsville.

66. Testimony on Rice's bootlegging background and construction of Martinsville Speedway from Johnson, interview by author; Frank Mundy in Golenbock, *NASCAR Confidential*, 28, 31; and Waid and Thompson, "Martinsville Speedway," 109.

67. Golenbock, *NASCAR Confidential*, 4–10; *NSSN*, September 3, 1947.

68. Golenbock, *NASCAR Confidential*, 31.

69. Testimony on bootlegging activities and construction of the Charlotte Speedway from David Allison in McCredie, "First NASCAR Race," 121.

70. Testimony on Gene Sluder's bootlegging involvement from Johnson, interview by author; information on the Burgess brothers and the construction of Hickory Speedway in Washburn, *Hickory Motor Speedway*, 13–19.

71. Golenbock, *NASCAR Confidential*, 8.

72. Wheeler, interview by Daniel.

73. Golenbock, *NASCAR Confidential*, 8.

74. Ibid., 31.

75. *History of Racing Asheville* (audio CD), pt. 1.

76. Wheeler, interview by Daniel.

77. Pirkle, interview by author.

78. *PP*, December 2001; Day, interview by author.

79. *NSSN*, January 15, 1947.

80. Based on 1947 reporting in *NSSN*, *ISN*, *AC*, *CO*, *GNI*, *SH*, and *GDN*.

81. *GNI*, June 7, 1947.

82. *NSSN*, May 7, 1947.

83. *ISN*, May 2, 1947.

84. *GDN*, June 14, 1947.

85. *ISN*, May 2, 1947.

86. *PP*, February 2002, 12.

87. *ISN*, October 10, 31, 1947.

88. *ISN*, July 12, 1946.

89. *ISN*, July 5, 1946; August 2, 30, 1946.

90. *PP*, March 1999, 7–8; also see *ISN* and *NSSN* over the summer of 1947 for Nunis promotions.

91. *ISN*, March 14, 1947; November 14, 1947.

92. *NSSN*, June 11, 1947.

93. *ISN*, May 30, 1947; *NSSN*, March 12, 1947.

94. *ISN*, February 28, 1947; May 30, 1947; June 20, 1947; August 8, 1947; *NSSN*, March 26, 1947; June 11, 1947.

95. Neely, *Daytona, U.S.A.*, 52.

CHAPTER 4

1. Kahn's description in White, "NASCAR."

2. This standard description of NASCAR's organizational meeting can be found in most books on NASCAR's history, especially Fielden, *Forty Years of Stock Car Racing*, 1:5–9; Golenbock, *American Zoom*, 69–72; and Wilkinson, *Dirt Tracks to Glory*, 24–27.

3. Identical articles, probably written by a France publicist, advertising the event—complete with misspelling of the Streamline Hotel—appeared in both *ISN*, December 5, 1947, and *NSSN*, December 3, 1947.

4. Golenbock, *NASCAR Confidential*, 40–41.

5. Wilkinson, *Dirt Tracks to Glory*, 25–26.

6. Parks, interview by Daniel.

7. Hinton, *Daytona*, 83.

8. "Stock Car Racing Leaders Form New National Association."

9. Neely, *Daytona, U.S.A.*, 58.

10. Ibid., 56.

11. Ibid., 57.

12. *ISN*, January 16, 1948.

13. White, "NASCAR," 10.

14. *NSSN*, January 21, 1948.

15. "Baker, 'Cannonball' (Erwin G.)," <http://www.hickoksports.com/biograph/bakercan.shtml>.

16. Logo can be seen in NASCAR ads in the racing press such as *NSSN*, March 17, 1948.

17. Fielden, *High Speed at Low Tide*, 99–100.

18. *ISN*, February 6, 1948.

19. Fielden, *High Speed at Low Tide*, 100.

20. *NSSN*, June 23, 1948; July 14, 1948; *ISN*, March 5, 1948.

21. McCredie, "First NASCAR Race," 121.

22. *NSSN*, March 31, 1948; and December 15, 1948.

23. *NSSN*, October 13, 1948.

24. *NSSN*, September 3, 1947.

25. *NSSN*, April 28, 1948.

26. Flock, interview by Daniel; Wilkinson, *Dirt Tracks to Glory*, 32–37.

27. Edelstein, *Full Throttle*, 17–33; Morris, *Timber on the Moon*.

28. Chapin, *Fast as White Lightning*, 52.

29. Edelstein, *Full Throttle*, 35–45; Morris, *Timber on the Moon*.

30. *GNI*, April 4, 5, 1948; May 10, 1948; July 3, 6, 1948; November 8, 1948.

31. *NSSN*, March 17, 1948.

32. *NSSN*, May 5, 1948.

33. *ISN*, September 24, 1948; March 17, 1948.

34. *NSSN*, April 7, 1948.

35. *SH*, September 5, 1947.

36. Wheeler, interview by Daniel.

37. *WJP*, April 8, 1948.

38. *WJP*, September 16, 1948.

39. See 1948 issues of *WJP*.

40. *GNI*, July 26, 1948.

41. Fielden, *Forty Years of Stock Car Racing*, 1:18.

42. Smith, interview by Daniel.

43. Chapin, *Fast as White Lightning*, 73.

44. *ISN*, December 31, 1948; Fielden, *High Speed at Low Tide*, 105.

45. Fielden, *High Speed at Low Tide*, 106–107.

46. Newspapers in 1948 were full of complaints about the inability to get new cars. For an example, see *GNI*, March 21, 1948.

47. *NSSN*, June 23, 1948.

48. *ISN*, January 21, 28, 1949.

49. *ISN*, May 10 1949.

50. "O. Bruton Smith," <http://www.referenceforbusiness.com/biography/S-Z/ Smith-O-Bruton-1927.html>.

51. *CO*, June 10, 12, 1949.

52. *CO*, June 18, 1949.

53. Fielden, *Forty Years of Stock Car Racing*, 1:7.

54. *CO*, June 18, 1949.

55. *NSSN*, June 29, 1949.

56. *CO*, June 21, 1949.

57. *PP*, March 1999.

58. Petty, *King Richard I*, 64–65; Golenbock, *Last Lap*, 17.

59. McCredie, "First NASCAR Race," 122–23.

60. Ibid., 125.

61. Ibid., 125–27; Fielden, *Forty Years of Stock Car Racing*, 1:8–9.

62. Petty, *King Richard I*, 69–70.

63. McCredie, "First NASCAR Race," 124.

64. Ibid., 124–27; Fielden, *Forty Years of Stock Car Racing*, 1:9.

65. Frank Mundy makes this accusation in Golenbock, *NASCAR Confidential*, 29.

66. Fielden, *Forty Years of Stock Car Racing*, 1:11–17; *NSSN*, November 2, 1949.

67. Fielden, *High Speed at Low Tide*, 111.

68. Packard, "Millions in Moonshine," 105.

69. *NSSN*, December 21, 1949.

70. Fielden, *High Speed at Low Tide*, 109.

71. Fielden, *Forty Years of Stock Car Racing*, 1:11–32.

72. Bledsoe, *World's Number One*, 94; Fielden, *Forty Years of Stock Car Racing*, 1:32.

73. Bledsoe, *World's Number One*, 98.

74. Ibid., 98–101.

75. *GNI*, July 3, 1949.

76. *GNI*, July 10, 1949.

77. Golenbock, *NASCAR Confidential*, 12.

78. *NSSN*, August 24, 1949.

79. Golenbock and Fielden, *Stock Car Racing Encyclopedia*, 642; Fielden, *Forty Years of Stock Car Racing*, 1:82–106.

80. Golenbock and Fielden, *Stock Car Racing Encyclopedia*.

81. *ISN*, May 24, 1949; June 14, 1949; July 12, 1949; Pearson, "Bowman Gray Stadium."

82. *ISN*, September 27, 1949.

83. *ISN*, August 16, 1949.

84. Wheeler, interview by Daniel.

85. Jarrett, interview by Daniel.

86. *AC*, October 16, 1949.

87. Fielden, *Forty Years of Stock Car Racing*, 1:18.

88. *AC*, October 23, 24, 1949.

89. *NSSN*, November 2, 1949.

90. *AC*, October 24, 1949.

91. *AC*, November 11, 1949.

92. *AC*, November 21, 1949.

93. Bledsoe, *World's Number One*, 94.

CHAPTER 5

1. Golenbock and Fielden, *Stock Car Racing Encyclopedia*.

2. Ibid.

3. *1951 NASCAR Yearbook*.

4. *NSSN*, January 25, 1950.

5. *1951 NASCAR Yearbook*, 100–102.

6. *NSSN*, March 29, 1950; August 16, 1950.

7. *NSSN*, August 16, 23, 1950; *History of Racing Asheville* (audio CD); "Official Souvenir Program, Championship Modified Stock Car Races, Asheville-Weaverville Speedway."

8. Washburn, *Hickory Motor Speedway*, 13–38.

9. *NSSN*, January 11, 1950.

10. *NSSN*, April 5, 1950.

11. *1951 NASCAR Yearbook*, 71, 102.

12. *NSSN*, April 12, 1950; October 11, 1950; June 21, 1950; Higgins and Waid, *Junior Johnson*, 13–14; *NSSN*, July 14, 1954.

13. King, interview by Daniel.

14. Fielden, *High Speed at Low Tide*, 27, 49, 73.

15. Weir, "Changing Times Test Track 'Too Tough to Tame.'"

16. King, interview by Daniel.

17. The better accounts of the construction of Darlington include Kelly, "Darlington"; Granger, "1950 Southern 500"; and Kirkland and Thompson, *Darlington International Raceway*, 17.

18. *NSSN*, February 15, 1950.

19. *NSSN*, March 22, 1950.

20. *NSSN*, July 5, 1950.

21. Granger, "1950 Southern 500," 115.

22. Ibid., 123.

23. Ibid., 115.

24. *NSSN*, August 9, 1950.

25. Kelly, "Darlington," 114.

26. Quoted in Granger, "1950 Southern 500," 118.

27. Quoted in ibid., 125.

28. Ibid., 120–25.

29. *NSSN*, April 5, 1950.

30. Granger, "1950 Southern 500," 116–26.

31. Ibid.

32. Yunick, *All Right You Sons-a-Bitches*, 61–62.

33. *NSSN*, May 2, 1951.

34. *PP*, March 1999, 7–9.

35. Wheeler, interview by author.

36. *PP*, March 1999, 8.

37. Wheeler, interview by author.

38. *1951 NASCAR Yearbook*.

39. Ibid.

40. *NSSN*, July 1, 1953.

41. *1951 NASCAR Yearbook*.

42. Edeslstein, *Full Throttle*, 70–72.

43. Ibid., 81.

44. *NSSN*, October 14, 1953.

45. *NSSN*, February 8, 1950.

46. *NSSN*, May 10, 1950.

47. *NSSN*, August 30, 1950.

48. *1951 NASCAR Yearbook*, 19; *NSSN*, December 20, 1950.

49. *NSSN*, October 3, 1951.

50. Fielden, *Forty Years of Stock Car Racing*, 1:23–41.

51. *NSSN*, May 10, 1950; Edelstein, *Full Throttle*, 62.

52. Yunick, *All Right You Sons-a-Bitches*, 37.

53. Ibid.

54. Fielden, *Forty Years of Stock Car Racing*, 1:45.

55. Ibid., 45–67.

56. *NSSN*, January 30, 1952.

57. Yunick, *All Right You Sons-a-Bitches*, 41.

58. Fielden, *Forty Years of Stock Car Racing*, 1:65–78.

59. Ibid., 79–171.

60. *NSSN*, October 27, 1954.

61. Yunick, *All Right You Sons-a-Bitches*, 49.

62. "History of the Hudson Motor Company," <http://hetclub.com/history/history .htm>.

63. Yunick, *All Right You Sons-a-Bitches*, 50–52.

64. *NSSN*, May 9, 1951.

65. *NSSN*, June 6, 1951.

66. *NSSN*, July 25, 1951.

67. Quoted in Fielden, *Forty Years of Stock Car Racing*, 1:43.

68. *NSSN*, December 24, 1952.

69. *NSSN*, November 3, 1954.

70. Yunick, *All Right You Sons-a-Bitches*, 37; *NSSN*, February 4, 1953.

71. *NSSN*, February 4, 1953.

72. Yunick, *All Right You Sons-a-Bitches*, 40.

73. *NSSN*, January 18, 1950.

74. *NSSN*, March 29, 1950.

75. *NSSN*, May 17, 1950.

76. Yunick, *All Right You Sons-a-Bitches*, 39.

77. Fielden, *Forty Years of Stock Car Racing*, 1:75.

78. Ibid., 101, 169; Golenbock, *Last Lap*, 24.

79. Yunick, *All Right You Sons-a-Bitches*, 29.

80. Fielden, *Forty Years of Stock Car Racing*, 1:53.

81. Chapin, *Fast as White Lightning*, 88.

82. Ibid., 86–87.

83. *AC*, June 12, 1950; *NSSN*, June 14, 1950.

84. Chapin, *Fast as White Lightning*, 65–66.

85. Ibid., 65.

86. Ibid., 88.

87. *RNO*, September 9, 1953.

88. *AC*, June 13, 1950.

89. *RNO*, August 20, 1953.

90. *RNO*, September 25, 1953.

91. *NSSN*, October 22, 1952.

92. Fielden, *Forty Years of Stock Car Racing*, 1:109.

93. *NSSN*, August 20, 1952.

94. Fielden, *Forty Years of Stock Car Racing*, 1:170.

95. *NSSN*, April 4, 1951.

96. Fielden, *Forty Years of Stock Car Racing*, 1:66, 101, 149.

97. *NSSN*, March 31, 1954; Fielden, *Forty Years of Stock Car Racing*, 1:145.

98. Golenbock, *Last Lap*, 25; *NSSN*, August 11, 1954.

99. Yunick, *All Right You Sons-a-Bitches*, 26.

100. Golenbock, *Last Lap*, 24.

101. Yunick, *All Right You Sons-a-Bitches*, 29, 26.

102. Chapin, *Fast as White Lightning*, 90.

103. Golenbock, *Last Lap*, 24.

104. *NSSN*, May 27, 1953.

105. Chapin, *Fast as White Lightning*, 91.

106. Yunick, *All Right You Sons-a-Bitches*, 26.

107. Golenbock, *Last Lap*, 21.

108. Jensen, *Cheating*, 58; Yunick, *All Right You Sons-a-Bitches*, 26.

109. *NSSN*, June 28, 1950.

110. Fielden, *Forty Years of Stock Car Racing*, 1:86.

111. Chapin, *Fast as White Lightning*, 90–91.

112. Golenbock, *Last Lap*, 37–38.

113. Ibid., 54.

114. Fielden, *Forty Years of Stock Car Racing*, vol. 1.

115. Golenbock, *Last Lap*, 38.

116. *NSSN*, November 3, 1954; July 20, 1955.

117. "Daredevil Driver."

CHAPTER 6

1. O'Reilly, "Bill France, Sr.," 31–32.

2. *WSJ*, July 8, 1956.

3. Petty, *King Richard I*, 124.

4. Rodengen, *Iron Fist*, 248.

5. Fielden, *High Speed at Low Tide*, 192–93.

6. Golenbock, *Last Lap*, 60–61; Fielden, *High Speed at Low Tide*, 192–96.

7. Fielden, *Forty Years of Stock Car Racing*, 1:176–254.

8. Rodengen, *Iron Fist*, 276–77.

9. Golenbock, *Last Lap*, 61.

10. Rodengen, *Iron Fist*, 210–11.

11. Ibid., 214.

12. Ibid., 199–215.

13. *NSSN*, August 25, 1954.

14. Rodengen, *Iron Fist*, 248–49. Rodengen mistakenly credits Tony Bettenhausen with the victory at Milwaukee, but it was Mundy; see *NSSN*, August 25, 1954.

15. Golenbock, *NASCAR Confidential*, 57.

16. Rodengen, *Iron Fist*, 253.

17. Ibid., 249.

18. Ibid., 269–70.

19. Ibid., 273.

20. *WSJ*, July 8, 1956.

21. Rodengen, *Iron Fist*, 253.

22. Golenbock, *Last Lap*, 62.

23. Golenbock, *NASCAR Confidential*, 58.

24. Fielden, *Forty Years of Stock Car Racing*, 1:172–254.

25. Fielden, *High Speed at Low Tide*, 209–12.

26. Golenbock, *NASCAR Confidential*, 69; Golenbock, *Last Lap*, 63.

27. Higgins and Waid, *Junior Johnson*, 39–40.

28. Golenbock, *Last Lap*, 62–63.

29. Fielden, *Forty Years of Stock Car Racing*, 1:172–208.

30. *NSSN*, January 18, 1956.

31. Yunick, *All Right You Sons-a-Bitches*, 55, 65.

32. Duntov, "Thoughts Pertaining to Youth, Hot Rodders and Chevrolet."

33. Levine, *Ford*, 208.

34. Yunick, *All Right You Sons-a-Bitches*, 55–65.

35. Ibid.

36. Ibid., 63–64.

37. Ibid.

38. *NSSN*, September 7, 1955.

39. Yunick, *All Right You Sons-a-Bitches*, 66–67.

40. Cotter and Pearce, *Holman-Moody*, 30.

41. Levine, *Ford*, 209.

42. Cotter, *Holman-Moody*, 32.

43. Levine, *Ford*, 209.

44. Ibid.

45. Ibid., 212.

46. Edelstein, *Full Throttle*, 92–98.

47. Ibid., 99.

48. *NSSN*, September 7, 1955; Fielden, *Forty Years of Stock Car Racing*, 1:199–200.

49. Levine, *Ford*, 216.

50. *NSSN*, February 8, 1956.

51. Fielden, *High Speed at Low Tide*, 209.

52. Fielden, *Forty Years of Stock Car Racing*, 1:209.

53. Granger, "Buck Baker," 43.

54. Golenbock, *Last Lap*, 62–63.

55. *WSJ*, July 8, 1956.

56. Ibid.

57. Jensen, *Cheating*, 52.

58. Levine, *Ford*, 222.

59. Rodengen, *Iron Fist*, 275.

60. *WSJ*, July 8, 1956.

61. Levine, *Ford*, 217–26; Cotter, *Holman-Moody*, 33–36.

62. Fielden, *Forty Years of Stock Car Racing*, 1:250–51.

63. *NSSN*, October 31, 1956; Fielden, *Forty Years of Stock Car Racing*, 1:250–51.

64. Rodengen, *Iron Fist*, 283–84.

65. Fielden, *Forty Years of Stock Car Racing*, 1:255–58; Yunick, *All Right You Sons-a-Bitches*, 70.

66. *NSSN*, May 22, 1957.

67. Yunick, *All Right You Sons-a-Bitches*, 71.

68. Petty, *King Richard I*, 129.

69. *NSSN*, February 20, 1957.

70. *NSSN*, May 22, 1957.

71. Levine, *Ford*, 234.

72. *NSSN*, September 25, 1957.

73. *NSSN*, March 6, 1957.

74. Fielden, *Forty Years of Stock Car Racing*, 1:172–295.

75. Ibid., 255–95.

76. Levine, *Ford*; Yunick, *All Right You Sons-a-Bitches*, 55–66.

77. *NSSN*, February 6, 1957.

78. *NSSN*, April 20, 1955; June 15, 1955.

79. *NSSN*, July 6, 1955. In 1955 a major Davy Crockett fad swept the nation with the release of a Walt Disney movie, starring Fess Parker, about the frontier legend.

80. *NSSN*, December 28, 1955; January 25, 1956.

81. *NSSN*, February 29, 1956.

82. Edelstein, *Full Throttle*, 104.

83. Fielden, *Rumblin' Ragtops*, 46, 84.

84. Edelstein, *Full Throttle*, 104.

85. Fielden, *Rumblin' Ragtops*.

86. *NSSN*, February 20, 1957.

87. Yunick, *All Right You Sons-a-Bitches*, 67.

88. Rodengen, *Iron Fist*, 284.

89. Yunick, *All Right You Sons-a-Bitches*, 69.

90. "Traffic Fatality Rates," <www.volpe.dot.gov/infosrc/journal/2005/pdfs/vj05 intro.pdf>.

91. Coffey and Layden, *America on Wheels*, 184.

92. *NSSN*, March 2, 1955.

93. *NSSN*, June 1, 1955.

94. *NSSN*, July 20, 1955.

95. *NSSN*, June 15, 1955.

96. *NSSN*, June 29, 1955; August 17, 1955.

97. *NSSN*, August 10, 1955.

98. Ibid.

99. *NSSN*, August 24, 1955.

100. *NSSN*, January 12, 1955.

101. *NSSN*, February 8, 1956.

102. Fielden, *Rumblin' Ragtops*, 48.

103. *NSSN*, March 3, 1955; April 25, 1956; June 13, 1956.

104. Fielden, *Forty Years of Stock Car Racing*, 1:270.

105. *NSSN*, May 22, 1957.

106. Levine, *Ford*, 236–45.

107. Yunick, *All Right You Sons-a-Bitches*, 73.

108. Cotter, *Holman-Moody*, 39, 47.

109. *NSSN*, July 17, 1957.

110. *NSSN*, June 12, 1957.

111. *NSSN*, July 17, 1957.

112. *NSSN*, August 7, 1957.

113. Higgins and Waid, *Junior Johnson*, 35–37.

114. *NSSN*, September 4, 1957; Fielden, *Forty Years of Stock Car Racing*, 1:286–87.

115. Yunick, *All Right You Sons-a-Bitches*, 75–76; Fielden, *Forty Years of Stock Car Racing*, 1:285–86; *NSSN*, September 4, 1957.

116. Yunick, *All Right You Sons-a-Bitches*, 257–59.

117. *NSSN*, March 14, 21, 1956.

118. Russell, "Racing vs. Religion," <www.historichillsborough.org/images/Speedway-Complete.pdf>.

119. Ibid.

120. Fielden, *Forty Years of Stock Car Racing*, 1:279, 298.

121. Ibid., 281–82.

122. *NSSN*, September 11, 1957.

123. Ibid.

124. Fielden, *Forty Years of Stock Car Racing*, 1:209–54, 297–336.

125. Ibid,, 301–2.

126. Ibid., 297–336.

127. Ibid., 297–335.

128. Higgins and Waid, *Junior Johnson*, 40.

129. Ibid.

130. Ibid., 42–43.

131. Ibid., 44.

CHAPTER 7

1. Jarrett, interview by author; Fielden, *Forty Years of Stock Car Racing*, 2:37–38.

2. Jarrett, interview by author.

3. Ibid.

4. Neely, *Daytona, U.S.A.*, 94–95; Zeller, *Daytona 500*, 16; *NSSN*, November 13, 1957.

5. *NSSN*, March 26, 1958.

6. Neely, *Daytona, U.S.A.*, 100.

7. *NSSN*, May 7, 1958; Neely, *Daytona, U.S.A.*, 97.

8. Zeller, *Daytona 500*, 19; Neely, *Daytona, U.S.A.*, 100.

9. Hinton, *Daytona*, 101–3; Neely, *Daytona, U.S.A.*, 100; Zeller, *Daytona 500*, 19.

10. Neely, *Daytona, U.S.A.*, 97.

11. *NSSN*, February 4, 11, 1959.

12. Hinton, *Daytona*, 104.

13. *NSSN*, February 11, 1959.

14. Yunick, *All Right You Sons-a-Bitches*, 154–55.

15. *NSSN*, February 18, 1959.

16. Ibid.

17. Ibid.

18. Zeller, *Daytona 500*, 24.

19. *NSSN*, February 25, 1959.

20. *NSSN*, March 4, 1959; Hinton, *Daytona*, 106–9; Petty, *King Richard I*, 158–59; Zeller, *Daytona 500*, 24.

21. *NSSN*, April 8, 1959.

22. *NSSN*, April 29, 1959.

23. *NSSN*, April 15, 1959.

24. Fielden, *Forty Years of Stock Car Racing*, 2:34, 74, 103, 122, 148, 165, 194, 212.

25. Higgins and Waid, *Junior Johnson*, 48.

26. Fielden, *Forty Years of Stock Car Racing*, 2:103, 122, 148, 165, 194, 212, 248, 269.

27. *NSSN*, February 27, 1963; Hinton, *Daytona*, 120.

28. Yunick, *All Right You Sons-a-Bitches*, 294.

29. Jarrett, interview by author.

30. *NSSN*, April 9, 1958.

31. Fielden, *Forty Years of Stock Car Racing*, 2:53.

32. *CO*, April 23, 1959; *NSSN*, April 9, 1958.

33. Edelstein, *Full Throttle*; Morris, *Timber on the Moon*.

34. Edelstein, *Full Throttle*, 128.

35. Ibid., 130.

36. Edelstein, *Full Throttle*, 132; Morris, *Timber on the Moon*, 89–90.

37. Edelstein, *Full Throttle*, 135–38; Morris, *Timber on the Moon*, 24–27.

38. Edelstein, *Full Throttle*, 134; Morris, *Timber on the Moon*, 92.

39. Edelstein, *Full Throttle*, 135.

40. Ibid., 141–42.

41. *CO*, June 19, 1960; Morris, *Timber on the Moon*, 93–94.

42. Morris, *Timber on the Moon*, 94–95; *CO*, June 17, 1960.

43. *CO*, June 16, 1960.

44. *CO*, June 17, 1960.

45. *CO*, June 18, 1960.

46. *CO*, June 19, 1960.

47. Fielden, *Forty Years of Stock Car Racing*, 2:52.

48. *CO*, June 19, 1960.

49. *CO*, June 20, 1960; Fielden, *Forty Years of Stock Car Racing*, 2:72.

50. Morris, *Timber on the Moon*, 95.

51. *CO*, June 19, 20, 1960.

52. *CO*, June 20, 1960; Edelstein, *Full Throttle*, 146.

53. *CO*, June 21, 1960.

54. Ibid.

55. Fielden, *Forty Years of Stock Car Racing*, 2:87–88, 117–18.

56. Edelstein, *Full Throttle*, 156–63.

57. Ibid., 151.

58. Ibid., 167

59. Golenbock, *Last Lap*, 139.

60. *CO*, August 10, 1961.

61. Fielden, *Forty Years of Stock Car Racing*, 1:7.

62. Golenbock, *Last Lap*, 220.

63. Ibid., 69.

64. Jarrett, interview by author.

65. Petty, *King Richard I*, 149.

66. *ACT*, August 10, 1961.

67. *CO*, August 10, 1961.

68. Fielden, *Forty Years of Stock Car Racing*, 2:94.

69. Ibid., 93–100; Jarrett, interview by author.

70. *CO*, August 10, 1961.

71. Edelstein, *Full Throttle*, 171.

72. *CO*, August 10, 1961.

73. Fielden, *Forty Years of Stock Car Racing*, 2:97; *CO*, August 13, 1961.

74. *ACT*, August 11, 1961.

75. Golenbock, *NASCAR Confidential*, 96.

76. *ACT*, August 11, 1961.

77. Ibid.

78. *CO*, August 12,1961.

79. Edelstein, *Full Throttle*, 177.

80. Fielden, *Forty Years of Stock Car Racing*, 2:99–100; *CO*, August 22, 1961; Edelstein, *Full Throttle*, 177–87.

81. *ACT*, August 14, 1961.

82. Ibid.; Fielden, *Forty Years of Stock Car Racing*, 2:127–28.

83. *CO*, August 23, 1961; Jarrett, interview by author.

84. Information on infield experience comes from conversations with Don Good and Monica Jernigan.

85. *WSJ*, May 30, 2006; "Hamrick, Warren NASCAR Legends," <http: www.close finishes.com/cgi-script/csArticles/articles/000007/000007.htm>.

86. *NSSN*, March 7, 1962.

87. Fielden, *Forty Years of Stock Car Racing*, vols. 2, 3.

88. *NSSN*, January 16, 1963.

89. *NSSN*, February 27, 1963.

90. Ibid.

91. Fielden, *Forty Years of Stock Car Racing*, vols. 2, 3.

92. *NSSN*, January 20, 1965.

93. Fielden, *Forty Years of Stock Car Racing*, vol. 2.

94. *NSSN*, June 13, 1962.

95. Fielden, *Forty Years of Stock Car Racing*, 2:185–223.

96. *NSSN*, March 13, 1963.

97. *NSSN*, March 27, 1963.

98. Fielden, *Forty Years of Stock Car Racing*, 2:188–89.

99. Ibid.

CHAPTER 8

1. Kelly, *Fireball*, 183.

2. Ibid., 187.

3. Golenbock, *NASCAR Confidential*, 142.

4. Fielden, *Forty Years of Stock Car Racing*, 2:140, 184; Edelstein, *Full Throttle*, 91–202.

5. Quoted in *NSSN*, October 6, 1965.

6. Higgins and Waid, *Junior Johnson*, 57–63.

7. Wolfe, "Last American Hero."

8. Rash, *World Made Straight*, 200.

9. Golenbock, *Last Lap*, 152; Pearson, interview by author.

10. Yunick, *All Right You Sons-a-Bitches*, 300.

11. *NSSN*, May 13, 1964.

12. Hellman, "Cool Fireball Named Roberts."

13. Petty, *King Richard I*, 180–81.

14. Jarrett, interview by author; Jarrett, interview by Daniel.

15. Fielden, *Forty Years of Stock Car Racing*, 3:50.

16. *NSSN*, March 2, 1966.

17. *NSSN*, January 2, 1963.

18. Golenbock, *NASCAR Confidential*, 90–113.

19. Fielden, *Forty Years of Stock Car Racing*, 2:114–15.

20. *NSSN*, July 1, 1964.

21. Petty, *King Richard I*, 197–99.

22. Fielden, *Forty Years of Stock Car Racing*, 2:246–47.

23. Petty, *King Richard I*, 198.

24. *NSSN*, February 12, 1964.

25. *NSSN*, February 12, 19, 1964.

26. *NSSN*, February 26, 1964.

27. *NSSN*, March 11, 1964.

28. Fielden, *Forty Years of Stock Car Racing*, 2:235–90.

29. Ibid.

30. Ibid.

31. Petty, *King Richard I*, 196.

32. Golenbock, *Miracle*, 101.

33. Ibid., 71–72.

34. Chapin, "Curtis Lives!"

35. Individual driver records can be found listed alphabetically in Golenbock and Fielden, *Stock Car Racing Encyclopedia*.

36. Fielden, *Forty Years of Stock Car Racing*, 2:241–89, 3:7–110.

37. *NSSN*, November 9, 1966.

38. *NSSN*, June 10, 1964.

39. *NSSN*, October 21, 1964.

40. *NSSN*, November 25, 1964.

41. Golenbock, *Miracle*, 65–66.

42. Golenbock and Fielden, *Stock car Racing Encyclopedia*, 135.

43. Davis, interview by Daniel.

44. Biographical information on Scott can be found in ibid.; Smith, "Wendell

Oliver Scott"; Bledsoe, *World's Number One*, 228–30; Donovan, *Hard Driving*; and *American Stock* (video), pt. 4.

45. Wilkinson, *Dirt Tracks to Glory*, 115.

46. Bledsoe, *World's Number One*, 228.

47. *American Stock* (video), pt. 4.

48. Wilkinson, *Dirt Tracks to Glory*, 119

49. *American Stock* (video), pt. 4.

50. Bledsoe, *World's Number One*, 230.

51. *American Stock* (video), pt. 4.

52. Wilkinson, *Dirt Tracks to Glory*, 119.

53. Fielden, *Forty Years of Stock Car Racing*, 3:28.

54. Wilkinson, *Dirt Tracks to Glory*, 119.

55. Ibid., 66.

56. Petty, *King Richard I*, 204.

57. Golenbock and Fielden, *Stock Car Racing Encyclopedia*, 374.

58. *American Stock* (video), pt. 4.

59. Ibid.

60. Wilkinson, *Dirt Tracks to Glory*, 119; Fielden, *Forty Years of Stock Car Racing*, 2:243.

61. Wilkinson, *Dirt Tracks to Glory*, 119.

62. Granger, "Jack Smith," 87.

63. Yunick, *All Right You Sons-a-Bitches*, 302.

64. Fielden, *Forty Years of Stock Car Racing*, 2:239.

65. Ibid.

66. *NSSN*, July 15, 1964.

67. *NSSN*, February 27, 1963.

68. *NSSN*, July 15, 1964.

69. *NSSN*, January 22, 1964.

70. Ibid.

71. *NSSN*, May 27, 1964.

72. Kelly, *Fireball*, 177.

73. *NSSN*, September 30, 1964.

74. *NSSN*, January 13, 1965.

75. *NSSN*, October 20, 27, 1965.

76. Petty, *King Richard I*, 209.

77. Kelly, *Fireball*, 198; Yunick, *All Right You Sons-a-Bitches*, 81–82.

78. "Timelines," <http://www.fireballroberts.com/Timelines6070.htm>; *NSSN*, August 3, 1966.

79. *NSSN*, May 12, 1965.

80. *NSSN*, June 16, 1965.

81. *NSSN*, October 27, 1965.

82. *NSSN*, October 28, 1964.

83. *NSSN*, October 21, 1964.

84. *NSSN*, November 4, 1964.

85. Ibid.

86. *NSSN*, December 9, 1964.

87. *NSSN*, November 25, 1964.

88. Fielden, *Forty Years of Stock Car Racing*, 3:11, 19.

89. *NSSN*, March 3, 1965.

90. Petty, *King Richard I*, 201–2.

91. Fielden, *Forty Years of Stock Car Racing*, 3:12.

92. *NSSN*, February 24, 1965.

93. *NSSN*, March 3, 1965.

94. *NSSN*, April 14, 1965; May 12, 1965.

95. *NSSN*, August 4, 1965.

96. *NSSN*, May 12, 1965.

97. *NSSN*, May 19, 1965; Fielden, *Forty Years of Stock Car Racing*, 3:12.

98. *NSSN*, June 23, 30, 1965; Fielden, *Forty Years of Stock Car Racing*, 3:42–59.

99. Edelstein, *Full Throttle*, 211–15.

100. *NSSN*, August 4, 1965.

101. Ibid.

102. Edelstein, *Full Throttle*, 219–22.

103. *NSSN*, October 6, 1965; November 3, 1965.

104. Edelstein, *Full Throttle*, 230–33.

105. Fielden, *Forty Years of Stock Car Racing*, 3:7–60.

106. *NSSN*, February 23, 1966.

107. Fielden, *Forty Years of Stock Car Racing*, 3:70–71.

108. *NSSN*, March 9, 1966.

109. *NSSN*, April 13, 1966.

110. Levine, *Ford*, 580.

111. *NSSN*, April 20, 1966.

112. *NSSN*, April 6, 1966.

113. Fielden, *Forty Years of Stock Car Racing*, 3:77–97.

114. Higgins and Waid, *Junior Johnson*, 74.

115. Fielden, *Forty Years of Stock Car Racing*, 3:65.

116. Ibid., 65–66.

117. Yunick, *All Right You Sons-a-Bitches*, 320–21.

118. Fielden, *Forty Years of Stock Car Racing*, 3:70–97.

119. Ibid., 96–97.

120. Ibid., 66.

121. *NSSN*, August 31, 1966.

122. Petty, *King Richard I*, 210.

123. "Adios Pancho."

124. Higgins and Waid, *Junior Johnson*, 69.

125. *NSSN*, November 10, 1965.

126. Higgins and Waid, *Junior Johnson*, 69.

127. Jarrett, interview by author.

128. Golenbock, *NASCAR Confidential*, 142–149.

129. Odom and Dorman, *Lynyrd Skynyrd*; Golenbock, *Last Lap*, 96.

130. Granger, "Bobby Isaac"; Wilkinson, *Dirt Tracks to Glory*, 2.

131. Yarborough, with Neely, *Cale*.

132. Golenbock, *Miracle*.

133. *NSSN*, July 6, 1966.

134. *ACT*, June 12, 1966.

135. *NSSN*, July 20, 1966.

136. Fielden, *Forty Years of Stock Car Racing*, 3:92.

137. Edelstein, *Full Throttle*, 247–48.

138. Fielden, *Forty Years of Stock Car Racing*, 3:98; Edelstein, *Full Throttle*, 249.

139. Fielden, *Forty Years of Stock Car Racing*, 3:99–100; Edelstein, *Full Throttle*, 249–51.

140. Edelstein, *Full Throttle*, 249–51.

141. Ibid., 251.

CHAPTER 9

1. *NSSN*, October 4, 1967; Fielden, *Forty Years of Stock Car Racing*, 3:166.

2. Fielden, *Forty Years of Stock Car Racing*, 3:112–58.

3. Petty, *King Richard I*, 205.

4. Fielden, *Forty Years of Stock Car Racing*, 3:147–54.

5. *NSSN*, September 6, 1967.

6. Petty, *King Richard I*, 206.

7. Golenbock, *Miracle*, 70–71; Fielden, *Forty Years of Stock Car Racing*, 3:91–100.

8. Golenbock, *Miracle*.

9. Fielden, *Forty Years of Stock Car Racing*, 3:157; Golenbock, *Miracle*, 79–80.

10. *NSSN*, July 17, 1968.

11. Golenbock, *Miracle*, 84.

12. Fielden, *Forty Years of Stock Car Racing*, 3:187.

13. Golenbock, *Miracle*, 107.

14. *NSSN*, October 18, 1967.

15. *NSSN*, November 29, 1967.

16. "Grand American," <http://thirdturn.armchairgm.com/wiki/Grand_Touring>.

17. *NSSN*, November 8, 1967; Fielden, *Forty Years of Stock Car Racing*, 3:242.

18. *NSSN*, January 31, 1968; Fielden, *Forty Years of Stock Car Racing*, 3:164.

19. Fielden, *Forty Years of Stock Car Racing*, 3:163–64; *NSSN*, November 5, 1969.

20. There are conflicting stories from Fonty Flock and others about who discovered the Talladega site. Smoky Yunick tells the story that Fonty Flock dreamed the idea up, found the suitable site, and even had blueprints of the speedway and that France stole the idea from him and left him in the lurch; Yunick, *All Right You Sons-a-Bitches*, 212. Jeff Frederick tells the story that Bill Ward, an Anniston, Alabama, insurance agent and part-time race driver, had the idea and scouted out the site and that France stole it from him; Frederick, "'If It Weren't for Bad Luck,'" 10. Ward—who raced in the first fifteen races at the speedway—told the same story to the *New York Times* in October 2007. France always claimed that while these individuals had talked about a much smaller project in that section of Alabama, he found the site on his own.

21. Paul Hemphill, *Wheels*, 204; Frederick, "'If It Weren't for Bad Luck,'" 9–10.

22. Frederick, "'If It Weren't for Bad Luck,'" 12.

23. Ibid., 11; "Timeline of George Wallace's Life," <http://www.pbs.org/wgbh/amex/wallace/timeline/index_2.html>.

24. Frederick, "'If It Weren't for Bad Luck,'" 15.

25. Ibid., 19.

26. Ibid., 24.

27. Ibid., 21.

28. Ibid., 23.

29. Fielden, *Forty Years of Stock Car Racing*, 3:210–11.

30. *NSSN*, August 27, 1969; September 3, 1969.

31. Petty, interview by author.

32. *NSSN*, May 29, 1969.

33. *NSSN*, May 1, 1969.

34. Fielden, *Forty Years of Stock Car Racing*, 3:211.

35. Golenbock, *Miracle*, 89.

36. Fielden, *Forty Years of Stock Car Racing*, 3:211.

37. Ibid., 249–50.

38. Granger, "Boycott of Talladega," 9.

39. *NSSN*, August 27, 1969.

40. Fielden, *Forty Years of Stock Car Racing*, 3:211–12.

41. Carey, "Talladega Story," 13.

42. Ibid., 12.

43. *NSSN*, September 17, 1969.

44. *CO*, September 13, 1969.

45. Granger, "Boycott of Talladega," 11.

46. *CO*, September 14, 1969.

47. *CO*, September 13, 1969.

48. Granger, "Boycott of Talladega," 8.

49. *CO*, September 14, 1969.

50. Ibid.

51. *NSSN*, September 24, 1969.

52. *CO*, September 14, 1969.

53. Granger, "Boycott of Talladega," 16.

54. Ibid., 17.

55. Carey, "Talladega Story," 15.

56. *CO*, September 15, 1969.

57. Fielden, *Forty Years of Stock Car Racing*, 3:214.

58. Carey, "Talladega Story," 15.

59. Granger, "Boycott of Talladega," 18.

60. Wheeler, interview by author. Isaac later gave the watch to Wheeler, who wears it to this day.

61. *CO*, September 15, 1969.

62. Ibid.

63. *NSSN*, September 24, 1969.

64. *NSSN*, October 22, 1969.

65. *CO*, September 15, 1969.

66. Fielden, *Forty Years of Stock Car Racing*, 3:255–57.

67. *NSSN*, February 18, 1970.

68. Fielden, *Forty Years of Stock Car Racing*, 3:266.

69. Ibid., 266–67.

70. *NSSN*, December 10, 24, 1969; August 5, 1970.

71. Fielden, *Forty Years of Stock Car Racing*, 3:270.

72. *NSSN*, August 5, 1970.

73. *NSSN*, March 25, 1970; April 8, 1970.

74. Granger, "Boycott of Talladega," 20.

75. Daniel, *Lost Revolutions*, 99.

76. *NSSN*, February 18, 1970.

77. Fielden, *Forty Years of Stock Car Racing*, 3:310–11.

78. *NSSN*, June 7, 1970.

79. *NSSN*, June 30, 1971.

80. Golenbock and Fielden, *Stock Car Racing Encyclopedia*, 798–99, 831–33, 791–93, 813–15, 751, 824–30, 899–906.

81. Golenbock, *American Zoom*, 68.

82. *NSSN*, February 18, 1970.

83. *NSSN*, November 25, 1970.

84. Fielden, *Forty Years of Stock Car Racing*, 3:318.

85. Golenbock, *American Zoom*, 122.

86. Ibid., 134.

87. Myers, "Graceful Evening at the Mansion."

88. *NSSN*, April 7, 14, 1971.

89. *NSSN*, October 13, 1971.

90. Bolton, "President Nixon Receives Racers."

91. *NSSN*, October 25, 1972.

92. Bledsoe, *World's Number One*, 215–21.

93. Petty, interview by author.

94. Bledsoe, *World's Number One*, 215–25. The "Racer's Prayer" is still used at many racetracks.

95. Petty, interview by author.

96. "Motor Racing Outreach," <http://www.go2mro.com/>.

97. Bledsoe, *World's Number One*, 224.

98. Higgins and Waid, *Junior Johnson*, 52.

99. Golenbock, *Miracle*, 113.

100. *NSSN*, January 21, 1970.

101. Golenbock, *Miracle*, 90.

102. *NSSN*, February 18, 1970.

103. Petty, *King Richard I*, 216–19.

104. *NSSN*, April 8, 1970.

105. "Public Cigarette Smoking Act," which reads: "After January 1, 1971, it shall be unlawful to advertise cigarettes and little cigars on any medium of electronic com-

munication subject to the jurisdiction of the Federal Communications Commission";
<http://www.law.cornell.edu/uscode/15/usc_sec_15_00001331----000-.html>.

106. Economaki, with Argabright, *Let 'Em All Go*, 221.

107. The Wilkes County section of the highway is now named in honor of Johnson.

108. Higgins and Waid, *Junior Johnson*, 83–84.

109. *NSSN*, December 16, 1970.

110. Fielden, *Forty Years of Stock Car Racing*, 3:265, 336.

111. *NSSN*, November 10, 1971.

112. Fielden, *Forty Years of Stock Car Racing*, 4:45.

113. Higgins and Waid, *Junior Johnson*, 84.

114. "Ralph Seagraves Dies," <http://www.motorsport.com/news/article.asp?ID=21357&FS=NASCAR*>.; "T. Wayne Robertson, 47, Leader in Development of Motor Sports," <http://query.nytimes.com/gst/fullpage.html?res=9400E5061738F934A25752C0A96E958260>.

115. Economaki, with Argabright, *Let 'Em All Go*, 244.

116. Woody, "End of Tobacco Road."

117. *NSSN*, January 12, 1972.

118. *NSSN*, January 12, 19, 1972; October 25, 1972; November 15, 1972; December 6, 1972.

CONCLUSION

1. Yunick, *All Right You Sons-a-Bitches*, 278.

2. Hagstrom, *NASCAR Way*, 43.

3. Ross and Szymanski, *Fans of the World Unite*.

4. Hagstrom, *NASCAR Way*, 202.

5. Ross and Szymanski, *Fans of the World Unite*.

Bibliography

INTERVIEWS

Conducted by author, audiotapes and transcripts at NASCAR Collection,
Special Collections, D. Hiden Ramsey Library, University of North Carolina
at Asheville

J. B. Day, July 25, 2005

Chris Economaki, June 16, 2005

Ned Jarrett, September 14, 1998

Junior Johnson, October 17, 2005

David Pearson, April 21, 2003

Richard Petty, September 23, 1998

Gordon Pirkle, November 8, 2005

H. A. "Humpy" Wheeler, July 27, 2005

Conducted by Pete Daniel, videotapes and transcripts at James G. Kenan Research
Center, Atlanta History Center, Atlanta, Ga.

Millard Ashley, September 2, 2000

Clay Call, July 21, 2001

Deborah Scott Davis, September 2, 2000

Frances Flock, July 22, 2001

Ray Fox, September 2, 2000

Jim Hunter, September 4, 2000

Ned Jarrett, July 28, 2001

Junior Johnson, July 21, 2001

Harold King, September 2, 2000

Sam Packard, February 19, 2001

Raymond Parks, August 27, 2000

Louise Smith, August 27, 2000

H. A. "Humpy" Wheeler, August 28, 2000

Henry "Smokey" Yunick, February 17, 2001

Conducted by Ben Shackleford, videotape and transcript at James G. Kenan
Research Center, Atlanta History Center, Atlanta, Ga.

Henry "Smokey" Yunick, December 13, 2000

Conducted by Suzanne Wise, videotape at Stock Car Racing Collection, Belk
Library, Appalachian State University, Boone, N.C.

Donald Johnson

Max Welbourn

NEWSPAPERS AND PERIODICALS

American Racing Classics

Asheville Citizen-Times

Atlanta Constitution

Charlotte Observer

Circle Track

Grand National Illustrated

Greensboro Daily News

High Point Enterprise

Illustrated Speedway News

National Speed Sport News

Pioneer Pages (publication of the Georgia Automobile
    Racing Hall of Fame Association)

Raleigh News and Observer

Spartanburg Herald

Speed Age

Sports Illustrated

Stock Car Racing

Wilkes Journal-Patriot

Winston-Salem Journal

BOOKS

Bledsoe, Jerry. *The World's Number One, Flat-Out, All-Time Great Stock Car Racing Book*. Asheboro, N.C.: Down Home Press, 1975.

Blount, Roy, ed. *Roy Blount's Book of Southern Humor*. New York: W. W. Norton, 1994.

Bragg, Rick. *All Over but the Shoutin'*. New York: Pantheon Books, 1997.

Carr, Jess. *The Second Oldest Profession: An Informal History of Moonshining in America*. Englewood Cliffs, N.J.: Prentice-Hall, 1972.

Cash, W. J. *The Mind of the South*. New York: Vintage Books, 1969.

Chapin, Kim. *Fast as White Lightning: The Story of Stock Car Racing*. New York: Three Rivers Press, 1998.

Clark, Thomas D. *The Emerging South*. New York: Oxford University Press, 1961.

Cobb, James C. *Industrialization and Southern Society, 1877–1984*. Chicago: Dorsey Press, 1988.

Coffey, Frank, and Joseph Layden. *America on Wheels: The First 100 Years, 1896–1996*. Los Angeles: General Publishing Group, 1996.

Cotter, Tom, and Al Pearce. *Holman-Moody: The Legendary Race Team*. St. Paul, Minn.: MBI Publishing, 2002.

Dabney, Joseph Earl. *Mountain Spirits: A Chronicle of Corn Whiskey from King James' Ulster Plantation to America's Appalachians and the Moonshine Life*. New York: Scribner, 1974.

Daniel, Pete. *Lost Revolutions: The South in the 1950s*. Chapel Hill: University of North Carolina Press, 2000.

Donovan, Brian. *Hard Driving: The Wendell Scott Story: The American Odyssey of NASCAR's First Black Driver*. Hanover, N.H.: Steerfort Press, 2008.

Economaki, Chris, with Dave Argabright. *Let 'Em All Go: The Story of Auto Racing by the Man Who Was There*. Fishers, Ind.: Books by Dave Argabright, 2006.

Edelstein, Robert. *Full Throttle: The Life and Fast Times of NASCAR Legend Curtis Turner*. New York: Overlook Press, 2005.

Fielden, Greg. *Forty Years of Stock Car Racing*. 4 vols. Surfside Beach, S.C.: Galfield Press, 1992.

———. *High Speed at Low Tide*. Surfside Beach, S.C.: Galfield Press, 1993.

———. *Rumblin' Ragtops: The History of NASCAR's Fabulous Convertible Division and Speedway Division*. Pinehurst, N.C.: Galfield Press, 1990.

Flink, James J. *The Automobile Age*. Cambridge, Mass.: MIT Press, 1988.

Gabbard, Alex. *Return to Thunder Road: The Story behind the Legend*. Lenoir City, Tenn.: Gabbard Publications, 1992.

Golenbock, Peter. *American Zoom: Stock Car Racing—From the Dirt Tracks to Daytona*. New York: Macmillan, 1993.

———. *The Last Lap: The Life and Times of NASCAR's Legendary Heroes*. New York: Macmillan, 1998.

———. *Miracle: Bobby Allison and the Saga of the Alabama Gang*. New York: St. Martin's Press, 2006.

———. *NASCAR Confidential: Stories of the Men and Women Who Made Stock Car Racing Great*. St. Paul, Minn.: Motorbooks International, 2004.

Golenbock, Peter, and Greg Fielden. *The Stock Car Racing Encyclopedia: The Complete Record of America's Most Popular Sport*. New York: Macmillan, 1997.

Gorn, Elliot, and Warren Goldstein. *A Brief History of American Sports*. New York: Hill and Wang, 1993.

Hagstrom, Robert. *The NASCAR Way: The Business That Drives the Sport*. New York: Wiley, 1998.

Hall, Jacquelyn, et al. *Like a Family: The Making of a Southern Cotton Mill World*. Chapel Hill: University of North Carolina Press, 1987.

Hemphill, Paul. *Wheels: A Season on NASCAR's Winston Cup Circuit*. New York: Simon and Schuster, 1997.

Higgins, Tom, and Steve Waid. *Junior Johnson: Brave in Life*. Phoenix: David Bull Publishing, 1999.

Hinton, Ed. *Daytona: From the Birth of Speed to the Death of the Man in Black*. New York: Warner Books, 2001.

Jensen, Tom. *Cheating: An Inside Look at the Bad Things Good NASCAR Winston Cup Racers Do in Pursuit of Speed*. Phoenix: David Bull Publishing, 2002.

Kelly, Godwin. *Fireball: Legends Don't Fall From the Sky*. Daytona Beach, Fla.: Carbon Press, 2005.

Kirkland, Tom, and David Thompson. *Darlington International Raceway*. Osceola, Wis.: MBI Publishing, 1999.

Levine, Leo. *Ford: The Dust and the Glory; A Racing History*. Warrendale, Pa.: Society of Automotive Engineers, 2000.

Malone, Bill. *Country Music, U.S.A.* Austin: University of Texas Press, 1968.

Morris, D. L. *Timber on the Moon: The Curtis Turner Story*. Charlotte, N.C.: Colonial Press, 1966.

Mull, J. Alexander, and Gordon Boger. *Recollections of the Catawba Valley*. Boone, N.C.: Appalachian Consortium Press, 1983.

Neely, William. *Daytona, U.S.A.: The Official History of Daytona and Ormond Beach Racing from 1902 to Today's NASCAR Super Speedways*. Tucson: Aztex Corp., 1979.

1951 NASCAR Yearbook. Daytona Beach, Fla.: National Association for Stock Car Auto Racing, 1952.

Ownby, Ted. *Subduing Satan: Religion, Recreation, and Manhood in the Rural South, 1865–1920*. Chapel Hill: University of North Carolina Press, 1990.

Petty, Richard, with William Neely. *King Richard I: The Autobiography of America's Greatest Auto Racer*. New York: Paperjacks, 1987.

Punnett, Dick. *Racing on the Rim: A History of the Annual Automobile Racing Tournaments Held on the Sands of Ormond-Daytona Beach, Florida, 1903–1910*. Ormond Beach, Fla.: Tomoka Press, 1997.

Raper, Arthur. *Preface to Peasantry: A Tale of Two Black Belt Counties*. Chapel Hill: University of North Carolina Press, 1936.

Rash, Ron. *The World Made Straight*. New York: Henry Holt, 2006.

Rodengen, Jeffrey. *Iron Fist: The Lives of Carl Kiekhaefer*. Fort Lauderdale, Fla.: Write Stuff Syndicate, 1991.

Ross, Stephen, and Stefan Szymanski. *Fans of the World Unite: A (Capitalist) Manifesto for Sports Consumers*. Palo Alto, Calif.: Stanford University Press, 2008.

Shifflet, Crandall. *Coal Towns: Life, Work, and Culture in Company Towns of Southern Appalachia, 1880–1960*. Knoxville: University of Tennessee Press, 1991.

Thompson, Neal. *Driving with the Devil: Southern Moonshine, Detroit Wheels, and the Birth of NASCAR*. New York: Crown, 2006.

Tullos, Allen. *Habits of Industry: White Culture and the Transformation of the Carolina Piedmont*. Chapel Hill: University of North Carolina Press, 1989.

Washburn, W. D. *Hickory Motor Speedway: The World's Most Famous Short Track*. Hickory, N.C.: Tarheel Press, 2003.

———. *Secrets on the Mountain*. Hickory, N.C.: Tarheel Press, 2002.

White, Rex, as told to Anne B. Jones. *Gold Thunder: Autobiography of a NASCAR Champion*. Jefferson, N.C.: McFarland and Co., 2005.

Wilkinson, Sylvia. *Dirt Tracks to Glory: The Early Years of Stock Car Racing As Told by Its Participants*. Chapel Hill, N.C.: Algonquin Books, 1983.

Williams, John A. *Appalachia: A History*. Chapel Hill: University of North Carolina Press, 2002.

Wright, Jim. *Fixin' to Git: One Fan's Love Affair with NASCAR's Winston Cup*. Durham, N.C.: Duke University Press, 2002.

Yarborough, Cale, with William Neely. *Cale: The Hazardous Life of the World's Greatest Stock Car Driver*. New York: Times Books, 1986.

Yunick, Henry "Smokey." *All Right You Sons-a-Bitches, Let's Have a Race*. Vol. 2 of *Best Damn Garage in Town: The World According to Smokey*. Daytona Beach, Fla.: Carbon Press, 2001.

Zeller, Bob. *The Daytona 500: An Official History*. Phoenix: David Bull Publishing, 2002.

MAGAZINE AND JOURNAL ARTICLES

"Adios Pancho." *Stock Car Racing*, September 1967, 16–20, 51.

Blount, Roy. "Million-Dollar Sunday Driver." *Sports Illustrated*, August 9, 1971, 16–17.

Bolton, Clyde. "President Nixon Receives Racers." *NASCAR Newsletter*,
     October 1, 1971. Found in "Politicians and Racing," vertical file, Stock Car Racing
     Collection, Belk Library, Appalachian State University, Boone, N.C.

Carey, Bob. "The Talladega Story." *Stock Car Racing*, December 1969, 12–15.

Chapin, Kim. "Curtis Lives!" *Sports Illustrated*, February 26, 1968, 50–60.

"Daredevil Driver." *Time*, December 8, 1952, 38–41.

Frederick, Jeff. "'If It Weren't for Bad Luck I'd Have No Luck at All': NASCAR,
     Southern Boosterism, and Deep South Culture in Talladega, Alabama." *Gulf
     South Historical Review* 20, no. 2 (2005): 7–36.

Gorn, Elliot J. "Gouge and Bite, Pull Hair and Scratch: The Social Significance of
     Fighting in the Southern Backcountry." *American Historical Review* 90 (1985):
     18–43.

Granger, Gene. "Bobby Isaac: GN Champion." *Circle Track*, May 1971, 36–40.

———. "The Boycott of Talladega." *American Racing Classics*, January 1993, 6–21.

———. "Buck Baker." *American Racing Classics*, October 1992, 32–45.

———. "Jack Smith." *American Racing Classics*, April 1992, 87.

———. "The 1950 Southern 500." *American Racing Classics*, October 1992, 112–15.

Hall, Randal. "Before NASCAR: The Corporate and Civic Promotion of Automobile
     Racing in the American South, 1903–1927." *Journal of Southern History* 3
     (August 2002): 629–68.

Hellman, Barbara. "A Cool Fireball Named Roberts." *Sports Illustrated*, February 10,
     1964, 31–39.

Kelly, Godwin. "Darlington: The First Superspeedway." *American Racing Classics*,
     January 1992, 111–13.

McCredie, Gary. "The First NASCAR Race." *American Racing Classics*, April 1992,
     118–27.

Myers, Bob. "A Graceful Evening at the Mansion." *NASCAR Newsletter*, April 15, 1971.
     Found in "Politicians and Racing," vertical file, Stock Car Racing Collection,
     Belk Library, Appalachian State University, Boone, N.C.

O'Reilly, Don. "Bill France, Sr." *American Racing Classics*, January 1993, 30–37.

Ownby, Ted. "Manhood, Memory and White Men's Sports in the Modern South."
     In *The Sporting World of the Modern South*, edited by Patrick B. Miller, 326–42.
     Urbana: University of Illinois Press, 2002.

Packard, Vance. "Millions in Moonshine." *The American*, September 1950, 46–47,
     100–105.

Pearson, Harold. "Bowman Gray Stadium." *American Racing Classics*, April 1992,
     111–17.

Pillsbury, Richard. "Carolina Thunder: A Geography of Southern Stock Car Racing."
     Journal of Geography 73 (1974): 43.

Smith, Mike. "Wendell Oliver Scott." *American Racing Classics*, November 1994,
     87–95.

"Stock Car Racing Leaders Form New National Association." *Speed Age*,
    February 1948, 10, 28–29.
Waid, Steve. "An Interview with Clay Earles." *Grand National Illustrated*,
    September 1982, 10–12.
Waid, Steve, and Dick Thompson. "Martinsville Speedway." *American Racing
    Classics*, July 1992, 108–19.
White, Ben. "NASCAR: The Beginning." *American Racing Classics*, January 1992,
    6–13.
Wolfe, Tom. "The Last American Hero Is Junior Johnson. Yes!" *Esquire*, March 1965,
    73–74, 138–54.
Yates, Brock. "Who the Hell Do You Think You Are? Curtis Turner?" *Car and Driver*,
    November 1966.

AUDIO AND VIDEO

American Stock: The Golden Era of NASCAR, 1936–1971. Pt. 4, *Wendell Scott*. Video.
    Westport, Conn.: Stonebridge Productions, 2005.
The Fifty: Sincerely Bill France. Video. Indianapolis: Ligner Group Productions for
    ESPN Video, 1998.
History of Racing Asheville. Audio CD. On deposit at Buncombe County, North
    Carolina Public Libraries, West Asheville Branch.
Padrush, David. *Rumrunners, Moonshiners, and Bootleggers*. Video. New York: Big
    Rock/Pinball Productions, 2002.
Yanacsek, Bill. *North Carolina Moonshiners*. Video. N.C.: Carolina Racing, ca. 2000.

WEBSITES

"Anne France." NASCAR.com. <www.nascar.com/2002/kyn/women/02/02/France/>.
    December 16, 2007.
"Baker, 'Cannonball' (Erwin G.)." Hickok Sports.com. <http://www.hickoksports
    .com/biograph/bakercan.shtml>. December 15, 2008.
"Baptist Faith and Message." 1925. SBC.net. <http://www.sbc.net/bfm/
    bfmcomparison.asp>. December 14, 2008.
Duntov, Zora. "Thoughts Pertaining to Youth, Hot Rodders and Chevrolet."
    <www.idavette.net/HistFact/zpaper53.htm>. October 6, 2007.
"Edwin Keith 'Banjo' Matthews." Legends of NASCAR.com. <http://www
    .legendsofnascar.com/Banjo_Matthews.htm>. December 11, 2008.
Glier, Ray. "Talladega Nightmares for the Chase." *New York Times*, October 7, 2007,
    <http://www.nytimes.com/2007/10/07/sports/othersports/07nascar.html>.
    June 18, 2008.
"Grand American." <http://thirdturn.armchairgm.com/wiki/Grand_Touring>.
    December 21, 2008.
"Hamrick, Warren NASCAR Legends Who Will Be Missed." <http: www
    .closefinishes.com/cgi-script/csArticles/articles/000007/000007.htm>.
    January 11, 2009.
"History of the Hudson Motor Company: Good Value and Performance with Solid
    Engineering!" <http://hetclub.com/history/history.htm>. December 18, 2008.

"Motor Racing Outreach." Motor Racing Outreach.com. <http://www.go2mro
.com/>. December 21, 2008.

"O. Bruton Smith." <http://www.referenceforbusiness.com/biography/S-Z/Smith-O-
Bruton-1927.html>. December 13, 2007.

Odom, Gene, and Frank Dorman. *Lynyrd Skynyrd: Remembering the Free Birds
of Southern Rock*. New York: Random House, 2002. Excerpt at <http://www
.randomhouse.com/catalog/display.pperl?isbn=9780769102863&view=excerpt>.
January 11, 2009.

"Public Cigarette Smoking Act." <http://www.law.cornell.edu/uscode/15/usc_sec_15
_00001331----000-.html>. June 24, 2008.

"Ralph Seagraves Dies." Motorsport.com. September 28, 1998. <http://www
.motorsport.com/news/article.asp?ID=21357&FS=NASCAR*>. June 25, 2008.

"Robert 'Red' Byron." Living Legends of Auto Racing.com. <http://www.living
legendsofautoracing.com/drivers_pages/drivers_red_by.html>. December 14,
2008.

Russell, L. D. "Racing vs. Religion: A Brief History of Occoneechee Speedway."
Historical Hillsborough.com. <www.historichillsborough.org/images/Speedway-
Complete.pdf>. October 31, 2006.

"T. Wayne Robertson, 47, Leader in Development of Motor Sports." Obituary. *New
York Times*, January 17, 1998, <http://query.nytimes.com/gst/fullpage.html?res=
940DE5D61738F934A25752C0A96E958260>. June 25, 2008.

"Teeter Tots." <http://freepages.genealogy.rootsweb.ancestry.com/~teeterkinmy/
teetertot.html>. December 8, 2008.

"Timeline of George Wallace's Life." PBS.org. <http://www.pbs.org/wgbh/amex/
wallace/timeline/index_2.html>. May 30, 2008.

"Timelines." Fireball Roberts.com. <http://www.fireballroberts.com/Timelines6070
.htm>. December 11, 2008.

"Traffic Fatality Rates." John A. Volpe National Transportation Systems Center.
<www.volpe.dot.gov/infosrc/journal/2005/pdfs/vj05intro.pdf>. October 17, 2006.

Weir, Tom. "Changing Times Test Track 'Too Tough to Tame.'" *USA Today*, May 5,
2005, < http://www.usatoday.com/sports/motor/nascar/2005-05-05-darlington-
future_x.htm>. October 12, 2005.

Woody, Larry. "The End of Tobacco Road: NASCAR Will End the 31-Year Winston
Era and Opt for a Breath of Fresh Air with Nextel." *Auto Racing Digest*,
December 2003, <http://findarticles.com/p/articles/mi_m0FCH/is_1_32/ai
_109579105/pg_2?tag=artBody;col1>. June 25, 2008.

MISCELLANEOUS

"Official Souvenir Program, Championship Modified Stock Car Races, Asheville-
Weaverville Speedway, Sunday, August 20th 1950." On deposit, West Asheville
Library, Asheville, N.C.

Acknowledgments

Writing this book has been one of the great pleasures of my life. I am deeply indebted to many folks who helped me along the way with guidance, inspiration, and support.

A number of individuals deeply connected to NASCAR racing graciously granted interviews that helped me better understand the sport's history. I will never forget my first of such meetings with the aptly nicknamed "Gentleman" Ned Jarrett and the drive to his house, where I swear Dale Earnhardt was on my rear bumper; the hour and a half interview with Richard Petty, during which he sat at his desk—in cowboy hat and sunglasses—under a portrait of Robert E. Lee; breakfast with Junior Johnson and friends at his farm shop; the sound of Chris Economaki's distinctive voice when he told me "Dan, it's all about the con" in a phone interview; my conversation with David Pearson, in which he challenged the facts as I had written them in an encyclopedia article on his life and career—he was right and I corrected it; talking southern history with Humpy Wheeler in his huge office at Lowe's Motor Speedway and getting to actually see the Rolex watch Bobby Isaac gave him; and wonderful afternoons spent talking racing history with Bobby Allison, Jack Ingram, Paul Call, Gordon Pirkle, J. B. Day, Dr. Don Tarr, and the incredibly helpful Doug Stafford.

I also owe a debt of appreciation to the many individuals whose professional work or advice contributed to my research in significant ways. Journalists Ed Hinton and the late Bob Terrell along with the late, great photographer Don Hunter gave me leads that proved invaluable. Tom Higgins inspired me with incredible stories of his days as a NASCAR journalist and helped steer this project in significant ways. Archivists Betty Carlan and Suzanne Wise provided crucial research assistance and contact information; no one can do proper research on this topic without their help, which they offer with professionalism and grace. A number of friends and professional colleagues—including Pam Grundy, Richard Starnes, Duane Davis, Jonathan Bass, Jenny Brooks, Craig Pascoe, Jim Cobb, Tom Lawton, and Geoff Cantrell—advised me on this project and read and commented on drafts of this work and hopefully helped keep me from making a complete fool of myself. As usual, Paul Bergeron took his editor's pen to my work, and it is much the better because of his advice. The research of three of my students at the University of North Carolina at Asheville—Ted Vogel, Will Tate, and Bryan Greene—further enriched my work. Jan Loveday provided much-needed, and appreciated, technical advice on preparing the photographs.

This book is built on the research of many historians and journalists. I am especially indebted to the earlier research on the history of NASCAR done by Pete Daniel, Neal Thompson, Jeff Frederick, Randal Hall, and Peter Golenbock. We all stand on the shoulders of Greg Fielden, whose tireless and comprehensive research provides the starting point for all historical work on this subject.

My editor at the University of North Carolina Press, David Perry, believed in this project early on and kept me moving through the process even when I wanted to give it up. I also owe many thanks to the fine and professional folks at UNC Press.

This work would also not have been possible had it not been for the support and encouragement of friends and family. Longtime friends and "racin' buddies" Larry Ward, Tim Harris, Johnny Ward, Clyde Kintner, Mike Kellis, Daniel Hinson, Von Foreman, and the late Dale Ammons helped turn me from an observer into a fan. I cannot thank Buster Watts enough for all his support over the years and the invaluable insights into racing fandom he provided. While my brothers David and Jon Pierce do not often understand their "gearhead" younger brother, their belief in me has often sustained me over the long haul. I am especially grateful to Jon, his wife, Jane, and Steve and Lee Noblitt, who generously allowed me to use their condo at Seabrook Island for a writing retreat. I must apologize to my mom, Archie Pierce—and to my late father, the Reverend C. R. Pierce Jr.—for some of the language in this book, but I assure you that there is nothing in it that I did not hear a long time ago from Uncle Emmett. Thanks, Mom, for being my greatest fan and for all you did to make this book a possibility. I am also blessed with incredible children in Anna Clare, Taylor, Sully, and Coulter, whose love, astounding accomplishments, and strength of character help drive me to greater things. Although it is an overused cliché, my wife, Lydia, is my rock. Her encouragement, support, and constant and unconditional love kept me going when things got difficult, and her pride in my accomplishments make it more than worth the effort.

Finally, this book would never have been written had it not been for my best friend, Don Good, and his father, Wayne Good. Wayne Good grew up in Hickory, North Carolina, in a family that had some firsthand experience with moonshine; served in the Korean War; spent much of his life as a truck driver; and was the only individual I ever knew personally who had a handgun with the serial number filed off. While he did not leave his son much in the way of material wealth when he passed away, he did instill in Don an intense love for stock car racing developed over many years of trips to Hickory Speedway for the Saturday night races and weekend camping trips to the infield at Charlotte, Rockingham, and Darlington. I often thought of Wayne when I sought to envision the working-class fans who laid the foundation for NASCAR and helped make it what it is today.

Although Don Good and I formed a lifelong friendship in 1974 as potluck roommates at Western Carolina University, I never really understood his passion for this sport. Despite his best efforts, it took twenty years of persistence to get me to a race, and one race was all it took. After that first transformative race at Bristol Motor Speedway, Don took it upon himself to educate me on the sport's history and hooked me on that as well. His careful fact checking and probing questions have proven invaluable to this project, but most of all his deep love and respect for this sport inspired me at every juncture. Don and I have shared so many incredible NASCAR-related experiences over the years that formed the core of my education in the sport's history and its significance. We've sat together for memorable races in NASCAR's top division at Bristol, Martinsville, Charlotte, and Darlington, where we remained in the stands long after Terry Labonte had won the last Southern 500, mourning the end of that great event until track workers forced us to leave. We've been "short trackin'" together at New Asheville and Bulls Gap and spent an unforgettable evening eating barbecue sandwiches from Lexington Barbeque and watching the unparalleled Saturday night show at Bowman Gray Stadium. We've also talked racing together with Richard Petty in his office, with Ned Jarrett at his charity golf tournament, with Bobby Allison at the dedication of a historical marker for the first NASCAR race, with Dr. Don Tarr in his Tennessee home, with Betty Carlan over biscuits and gravy at the McCaig-Welborn Library, with all the wonderful folks in the Old Time Racers' Club, and with Paul Call and Suzanne Wise in the stands at North Wilkesboro Speedway. If there is anything of value in this book to the study of NASCAR history, it is due to Don's inspiration. In honor of their contributions to my work, this book is dedicated to Don Good and in memory of his father, Wayne Good.

Index